Christians versus Muslims in Modern Egypt

Christians versus Muslims in Modern Egypt

The Century-Long Struggle for Coptic Equality

S. S. HASAN

OXFORD
UNIVERSITY PRESS
2003

OXFORD
UNIVERSITY PRESS

Oxford New York
Auckland Bangkok Buenos Aires Cape Town Chennai
Dar es Salaam Delhi Hong Kong Istanbul Karachi Kolkata
Kuala Lumpur Madrid Melbourne Mexico City Mumbai Nairobi
São Paulo Shanghai Taipei Tokyo Toronto

Published by Oxford University Press, Inc.
198 Madison Avenue, New York, New York 10016

www.oup.com

Library of Congress Cataloging-in-Publication Data

Hasan, Sana.
Christians versus Muslims in Modern Egypt : The century-long struggle for Coptic equality / S. Hasan.
p. cm.
Includes bibliographical references and index.
ISBN 0-19-513868-6
1. Coptic Church—Egypt—History—20th century. 2. Egypt—Church history—20th century. 3. Egypt—Politics and government—1970– 4. Christianity and other religions—Islam. 5. Islam—Relations—Christianity. I. Title.

BX133.2 .H37 2002
281'.72'0962—dc21 2002022039

9 8 7 6 5 4 3 2 1

Printed in the United States of America
on acid-free paper

For Oxford University's crown jewel
Edward Roger Owen,
with gratitude for his infinite patience
and loving concern

and

In memory of his friend and mine,
Magdi Wahba,
a Copt who incarnated the spirit
of Egypt's belle époque

One can exercise one's tolerance, out of charity or out of love of peace, when someone attacks one's individual rights. But, as far as our collective rights are concerned, one cannot, because these concern us more than personally. They concern the whole community; for that reason, one must act so that the strong party does not devour the weaker party.

—His Holiness Pope Shenuda III

The nation has orphaned them, but God hems them in.

—Mark Gruber, a Benedictine monk

Acknowledgments

I would like to thank His Holiness Pope Shenuda III for opening up his church to me. Without his endorsement of this project, it would have been impossible.

The reader might wonder how, as a Muslim—albeit only nominally—and as a woman, could I penetrate this hermetically closed universe, which shuts itself off not only from the gaze of the enemy and potential informant but also, as a monastic institution, from that of the female? With regard to the former handicap, I found that once I had won the pope's heart and hence his confidence, his letter or recommendation was sufficient, in a hierarchic and authoritarian context where his least wish is a command for his subordinates to overlook my religious affiliation. It then became a matter of establishing a rapport with the more open minded bishops, who would be amenable to engaging in a frank discussion of sensitive church issues.

As to my gender, I had anticipated that in such an exclusive male preserve it would be difficult not only to gain access to the monks, monk-priests, and bishops hailing from the monasteries but even more so to get them to take a woman seriously enough to engage in discussion and to confide in. And indeed, one of the jokes that I repeatedly heard from clergy was about an Egyptian pope who had been foolish enough to confide in one of the nuns that he had only one "egg." When this nun spread the "secret" to her friends in the nunnery, the story was changed to his having three eggs and so on down the line until the entire nunnery was buzzing with the rumors that the pope had thirty-nine "eggs." This kind of joke and other less humorous attacks on women, which I frequently encountered in church-servant circles and amid the bishops, led me to anticipate great difficulty in carrying out my research. However, in the end I believe that the chance for legitimate contact with a woman, in a church where merely allowing a consecrated woman (*mukharasa*) to drive a priest who had suffered a heart attack around in Chicago was enough to have the latter defrocked, proved sufficiently alluring to make me privy to their time and confidence.

I would like to thank the bishops who gave me their trust, particularly Bishop Serapion, Bishop Moses, Bishop Arsanios, Bishop Bula, Bishop Murqus, Bishop Fam, Bishop Bachum, Bishop Thomas, Bishop Tackla and the late Bishop Athanasios. Because of the frank conversations we had about the challenges and difficulties facing the church, this book has been greatly enriched. I hope they will not feel I betrayed their trust. Even bishops, like Bishops Bishoi and Isaiah, who did not give me their trust gave me their hospitality, and I thank them for that.

Clearly any conclusions reached in these chapters on the basis of information the bishops provided me with are entirely my own. I know that some Copts may disagree with my observations, others may be shocked because they are not used to such open discussions of church problems, and still others may be offended at the pope's treatment of his predecessor, Pope Kyrilos VI, as well as Bishop Samuel. Some may claim that certain things I've written are untrue. I therefore wish to assure one and all that no matter how much we may differ in our interpretation of what is going on in the present-day church this is truly a work of *agape*. I may also not agree with the church's views on sex, marriage, and divorce, or the subordination of women, but I have great admiration for the efforts it is exerting on behalf of its people. I applaud the proud defiance of Pope Shenuda III and the stubborn tenaciousness of the church leadership and I care deeply for many of the bishops. They are indeed ḥilwin (lovely) as their devotees say. I would also like to thank the many Khuddam (church servants) who added to their heavy workloads by showing me around. I hope they will forgive me for saying that they are too numerous to name. But I owe special thanks to Arsani (Michel) Ghabur and Raef Henawi of Minia for offering me the hospitality of their homes.

Aside from my spiritual mentors, I have my intellectual mentors to thank. I would like to thank Professor Michael Walzer of Princeton University's Institute For Advanced Studies, who guided my first faltering footsteps in his political theory course for undergraduates, at Harvard, and has lent me a hand in my intellectual endeavors ever since. To his own fascinating book on radical Protestantism in England and America I owe much of the inspiration for this work. And to him personally I owe the many passionate discussions we had in his apartment in New York during my visits from Egypt, while I was doing the fieldwork for this book. He also patiently plowed through the somewhat incoherent notes of my observations recorded during my fieldwork in Egypt.

In January 1995, when I heard that Harvard University had acquired Professor Roger Owen, I wrote to him from Egypt and asked him if he would be willing to read for me the first draft of this book, which I had just completed. He immediately responded affirmatively and I traveled with the manuscript to Cambridge in April 1995 for what I had then booked as a one month's stay. A week after my departure, I learned that the secret police had visited my home in the middle of the night in search of me and when they did not find me they had ransacked my apartment in search of the manuscript.

This was not my first close call with the Egyptian authorities. After I returned to live in Egypt in 1987, following my receipt of political asylum in the United States when I was stripped of my Egyptian passport and banned from entrance to the country because of my political engagement in the cause of peace with Israel, I once more had problems on account of the appearance of *Enemy in the Promised Land* (Pantheon, 1987) at Cairo International Book Fair. Soon thereafter I was stopped at the Cairo airport, on my way to Berlin, and told that I could not leave the country because I had been placed on the black list by Amn el-Dawlah (State Security Authority). I therefore decided in 1995, after narrowly missing arrest by the secret police, that I had had enough of these "cat and mouse" chases and would settle definitively in the "Land of the Free."

It was as an Associate of the Center for Middle Eastern Studies at Harvard University, of which Roger Owen had become the director, that I completed this work in the academic year 1997–1998. I am grateful that he remained throughout this enterprise tough, skeptical, and relentlessly critical so as to tease the best out of me, yet sufficiently encouraging to keep up my morale for the long haul. All the while he was inordinately generous with his time.

Last but by no means least, I am indebted to my editor, Cynthia Read, at Oxford University Press, who was invariably friendly and accessible—as well as extraordinarily insightful. I also wish to thank the Guggenheim Foundation for funding the fieldwork in Egypt. I would also like to thank David Giovacchini of Widener Library's Arabic division and William Granara, professor of Arabic at Harvard University, for helping me with the transliteration. I would also like to thank Aris Boushra for helping me with the Arabic material in Cairo.

Contents

PART IV: THE CHURCH AS SOCIOECONOMIC ENTREPRENEUR

PART V: THE CHURCH AS CULTURAL AGENT

PART VI: THE POLITICS OF IDENTITY

PART VII: THREE QUESTIONS FOR THE TWENTY-FIRST CENTURY

Glossary

Khedive is a Persian word meaning grand seigneur. The khedivate was established in Egypt by the Ottoman ruler of Egypt Muḥammad Ali, who arrogated to himself the title of Khedive. It was not until his grandson Ismail took over in 1865 that legal recognition of the title was obtained from the sultan of the Ottoman Empire. Only then did primogeniture become the basis of succession. Before that, the throne had been passed on to the oldest male relative, in accordance with Ottoman law.

Mamluks were slaves, mostly imported when they were still children from Georgia and other places in the Caucasus. They were educated to be administrators and rulers of Muslim domains. Muḥammad Ali also had a good number of Greek Mamluks who were captured by his forces when they intervened on the sultan's behalf to put down insurgents during the Greek War of Independence. In time, Mamluks became indistinguishable from free-born members of the Ottoman ruling class.

Sultan refers to the sovereign of a Muslim state.

Dhimis were non-Muslims who were exempt from army duty but as "protected people" had to pay a poll tax (jizyah).

All other words or terms in Arabic used throughout the text are translated in the initial instance.

Egyptian Class Structure

Prior to the 1952 Revolution

THE UPPER CLASSES. A "Turco-Egyptian" landed aristocracy. An haute bourgeoisie consisting of a native agrarian bourgeoisie and a mostly foreign commercial and industrial bourgeoisie made up of Greeks, Italians, Armenians, and Jews.

THE MIDDLE CLASSES. An upper middle class consisting of native and foreign professionals and a native agrarian middle class. A lower middle class consisting of native and foreign shopkeepers and government and private sector employees.

THE LOWER CLASSES. An upper lower class consisting of mostly foreign skilled workers, with a sprinkling of natives, and of native artisans. A lower lower class of native lumpenproletariat, agricultural workers, and domestic workers.

After the 1952 Revolution

THE UPPER CLASSES. A native haute bourgeoisie consisting of a commercial and industrial "state bourgeoisie" and of the offspring of the pre-revolutionary upper classes.

THE MIDDLE CLASSES. A native upper middle class of professionals and a native rural middle class. A native lower middle class consisting of government employees, small shopkeepers, and some professionals.

THE LOWER CLASSES. A native upper lower class consisting of an industrial lower class and native artisans and skilled workers. A lower-lower class consisting of a lumpenproletariat, agricultural workers, and domestic workers.

Christians versus Muslims in Modern Egypt

Introduction

Though the problems faced by the Christian minority are for many Egyptians a taboo subject, there can be no doubt that the condition of the Copts steadily deteriorated, during the second half of the twentieth century, as Egypt was ineluctably drawn to the Islamic orbit. The Coptic Orthodox Church took upon itself the role of bolstering the battered self-image of Egyptian Christians as well as of equipping them with the values and skills that would enable them to succeed economically despite discrimination. That the church has been able to assume this challenge as well as to confront the danger posed by the resurgence of Islamic militancy, in the 1970s, is attributable to a reform movement known as the "Sunday School Movement." This book is about a generation of Egyptian Christians, the "Sunday School generation," part of the new urban middle class that surfaced in the 1940s and early 50s, with a reform project to reconstitute Coptic culture as well as to reinvigorate their community by upgrading its educational and socioeconomic level. They found in the church the main outlet for their reforming zeal and proceeded to use it as a safe haven, outside the reach of the Muslim state, from which to launch their project.

The Orthodox Church renaissance had its own autochthonic roots; it was not just a reaction to Islamic belligerence. It was a rebellion against the old church guard by the first generation of middle-class university graduates, an attempt to bring up to date what they had come to regard as a decrepit, venal, and obscurantist institution.

The radical restructuring of the Egyptian Orthodox Church and the simultaneous attempt at character transformation of the Coptic community at large accompanied a broader historical process, namely Egypt's socioeconomic modernization, begun in the nineteenth century. The Sunday School generation, was both a product of Egypt's modernization and an agent of it. The emphasis here is on the *process* of modernization, not on modernity itself, the latter yet to be attained.

For this generation, the word *reform* did not suggest anything modern; what they sought was a *revival*, not a *revolution*—a revival of the Apostolic Church, in particular the Church of Alexandria, and of the Catechetical School of Alexandria, which had by the third century AD acquired renown throughout the Christian world as a result of the work of two of its great scholars, Clement and Origen.

Yet if we are to judge that generation by what it accomplished, rather than by its own motives and purposes, there can be no doubt that it put in motion a revolutionary process, the transformation of a traditional community into a modern one. The changes this generation proposed, in the name of a mythical past, represented such a drastic break with custom that despite their acknowledgment of precedent, their reforms resulted in improvement rather than revival—a radical change for the better.

During the reign of Pope Shenuda III (1971–) the responsibilities of the church for the welfare of the Coptic community expanded immeasurably. In addition to the church leaders' arrogating to themselves *exclusive* political representation of their community, their conception of their role changed irrevocably: from the traditional praying and giving out alms to the poor in their locality to promoting the economic and cultural efflorescence of the Coptic community as a whole.

The structural revolution that Shenuda's generation sought necessitated an ideology, as a kind of mental and moral discipline—an ideology that was to be indoctrinated not only within the church but also within the Coptic household, the Coptic school, the Coptic youth center, the Coptic university hostel, the Coptic vocational center, and the Coptic recreational centers. It was the genius of these Orthodox reformers that they perceived the ideological need of their community to relate to indigenous cultural traditions and that they were able to communicate these old legends in a novel and historically relevant manner. The "founding myth" for them became the glorious history of the Orthodox church—particularly its monastic movement, launched by St. Antony, an Egyptian by birth, in the third century AD. In grounding their ideology in that myth, the reformers of the 1940s and early 1950s were able to evoke a response that the secular Coptic elite, even the consummate politicians among them, could not. They also performed an invaluable service for future generations, whose self-esteem would be threatened by the resurgence of Islamic supremacist theories.

As we shall see in the following chapters, the communal framework, which was gradually built up in the 1940s and early 1950s by a middle-class leadership, was based on a shared affection for legendary local figures—the Coptic saints and martyrs of ancient times. Thus, Coptic Orthodox hagiography is very different from that of the Catholic Church, inasmuch as it centers on the life histories of such local heroes as Barsum the Naked, an Egyptian hermit; Abanob, a twelve-year-old Egyptian boy martyred by the Romans; Black Moses, an African bandit turned ascetic, and other local saints—many of whom are not recognized by or even known to the Catholic Church. The reverence of the middle- and lower-class Copts for their local saints and martyrs and their shrines, which are believed to have healing powers and to afford protection against demons and evil spirits, is scorned by the ancien régime upper class, who consider, such beliefs to be superstitions.

My focus is the middle class, which searched for these roots. Convinced that the social welfare of its community depended on its connection to its own indigenous culture, it made an earnest effort to wrest meaning from its religious heritage. I deal only minimally with the upper class, a landed aristocracy that had played an important role in community affairs in the first half of this century through its dominance of the communal council known as the Maglis Milli.

The upper class had no notion of an indigenous culture; the culture of the neocolonial society, in which this ancien régime aristocracy was embedded, tended to be international and devoid of specificity. The upper class contributed neither to the constituency of the church nor to its leadership—not even its communal leadership—in the period during which this study was undertaken. Under Shenuda III, the clergy had finally succeeded in ousting the secular lay leadership from its preeminence in communal affairs, taking over both its role as political representative and provider—in short, it became an agent of modernization.

Some scholars may question the usefulness of such a paradigm, in that the theory of modernization has come under considerable criticism. I myself believe it is relevant to this context, inasmuch as the reformers, drawn from the ranks of a newly educated middle class, had absorbed the modernist aspirations of the state. They sought, by restructuring the religious space, a form of modernization that differed from that which the state was trying to introduce in the middle-class urban complexes to which families had migrated from their villages and small towns in search of better job opportunities and a university education for their sons.

Although modern enterprise is generally associated with the Calvinist ethic of industriousness and frugality, which Max Weber demonstrated was admirably suited to the needs of a capitalist order, I suggest in this book that it is not the particular ideology that matters for purpose of socioeconomic change so much as the ability to mobilize a constituency by drawing on the symbols and myths that are emotionally relevant to that constituency. I try to show the way in which social change can be brought about by means of an ideology that may be perceived by some as reactionary.

Just as we associate the phenomenon of revolution, which gave birth to the modern state in Europe, with the concept of an ideology, the rebellion against the old guard that preceded the emergence of a modern church in Egypt is also linked to one. What distinguishes the Orthodox reform movement from the Protestant one, however—particularly from Calvinism in Geneva and Puritanism in England and America—is that the ideology that inspired it was not modern. On the contrary what was needed, it would seem, in Egypt to modernize the Coptic community effectively was a revitalization of tradition.[1] Inasmuch as ancient legends were resurrected and used as props by the Orthodox reformers to bring about a fundamental change in the social order, we can speak of a "revolutionary traditionalism," to borrow a term applied by S. A. Arjomand to Shiite radicalism in modern Iran.[2]

Christian, Muslim, and Jewish ultra-Orthodox myths all share one thing—orientation to the past.[3] One tends to think of such a reverence for tradition as antithetical to change, as a blind adherence to customary ways, which does not encourage man-made transformations. The intensely personal relations that characterized a traditional society preclude, one assumes, an impersonal commitment to ideas and ideologies as well as to legal-rational organizations. The real question, then, is how a highly corporate church like the Egyptian Orthodox Church, in which patriarchy and personal loyalty form the basis of relationships, and hierarchy is such a fundamental organizing principle that even a bishop has to prostrate himself before the pope, can accomplish modernization.

The answer is not immediately obvious, because unlike Calvinism, modern orthodoxy did not criticize hierarchy or evince any particular talent for organizing men or any capacity for sending them into battle against Satan and his allies—even if the ruler of the Muslim state happened to be one of those allies, as President Anwar Sadat was perceived by many of the clergy I interviewed. One must try to discern, therefore, elements within the Orthodox tradition that could contribute to social reconstruction. Or was change possible only because the reformers, though "sons of the Church" as pious Copts refer to themselves, were essentially outsiders—laity—and were rebels against the old church guard? Even if some of them chose later to join the monasteries, their motive was to change the church, which had become stagnant, from within. Perhaps their very alienation from the old church order enabled them not only to act as creative entrepreneurs, adapting different strands of Orthodoxy to existing needs, but also to borrow from Western values and institutions. Protestant values, like punctuality, industriousness, and reliability in work, and modern institutions, medical and educational centers, were forms of organization copied not only from the modernizing state but from the Western Protestant and Catholic missions which combined modernity with religiosity.

In the area of social change but also in the religio-cultural sphere these rebels against the old guard were engaged in a creative process—not a simple return to their origins. This necessitated a reinterpretation of religious fundamentals and the conquest of a religious space in which to carry out their reform projects: successively, the Sunday schools, the monasteries and seminaries, and the upper reaches of the church hierarchy.

From this perspective, one can understand that the actions the reformers undertook were not just the defense of a traditional community against the seduction of modernism or of Islam but a dynamic reformulation of a religious identity and a social restructuring of a traditional community meant to provide a new framework for Coptic lives in the modern age. At the same time, they aimed to preserve and revitalize ancient bonds, as a defense of the community against assimilation into the modern secular nation-state and later into the emerging Islamic one.

In short, I seek to demonstrate that it would be a mistake to define this religious movement as solely traditional. In fact, it was no less innovative and productive of a modern ethic than the nationalist movement. I offer a revisionist theory of modernization, with the paradoxical argument that not only is it at times unnecessary to rid oneself of hierarchy and tradition to achieve social change but that these very hierarchical structures and traditions may be effectively manipulated for modern purposes.

There is no attempt to suggest here that the church fathers merely manipulated these symbols to mobilize their followers. Clearly, they themselves were true believers. I am merely arguing that it is doubtful whether the present church fathers would be able to make the kind of demands they make on the time of a virtual army of lay volunteers or to harness their energy and expertise toward socioeconomic goals if they did not command the traditional aura they do, which makes it hard to refuse their requests.

We know that as early as the 1960s, Western social theorists had begun to question the validity of too rigid a dichotomy between tradition and modernity. Highly regarded scholars came under attack both for contributing to a misunderstanding of modern societies by neglecting the study of their traditional features and for underestimating the potential for modernization within traditional societies. The melting pot theory, for instance, was revised in favor of a theory that underlined the survival in the United States of such traditional features as ethnic and religious solidarities. Third World theorists, on the other hand, who presumably had a greater knowledge of nonwestern societies, criticized the belief that the achievement orientation, the attitude of mastery toward one's physical and human environment, and individualism—attitudes, in short, that are believed to have led to western technological achievements and to the growth of modern administration and political democracy—were incompatible with the norms, institutions, and behavioral patterns of traditional societies. Studies like those of Lloyd and Suzane Hoeber Rudolph on India, which show how Gandhi was able to mobilize latent qualities within a traditional society, served as useful correctives to parochial western judgments and narrow perspectives.[4]

I do not want to reduce all differences between modern and traditional societies to the prejudice of the viewer, as Edward Said seems at times to do in his critique of the Orientalists,[5] despite his compelling basic premise that dominant nations and races need to justify their subjugation of others by attributing to themselves superior moral and intellectual merit. Anyone familiar with the white supremacist stereotypes of blacks as lazy, childlike in the pursuit of enjoyment, and sexually permissive—hence incapable of modern organization or self government—in contrast to the white man's industriousness, self-control, and orderly (mature) behavior or with our understanding of Asia (both Far and Near East), as fatalistic, corporate, and inegalitarian as opposed to the masterful, egalitarian, and individualistic West, will easily concede this. While there is some truth to such portrayal of "the Orient," we must try to get away from both the reality and the myths of our western cultures to be able to perceive new historical possibilities.

As Lloyd and Suzane Hoeber Rudolph have shown us, a culture is never monolithic, nor does it ever command a total compliance among all members of a particular nation. It is necessary, therefore, to explore variations within a particular culture, as they have done in the case of India, to detect the potential for change.

Two considerations have dictated my choice of subject matter: First, the virtual absence of any social-scientific studies of the contemporary Coptic community based on fieldwork and the tendency of the few studies that do exist to rely on secondary material. (One of the notable exceptions is the excellent fieldwork of Dina el-Khawaga, which is embodied in her article "Le renouveau Copte actuel; Raison d'émergence et mode de fonctionnement," *Dossier du CDEJ*, 1991, and some of the essays in Nelly van Doorn Harder and Kari Vogt, eds., *Between Desert and City: The Coptic Church Today* (Oslo, 1997.) However, the latter work was not yet published at the time I undertook this study. On the whole, despite the abundance of writings on the history of the Coptic Church and its liturgy, on the Egyptian monasteries and Egypt's saints and martyrs, very little attention was paid to the modern Coptic experience until the resurgence of Islamic militancy in the mid-1970s. Second, and perhaps more important, the failure to deal with anything outside of the Coptic "problem"—that is to say, the failure to view the modern Coptic experience as interesting and worthwhile for its own sake. As an unfortunate result, the studies we do possess tend to be reductionist, inasmuch as they view the Copts through the prism of their relationship to the Muslims. This is true even of the best of these studies, notably the seminal and pioneering work of the Egyptian historian Tariq al-Bishri, *Muslim and Copts within the Framework of National Community*,[6] and the equally impressive research on Coptic-Muslim relations in the first half of this century by the American scholar B. L. Carter. A byproduct of the focus on Coptic-Muslim relations in Carter's *The Copts in Egyptian Politics*,[7] as well as in the work of al-Bishrī and others,[8] is their concern with the elites that dominate the political orbit, rather than with the average members of the community.[9]

By contrast, my study, as a communal study, shifts the attention away from the state and the upper-class actors who dominated its institutions until the 1952 revolution in Egypt to small groups of middle-class people, and their new networks and institutions, within the Sunday School Movement. Second, it parts company both with social scientists, who look on such groups as "traditional groups" that have failed to be successfully integrated into the newly emerged, more modern social structures of the nation-state, and with those who see communalism as comprising identities forcibly repressed at the time of the formation of nation-states (often by outside powers), which later erupted in the form of a virulent nationalism, based on religion or ethnicity. In the following chapters, I argue that the Coptic Orthodox reform movement, the Sunday School Movement, cannot be properly understood if it is merely seen as the expression of traditional forms of identity.

In studying the communal action of the middle class and its clerical leaders, I have relied principally on primary sources, which in addition to my own interviews consisted of taped and videotaped memoirs of church-servants and deacons active in the formative years of the 1940s and early 1950s, unpublished and published clerical writings, and private correspondence, entrusted to me, of bishops with the pope. Through the latter, and through my private conversations with the pope and the bishops, I was able to get a sense of the different and sometimes conflicting opinions within the church on the most appropriate strategy for dealing with the state, in a given context, as well as problems within the Coptic community or within Church itself.

My secular upbringing had left me totally ignorant of all sacred texts and traditions. I had therefore to take the time to acquaint myself with the study of both Christianity and the specific Coptic Orthodox heritage. In a world so rich in symbols and metaphors, I was as much a stranger as I had been years prior in my encounter with Israel, where my intended three months' stay extended to three years, as I very quickly discovered that my initial contacts with cabinet ministers, army generals, and prominent intellectuals, with whom I could share a language (English), did not even begin to tell me the story of a country whose grass roots I had yet to explore. My intended one year foray into the labyrinthian realm of Coptic Egypt also stretched out into three. In a world so alien, to avoid getting lost in my search for meaning, I had to learn a new language: not Hebrew this time, which I had tried to master to reach the lower classes in Israel's factories, farms and sculleries, but a language every bit as difficult. For without learning the legends, myths, and symbols of this church, I could not grasp the subtle allusions to the current plight of the Copts that were made in church meetings and private conversations. Discovering hidden meanings among deceptively simple and straightforward statements, was like scratching through layers of a palimpsest.

Mastery of this metaphoric language required a discipline and perseverance no less taxing than did Hebrew; I had to set myself a daily program of reading long and, to me, boring religious texts: hagiographies, homilies, printed sermons, Orthodox canonical laws and Orthodox Church history, a plethora of episcopal publications on everything from sex to cigarettes, to how to deal with psychiatric and matrimonial problems. Once I had mastered it, I was finally able to penetrate the restructured religious space that the vast majority of middle-class and lower-class Copts today inhabit. My research was not limited to the power relations within the church or between the church and the state or to the economic strategies adopted to ensure the upward mobility of the Copts, but it was in large part focused on meaning. For the Copts today, the matrix of meaning is not rooted in the national language, as it was in the first half of the twentieth century. To understand it, one must look up religious references. Though they may share, at the material level, the same strategies as their Muslim compatriots for coping with job-related and housing problems, each community navigates the universe of meaning by means of its own compass.

The mnemonic maps that guide the present-day Copts consist of a multiplicity of layered narratives, which keep alive the memory of past events, some as oral narratives, some as visual texts—the iconographies—and some as written texts. But the Coptic martyrologies and hagiographies are not only preserving the past. Their experience whether through listening, reading, or seeing is creative of new meaning through the interaction between the text and the current context. Thus, Coptic religious memory is continuously being reconstructed to guide the faithful through treacherous paths and help them cope with difficulties and take on new challenges.

It is this mnemonic map that President Sadat was unable to make out, because like many of his Muslim compatriots he did not undertake this enterprise equipped with the necessary cultural baggage. When Sadat, among others, accused the Copts of trying to set up a nation of their own, he was not wrong. That nation, however, was not a geographical entity with a capital in the Upper Egyptian province of Assiut, as he conceived it. Its topography was invisible to him, because it lay in the religio-cultural realm. The politics Copts were engaged in was a different sort of politics, namely a politics of identity.

But there is also a practical side to the church reform movement. It did not only take upon itself the task of restoring to the Copts their ancient heritage to shore up their self-esteem; it sought to endow them with the know-how to succeed in a modern economy. It needed, therefore, to create an administrative machinery to undertake this task.

Any study of church developmental work must therefore, ipso facto, be a study of its administration. Coptic Egypt is divided into dioceses, which in effect function as a series of autonomous, self-governing principalities. The bishop, as Christ's vicar on earth, is privy to hand-kissing and is addressed as *Saidna* (our lord). He is a prince of sorts, with vast powers and prerogatives. Focusing on his role as chief administrator, I have engaged in fieldwork in twenty-two dioceses (a little under half of all the dioceses at the time I began my fieldwork in 1992, if one excludes the overseas dioceses, which I did not attempt to cover). In the interest of brevity I later deleted my observations about a few of these dioceses to reduce the size of the manuscript.

I may appear to have neglected the role of the women in the church, but only because this is a highly patriarchal church in which women have been kept from positions of influence and power within the church hierarchy—even if since the 1970s, with the takeover of the helm of the church by Shenuda's reform-minded generation, women have been allowed to engage in social work and a new order of consecrated women (mukharasat) incorporated them into the clerical body.

Since Egypt is considerably more developed economically and culturally in the north than in the south, and since I was mainly interested in assessing the extent to which the bishops were contributing to the development of their communities, I selected for study only one-third of the dioceses in the more developed part of the country (Lower Egypt). These were Shubra al-Kheima, Tanta, Kafr al-Sheikh, and Damanhour. I studied over two-thirds of the bishoprics of Upper Egypt, the poorest and least developed part of the country. There, one has more of a chance to see the developmental processes at work, because many of these dioceses were, in 1992, no more than two to three years old. In that area I undertook the study of Banī Suwayf, Minya, Qusia, Abnub, Assiut, Abu Tig, Tima, Tahta, Sohag, Akhmim, Girga, Naga Hammadi, Dishna, Kena, Qus, Luxor, and Aswan. Because of the proximity of many of these Upper Egyptian dioceses to each other—most of them were on the average no more than 20 to 40 minutes apart by car—it proved possible for me to cover several dioceses simultaneously, without having to reside in each and every one of then. Thus, by residing in Assiut I was able to do the fieldwork in Qusia as well. By residing in Tima I could cover Tahta, by residing in Sohag, Akhmim; by residing in Girga, Naga Hammadi; by residing in Luxor, Qus; and so on.

For the same reason, I invested more time and did most of my fieldwork in the smallest, poorest dioceses within Upper Egypt rather than in the relatively more affluent ones centered around the big towns of Assiut, Luxor, and Aswan (even though I included them in my observations for comparative purposes). Similarly, though I used my observations of the remarkable work carried out in Cairo by the bishop of Social Services, Bishop Serapion (who has since been consecrated bishop for Southern California) as a comparative basis for the progress achieved in other areas of Lower Egypt, I did not focus on Cairo as such, because I was investigating the manner in which bishops ruled their dioceses and Cairo is not a diocese ruled by Bishop Serapion, but rather lies within the pope's jurisdiction.

Although I first met Pope Shenuda III on November 13, 1991, at his twentieth anniversary of investiture, I could not begin the fieldwork before obtaining a letter of recommendation from him. It took a long time to gain his trust. I finally obtained this letter, which was a door opener to the dioceses, in January 1992. I did fieldwork in 1992, 1993, and 1994, and I wrote the first draft of this book in Egypt in the academic year 1994–1995, while watching for any new developments.

In addition to acting as a participant observer in the Orthodox-Christian community at large, in its various activities, devotional, educational, and economic, I interviewed all levels of the church leadership from the church-servants and church-servants turned priests (228 of them) to the bishops (25 of them) to the pope, with whom I carried out six interviews, each ranging in time from 2 to 3 hours.

This book is based on those interviews plus video and audiotaped interviews with previous generations of church servants and bishops now deceased, which I borrowed from their friends or family members or from the collection of the Bishopric of Youth headquarters in Cairo, as well as on homilies and talks of the pope, bishops, and church servants which I recorded myself, in addition to church publications in Arabic. Because of the voluminous amount of such publications, I ask the reader's indulgence for having only reported the overall theme of these books and pamphlets and hence not providing page numbers.

As a result of this study, I myself have become fully convinced that the church reform movement has on the whole generated a dynamic and competent new leadership, and that most Copts are successfully reconstituting their lives, as a function of a communitarian space that seeks to attract them and a national space that, if it does not exclude them, at the very least marginalizes them. Wherever I went, I found standing room only in the churches, the overflow of worshipers was such that chairs had to be set up, under an open sky, outside the main entrances to the church. Church literature was avidly read, to judge from the number of times *Kirasa* (the church newsletter) was sold out, and stocks of new releases, both books and manuals, were depleted equally rapidly. Much the same enthusiastic response applies to the taped weekly sermons and homilies of the Pope and the bishops.

One has only to compare this with the eyewitness accounts of those who were active in church service in the 1940s and 1950s, accounts that fortunately have been preserved for us in a number of taped interviews. In them, one hears of empty churches containing only a few illiterate old men and women, of neglected and abandoned monasteries that had become a dumping ground for the poor and ignorant—in short those with no job prospects. In contrast, all the monasteries I visited were teeming with monks hailing from Egypt's technocratic elite of engineers, agronomists, doctors, and the like who had sacrificed lucrative professions.

It is in Coptic participation in a plethora of church activities, the ever-growing space allotted to religion during leisure time, and the significance accorded to clerical interpretations of mundane subjects and the heed paid to their counsel on how to solve financial and employment problems, make career choices, and resolve disputes over inheritance as well as to their prescriptions of good Christian behavior in marital conflicts that the meaning of Coptic life today must be sought.

However, to prove the success of the church endeavor, I would have needed the resources to engage in teamwork, with a group of qualified social scientists stationed in the different towns and villages of the dioceses under study, and to trace the difference over time in church activities and church attendance, subscription to religious publications, and the like. Both because of a previous lack of interest on the part of the churches and the absence of qualified people to gather these statistics and keep records, I would have had to begin with a tabula rasa and to follow up my initial study some five years later. Even if I had the means to hire a qualified team of researchers to survey the different cities and villages throughout the country, a major problem of methodology would have been that no survey has been conducted in the past that would have enabled us to compare our findings with the situation before the church reform movement was launched in the 1940s.

The unavailability of such an earlier study, which would have provided a comparative perspective for my observations, and the fact that my Guggenheim grant did not make allowances for research assistants compelled me to narrow the scope of my study. I focused, therefore, on the avowed objectives of the reform movement and the means by which these were being pursued. In other words, I concentrated on monitoring the process of modernization, rather than on assessing the extent to which modernity has been attained.

To sum up, if modernity, as stated at the outset of this chapter, was not in any sense the intentional objective of the church reformers, the by-product of their activity was to set in motion the change of a traditional society of non-participants into one in which a large number of men, women, and even children are motivated to serve their community on a voluntary basis. Thus, reform Orthodoxy tried to teach previously passive men (doubly so in that they belonged to a downtrodden and fearful minority) the methods of social and economic organization that would bring them into the modern age and enable them to claim their rightful place in the state.

PART I

The Historical Background

Prologue

The "True Egyptians"

The Copts perceive Egypt's geography in their own way, through their own religious memory of the journey of the Holy Family in flight from Judah and the early Christian luminaries, saints, and martyrs who resided in Egypt. Its spatial dimension is therefore experienced differently by them than by their Muslim compatriots, inasmuch as, to borrow a conceptual term introduced to us by Pierre Nora, their sites of memory (*lieux de mémoire*) are a merger of both places and topics, the concrete and abstract.[1] Rituals and commemorations of specific events, of sufferings and sacrifices with which that community can identify, are as much part of these sites of memory as are certain landscapes and material remnants of Christian civilization in Egypt during late antiquity. In short, the Copts' collective memory is both action and representation in Maurice Hallwach's sense.[2] Coptic history, in turn, is a combination of both written and oral history, which can be continuously reconstructed, or in Benedict Anderson's terms "imagined" to answer their circumstances and suit the times.[3]

Who Are the Copts?

The word *Copt* is derived from the Greek word *Aigyptos* (Egyptian). Hence a Copt, until the Arab conquest of Egypt in the seventh century and its subsequent Islamization, simply meant an Egyptian. That word was synonymous with the word Christian, the religion of the majority at the time. The Arabs in turn used the word *Copt* (in Arabic *Kibt*) to refer to the inhabitants of the Nile valley.

In the closing decade of the twentieth century, when this study was undertaken, the Copts were the largest Christian minority of any country in the Middle East. Their exact number could not be determined for two reasons: the sloppy manner of gathering statistics in the less developed part of the country (Upper Egypt), where anyone with a name that was not distinctly Christian might be put down on record as Muslim, and the absence of any government interest in organizing a census under a professional team of social scientists, for fear that the discovery that the Copts constitute more than 6 percent of the Egyptian population (the official estimate)[4] would upset the tenuous intercommunal peace. The researcher is therefore left with the choice of two widely disparate estimates: the official one, which is as low as 6 percent, and that of the Orthodox Church, which is as high as 20 percent. And while the Orthodox Church's estimate may be inflated, the government estimate may be too low. Although the government count of the number of Copts in proportion to the total population yields a percentage that is close to the census undertaken by the British authorities at the beginning of the twentieth century,[5] and the British cannot be accused of doctoring their findings out of a bias in favor of the Muslims, the British census offers the scholar little comfort. The British presumably had to rely on the collaborative effort of the local population, at a time when the accuracy of reporting and the methods of gathering such information were even more slipshod than they are at present. Hence the scholar has the choice of picking a figure in between, say, 8 to 12 percent, or of consoling himself with the thought that even if one accepts the low government estimate of 6 percent there is still the fact that the Christian population of Egypt is as large as the Jewish population of the entire state of Israel.

Regardless of the actual number of Copts in fin de siècle Egypt—or even the humanitarian issue of their relationship as a minority to the Muslim majority—I believe that the historical particularity of the Coptic nation and its contribution to world civilization is in itself a rewarding subject of study. This prompts the question whether the Copts can be referred to as a nation, in the sense that, say, the Jews of Israel claim this status. This question must of necessity be raised, because the Islamic revival in the last three decades of the twentieth century has led to the politicization of the Coptic ethnic identity.

The British occupants repeatedly stressed the absence of notable differences between Christian and Muslim Egyptians. And both Christians and Muslims who want to stress Egypt's national unity quote Lord Cromer, the British high commissioner, who said that a Copt was an Egyptian who prayed in a church and a Muslim was one who prayed in a Mosque.[6] Cromer was not the only British observer writing at the beginning of the twentieth century to point out the similarities between Christians and Muslims in Egypt. Lady Duff Gordon, in her *Letters from Egypt*, stresses similarity of some of their customs, such as the veiling of women,[7] and E. W. Lane, in his *Manners and Customs of the Modern Egyptians*,[8] points out that they visited each other's religious shrines and that the Muslims sought out Coptic priests, whom they believed to possess special healing powers. (This, according to my own observations, is true to the present day.) Sir John Bowring noted that Christian women were as secluded as Muslim women, that they too were confined to harems, that both Muslims and Christians circumcised their boys and subjected their daughters to clitorectomy, and that in the more remote parts of the country the Copts even practiced polygamy. "In the rural districts, the habits of the Copts are scarcely distinguishable from those of the Arabs. . . . They adopt with the Muslims all the superstitions of the country, whether these superstitions be of Mohammedan or Christian origin."[9] I myself recall being surprised, when once on a trip to Upper Egypt to visit the Monastery of the Martyrs in Akhmin, I observed that all the Christians, in a weaving workshop run by Dutch and German sisters for girls of modest means, were veiled. Among the profusion of colors and designs, it took me a few moments to discern the crosses which, like the girls themselves, were so deftly interwoven into the overall pattern as to pass unnoticed.

If we move from the period of British occupation to the present, we will find then, as now, that the Christians spread out across the geographical regions of Egypt and its social strata. The Copts have remained heavily concentrated in the Upper Egyptian provincial capitals of Assiut and Minya, where they represent over 30 percent of the population (roughly around 350,000 to 400,000 souls) and in the capital, where their number is estimated at half a million. While there is nothing even approaching the phenomenon of the Jewish ghetto, because of the absence of the kind of persecution that caused it, one does find large concentrations of Christians in certain Cairene districts like Shubra, Faggala, and Daher—which date back to the end of the nineteenth century when the rural emigrants began to arrive and recreated the patterns of village kinships they had left behind.[10]

In Upper Egypt the number of Christians seems to have dropped from 75 percent, according to the 1917 census, to the current estimate of anywhere from 50 to 60 percent, as migration toward the more urbanized and industrialized lower Egypt continues—a trend that was set in motion in the late nineteenth century by exorbitant taxes from which the peasants fled after losing land they had mortgaged to moneylenders.[11] But the majority of the Copts remain peasants who see themselves as an integral part of the Nile Valley. Just as in monarchical Egypt of the first half of the twentieth century Copts figured among the landed aristocracy, in republican Egypt of the second half of the twentieth century they were heavily represented amid the richest strata of the population as entrepreneurs, industrialists, retailers, merchants, and professionals. But they were also to be found among the poorest strata, not only as landless cultivators, but, in the urban conglomerates, as garbage collectors. They are particularly salient in that occupational group, because of their ability to raise pigs on the rotten vegetables that figure among the garbage—something Muslims shy away from due to Islam's injunction against the eating of pork.

In short, the geographical and occupational profile of Egypt's Christian minority has not changed all that much over time. Like the Jews, they have been prominent in the field of finance, especially banking. Hence, it is not surprising to find Copts heavily represented in the modern business sector, not only in big business but also as small-scale owners of photocopy centers, computer shops, typing and fax service units, jewelry stores, and pharmacies. And like Jewish families of old, Coptic families are tight-knit—divorce is prohibited by the church, with very few exceptions.

Both their intense family relations and their passionate attachment to their church have constituted assets. Christian children tend to be homebound and to spend time at their homework under the vigilant eyes of their mothers, and Christian fathers are more likely to spend their evenings in the bosom of their families than in the all-male coffee houses that keep Muslim fathers of modest means outdoors in the evenings. This results in an overrepresentation of the Copts in higher education and in their prominence in the prestigious professions; in postrevolutionary Egypt these are medicine and engineering. But Copts have remained underrepresented in such government-appointed positions of authority as governor, army officer or general, police chief, and school director or university dean, as well as in the powerful cabinet posts. One cannot but detect in their failure to obtain such positions the reluctance of the heads of state—no matter how liberally inclined they personally might be—to offend the Muslim sensibilities of the majority.

Religiously, the Copts are still overwhelmingly Orthodox. About 90 percent of them remain Orthodox today, despite the defection at the turn of the century of a number of prominent Coptic families, who were either attracted to the more modern Protestant churches, or converted to Catholicism—often as a result of the influence of the private French Catholic schools they had attended.

There remains the question of race. The Copts take pride in portraying themselves as the original inhabitants of the Nile valley, and believe that they are the "true Egyptians" because they have succeeded thanks to their endogamous rules of marriage in preserving their racial purity since pharaonic times, in contrast to the Muslims who are the product of miscegenation. Muslims, in their view, are basically Copts who converted to Islam, either under pressure or for tax advantages, and intermarried first with the Arab invaders, then with the Mamluks (slaves imported as boys from Caucasia, later part of the Soviet Union, who were manumitted after being trained as soldiers and administrators) and still later with the Ottoman rulers with their motley collection of peoples from Eastern Europe. Yet there is no way to distinguish Copts physically from their Muslim compatriots. It is true that in certain areas of Upper Egypt one is sometimes struck by the similarity of a Coptic physiognomy with personages depicted on pharaonic murals and that perhaps the Copts are more uniformly dark-skinned and dark-eyed than their Muslim counterparts, whose color—especially among the upper classes—has been whitewashed through intermarriage with the Muslim Circasians,

Georgians, and Albanians who ruled them for centuries. But even this statement can be made only tentatively, because in the twentieth century there was some intermarriage in the upper reaches of Coptic society with Europeans.

Coptic Mythical History

If there is no such thing as a racial or social specificity to Egypt's Christian population, what then constitutes their nationhood? To answer this, I invoke the concept of mythical history, which I do not necessarily mean to suggest something that did not really happen, but rather something that in the course of time aquired mythical stature. Coptic identity is closely linked to the fact that the Christians share a distinct history of origin: Certain events such as the persecutions the early Christians of Egypt suffered, certain local figures such as the legendary bandit turned saint, by the name of Black Moses, or the Egyptian boy-hero, Abanob, who was martyred by the Roman soldiers at the age of twelve; and certain localities such as the banks of the Nile at Biba, in the Delta region and the sacred mountains at Dronka, near Assiut in Upper Egypt, which are connected to what is believed to be the trek of the Holy Family on a donkey, across Egypt, are charged with meaning for every child born to a Coptic family. This cultural baggage, which Copts carry into adulthood and indeed to the grave, separates them from the Muslims who neither share it nor suspect it exists—or even if they did would care to learn why it is so emotionally loaded for their Christian compatriots. The Muslims have their own heroes: men of action like Saladin, who figures prominently in the Egyptian televised epics. But the folk heroes of the Copts are hermits, like Paul of Thebes, who escaped the persecuting third-century Roman emperor Decius by withdrawing to a solitary cave in the desert, and others less fortunate who were martyred.

Furthermore, the rhythm of a Copt's every day life, with its numerous fasts and feasts, as well as the ritual prescriptions governing a Copt's relationship to the place of worship—especially the rules concerning, the positioning of woman behind the men during prayer, their banishment from the alter, the restrictions on their entry into the church during menstruation and after childbirth—bear far more similarity to those of Orthodox Judaism, from which Orthodox Christianity stems, than to those of Islam. Egyptian monastic tradition has always given the Old Testament a very prominent place. The current movement of monastic revival requires memorization of all the psalms and intensive reading of the prophetic literature and history[12] an uncommon thing among modern western Christian institutions. (A Coptic monk must recite all 150 of the psalms of David daily.)

The Coptic clergy was not able to preserve the Coptic language for the Copts the way the Jewish clergy was. Perhaps Islam was more accommodating to other faiths, given its own syncretism, than Christianity was to Judaism and, by thus being less threatening, did not call for the fierce resolve that preserved Judaism for future generations. But the Coptic cultural legacy, namely the historical memory of their martyrdom and the shared pride in their scholarly contributions to early Christendom and their spiritual contributions to monasticism, which began in Egypt, was preserved and passed on from generation to generation. To this day the two main Coptic traditions remain monasticism and martyrdom.

This book is, in large part, about the way in which the history of the first generations of Christians in Egypt was remembered, recovered, and reconstructed by the generation of the 1940s and early 1950s, to weld the Copts into a unified nation, resistant to the growing encroachments of Islam. That particular interpretation of history, in which hagiography and the cult of the Egyptian martyrs figures so prominently, made possible the rebirth of the Coptic Church and community, in much the same way as the historical memory of Jewish tribulations served national reconstruction in the state of Israel. And just as the Jews have their own new year, Rosh Hashana, which begins in September, September marks the beginning of a new year for the Copts in which they commemorate their martyrdom as Christians under the pagan Roman emperor Diocletian. On that day the Copts are conscious of their separate identity as a community, a church, a nation, and a threatened minority.

Just how relevant the martyr stories are for the current period may be gauged from the response of Bishop Arsanios to an incident of communal strife in his diocese, involving thirteen Copts who were shot down in 1995 by Islamic militants while attending Mass at St. George's Church in Abu Korkas. He told me that he had wanted to have posters made of the thirteen victims in the guise of martyrs forming a halo around the Christ figure, because raising the status of the victims to that of the martyrs of old would provide some consolation to their families. These posters were to be put up in all the churches of his diocese during the memorial services held for them. But the Muslim governing authorities of Minya saw this as a provocation and forbade it.[13]

Many Coptic stories are written apocryphally to reflect the reality of the changing historical eras, which make these texts as relevant to the present as they were to the past. In a brilliant interpretation of the metonymic logic applied to the story of the martyr Victor, the son of Romanos, Safinaz-Amal Naguib unravels the process by which new meaning is derived by the reader from the encounter between text and context.[14] Romanos, Victor's father, was the emperor Diocletian's trusted vizier, and when Diocletian decided to impose idolatry on his kingdom, Romanos conspired with Diocletian to have the patriarch who opposed him killed. Of immediate contemporary relevance to the current pope, Shenuda III's reign are the problems of apostasy and the forcible removal of the patriarch who stands fast against the pagan ruler.

Not only the martyr stories, but also stories of miracles are rewritten apocryphally to give encouragement in dark times. Recently, with the upsurge of bloody attacks by Islamic militants, such stories have been put to good use by the church leadership.

1

When Egypt Was Christian

The following three chapters are a very rough historical sketch, based on a few of the better known works. Those who are well versed in Egyptian history are advised to skip chapters 1–3 of this book.

To shed some light on Coptic myths and the commemorations of suffering and sacrifice that reproduce the Coptic past, I will attempt to outline in a rudimentary fashion the main personalities and events of the third to fifth centuries AD that captivate the imagination of Egyptian Christians to this day.

The Greeks of Egypt were the first converts to Christianity and the first proselytizers among the native population. Alexander the Great arrived in Egypt in October 332 BC; the priests of Memphis (modern Luxor) offered him the crown of Upper and Lower Egypt, and after seven months, in April of 331, he left Egypt to engage in further conquests. He was never to return; he died eight years later in the year 323 BC in Babylon. However, his legacy, the prosperous capital city of Alexandria, which he had founded in April 331, was to become, under the Ptolemaic dynasty, the home of some of the greatest scholars of the age: Euclid the geometer, Erastosthenes the geographer, and Philo the New Platonist, a Jew who resided in Alexandria in the first century AD (after the Greeks, the Jews constituted the largest foreign community in Alexandria).[1]

By the third century, Alexandria was not only a major center of classical Greek culture but the intellectual capital of Christianity in the Eastern Mediterranean. Though Christianity is generally traced back by the Copts to the arrival of the Apostle Mark to Egypt, sometime in the first century AD (he is considered the founder of the first church in Egypt and its first patriarch), it only became an intellectual force in Egypt toward the end of the second century, when the Greek philosopher Titus Flavius Clement (c. AD 160–215) became the main Christian instructor at the Catechetical School of Alexandria, which he was eventually to head. Clement, who was converted to Christianity shortly after he came to Alexandria, wrote several important treatises, whose main appeal to the well-educated Alexandrians lay in their interpretation of biblical themes in allegorical and mystical terms familiar to those imbued with Greek culture. For while Clement attacked the great philosophers of ancient Greece for failing to criticize the superstitions of pagan cults and myths, he nonetheless acknowledged his debt to Aristotelian logic and Platonic metaphysics, as well as to the ethics of the Stoics. In this way, Clement's erudition served the early church well, although his converts were mainly limited to the cosmopolitan Greeks—outside of a small number of Greek-speaking Jews and natives.

Although Clement, or Clement of Alexandria as he came to be called, was a Greek, he was adopted by later generations of Egyptian Orthodox clergy, together with his pupil Origen, as one of their own. These two luminaries, to whom the Catechical School of Alexandria owed its luster, figure prominently among the assets of the Egyptian Orthodox Church. Origen, a Greek who unlike his master was born in Alexandria (c. AD 185), not only matched Clement's erudition but had the kind of fearless mettle that could ascend easily to martyrdom for the faith. He might have joined the hagiography of saints, had he not been so impetuous as to castrate himself to avoid being tempted by his female students—an excess of zeal that was later used against him. The story goes that even when Origen was just a boy he exhorted his father Leonides to accept martyrdom for the faith. Leonides was duly beheaded and only the ploy of Origen's mother, who hid his clothes to prevent her son from rushing out after him to share his fate, saved his life. Origen later died from the aftereffects of the merciless torture to which he was subjected during a wave of Christian persecution.

Like his master Clement, Origen was a prolific writer, whose works, particularly his *Exhortation to Martyrdom* and his *Commentaries on the Old and New Testaments*, brought him fame throughout the Christian world. But although, like Clement, he was familiar with the works of all the Greek philosophers, he did not feel the need to invoke the authority of some illustrious Greek philosopher to justify a Christian principle—an indication of the growing self-confidence of the Egyptian church, which was no longer intimidated by Greek culture, as it had been when Clement first arrived in Alexandria.

Though Origen contributed to the importance and influence of the Church of Alexandria, he also aroused the jealously of the patriarch, an ambitious man, because Origen, rather than he, was invited by the eastern churches to resolve their theological conflicts. The patriarch therefore had him excommunicated. The grounds for his excommunication are of interest to us: the council of bishops who judged him reproached not only his self-castration but also his heretical teachings, mainly his denial of eternal punishment. This judgment marks a turning point in Egyptian church history, as the first self-assertive attempt by that body to draw the boundary between itself as *Orthodox* and others as heretical. This attitude would eventually lead to the Great Schism that separated it for centuries from the mainstream of Christianity. Both Origen and his master Clement of Alexandria were far too cosmopolitan, erudite, and syncretic in their biblical interpretations to fit in with Orthodox Church dogmatism. Hence it comes as no surprise that the Orthodox Church was to remove from Clement, some years later, the title of Saint, on the grounds of certain "heretical" statements he had made.

Second, though Origen's own reputation did not suffer from his banishment from Alexandria—he continued to be courted by the prelates of many of the eastern churches—the influence of the Catechetical School began to decline as a result and never recovered. Thereafter, the Catechetical School was eclipsed by the Church of Alexandria, and the patriarch, not the head of the school, occupied center stage. Though on occasion the patriarchs were also great theologians, proselytizing in Egypt took on a more plebeian character: Christianity was no longer just the religion of the Greek elite but began to be preached to the masses in their native tongue, demotic, an Egyptian vernacular derived from an amalgam of the Pharaonic and Greek languages (24 out of 31 letters in the Coptic alphabet are borrowed from Greek).

It was Dionysios, a student of Origen, who initiated the policy of preaching Christianity to the natives in their own language, once he became patriarch. All the great church fathers, however, continued to write in Greek. These included St. Anthony, St. Pachomios, and St. Shenoute of Atripe—three monks with whom Coptic literature was born outside of Alexandria in the fourth century AD, as well as St. Athanasios, a fourth century patriarch who was born in Alexandria in 296 AD. In fact, Egypt remained bilingual until the Arab conquest in 642 AD: documents from that period show that not only Coptic was used but also Greek.

At the beginning of Patriarch Dionysios's reign, which coincided with a wave of empire-wide Christian persecution in 249 AD, under the newly instated Roman emperor Decius, only four native martyrs were recorded among the hundreds that were killed—even if one of them was none other than the famed Apollonia, who became the patron saint of those who suffered from toothache, on account of her broken jaws. Essentially, the church Dionysios inherited had remained the church of the Greeks living in Alexandria and in some of the northern provinces. But by the time of the next wave of persecution under emperor Diocletian, a great number of the martyrs were native Egyptians.

The present day Copts have linked their calender, which is a solar calendar derived from the pharaonic one and using the pharaonic names for the various months, to their experience of persecution and martyrdom under Diocletian. Thus, the first year of their calendar, referred to as the first year of the martyrs, begins with 284 AD, the year of Diocletian's accession to the throne of Rome.

This period, which has become known as the Era of the Martyrs, does indeed mark a new era in Egyptian history, inasmuch as it gave birth to a native church distinct from the originally Greek church of Alexandria. Mass conversions in Egypt had, however, to await the advent of Constantine the Great to the throne of Rome in 312 AD. Constantine, who was influenced by his Christian mother (St. Helena), came to look on Christianity as the ideology that would unify all the different groups of peoples and races within the Roman Empire and thus prevent its further disintegration. Already, when he was only emperor of the western part of the empire, he issued, together with Licinius, the ruler of the eastern portion of the Roman Empire, the Edict of Milan, which granted freedom of religious worship to everyone within the empire. In 324, after defeating Licinius in battle, he became the sole ruler of the entire empire and began to put into effect a policy of conversion of pagans to Christianity throughout the empire. As a result, partly because of increased missionary activity throughout Egypt, and partly because of the effort to preach the gospel to the natives in their own tongue, Christianity began to spread rapidly.

In the fourth century, the diocese of Alexandria was one of the most important in all of Christendom. The patriarch of Alexandria was the only one to bear the title of pope. This position was greatly strengthened by Athanasios, who managed to bring the monasteries under his control when he became patriarch. And the Catechetical School of Alexandria was still one of the main centers of Christian learning. But this was destined to begin changing with the founding of Constantinople, sometime around 330 AD, by Emperor Constantine. He had decided that Rome was not the best center for an empire that extended from the Rhine to the Euphrates and that the town of Byzantium, by the strategic straits of the Bosporus, was better situated. Even if the effect was not immediately obvious, the transformation of Byzantium into Constantinople was to shift the center of Christianity away from Alexandria and, inadvertently, to cause the rift in the domain of Christendom known as the Great Schism. The Orthodox Church of Egypt, accustomed as it had become to a position of preeminence, could not tolerate a rival authority.

At first the Egyptians managed to hold their own in the game of power politics by prevailing in the theological disputes that plagued the era. In large part, this was due to the brilliance of one of the greatest theologians of the fourth century, and indeed of any century, Athanasios. When the first theological controversy over the views advanced by an Egyptian priest, named Arius, that in the Trinity the Father was superior to the Son as the Son was, in turn, to the Holy Ghost, wrenched the church, the Council of Nicea was convened in 325 by Emperor Constantine to resolve it. The then patriarch of Alexandria, Alexander, took Athanasios with him so that he might convince the other prelates of the folly of Arius's views. And indeed Athanasios carried the day by the power of his rhetoric, although Arianism remained a potent challenge for a long time thereafter. But at the next ecumenical council, which met in Constantinople in

381, the See of Constantinople was declared superior to that of Alexandria, despite the fact that the decisions arrived at in Nicea were reconfirmed. This demotion infuriated the Egyptians.

Still, the Egyptians were able to hold their own into the fifth century, thanks to the presence of another strong personality and acute theologian in their midst, Patriarch Cyril, who took the reigns of the church in AD 412. It was in his era that the next great theological disputes took place. The issue this time was not the nature of the Trinity but that of the Virgin Mary, whom Nestorius the bishop of Constantinople decided should only be called Christ-bearer (Christokos), not God-bearer (Theotokos), as she was then called, since she herself was not divine. This view, which came to be known as the Nestorian heresy, was vehemently opposed by Patriarch Cyril, who claimed it smacked of an earlier heresy, Arianism. Cyril was perhaps less irked by the theological argument than by the fact that it was advanced by his great rival, the bishop of Constantinople.

At any rate Cyril, who from the outset had shown a combative temperament, decided to make this issue his own crusade. He departed for the Council of Ephesos, which had been summoned by Emperor Theodosius in AD 431 to resolve the question, accompanied by a large contingent of Egyptian bishops and monks, among whom figured the monk Shenoute, after whom the current pope is named, because he was considered by later generations to be the glory of militant Christianity. And historians generally recognize that it was thanks to this intimidating Egyptian presence that the council members ruled against Nestorius, who was condemned, and that God-bearer, the appellation of the Virgin, was reconfirmed.

Cyril's influence continued over both the churches of the West and East throughout his lifetime, so that his successor Dioscoros inherited a very powerful position. Christianity reigned supreme throughout Egypt. Even in the north of the country, the influence of the great pagan philosophies that had once competed with Christianity had been all but eliminated.

Already by the end of the fourth century, paganism had been outlawed by the emperor of Rome and the once-persecuted Christians of Egypt had thus been able to turn the table on their erstwhile foes, with Patriarch Theophilus taking the lead in instigating the mobs to storm the Serapion (the Greek temple, which housed a library containing one of the world's largest collection of books of learning, some forty thousand), one of the greatest acts of vandalism in history. When Theophilus was succeeded by his nephew Cyril, in 412, the attacks were no longer limited to objects that symbolized the hated paganism but aimed at persons. Cyril had the renowned pagan mathematician and philosopher Hypatia killed. A group of monks dragged her off the chariot that was bringing her back from one of her lectures and stoned her to death. Cyril's violence was not only directed at pagans; he incited the mobs to invade the Jewish homes and drive their inhabitants out of the city of Alexandria, to punish them for having spilled Christian blood in a quarrel. When the prefect of the city protested against this behavior, Cyril had a battalion of monks stationed near Alexandria give him a beating. Nor was this the only time the monks engaged in such unchristian behavior. It is fair to say that since the imperial edict against paganism of 392, not only pagans but also heretics and people of other religious persuasions became fair game.

Thus the church that emerged in the fifth century under Cyril's successor, Patriarch Dioscoros, was very different from the early Christian Church: The head of the church enjoyed great temporal power, in part because he had inherited a wealthy see. Furthermore, the patriarch of Egypt, unlike all others outside of Constantinople, had direct jurisdiction over his bishops (elsewhere, the bishops were responsible to and could be called into account only by a synod of archbishops). The Church of Egypt was so strong that the next time a theological dispute broke out, over the heretical views of a monk from Constantinople called Eutyches (in contrast to Nestorius, who claimed that while the human nature of Christ was born of Mary the divine was not; he claimed that Christ was of one substance with God, but not with humankind), Patriarch Dioscorus, who supported Eutyches, succeeded in having the bishop of Constantinople deposed at the second Council of Ephesos in 449.

This was to be the last time, however, that the church of Egypt could exercise its power in so blatant a fashion. Its influence at Ephesos had been largely a function of the weakness of the presiding emperor, Theodosius II. But in 450 the emperor died, and his successor, his sister Pulcheria, was determined to undo the accomplishments of the Council of Ephesos, which had been nicknamed the Robber Council because of the intimidating tactics of the monks of Egypt. At the Council of Chalcedon in 451, the patriarch Dioscoros was brought to trial, excommunicated, and sent into exile, and the decisions of the previous council were reversed.

In essence, what this meant was that the council adopted what came to be known as the doctrine of Diphysitism (the dual nature of Christ), whereas the Egyptians adhered to the doctrine of Monophysitism (a single nature in which both were fused). This hairsplitting doctrinal difference became the basis of a permanent rift between the Church of Egypt and the rest of Christendom.

The doctrines of the Council of Chalcedon had, however, been accepted by the Byzantine Church (referred to as Melchite). A Melchite patriarch was imposed on Alexandria, an act that divided that city between the members of the Monophysite church and those of the "foreign" church. The Greeks who were pro-Chalcedonian prevailed in the churches near the harbor, while the Copts who were Monophysites prevailed in those near the Serapeion. The successive waves of persecution of Monophysites, between the fifth and seventh centuries, reinforced the hostility of the native population to the imperial Byzantine power and predisposed it to support the Arab armies that defeated the Byzantine forces at Babylon in 641 as liberators from oppression.

The Council of Chalcedon was detrimental to the subsequent development of the Egyptian Church because, ever since, the Egyptian Monophysites have been considered schismatic by the other main centers of Christianity, Rome and

Constantinople. Furthermore, that council demoted Alexandria to fourth in rank, after the see of Antioch. Asia Minor also replaced Alexandria as the nexus of the intellectual life of the Eastern Mediterranean in late Antiquity. Egypt which through Alexandria had been in touch with the theological developments in other areas, was cut off from them after the fifth century. Coptic theological literature—apart from some hagiographical and homiletic gems producted by the monasteries, particularly St. Macarios—became mainly defensive and conservative, even if some of that apologetic discourse achieved great brilliance later in the Middle Ages, when the threat of Islam to the Coptic cultural heritage replaced that of the Byzantines. But the intellectual ferment of the Reformation and the biblical criticism that grew out of it bypassed Egypt, as did, in modern times, the western vision of a family of churches mutually responsible for each other—a vision that itself was the outgrowth of age-long disputes and dialogues among Protestant churches and between them and the Catholic Church. The Coptic Church, which never forgot its humiliation at Chalcedon, maintained its isolation from other Christians until the late twentieth century; the only way it could be entered was through baptism.

Because Egyptian national pride had been wounded at Chalcedon, thereafter Monophysitism became an expression of Egyptian religious nationalism, one in which xenophobia was always latent.[2] This sentiment, an esteemed Coptic scholar has argued, made it possible for the Copts to unite with the Muslims against the Christian powers from earliest times right through the British occupation of Egypt in the late nineteenth century and early twentieth century.[3]

2

The Dawn of a New Era

The Arab rulers were willing, on the whole, to allow Christians and Jews to practice their own religion and be governed by their own religious laws, since the Koran recognized the validity of these two religions (Suras 2 and 5 maintain that anyone who believed in God and performed good deeds, whether Jew or Christian, would be rewarded by God). Nonetheless, conversions to Islam gained in momentum between the seventh and ninth centuries, at times under pressure, at others for financial and tax advantages, so that by the ninth century the Coptic peasantry had largely intermingled with the Arab invaders and Coptic was being replaced by Arabic.

The Dark Ages: Mamluk Rule

The period of Arab rule was one of relative tolerance, apart from the reign in the tenth century of the insane Fatimid caliph al-Hakim, who claimed he was divine and, although or perhaps because he was born of a Christian mother, persecuted the Copts by issuing an edict that all Christian males had to wear a cross weighing five rotl (about 5 pounds) around their necks and black turbans, and by decreeing that they should not ride horses—only asses and mules. But such instances of persecution were the exception rather than the rule under the Arab rulers, while under the Caucasian slave dynasties, the Mamluks, that followed them, ruling Egypt from 1250 until the Ottoman conquest in 1517, all manners of disabilities were imposed on the Copts from being required to ride their mules backwards to wearing a bell around their necks when using the public baths.

The importation of boy slaves, from the Caucasian regions of what later became part of the Soviet Union, who were converted to Islam, trained for the army and administration, and manumitted once they reached adulthood so they could be used in the service of the state, began under the Arab Ayyubid dynasty. But this type of administration was vastly expanded and systematized later under the Mamluks themselves, when they in turn became the rulers of Egypt. It was under the Mamluks that the Copts suffered their darkest hour. In one instance, in 1320, even their churches were attacked and looted. This triggered a Coptic uprising against their Muslim rulers, in which the latter's mosques, palaces, houses, and shops were burnt and looted until the revolt was bloodily put down.

Since the Arab conquest, the Egyptian state had relied on the Copts for a poll tax known as *Jizyah* which, as Dhimis (protected people exempt from army duty), they had to pay. They, in turn, relied on the government for the protection of their lives and property. There were instances when the government failed to keep its part of the bargain, particularly during the reign of the Mamluk princes' dynasties. In the anarchical late Mamluk era, which was characterized by a nearly total breakdown of the central authority, competing Mamluk princes and their retainers plundered homes and shops and killed at will. To be sure the Muslim subjects also suffered in periods of oppressive governments—above all from tax extortion. But it remains true that the social and civil inferiority of the Jews and Christians made them an easy prey.

In the eighteenth century, non-Muslims were organized, into religious communities known as Millets, with a semi-autonomous status officially recognized by the Ottoman sultan. These were headed by an ecclesiastical authority, which acted as an intermediary between the community and the state. On the whole, the Millet system, based on the separation of the ethnic groups from each other, worked well in containing ethnic conflict within the empire. But while Muslims accepted the idea that the Copts should be tolerated, and often recalled that one of the Prophet's own wives had been a Copt and that he had preached a special regard for them, it was understood that non-Muslims should not exercise power over Muslims.

The Emancipation of the Copts in the Nineteenth Century

At the turn of the nineteenth century, Egypt began to modernise under the aegis of a new Macedonian dynasty founded by Muḥammed Ali, known as al-kabir (the Great). He had been sent by the Ottoman sultan at the head of armed forces from the East European provinces of the empire to reassert the sultan's control over the rebellious Mamluks. In his endeavor to modernize the army, the economy, the bureaucracy and the educational system, Muḥammed Ali opened Egypt up not only to the unemployed French officers, the debris of the defeated Napoleonic armies who became upper-echelon administrators, technicians, and teachers, but also to impoverished Greeks and Italians. The latter, together with the Armenians, many of whom came down from Istanbul and Smyrna, became shopkeepers, retailers, grocers, foremen, skilled laborers, carpenters, and plumbers.[1]

In short, Muḥammed Ali sought out talent, regardless of religious persuasion, for his administration and army, as well as for his medical, educational, and commercial ventures. The Copts had neither the training nor the technical expertise to be able to compete with the Europeans for administrative and managerial jobs, nor did they have the familiarity with European markets that gave even the unlettered Greeks and Italians an edge in an economy newly tied to Europe, through the export of cotton. They did, however, have certain traditional skills: their knowledge of accounting and surveying gave them an advantage over the Muslims, who had always shied away from these professions. Thus, they were able to play a part in Muḥammed Ali's endeavor to transform a largely subsistence agriculture into an export-oriented one. This transformation was based on the cultivation of long staple cotton, which a French agricultural engineer had introduced to Egypt during Muhammed Ali's reign.[2]

At the time Muḥammed Ali seized power (in 1805), Egypt's system of tax collection was chaotic, due to the arbitrary tax levies by rival groups of Mamluk princes, whose frequent descent on the villages resembled looting raids far more than they did tax collections. To reorganize the administration and make it an effective instrument of government, Muḥammed Ali most urgently needed the funds that a good system of taxation would provide. For this he had to rely on the Coptic land-surveyors, tax collectors, and scribes. But corruption flourished in his administration; indeed it was one of the chief avenues of personal enrichment. Thus, their expertise not only enabled the Copts to carve out a niche for themselves in the administration, but also to use and misuse it as a means of self-enrichment. In this way, by the end of the nineteenth century, a well-to-do Coptic stratum had emerged in the countryside.[3]

Corruption was the general standard of conduct: The Copts were no more venal than their Turkish overlords. Muḥammed Ali tried to curb misappropriations of tax revenues by periodically arresting the culprits. Any official, Coptic or Muslim, caught embezzling was removed from office, forced to reimburse the government, and in some instances publicly flogged as an example to others. The ancestor of Boutrous Boutrous Ghālī, the former secretary-general of the United Nations, a certain Mualim Ghālī, who was the chief of the Coptic guild responsible for the collection of taxes throughout the country, was repeatedly arrested on charges of malversation. However, since Muḥammed Ali's practice was generally to reinstate the high officials after they had paid their fines, they resumed their corrupt practices as soon as he relaxed control, because he was preoccupied with other matters of state.[4] To aggravate this situation, there was as yet no regular budget and the amounts of receipts and expenses were unknown to all except the Copts, who kept the accounts, and therefore had many opportunities to defraud the state.

Outside of corruption, they, like the Muslims in the administration, made their fortune by receiving state lands from the khedive and from the Ottoman ruling class, whose large landed properties they managed, as a recompense for their services. By the reign of Muḥammed Ali's grandson Ismail (1863–1879), the Coptic tax collectors and land-surveyors, many of whom received large bribes for underreporting the extent of an owner's landed property, had emerged as big landowners in their own right. They had also begun to make their weight felt in state institutions. For example, they were represented in the Consultative Council Khedive Ismail had set up in 1866, primarily to legitimize his own need to increase taxation, since Egypt was tottering toward bankruptcy on account of an ambitious development program encompassing the building of schools, hospitals, railways, telegraph lines, dams, and canals and of a huge public debt incurred for the building of the Suez Canal. The Coptic dignitaries added their voice to those of their Muslim colleagues in the council who were demanding the right to control the state budget, which was unprecedented in the khedival administration. Already under Khedive Ismail's predecessor Said the Copts had been admitted for the first time into the ranks of officers in the army and now, under Ismail, Copts also began to reach high offices in the administration. The turn of the century would usher in the first Coptic prime minister, Boutros Ghālī, a descendent of Mualim Ghālī, who himself had reached the post of khedival secretary under Muḥammed Ali.[5]

From Tolerance to a Quest for Equality

Although the Muḥammed Ali dynasty freed the Copts from much discrimination, such as the interdiction to bear arms or testify against a Muslim in court, and the restrictions on their behavior and dress, Muslim attitudes on the whole remained prejudiced. Christian displays of wealth or power aroused resentment. The appointment of Christians to high office was always controversial: Among the arguments advanced was that non-Muslims could not be trusted to pursue one of the goals of the state, namely Islam. Thus, though Christians gained a foothold in the corridors of power, their position remained precarious.

However, the Coptic upper class, emboldened by the dramatic improvements in their condition throughout the nineteenth century, became increasingly vocal in their demands for equality in the first decade of the twentieth century. Their struggle centered on four demands: equality in appointments to and promotions within the civil service, the appointment of more Copts to Egypt's representative bodies, Sunday as the day of rest for Christians, and Bible instruction to match Muslim religious instruction in public schools.[6] In 1911, a conference was convened in Assiut, which was attended by many prominent Copts, who were later to play a major role in the nationalist movement, to promote these aims. But Muslim public opinion was not yet ready to accept these demands. A counter-conference was convened, which reported that to give in to them would allow the Copts to form a separate nation "whose pretensions will grow until they concentrate all power in Coptic hands. And the Copts will do this by relying on the fact that the occupying power is Christian."[7]

In truth, the Copts got little support from the British in achieving their aims, and Coptic expectations for special treatment at the hands of their fellow Christians were disappointed. Appeals for special treatment, particularly for jobs, made in the name of the Savior, were extremely distasteful to the British. Indeed, the loss of the senior positions they had held under Khedive Ismail, was one of the Copts' chief complaints against the British.[8] Particularly when it came to the upper echelons of the provincial administration, the British made it explicit that they did not find Copts suitable for such jobs.

Futhermore, the British made little distinction between Copts and their Muslim compatriots. As the British agent Lord Cromer saw it, Christianity had conferred on the Copts very little moral benefit.[9] Quite apart from such value judgments, the British had no compelling reasons to pamper them. Unlike in India, where ethnic and religious divisions were used both as a means of facilitating the administration of a huge and politically fragmented area and as a way of preventing the emergence of a unified opposition to British rule, in Egypt the Coptic minority was too small to be worthy of their consideration (6% of the population as opposed to India, where the Muslim minority made up 30% of the population). Furthermore, they were not concentrated in any particular geographic area, as the Muslims were in India. Nor were they even a majority in any given province.

Lord Cromer was not averse to using the minority issue to persuade the foreign office to extend an occupation some liberal British policymakers wished to be temporary (as when he made the spurious argument of the need to extend British hegemony to Upper Egypt, to protect the Copts from the danger of Egypt's invasion by the Mahdi of the Sudan). But he understood that it was not in British interest to jeopardize Muslim support for British rule by courting the minority. And his successor, Lord Gorst, was even more determined to cultivate Muslim support.[10] Coptic dissatisfaction with this British attitude no doubt played a role in their decision to join the anti-British nationalist movement. As one British official put it, they had rightly calculated that in the long term it was more important for them to gain Muslim tolerance by proving their loyalty to the national cause than to count on the "remote and not always effective alien Christian support."[11]

But it would be a mistake to reduce the Coptic anti-British attitude to a matter of tactics. The Coptic community had been wary of foreigners ever since the fifth century when their church had seceded from the rest of the Christian world. The national church of Egypt was extremely xenophobic, and western Christianity had responded in kind, beginning with the Crusaders, who had made no distinction between Muslims and Christians when they entered Egypt in the tenth century, slaughtering the two indiscriminately. The nineteenth and early twentieth century missionaries, albeit with less sanguinary forms of persecution, refused to tolerate the "soul-destroying heresy of the Copts."[12]

Coptic Assimilation

At the end of World War I, groups of Egyptian dignitaries, encouraged by U.S. President Woodrow Wilson's Fourteen Points, began to meet to discuss the question of how Egypt was to obtain her independence from Britain. When they decided to form a delegation (*Wafd*) to present this demand directly to the British government in London, only two Copts figured in the group that had coalesced around the leader of the nationalist movement, Saad Zaglul. The two Copts, out of a delegation that comprised twelve Muslims, were both from wealthy Upper Egyptian families: Sinut Ḥannā, from Banī Suwayf, and George Khayat, from Assiut.[13] The majority of the Copts had not yet reconsidered their attitude towards independence, which would deprive them of British protection. They had kept aloof from the first nationalist movement led by a French-educated lawyer, Mustafa Kamāl, who, while he was imbued with French secular ideals of *liberté, egalité, fraternité*, equivocated about a radical rupture with pan-Islamism, because he considered the link to the Ottoman Empire to be a buffer against British designs on Egypt.

The post–World War I nationalists, however, had no interest in any pan-Islamic or even pan-Arab connection. For Mustafa Kamāl's successor to the leadership of the nationalist movement, Saad Zaglul, Egypt's interests superseded all others. When it was suggested to him that Egypt join forces with the Arab countries in their struggle for independence from British and French rule by sponsoring the Arab League, he replied, derisively, "Zero plus zero amounts to zero."[14]

Saad Zaglul's secularism paid off. The two-month nationalist agitation, a response to the British high commissioner's refusal to allow Zaglul's delegation to travel to London to present its demands for national independence and to Zaglul's exile, was a triumph of Muslim-Coptic cooperation. The demonstrators, who bore banners inscribed with a crescent intertwining a cross, were urged on by priests and sheikhs, sharing pulpits in churches and mosques.

The Copts played a very important and visible role in all aspects of this anti-British movement, which came to be known as the 1919 Revolution, from organizing strikes and demonstrations to planning and carrying out terrorist acts. Their role in anti-British propaganda was invaluable both at home and abroad. At home, for example, when the news broke that the British had exiled the nationalist leader Saad Zaglul, Father Sergios led a huge protest demonstration to the Islamic university, al-Azhar. A fiery orator, he was the first Christian ever permitted to speak from its pulpit.[15] Abroad, the Wafd relied on the oratorical skills and perfect command of foreign languages of two Copts: The Oxford-educated Makram Ebeid, who proselytized their cause in England, and the

French-educated Wasif Ghālī, son of the late prime minister, who took their case to Paris.[16] To a lesser extent, they relied on George Khayat's connections with the Americans. (He had been converted from Orthodoxy to Protestantism by the American Presbyterian missionaries in Assiut and had acted as the American consul there.) But America, barely out of its isolationism, was not yet a world power on a par with Britain and France, two countries of primary importance in determining Egypt's future.

After the revolution, when the issue of who was to lead the negotiating team to England came up—the moderate prime minister, Adli Pasha, an aristrocratic Turko-Egyptian in favor of compromise with the British, or the radical nationalist leader, Saad Zaglul—all the original members of the Wafd defected to the prime minister's camp with the exception of three Copts, Sinut Ḥannā, Wasif Ghālī, and Wisa Wasef.[17] Of all the Copts in the party these three were the most loyal, staying with the party until their deaths in the 1930s. Others left the party, and later returned. They, together with the new Coptic recruit Makram Ebeid, who was to rise to become the number two man in the party, were so successful in their anti-Adli campaign that the prime minister's negotiation efforts collapsed and he resigned from office. When the British retaliated by threatening them with banishment, unless they ceased all political agitation and retired to their villages, two of them, Sinut and Ebeid, who were openly defiant, came to share Zaglul's second period of exile. Many others, including an important new recruit, the large landowner Fakhri Abd al-Nur, who published a manifesto calling for a boycott of British goods, were to continue the struggle at home. By July 1922, he had become an important member of the Wafd's inner circle. He and three other Copts, Murqus Ḥannā, Wasif Ghālī, and George Khayat, who had rejoined the Wafd, were arrested and imprisoned by the British.[18]

All of these Copts, as members of the prominent land-owning families of Upper Egypt, not only were able to help the Wafd with their oratorical and writing skills but, equally important, contributed funds and rallied their tenant-farmers in their home provinces.

One of the nationalist tactics had been to make it impossible for the British to govern without Zaglul by compelling all Egyptians to turn down any offer of the post of prime minister. This united front held together, despite what was widely interpreted as a British attempt to detach the Coptic community from the nationalist camp by appointing, in 1919, a Copt to replace Adli as prime minister. The fact that Yūsuf Wahba was not regarded as having the aptitude of the late prime minister Boutros Ghālī only made British motives more suspect.

Wahba's acceptance of the post was vehemently denounced in the Coptic press. Several hundred Copts signed a letter repudiating him and more than two thousand held a protest meeting at the patriarchate, at which one of the speakers was Father Sergios. He denounced any Copt who accepted cabinet office. When all this pressure, including several Coptic delegations sent to persuade Wahba to resign, failed to bring about a result, an attempt was made on his life in December 1919. A Copt volunteered for the task, so that no intercommunal tension should result from this action. Finally, in May 1920, Wahba was compelled to step down. And the British, failing to find any credible interlocutor for negotiations, ended up, in 1922, by issuing unilaterally a proclamation of Egypt's independence.[19]

Coptic opposition to the British did not end there, however, because among the prerogatives the 1922 treaty had reserved for Britain was the right to protect Egypt's minorities. Although there was some justification for British concern, given the recent massacre of Armenians in Turkey, the Egyptians feared that the British would use this reservation as a pretext to intervene in Egypt's affairs, as they had done in the past. It is a measure of the degree to which the Copts trusted the nationalist leader, Saad Zaglul, that they were adamant in their insistence not to be designated as a minority along with the foreign permanent residents of Egypt like the Greeks, Italians and Armenians, as well as in their demand that Britian's prerogative to protect Egypt's minorities be annulled. They did not want to appear, in the eyes of their Muslim compatriots, to be seeking foreign protection. Even the conservative Coptic newspaper *al-Watan*, which was closely tied to the patriarchate, criticised this prerogative.[20]

When the Constitutional Committee, which included three Coptic dignitaries, had met in April of 1922 to draft Egypt's constitution, not one of the Copts took exception to the provision that made Islam the religion of state. In fairness, Muslim members of the committee were anxious to ensure freedom of worship and equality for Egypt's minorities, both Christian and Jewish. They had selected the Belgian constitution out of several European constitutions as their model, because Belgium in a context of diverse ethnic groups, had avoided sectarian problems. The chairman of the committee, former Prime Minister Rushdi Pasha, raised the issue of constitutional protection; he suggested several safeguards of the right to equality in civil and political life. These were incorporated in Articles 1, 12, and 13 of Egypt's constitution. Yet none of the aristocrats who made up the committee realized that the provision making Islam the religion of state negated these articles. Such an idea might have been too radical in any case for that conservative body of titled gentleman (pashas) handpicked by the palace. The Wafd, which had opposed the idea of an appointed committee and demanded the election of a constituent assembly featuring younger, more radical elements, had been overruled. Even if it hadn't, however, only its leader, Saad Zaglul, might have commanded enough respect to dissent publicly. But this would have had taxed his popularity—judging from the trouble he had, when the Wafd came to power two years later, keeping two prominent Copts in his cabinet.[21]

In the climate of the Muslim-Christian honeymoon that still lingered on after the 1919 revolution, it is doubtful whether even the Coptic politicians and intellectuals themselves understood the danger inherent in this clause. As perceptive a writer as Salama Musa, a secular socialist, declared that he was obliged to defend Islam, because it was the religion of his country. And the Wafdist politician Makram Ebeid said that he was a Muslim by country and a Christian by religion. At any rate, the clause making Islam the religion of state was incorporated into the constitution without a single objection being made.

There was more opposition to the issue of whether the Copts should have a certain number of reserved seats in Parliament. The most prominent Coptic proponent of proportional representation was Tewfik Doss Pasha, a member of the Liberal Constitutionalist Party. He suggested a proportional scheme that would give Egypt's minorities 20 percent of the seats in Parliament, and he was supported by Yūsuf Qattawi Pasha representing the Jewish community and by Bishop Yuanis representing the church. *Al-Watan* spoke out in favor of the scheme. But most Coptic politicians, whose interests transcended communal matters, agreed with Abd al-Hamid Badawi Pasha, the chief legal adviser to the constitutional subcommittee, who though himself a strong secularist argued against proportional representation. He feared that such a system would create permanent divisions based on religion in the body politic. He felt sure that if left alone, in time, religious differences would diminish in importance in the eyes of the electorate. A system of proportional representation, in his view, would divide Egypt along the lines adopted by the British in India, engendering ethnic and religious discord.[22]

The parties tended to divide on this issue along Wafdist and non-Wafdist lines. The Wafd continued to maintain a nationalist perspective: Zaglul insisted that Parliament should divide according to political issues, not ethnic or religious ones. All Wafdist Copts shared this view. They were confident that Copts would be elected, because of the interests they represented and skills they possessed. Perhaps prominent Wafdist politicians also feared the loss of their national influence, if they were perceived as representatives of an insignificantly small community. The minority parties, to one of which the Liberal Constitutionalist Tewfik Dos belonged, did not have the same grassroots support as the Wafd, to ensure votes for whoever was on their party list regardless of religious persuasion (the Wafd was able to get Christians elected in overwhelmingly Muslim constituencies and vice versa). Hence they tended to favor proportional representation. In the end, however, the Wafdist view of minority representation as a British plot to divide and rule prevailed. A vote was taken, and Dos's proposal was defeated by fifteen to seven, which was broadly perceived at the time as a victory for secularism and nationalism.[23]

All the Coptic Wafdist politicians maintained this stance until the signing of the second treaty of independence, in 1936, which made no mention of minorities. The Wafd had every reason to feel confident that no special guarantees would be needed to ensure the Christians equal participation: In the executive committee they set up in 1923 to prepare for party participation in the political life of the nation, the proportion of Copts to Muslims was six to eight. The Copts on the committee were Makram Ebeid, Wasif Ghālī, Wisa Wasef, Murqus Ḥannā,

George Khayat, and Sinut Ḥannā. A second group of Copts consisting of Fakhri Abd al-Nur, Rāghib Iskandar, and Salama Mikhail were designated to join them at the first plenary cession.

The Wafd also felt vindicated when the first election returns in 1924, which swept them into power, gave the Copts more seats than they would have received in a proportional representation scheme based on the census put together by the British in 1917, which had placed them at 6 percent of the population. The social origin of the Copts who had been elected was very similar to that of the Muslims: They were mostly wealthy landowners but–and this was reflective of the grass root linkages of the Wafd–there was a sprinkling of middle-class professionals, largely lawyers and a few doctors. Two-thirds of the districts that elected Copts were in Upper Egypt, where the majority of Copts resided, and one-third in Lower Egypt, which was sparsely populated with Copts—outside of Cairo with its two heavily Coptic districts of Shubra and Ezbekiah and Alexandria, with the al-Labban and Attarin districts. Still, that the Wafds were the only party able to get Copts elected in the Delta basin of Lower Egypt was a decisive indication of their strength.[24]

The Wafd also tried to have a Copt, Wisa Wasef, elected vice president of the chamber. And though the initial attempt failed, in 1924, it succeeded two years later. In the 1928 elections, the Wafd was able to secure for him the presidency of the chamber. In the Senate, which was restricted by electoral requirements to the well-to-do who were over 40 years of age, the Copts also held more seats than their proportion of the population. And indeed, whenever the Wafd won an election, as in 1924, 1929, 1936, and 1942, Coptic representation was adequate. It is fair to say that throughout its career the Wafd party placed more Copts in high office than did any other party, with the possible exception of al-Kutla, a splinter group that broke away from the mother party under Makram Ebeid's leadership in 1943.

It was not just the secularist leanings of the nationalist leader Saad Zaglul that had set the tone for this Muslim-Christian co-operation but also those of an entire generation of upper-class politicians, educated abroad or at the French Law School in Egypt, who were imbued with the European ideal of a separation of state and church. They believed in a western-style democracy, which would help Egypt achieve a more just and egalitarian society.

Many of these Egyptian leaders based their nationalism on the concept of Egypt as a distinct territorial unit, with an identify rooted in its unique historical experience, the pharaonic civilization, which had amalgamated other civilizations. Others went even farther, concentrating solely on the pharaonic heritage and ignoring the thirteen centuries of Arab and Islamic civilization. This interest in the pharaonic civilization as the core of Egypt's identity had been encouraged by the designs of the khedival ruling family, which wanted to carve out the Egyptian province of the Ottoman Empire for itself and to use it as a piece of real estate to pass on to its progeny. Already in the middle of the nineteenth century, European excavations in the Upper Egyptian region, where most of the pharaonic remains were found, had been sponsored by Khedive Said. Later, in 1922, the discovery of Tutankhamen's fabulous tomb, by an English explorer, did much to fuel national pride.

Two of the most outstanding Muslim intellectuals who contributed to the propagation of this pharaonic trend were the novelist Taha Husein, who became minister of education, and the writer Hassanein Heykal. Husein argued for a distinct national persona, in which the pharaonic civilization was far more important than the Arab one. Egypt, he also insisted, had far more in common with Mediterranean Europe than it had with its Arab neighbors: neither language nor religion could provide a sufficient basis for unity with them. Similar ideas were publicised by Heykal in the Liberal Party's newspaper al-Siyasa. The famous playwright Tewfik al-Hakim also endorsed the notion that Egypt should reject Arab culture in favor of a pharaonic one. Arguing that environment was the most important determinant of national character, he pointed out that the Nile valley had little in common with the geography of the Arabian peninsula and that the Egyptian peasant shared much with his pharaonic forebears. He stressed the ties of pharaonic Egypt, as the mother of the ancient world's civilization, to the civilizations of Greece and Rome.[25]

At the heart of such arguments was a desire to prove that Egyptian culture had much in common with that of the European Mediterranean basin, and hence the Egyptian mind was rational and intrinsically modern. Taha Husein said outright that the Egyptians thought and felt as Europeans, and both he and Musa repeatedly claimed that Egypt's links to the West were stronger than its links to the Arab East.

This view of Egyptians as direct descendants from the Pharaohs, untainted by Arab blood, naturally had considerable appeal for the Copts. They preferred to look back to a period when they shared in a heritage of high culture rather than to their more recent history of subjugation and subservience. Their foremost intellectual, Salama Musa, was representing much of the Egyptian intellectual elite—irrespective of religious persuasion—when he opined that Egyptians were superior to the Arabs by virtue of their pharaonic blood. He and many intellectuals, both Muslim and Coptic, hoped to obtain recognition for a distinctive Egyptian culture by writing in the Egyptian colloquial dialect rather than in literary Arabic.

A distinctive Egyptian culture created a common political ground for Muslims and Copts, one in which they were not only equal but in which the Copts formed a kind of natural aristocracy, because of their greater racial purity. Many of the European Egyptologists of the period, like the Frenchman Gaston Maspero, not only saw the Copts as direct descendants of the pharaohs but also propagated the viewpoint that Egyptian Muslims were Christians who had converted to Islam after the Arab conquest in the seventh century. As one Coptic aristocrat, Murqus Semeika, put it, all Egyptians were Copts; it was just a historical accident that made some Copts Muslims and other Christians.[26] Furthermore, the activities of European Egyptologists, in the first decades of the twentieth century, created an interest in the Greco-Roman period of Egyptian history, when Christianity first began to make inroads into Egypt. Semeika founded a Coptic museum to house Christian relics of that period, and societies were established to study Coptic history and language.

It was consistent with the spirit of the times that when the nationalist leader Saad Zaglul died, in 1927, the Wafd Party chose to bury him in a pharaonic-style tomb, despite the fact that some of the opposition parties disputed this, claiming that such a pompous burial site was contrary to the Islamic tradition of an unadorned tomb. Also, in 1930, the Sidky government moved several distinguished pharaonic mummies into Zaglul's pharaonic-style mausoleum to cohabit with him.

Pharaonism, by minimizing the importance of the religious divisions between Muslim and Christians, promised to broaden the political community to include the Copts.

3

The Vanished Dream

The Failure of Liberalism

Because of the heavy taxation of the peasantry, conscription, corvée, and debt foreclosures throughout the nineteenth century,[1] by 1907 an estimated 90 percent of the population were landless or held insufficient land to sustain their families.[2] This brought about one of the precursors to a capitalist mode of industrial development in the cities, through the separation of the peasant from his land and the transformation of labor into a salable commodity.

Egypt's mode of economic development did not, however, produce a class of local manufacturers and entrepreneurs able to expand on the basis of their own profits and provide jobs for these landless peasants in industry: A bourgeoisie did not grow out of the traditional urban middle class of merchants and traders; what did emerge was a new professional and white-collar middle class.

When Muḥammed Ali developed a long-staple cotton earmarked for export to Europe at the beginning of the nineteenth century, it was natural that he should prefer to deal with the Greeks and other Europeans, who had more familiarity with Western markets, than with Egyptian merchants. There is no reason to suppose, however, that after an initial period of adjustment, the traditional mercantile and commercial bourgeoisie would not have adapted successfully to changing circumstances. Indeed, in the past, following the sixteenth-century Ottoman conquest of Egypt, the merchant classes had been able to regain the lucrative transit trade with Europe, which they had lost as a result of the discovery of the Cape of Good Hope in 1497.[3]

Previous to that discovery, they had taken goods, which Venetian vessels brought to Egyptian ports, on camelback across the desert to the Persian Gulf, where they were loaded on Arab freights headed for India. Now, they took advantage of being part of a large unified area, under Ottoman sovereignty, which thrived on an intra-empire trade. The most important trading centers for Egypt became Turkey and Syria. And Egypt rapidly became the nexus of trading between Africa, the Orient, and Europe. In the eighteenth century, Egyptian traders were mainly involved with importing slaves, gold, ivory, rhinoceros hides, and tamarind from Africa and coffee from Arabia—commodities that had come to supersede the earlier spice trade with Asia.[4]

However, in the nineteenth century, Egyptian merchants and traders had not only to contend with the Europeans' better knowledge of European markets, but with the Capitulations a set of historic treaties and practices that granted foreigners tax exemptions, exemption from legal prosecution for financial irregularities in Egyptian courts of law, as well as all sorts of other privileges. These acted as a disincentive for native investors.

The British were not responsible for the head start foreigners received from their European connections, nor for the privileges granted to them by the Capitulations. These antedated the British occupation of Egypt in 1882. Indeed, the British even deplored the fact that the legal immunity granted by the Capitulations was abused by shady foreign speculators, loan sharks, and racketeers, as well as the inability of the Egyptian government to tax foreign businessmen.[5] But the British, in turn, did nothing to encourage indigenous industrial development. They would not allow the import of duty-free machinery for factories or permit local manufacturers to supply government stores. And the one large-scale industry with good prospects in Egypt because of the cultivation of high-quality cotton, namely the textile industry, was opposed by the British high commissioner, Lord Cromer, because it would reduce the amount of Lancashire textiles imported.[6]

Investment, encouraged by the climate of public order and fiscal stability during the first decade of British rule, did rise from LE 326,000 in 1892 to LE 87,176,000 in 1907. By World War I, it had reached LE 100 million.[7] And about 10 percent of this investment was channeled into industry by 1914. But most of it went into agricultural processing plants, such as those for cotton ginning and pressing, and sugar crushing and refining. The only other industry of note was the Greek-owned cigarette industry. This situation persisted up until the 1920s; most investment went into agriculture, with cotton remaining central to the economy and the most important commercial activities revolving around its cultivation and export. Processing and shipping facilities of this single crop, which defined Egypt's relationship to the world capitalist system, were mostly in the hands of foreigners or foreign residents, as were the credit institutions.

Aside from cotton, European investors were interested in the mining of raw materials; there were a few oil fields in the Red Sea area, and the British-owned Salt and Soda Company had been established for the extraction of soda and other minerals.[8] Almost 90 percent of this capital came from overseas; most of the remainder came from either foreign residents of Egypt—Greeks, Italians, and Armenians—or Jews, some of whom may have been lucky enough to acquire foreign passports with all the attendant privileges, such as tax exemptions (the most prized passport, obviously, was the British one). Furthermore, foreigners favored the employment of foreigners. Hence, the ethnic communities supplied the skilled labor and foremen.[9]

It was not until World War I cut Egypt off from its usual source of foreign imports, thus acting as an artificial tariff wall, that local industry at last had a chance. The year 1915 therefore saw the burgeoning of the first native industry centered on textiles, tied to the first native industrial bank, Banque Misr, and based on Egyptian rather than foreign capital. Also, La Filiature Nationale d'Alexandrie, owned by resident aliens, which Lord Cromer had tried to stifle, finally began to register some success.[10] (The foreign residents of Egypt were frequently in conflict with European interests represented by the British Chamber of Commerce. They even supported the revolution of 1919, because they looked forward to a nationalist government, headed by the Wafd parties that would free them from the competition of foreign products and from taxes on raw materials, semifinished products, and the machinery used in factories.)[11]

But the post–World War I years, which once more flooded the Egyptian markets with foreign imports, brought both the Filiature Nationale and the sugar industry close to bankrupcy. Massive unemployment loomed large in the postwar years as a consequence of both the bankruptcy of such local industries and the closure of the allied military bases and workshops, which had generated employment.

World War I also left behind a legacy of debauchery, the kind that inevitably accompanies the presence of foreign troops. The mushrooming of brothels during World War I, wherever the British and Australian troops were stationed, had given rise to a veritable slave trade, in which even the minister of religious endowments (Waqf) was implicated. Newspapers were full of stories about wives and daughters who had been sold into prostitution to ensure subsistence for needy families, as well as reports of black-marketing, profiteering, and other corruption involving high officials who exploited wartime shortages and hunger.[12] Both this blatant decay of public morals, which was blamed on western influence, and the inability and at times unwillingness of the government to deal with the spread of poverty and job anxiety were to sow the seeds in the postwar years of a clandestine Islamic protest movement, the Muslim Brotherhood.

One of the inevitable results of growing urban poverty was criminality, both by individuals and by organized bands known as *futūw'a*, which were made up of landless peasants who lived in the underworld of urban slums. The several thousand unemployed who were concentrated in the slums of Cairo in 1914 often participated in the looting of stores and groceries.[13] Such criminality typified the individualism of the new capitalist order. In the remote provinces of Upper

Egypt, characterized by self-sufficient subsistence economies, western-style crimes like rape and burglary had been virtually unknown. Violence tended to take the form of bloody family vendettas.

The worldwide depression of the late 1920s and 1930s also aggravated the problem; layoffs were the most common form of wage reduction. A government census counted 24,000 unemployed workers. But it is likely that this was a vast undercount, since many workers feared to register lest they be conscripted. Furthermore, the influx of rural migrants to the city continued and kept wages down.[14] Overcrowding and inadequate diet allowed disease to flourish. A doctor who inspected the Misr workers housing complex reported:

> The majority of these habitations, far from being proper for human beings, are not fit to shelter animals. The great majority of these houses are not equipped with toilets, running water or bathrooms, and therefore their residents relieve themselves outside. There results a pile of repugnant matter of every sort. In that way, they live in an atmosphere polluted by nauseating odours in which flies swarm.[15]

The employment prospects of the white-collar class were hardly any better. As early as the 1920s, the British had estimated that only 10 percent of school graduates would be able to find jobs in the government bureaucracy.[16] This situation was largely due to the fact that most Egyptians were too poor to use the services of professionals such as lawyers, dentists, physicians, and pharmacists or to sustain a sizable market for a local industry that might have provided employment for chemists, engineers, accountants, and so on. The business and commercial sector, as it existed in the 1930s, was still overwhelmingly in foreign hands, and these foreigners preferred to hire foreign residents rather than native Egyptians.

Following independence in 1922, there was pressure on the Egyptian government to alter this situation by insisting that Arabic replace French as the language of the financial and commercial establishments so that middle- and lower-middle-class Egyptians would be better able to compete for jobs. But not much came of it. There were some attempts in 1927 to enact laws requiring joint stock companies to include two Egyptian members on their boards. But such laws had virtually no impact on the problem of middle class unemployment, since the Egyptians appointed to these boards tended to be selected from the upper classes.[17]

This adverse job situation resulted in large part from the enormous expansion of education that followed the declaration of independence of 1922. While a mere one percent of the total state budget had been allotted to education under Lord Cromer, by the academic year 1930–1931 that figure had jumped to 10.9 percent. The student population at institutions of higher learning had grown by 45 percent since the preceding year, from 1,061 students in the academic year 1928–1929 to 1,540 students in the academic year 1929–1930.[18]

ample, it alleged that Upper Egyptian tax collectors, almost all of ts, were responsible for spreading false rumors among the peas- farious consequences of the treaty of independence that was being the British in 1936. In another issue, in which the Copts were g the nationalist movement to gain control over the Muslims, n analogy between the Jews in Palestine and the Copts, who were ng for a separate national home in Egypt.[30] In addition, the pro- tionalist press continued to harp on the theme of Coptic domina- by pointing to the two important portfolios held by Coptic cabinet e fact that the president of the senate was a Copt.

s, the Wafd held on to its united front. In the 1937 campaign, Ebeid in public and reiterated the theme of Muslim-Coptic nd Ebeid returned the compliment by comparing Nahhas to the nmad, a compliment that infuriated the opposition: *al-Siyāsa* ue-in-cheek why the Christian Ebeid did not, instead, compare rist.[31]

II brought about a recurrence of the economic crisis of the post- ars on a more massive scale. Unemployment loomed large as an end. By May 1944, fewer Egyptian workers were being em- ritish army and British officials were worried about Egypt's in- those laid off after the war. And indeed, in 1946 an estimated were unemployed as a result of the closures of the allied mili- s and bases. This set off a trend that continued until the 1952 gypt developed economies of scale: an increase in per capita pro- r decreased the number of workers needed, and purchasing power st enough to absorb the new products. Thus, Egypt's increased n did not really help solve her problem of middle- and lower-class . Added to this was the slow rate of post-war recovery and the rapid crease brought on by the inflationary spending during World War proliferation of workers' strikes throughout the 1940s.[32]

ects were no better for the middle classes. Continued urban mi- ned with the spread of literacy, built up frustrations in cities to vel on the eve of the 1952 revolution. Motivating this migration, tion had grown by 64 percent between 1915 and 1950, but her oduction had increased by only 30 percent.[33]

er the Wafd had made secondary education free, Mirit Ghālī, one the Coptic aristocracy and himself a Wafdist, warned, "There is ge of employment for these men. . . . [T]he masses of students n army of unemployed men who have nothing else to do but to al order in which they live."[34]

ailure of Liberal Nationalism to provide solutions to Egypt's grow- he field was left open to religiously oriented political movements damentalist Muslim Brotherhood. Its first cadres were formed in

By his own admission, Lord Cromer had opposed mass education beyond "the three R's" (reading, writing, and arithmetic). He had even gone so far as to reverse Khedive Ismail's policy of exempting children in secular governmental schools from tuition costs. By 1892, a total of 73 percent of all students were self-supporting, which meant that access to schools had been limited to children of the privileged classes.[19] On a higher level, Cromer repeatedly turned down native requests for the creation of an Egyptian university. He believed that he could thereby deny nationalism a following. "Whatever we do," he said, "education must produce its natural results, and one of the results both in Egypt and in India will be the wish to get rid of the foreigner." Britain's gravest error in India, in his view, had been her endowment of educational institutions and a measure of self-government to that country before its material prosperity had been ensured, thereby rendering the masses vulnerable to the irrational appeals of nationalist demagogues.[20]

In 1907, the year of Cromer's resignation, the illiteracy rate was estimated at 94.6 percent, and nearly a decade later that figure had improved only slightly, dropping to 92.1 percent.[21] Thus, there was a genuine need for the expansion of the educational facilities. But that need was also utilized by the parties as grounds for raising political capital among all classes of the population, on the mistaken assumption that while it cost the privileged classes a great deal to make economic concessions it would cost them nothing to grant free education.

Since the student population formed the single most important urban constituency, the parties frequently tried to woo it by issuing blanket permission to repeat state examinations to those who had failed. Thus, the ranks of university graduates swelled even further. Even the minister of Education Taha Husein, himself an upwardly mobile village boy who had been largely responsible for creating a higher education system that was as "free as water and air," was to decry the result of these policies:

> These thousands proclaim to us our failure every day, when they obtain university degrees and then demand government jobs: when we observe their failure in the examinations and the inevitable pressure on the government and parliament to alter the laws in order for them to avoid the delay of a year or two in obtaining government positions. It is unmistakable, when they resort to the usual weapons of frustrated people—strikes, demonstrations, letters to newspapers, club meetings and invasions of government offices.[22]

It was clearly impossible for the civil service to absorb these large numbers, despite its own considerable expansion from 15,000 employees in 1915 to 40,000 by 1930.[23]

The decade of the 1930s was also politically disastrous: It signaled the end of the liberal democratic experiment in Egypt. King Fouad hated the Wafd's leaders, because he suspected them of harboring republican sentiments. His flagrant violation of the nation's constitutional life and his ability to keep the Wafd Party out of power, despite its overwhelming popular mandate, as well as his flagrant corruption, were facilitated by his knowledge that he could always rely on the support of the British, who had placed him on the throne and were committed to his rule. He was not wrong in his estimation, for while the British considered the king "unreliable and untruthful," they preferred him to the Wafd since "his schemes . . . did not involve the elimination but rather the retention of British influence."[24]

The leadership of the Wafd, which gradually became disheartened by the apparently futile struggle against the British and the king—the latter had managed repeatedly to keep them from savoring their victory at the polls by exercising his prerogative to dissolve Parliament—finally agreed to a compromise with the British. That compromise was the Treaty of 1936, which, while it granted Egypt a greater measure of independence than did the 1922 treaty, still fell short of popular aspirations.

These were the depression years and the rag-tag middle class that formed the party's rank and file suspected the upper-class leadership, correctly, of having been prompted by growing urban unrest to liquidate the struggle against the British prematurely, out of fear that social discontent would insinuate itself into the nationalist movement. In the thick of the depression years, when hunger and epidemics ravaged the countryside, they had seen Wafdist large landlords get up in Parliament and argue against a government-sponsored campaign of family planning on the grounds that large families kept the price of agricultural labor down.[25]

Social Unrest and Religious Radicalism

The socioeconomic crisis triggered by the Great Depression and rendered worse by the indifference of the ruling class to the growing pauperization of large numbers of Egyptians disillusioned a segment of the middle-class youth with democracy. They turned away from the Wafd Party in the mid '30s and began to gravitate toward the new religious and semireligious groupings like the Muslim Brotherhoods, Shabab Muḥamed, and Young Egypt, which called for a social and economic order based on Islam. Their ideology included a strong anti-Christian and anti-Jewish element, inasmuch as they were opposed to their emancipation from the status of Dhimi.[26]

Perhaps the first to manipulate this climate of fanaticism for political gain, by resorting to the use of religious propaganda during election campaigns, was the Liberal Constitutionalist Party. It originated in the split in 1921 between the moderate nationalists, who accepted the leadership of Adli Pasha and the radical nationalists led by Zaglul. Until 1927, the Liberal Constitutionalist Party had limited itself to the claim that the Wafd was in the hands of a Coptic clique, in-

sinuating that there was a Coptic co
Ebeid, became secretary general of
nationalist leader Zaglul, it gainec
the Muslim leader of the party wh
a puppet in the hands of a sly and
In 1929, the Liberal Constitu
Copts of trying to sabotage the sec
negotiating. The slander in the pro
such a point that some Coptic poli
component of their names (Ebeid c
Farrag, another Wafdist politician, c
for *Messiah* in Arabic). In this way,
electorate that was not familiar wit
henceforth mistake them for Musli
a point of always referring to Ebeid a
one of the pro–Liberal Constitutio
both he and the Muslim head of the
and Copts in country and that entru
like entrusting a lamb to wolves.[28]
Occasionally, the Wafd meekly
in its duty toward Islam, by asking
whose membership was drawn from
since, they themselves were "atheist
attack for having a pharaonic-style m
cused the liberals of hypocrisy for c
did not believe in Islam. This in the
claim, not only because the seculari
but because the brother of one of it
former ʿAlī ʿAbd al-Rāziq, who had r
for a "sacrilegious" book disputing th
The Liberal Constitutionalists als
excessive references to Islam. Thus
ferred to Ebeid as a hypocrite for in
the Hadith into his political speeches
And the Coptic politician Fakhri Ab
beliefs by praying in mosques along
It is to the Wafd's credit that it
beyond calling it harmful to nationa
displaced the Liberal Constitutional
come president of the Chamber, it p
Liberal Constitutionalists' anti-Copt
Influenced by Nazi propaganda
Party began to inspire itself from anti

the Copts. For e
whom were Co
ants about the n
negotiated with
accused of usi
al-Siyāsa drew a
said to be work
Liberal Constit
tion of the Waf
members and
Despite th
Nahhas praise
brotherhood. A
prophet Muḥa
demanded ton
his friend to C
World Wa
World War I y
the war came
ployed by the
ability to abso
250,000 peop
tary enterpris
revolution, as
ductivity furth
did not grow
industrializati
unemploymen
cost-of-living i
II. Hence, the
The prosp
gration, comb
an explosive l
Egypt's popu
agricultural p
Shortly af
of the scions
simply no ra
. . . help form
resent the so
With the
ing social ills,
such as the fu

Ismailia in the 1930s under the leadership of a school teacher, Hassan al-Banna, and thereafter in Suez.[35] These two cities, by virtue of being ports, were dominated by foreign business. In addition to having to put up with abusive inspectors, Egyptian workers resented the fact that the Greek and Italian blue-collar workers received better pay and more fringe benefits than they did. In the Suez Canal zone, where the Brothers were anchored, Europeans who constituted a sizable portion of the workforce earned twice as much as did native Egyptians for the same work; moreover foreign workers had access to vacations, pensions, and medical care—none of which were accorded to Egyptians.[36]

Thus, it is not surprising that a central tenet of the Muslim Brotherhood program was the need to combat imperialism and to get rid of the corrupt monarchy that sought to perpetuate the British hold on Egypt. Although this theme was common to the Wafd party, what distinguished the Muslim Brotherhood was its claim that the struggle to rid the country of the British was not enough: Egypt had to be morally and spiritually regenerated as well. It exhorted the workers to behave as good Mulsims, by being charitable and morally inspiring to each other and to fulfill their obligations toward their employers. The Brotherhood paper, *al-Ikhwan al-Muslimun*, gave extensive coverage to a worker who had lent money to a fellow worker, when the latter was laid off by the Shubra el Kheima textile mills. It praised this as a true example of fraternal relations among Muslims.[37]

The Brotherhood opposed the capitalist view that workers could be hired and fired according to the laws of supply and demand. It had a fundamental antipathy toward capitalism, which it blamed for the spread of greed and materialistic values. However, at least until 1948, the Brotherhood leader Hassan al-Banna was willing to support workers against foreign Christian but not Muslim employers.

A major reason for the Brotherhood's popularity with the workers was its attack on foreign employers, whom it accused of exploiting Egypt's national wealth and humiliating her labor force. In 1934, when the Muslim Brotherhood emerged as a political force to be reckoned with, foreigners residing abroad were responsible for approximately 50 percent of the paid-up capital and debentures of companies operating in Egypt, which came to LE 99,317,000 (exclusive of Suez Canal shares); 86 percent of the capital was attributable to a foreign source, if foreigners residing in Egypt were included.[38]

The Muslim Brotherhood was not the only religious organization competing for the workers' allegiance in the 1930s, but it was the most important. Up until the 1940s, its only major rival for lower-middle-class and lower-class allegiance was the Wafd. The Communist Party in Egypt was then led by Egypt's permanent foreign residents, mostly Greeks and Ashkenazi Jews, and the movement was too intellectual to appeal to the illiterate workers. This began to change only after World War II, when a new native leadership surfaced and was able to gain a foothold in the working class districts. In contrast to the Communists, who strove to inculcate in the workers an understanding of society as divided by class conflict, the Muslim Brotherhood offered them the concept of one organic unit in which the various social strata—as opposed to classes—were interdependent and subject to mutual responsibility (*takaful ijtimā'i*). A state-regulated, modernized version of the traditional Islamic practice of giving alms (*zakat*) was to provide for the underprivileged within this system.

The Brotherhood also appealed to the semi-employed and unemployed lower-middle class, by criticizing the use of French in the foreign-owned commercial and financial institutions, which worked to the disadvantage of Egyptians from modest-income families. The upper class, both the topmost stratum composed of the remnants of the Ottoman aristocracy (referred to as Turko-Egyptians) and the lower stratum composed of native Egyptian large landowners was polyglot. Its members often chose to converse in French rather than Arabic. It was therefore not concerned about the use of French: members of the upper class often sat together with the foreigners on the boards of administration of Egypt's major banks and industries.

Coptic Disillusionment

The role played by the Muslim Brotherhood was a major factor in inciting communal tension. Though its founder, Hassan al-Banna, insisted in public that Islam called on Muslims to accept Jesus and his mission and to treat non-Muslims well, he believed that any authority exercised by non-Muslims over Muslims was against its teachings. According to him, the Copts had acquired far more power than they were entitled to.

The Brotherhood frequently criticized the Wafd for their hostility to Islam, which it laid at the door of "William" Makram, "the Egyptian Englishman and Muslim Christian."[39] Their inflammatory rhetoric led to an increase in the number of incidents involving the stoning of churches, the beating of priests, and the disruption of Christian funerals, weddings, and religious processions. Such incidents occurred most frequently in Upper Egypt, where the Copts were more visible. There were incidents in all the Upper Egyptian dioceses except Aswan, which had very few Copts. The Coptic press, both *al-Watan* and *Misr*, blamed the government for doing little to protect the Christians.[40]

There was some justification for this accusation; none of the parties was eager to be seen standing up for Christians. By the 1940s, the Brotherhood was simply too powerful a force for any party to defy openly. It had emerged as the master of the streets, with an armed underground and a following estimated in the millions. As such it was courted by all the parties—even the Wafd was rumored, in 1942, to be involved in secret talks with it.

It had become harder for the Copts to hold their own in elections. Election campaigns were no longer limited to verbal attacks but included physical assaults on Christians. During the 1943 by-election in the province of Girga, in Upper

Egypt, both churches and individuals were attacked in an attempt to prevent the election of the Copt Maurice Abd al-Nur, who hoped to accede to his late father's, Fakhri Abd al-Nur's, seat. Predictably he lost—despite his family name, the money he was able to put into his campaign, and the fact that one-third of his constituency was Christian. It was also becoming increasingly difficult for the Wafd Party to stand up publicly for Coptic candidates, unlike the situation in 1920s when Saad Zaglul had sent a famous Muslim preacher to help Maurice's father. The sheikh had made a round of the local mosques claiming that Fakhri Abd al-Nur was a better Muslim than the Muslims who cooperated with the British.[41]

The number of Copts expressing misgivings about British withdrawal from Egypt had also grown considerably, due to a growth of Muslim belligerence. Up until the signing of the 1936 Treaty of Independence, which omitted any mention of the British right to protect Egypt's minorities, all the Coptic Wafdist politicians had maintained their 1922 stance of objecting to the protection clause. But in 1946 the Coptic newspaper *Misr*, which had always been Wafdist, demanded that the new treaty with the British that was being discussed include a clause guaranteeing Egypt's minorities equality. A year later, it criticized the Coptic politician Ebeid for trying to arrange the withdrawal of British troops from Egyptian soil. This was a far cry from what its editor, Salama Musa, had written in the newspaper *al-Akbar* in 1922, when the provision granting the British the right of minority protection was under discussion: "Let Tewfik Dos know that the Copts prefer to sustain all the sufferings he fears . . . rather than to record in Egypt's constitution . . . that which makes them look like foreigners . . . and impute to their compatriots the charge of fanaticism."[42]

By 1946, tension had spread to Lower Egypt. There were several attacks on Coptic churches in Cairo that year, and the following year an angry mob burned down a church in Zagazig. (This was happening at the same time as the Brotherhood was carrying out a number of similar attacks on Jewish homes, shops, etc.). In fact, the Copts were so worried about the Brotherhood and their analogies between them and the Jews, that they expressed fears that they would meet a fate similar to that of the Jews in Europe.[43]

In 1948, the government itself became sufficiently worried, following the Brotherhood's assassination of the incumbent prime minister, to ban that organization. But the Brotherhood continued to operate underground. On the eve of the 1952 revolution, a Coptic church, school, and benevolent society were destroyed and three Copts were killed by a mob in Suez. The fact that the monarchy, which was fiercely anti-Wafdist, had chosen to ride the popular wave of enthusiasm for Islam merely fueled the flames of fanaticism.

PART II

The Sunday School Movement

4

Rebels and Saints

The Middle Class and Church Reform

Into the secular public spaces that had begun to emerge in the urban centers in the 1930s, mostly in Cairo and Alexandria, had come an influx of young Copts attracted by the prospects of a modern education. These middle-class Copts of recent rural origin, principally from Upper Egypt, the home of 70 percent of Egypt's Christians, vacillated between two competing modalities of solidarity: the religious one offered by the clergy, with the church as the communal meeting place, and the secular one offered by the Coptic upper class, with a political party (the Wafd) as the nexus connecting Coptic youth to each other. These young men from Egypt's villages and small towns were profoundly religious. They were shocked by the contempt of the upper class Wafdist leaders for the clergy whom they venerated. But, at the same time, they were fascinated by their western lifestyle and by the western-style reforms they advocated. Little by little, they allowed themselves to become seduced by the prospect of equality dangled before them by the Wafd Party, which featured such a visible upper-class Coptic presence among its leadership.

The gradual disillusionment of the Coptic upper classes with the Wafd was nothing by comparison with the sense of betrayal felt by these middle class recruits in the 1940s. They were the first generation of university graduates, a generation that had come of age in a period of secular slogans, which held out to it a promise of equality and political ascension. They now realized that unlike their Muslim compatriots, who graduated with them from the same universities, they had no chance to play a significant role in the polity.

Excluded from the political orbit, they withdrew into their own community. The failure of the experiment in pluralist democracy, which would have given both Christians and Muslims of modest social origins a chance to synthesize the nationalist sentiments that united them with the specificity offered them by the local churches and mosques, was to result in the 1952 revolution. This, ipso facto, accomplished the eclipse of the secular, Oxford- and Sorbonne-educated Coptic upper class, thereby opening the way for a new class—the middle class—which was more traditional, hence closer to the church, to play a key role in community affairs. As it sought compensatory networks outside the political space, it perceived the church as the only autonomous space that the state recognized as legitimate.

The vital role assigned to the church in community affairs made reform more imperative than ever: church corruption was blamed for the weakness of the community. The two most important leaders of the church reform movement, known as the Sunday School Movement, Pope Shenuda and Abbot Matthew the Poor, had earlier, in the 1940s, been involved in nationalist politics.

This new middle class was not the originator of the idea of church reform, which had been the aim of the upper class since the beginning of the century. There was no solution, in the view of the upper class, to the problems of clerical negligence and simony short of granting the laity a stronger voice in church affairs. To upgrade the community, the upper class had struggled for a long time to limit clerical responsibility to religious matters. Its desire to wrest control of community affairs from the clergy was the result of the influence of modern western political theory, particularly the ideas of Rousseau, Montesquieu, and Voltaire about the division of spiritual and temporal matters, which it had been introduced to in the French educational institutions. It ran into stiff resistance, however, from the hostile clergy, who came from poorer families and resented their rivals' opportunities for superior education in private foreign schools and in European universities.[1]

The fierce competition, between the clergy and the lay upper class, also played itself out around the issue of who was to represent the community before the state—a prerogative that for centuries had been the church's. But the wealthy, landed Coptic nobility that had arisen at the end of the nineteenth century had become politically assertive: it began to clamor in 1874 for khedival endorsement of the establishment of a communal council, which would be in charge of both communal and selected church affairs. In particular, it wanted to wrest control of the Christian properties in Mortmain away from the clergy. These were the source of considerable revenue, which was often subject to malversation. It wanted to see to it that these funds were used to provide the community with modern education and health services, as well as with all manner of philanthropic aid. Influenced by the modernizing endeavors of the state, the upper class had founded a plethora of organizations, beginning in the late nineteenth century, dedicated to raising the educational and health level as well as the standard of living of Copts of modest means. Of these the most renowned and successful was the al-Tewfik society, founded in 1890 and named after the reigning khedive, which persists to this day. These efforts were motivated by the same dissatisfaction with the performance of the clergy that led to the creation of the communal council in roughly the same period. The upper class strove not only to build schools, orphanages, and hospitals, but also to upgrade the educational level of the clergy, whom it viewed as ignorant, corrupt, and derelict in the performance of their duties.[2]

In their opposition to the upper-class claim to represent the community, the clergy were not only interested in protecting their personal power and prerogatives, but genuinely concerned that such changes would erode community cohesion and religious culture. They resolved, therefore, to prevent at all costs, what they termed *farnaget* (from the word Frank) *el kinisa* (the westernization of the church).

By the late 1940s, the project of church reform was no longer confined to the upper class; the middle class was fully involved in the struggle against the Orthodox clerical establishment. It too sought the deposition of Pope Yusab. When this pope, who had been the bishop of the diocese of Girga in Upper Egypt from 1942 to 1944, was enthroned in 1946, he had brought with him his valet, a semiliterate peasant named Melik, from one of the villages of his diocese. As the pope began to age, this unlettered but shrewd peasant became his closest confident and advisor in matters of church policy and of administrative decisions affecting the lay community. He soon began to exploit his ability to grant or deny people appointments with the pope in order to peddle influence for money. He is believed to have carried out such a lucrative trade selling offices to ambitious priests and monks that he was able to purchase four buildings in Alexandria and three in Cairo and to have accumulated IOUs from bishops totaling LE 21,000 Egyptian. That this trade was public knowledge is clear from the fact that the valet was so brazen as to undertake a civil suit in the Upper Egyptian city of Sohag against a bishop who failed to complete payment on his IOU.[3]

This was not the first time in the twentieth century that a movement was organized to unseat a pope. Pope Cyril V had been sent into exile at the beginning of the twentieth century by the Communal Council, and a reform-minded bishop had been brought down from Sanabo, in Upper Egypt, to govern in his place. But because there was as yet no educated middle class to support the reform movement, this act was regarded by the average tradition-bound folk as high-handed. They resented the attempt by the secular upper class who controlled the Communal Council to westernize the church, and they therefore greeted with jeers, at the train station, the arrival of the bishop whom they considered a usurper. Eventually, the exiled pope was able to garner enough support from them to send the reforming bishop packing, and to return to the papacy in a triumphal procession.[4]

The difference, in the 1950s, was that the movement to exile the pope had a much broader base of support. The question was only one of how—by force or by persuasion. A radical movement, known as the Coptic Nation (*al-Ummah al-Qibṭīyah*), which had been founded in the 1950s by some middle-class professionals largely in response to the mounting aggression of the Muslim Brotherhood, favored the use of force.[5] Because the Muslim Brotherhood championed an Islamic state, the Coptic Nation demanded a Coptic one. It had its own flag and its motto: "God is the king of the Copts, Egypt their country, the Gospels their law, and the Cross their insignia." It demanded a constitutional amendment naming the Copts a nation (*umma*). On the cultural side, its members sought to revive the defunct Coptic language. They studied it avidly and tried to speak it among themselves. They also tried to strengthen religious feelings and were strict in their own adherence to biblical injunctions.[6]

Their leader, the lawyer Ibrahim Hilal, was prepared to go to any length to achieve church reform. He planned, and carried out with co-members of the movement, the kidnapping of the pope and his confinement in a monastery—an act that was meant to be followed later by his assassination to eliminate any chance of his resumption of power (as had happened in the case of Pope Cyril V). But Hilal was arrested, together with leading members of his movement, and imprisoned before he could carry out the pope's execution.[7]

The majority of the pious middle-class youths, however, opposed the use of violence. Though they were equally determined to drag what they perceived as a stagnant and venal institution willy nilly into the twentieth century, they felt the solution was not to force a particular papal incumbent to resign, but rather to bring new blood into the church leadership as a whole. And they did not share the upper-class goal of limiting the role of the clergy in temporal matters; on the contrary, they sought to expand the role of the church in community affairs.

They succeeded where the upper class failed, because they did not seek to impose change from the outside as the upper class had done, using the Communal Council as its instrument of reform. Instead, they infiltrated the church and subverted it from within.

Their gradual rise to the top of the church hierarchy took twenty years. They fought a fierce battle to be recognized as a counter-elite that offered an important new reform project. The church leadership, as well as the monastic leadership, distrusted this newly educated generation that wished to upturn the traditional order of things and feared being displaced by it. But the lower rung of the church did not feel threatened: the diaconal corps welcomed them. Their ascent, therefore, took them first through the ranks of deacons.

Traditionally, the deacons were of humble social origin, usually from lower-middle-class families. Often, they had been consecrated for church service from childhood and had thereafter been supported by the church. These humble social origins, which they shared with the new generation of university graduates, made them far more appreciative of them than the upper-class members of the political parties had been. The latter, despite calling upon them to join the Wafd, looked down on these Coptic parvenus who spoke no foreign languages, had never traveled abroad, and lived in overcrowded, dirty urban neighbourhoods.

Prior to the entrance of the generation of university graduates into the diaconal corps, the deacons had a limited understanding of modernity. They had confined themselves principally to the adaptation of modern instruments of learning like the printing press and the newly created clerical institutions, seminaries and Sunday schools, to the propagation of Orthodox religious doctrine. Their dream was to return the church to its third century aura. It was to this end that they had recruited the university graduates: they needed their help in the teaching of Sunday schools. But the new recruits took this clerical dream of Coptic revival (*ihyāʾ Kibti*) and turned it into Coptic reform (*islah kibti*).[8]

The welcome extended to the middle-class university graduates by the diaconal corps enabled them in time to become a counter-elite and set themselves up as a third pole: by virtue of their religiosity, they offered a synthesis between two competing community structures, the first one centered on the church, with its newly created clerical institutions (seminaries, Sunday schools) and the other one centered on the secular urban institutions like the Coptic school, the Coptic hospital and the Coptic philanthropic associations. Both the secular and the clerical institutions were of nineteenth century origin.

But to seize control of the helm of the church, they would first have to be admitted to the monasteries, because Orthodox canonical law reserved the high church offices such as the bishoprics and the papacy for celibates. Yet the monks were not nearly as receptive to them as the deacons had been: They regarded with suspicion, it not outright hostility, this new breed of educated, aspiring monk. Initially, the only monastery willing to admit them was the Monastery of the Syrians, whose abbot, Father Tewfilios, though only a high school graduate himself, was exceptionally broad-minded.[9] Through its gates were to pass many of the most illustrious founders of the reformed church, including Pope Shenuda himself. Other illustrious founding fathers ordained in that monastery were Bishop Samuel and the Abbot Matthew the Poor.

Chastity

As Emmanuel Sivan has pointed out in his comparative study of Jewish and Muslim fundamentalism, the function of myths is not just to interpret the past in a way that strengthens group solidarity but to alter behavior. In other words, myths lead to action, and whether this action consists of a self-imposed exile from a corrupt order—in this case, the ailing mother church—or in an attempt to change it, forcefully or peacefully, depends on circumstances.[10]

To understand the way in which tradition served the purposes of modernization in Egypt, we have first to understand that the tradition in question was monastic tradition because Orthodox priests, who must be married to be allowed to hear the confessions of women, are barred from the higher echelons of the church, which are reserved for celibates. Popular sentiment holds monks to be on a higher spiritual plane than priests; they have not had their bodies defiled through sexual intercourse, nor their imaginations titillated by confessions of carnal sins. Even within a marriage, passion is frowned upon. As Bishop Moses once put it at a youth meeting I attended: "Some people look at romantic love within a marriage as a sign of its success, but the opposite is true: If he loves her that way, he will quickly tire of her. It is better to love in a calm, spiritual manner. Instead of letting one's emotions get hold of one, one should try to let one's soul control one's emotions."[11]

The Orthodox clergy's view of ejaculation as virtually an excretory function and their reference to the genitals as "the ugly organs" must be understood within the context of the Egyptian culture as a whole, which makes little distinction between love and lust. It is a culture that firmly upholds the superiority of traditional "arranged" marriages. Thus, in answer to a note written by a young man to Bishop Arsanios, in a general meeting I attended, to solicit his advice about how to deal with the parents of the girl he was in love with who refused to give her to him in marriage on the grounds that he was not wealthy, the bishop said, "You can only pray that they will have a change of heart, because marriage is *primarily* a relationship between families."

The lack of money for an apartment often compels newlyweds of modest means in Egypt to lodge with their families. Such joint family households offer them little opportunity for intimacy. The couples are obliged to avoid each other during the day and come together only at night, in their beds, for procreation. In such circumstances, sex has little chance to stand for anything other than itself, a mere physical act humans share with animals. Its larger context as an expression of affection or of a human need for playfulness is lost on most Egyptians. Bishop Arsanios, for example, like many bishops, had to live out his young manhood in the parental household—not only together with his mother, father, and celibate older sister, but also with his two older married brothers and their offspring. Each bedroom of his four-room apartment in Shubra formed the nucleus of a conjugal family.[12] In such crowded middle-class apartments, which served most bishops as homes, flirtation with a girlfriend would have been impossible, even if it had not been culturally taboo.

Popular bias in favor of chastity may also be seen in the way, each time a priest attains exceptional standing, he is enveloped with an aura of chastity. Such was the case in the 1950s of the late Father Bishoi, of a church called Sporting in Alexandria, whose spiritual merits were reputed to have been such that even Muslims were won over to the Christian faith. Stories circulated about how "he lived with his wife, like a brother with his sister," as though an admission that he had a normal sexual relationship would debase him. The same story can now be heard about his successor, Father Tadros who, in addition to having a reputation of impregnable virtue is one of the Orthodox church's most distinguished scholars.[13]

This consensus on the virtue of chastity has influenced the recruitment of popes and bishops: they have, almost invariably, been recruited within the monasteries. Church law does not stipulate that the pope must come from the monastery, only that he must be celibate, so that in theory a celibate pious layman is eligible for the post. Indeed Ḥabīb Jirjis, the founder of the Sunday School Movement, was considered for the post, but the accession of a layman to such high office has been very rare historically.

What is of interest for this book is not the study of Orthodox sexual mores per say, but rather the way in which these norms contributed to the character formation of the church leaders who were to double as the community leaders. For the most outstanding of these monks are recruited to become rulers of dioceses that resemble small principalities. I will try to show how monastic asceticism, embodied in the vows of chastity poverty and obedience, served the purpose of worldly asceticism.

The Coptic consensus on the superior merit of celibacy is rooted in the belief that men are endowed with a limited amount of energy which, if dissipated in the pursuit of pleasure, is no longer available for higher purposes. In the words of Bishop Arsanios, "Unlike a woman, a man expends a considerable amount of energy in the performance of sex, and every time he ejaculates it is as though he were losing one litre of blood."[14] This conviction is not as remote from western thinking as it may seem: Freud's theory of sublimation is, after all, based on the assumption that the repression of libidinal energy is a prerequisite for culture.

Furthermore, in a society such as Egypt's, where the question of the relationship between the sexes is so weighty, the honor accorded to those able to achieve sexual self-restraint is far greater than it would be in a sexually permissive western society, where most people would be indifferent to similar accomplishments—if they did not regard chastity as outright corny. To the extent that the Copts share in the broader Egyptian culture, they are also influenced by Islamic values, which are prevalent in the society at large and, in the last three decades of the twentieth century, have reinforced the value of chastity.

But not only sexual enjoyment is frowned upon by Orthodoxy; virtually anything that is a source of enjoyment falls under the law of self-restraint. Food is to be used as sparingly as medicine, as the pope once advised a young man who asked him if it was all right to gorge oneself during religious holidays,[15] and even speech is subject to the golden rule set by Saint Arsanios in the fifth century. He reportedly said that he often had cause to worry about things he had said, but for his silence he never had any regrets. In short, only what is deemed strictly essential for the body and soul is condoned.

Hence, the church attempts to ban cigarette smoking, which is viewed as an indulgence for its own sake, and abhors pop music, a form of enjoyment seen as a devilish medium for the intoxication of the senses. This fear of the loss of self-control also explains the ban on liquor. Unlike most other Christian communities, the Coptic community is not allowed to imbibe wine, outside of the Holy Communion. Even worship comes under the rule of self-restraint. "Orthodox worship," Bishop Moses once said, "entails emotions which are quiet, sensible emotions, controlled by the mind. The love of Christ should be like a light, not a fire. We don't want to be like the people in the West who get carried away during Mass and start clapping, screaming, and falling on the floor as though they were in a pop singers' arena."[16]

We should thus already be able to detect certain affinities with the Protestant ethic, in Orthodoxy's cultivation of the habits of orderly conduct, silence, and frugality in all things—even emotion. In the course of my research in Egypt, I witnessed the excommunication of Father Daniel, a monk-priest, who, in my opinion, could only be faulted for an excess of zeal. He had an unconventional, buoyant style of preaching, which made him enormously popular with the youth. They responded emotionally to his rousing sermons, sometimes going as far as to fling themselves onto the floor in a trancelike state, when they felt moved by the Holy Spirit and in one instance that I witnessed a teenager brought a batch of cocaine he had been taking and, in an act of remorse, flung the drug at Father Daniel's feet. Father Daniel's spontaneity of speech and manner and his freedom of movement—he walked up and down the podium when he sermonized and often placed his hand on the recumbent head of one of his parishioners—was extremely distasteful to the Orthodox establishment. It contrasted vividly with their own austerity of speech and frigidity of manner at the pulpit. So Bishop Moses, and other members of the committee who sat in judgment over him, whom I interviewed, castigated him for his "evangelical frenzies."

In fact, one could argue that the very nature of Orthodox worship adapted itself well to modern enterprise, because it never allowed for private passion: it is a highly collective emotion. This made it possible for the reformers to transmute this emotion into a new, impersonal discipline, one that demanded self-restraint, sustained commitment to the cause, and systematic activity. What was required of the prospective saint was total control—not only of his senses, but of his thoughts and feelings. For monastic asceticism was more than a mere control of the carnal self. Not only was an impure thought considered as grave a breach of the monastic code of ethic as outright fornication, but likewise feelings of anger and vexation. The layman turned prospective saint had, in addition to a life of purity and of ceaseless application, to keep a strict vigilance on his own aggressive instincts.

Once when Bishop Arsanios was on his way to confession (the pope is the father confessor of all the bishops), I asked him what he could possibly find to confess, since he seemed to me as close to sainthood as anyone could aspire to become. He answered that bishops were accountable not just for their actions but for their thoughts and feelings, and he had sinned by harboring feelings of vexation and resentment toward Bishop Bishoi, after the latter turned his back on him in response to his greeting. (Bishop Bishoi exhibited unchristian behavior because he disapproved of Bishop Arsanios's support for Father Daniel, who had recently been excommunicated. Bishop Arsanios was Father Daniel's confessor and had recruited him for the Monastery of the Romans, when he was its abbot, to take charge of the youth of the Diocese of Minia. During my stay, Bishop Arsanios had been compelled by the pope to resign from his monastic post of abbot on account of his loyalty to Father Daniel, his "son in confession." The Pope could not divest him of the title of bishop, as well, because bishops are considered "married" to their diocese and may only be removed for womanizing, corruption, heresy, or insanity).

According to Bishop Arsanios, one of the hardest things for the monks to get accustomed to is not sexual abstinence but keeping their tempers in check. Tempers in the monasteries are often frazzled, sensibilities hurt, and resentments seethe just underneath the surface of beatific composure. As part of their training, novices are constantly provoked by their seemingly overbearing superiors. One of the monks I interviewed in the monastery of the Syrians told me that Abbot Tewfilios used to take each newly arrived candidate for a walk around the monastic grounds, where he had secretly placed a loaf of bread beside a tree. If the monk-hopeful bent to pick it up, he would rebuke him harshly for not letting alone matters that did not concern him. If, on the other hand, he did not pick it up, he would reproach him for being unobservant. Bishop Arsanios also remembers how, when he was a novice at that same monastery, he had had to endure Abbot Tewfilios's irascible moods on a number of occasions. Bishop Arsanios had a good voice, and he liked to wake up at dawn to join in the singing of the hymns in praise of the Lord. One time, Abbot Tewfilios cut him off in the middle of a chant and shamed him publicly, in front of his brothers, by telling him he was singing too loudly—on purpose, to show off his good voice. Then, adding insult to injury, he treated him like a schoolboy, telling him to step out of the front row and stand in back of the chapel. The next day, when their paths crossed, Abbot Tewfilios asked him, with a twinkle in his eyes, if he had taken offense. He then admitted that he had deliberately picked on him to make an example of him to another novice, who was too proud to take this sort of treatment without protest.[17]

The novices were constantly and whimsically tested in that monastery, which produced some of the greatest church leaders of the new reform movement: Bishop Bimen of Mallawi, Bishop Athanasios of Banī Suwayf, Bishop Arsanios of Minya, Bishop Samuel, a pioneer in social services and ecumenical relations, and the pope himself. The rationale was that ministering to those who would come to depend on one later in life was as incompatible with indulging one's anger as was succumbing to lust. The training in self-control for the prospective saint had larger, political ramifications as well. Later, when some of these monks were selected to be bishops, they would be called upon not only to ease the suffering of members of their community but also to right their wrongs vis-à-vis a discriminatory state, without letting themselves fall prey to feelings of hatred toward the Muslims. This serenity, which bishops had to radiate in public life, was to be painfully acquired through an internal war with private anger.

To achieve this kind of utter self-control, to be able to make such a terrible demand on himself, the Orthodox would-be saint had to engage in a perpetual battle with Satan, who was known to use every trick to bring about the downfall, not only of prospective saints, but of the saints themselves. Saint Anthony had believed that it was through the intermediary of their bodies that humans were susceptible to the nefarious influence of demons; he had likened his own body to a house in which a war raged. Saint Pachomios, also, had much to say about the "wars" he had to wage against the evil spirits during his period of novitiate.[18] For both Saint Anthony, the Egyptian founder of monasticism, and Saint Pachomios, the Egyptian popularizer of that way of life, the demons and their master the Devil, who hovered in the air very near to humans, could take on visible forms as well. Saint Anthony, residing in the isolation of an old tomb, was reportedly attacked by demons incarnate in all manner of ferocious animals. He was terrified by the appearance of lions, leopards, wolves, and bears—in addition to visions of demons disguised as serpents, scorpions, wasps, and, not surprisingly, women.[19]

For the Orthodox, this bitter, unrelenting struggle with the Devil was not only unavoidable—it was the only morally worthy means of achieving virtue. Hence their disapproval of Origen, the great third-century luminary of the Catechetical School of Alexandria, for having castrated himself to avoid being tempted by his female students instead of engaging in battle against his libidinal instincts and learning to master himself.

Poverty

The monasteries, to which prospective saints went, were the culmination of their gradual but growing commitment as pious laymen in church service to asceticism; they gave institutional expression to their life of limited wants. Learning to live a life of limited wants was not only an excellent antidote against the virus of materialism that had contaminated virtually everyone in the new capitalist era with its nouveau riche ethos that measured men in terms of how much they made and objects in terms of how much they had cost; asceticism also immunized the prospective saints against the venality of Egyptian life.

In Egypt, the substitution of a public ethic for personal commitments and family obligations remains a goal that has yet to be achieved. Whether in the government bureaucracy or in private enterprise or—especially in earlier times—in the church, obligations to friends and family are often the grounds for bending the rules or for allocating jobs or money from public resources. The monastic requirement of shedding one's family and serving all people equally, even if it is not always strictly adhered to, nonetheless provides the needed legitimization for breaking with a traditional system of patronage. The act of lying face-down on the ground, covered by a sheet, and having the Prayer of the Dead read over one's body until one emerges from underneath the sheet reborn, with a new name, is not simply a ritual accompanying the consecration of a monk. It is a safeguard against the Egyptian tendency to regard loyalty to family and friends as overriding all other considerations and commitments. This safeguard is needed in the church context. Checks have not yet come into common usage in Egypt, and donations to the bishop consist of large cash sums, which are routinely handed to him during religious festivals or in fulfilment of a *nadr* (a solicitation that has been granted by God) and which are stashed away in the pocket of his habit. Since there is no way of holding the bishop accountable, it would be very easy for him to divert part of this cash away from educational and socioeconomic endeavors to the bank accounts of needy friends and family—as indeed is believed to have happened in the old days.

It is important to emphasize, therefore, that the movement of reform was not just an intellectual movement. The ouster of the old guard from the helm of the church, and its replacement by the first generation of university-educated monks and priests, was also, and perhaps primarily, a movement of moral regeneration after the corruption associated with Pope Yusab's reign led to his banishment to the Monastery of the Holy Family, in Upper Egypt, in 1955. Much the same skepticism regarding the ethics of superiors existed in the monasteries, because of rumors of corruption among governing bishops and abbots. This was easy to get away with, since not only were some monasteries, like the Monastery of the Holy Family, rich from bequests of arable land, but the budget of the monastery was a well-kept secret passed on from one abbot to the next. As the yearly budget of the monastery was not published, it was very difficult for the monks to prove the corruption of their superiors though they frequently rose in protest against them. In the Monastery of the Holy Family, in Upper Egypt, this occurred in 1936, 1937, 1939, 1947, and 1959. In the last instance, they actually locked their abbot out in defiance of the pope's wishes. These mutinies were often summarily dealt with by the expulsion of the most rebellious elements.[20]

A huge scandal had broken out in the early '20s over the claim that in 1919–1920 the Monastery of the Holy Family had earned a million and a half pounds from its cotton sales, which had vanished without a trace. In 1926 one of the large Coptic landowners, Suryal Jirjis Suryal, argued in the Senate that he had received numerous complaints from his constituents and demanded that the Communal Council be given the right to audit accounts of revenues from Coptic property left to the church (Waqf), as well as to oversee monasteries, churches, schools, voluntary associations, personal status courts and the Coptic press (a right that had been rescinded by Pope Cyril V). In his memorandum to the Senate, Suryal claimed that the monastery of the Holy Family had a huge income of LE 100,000 and only 35 monks to care for. Little of this income went into the monk's education or into improving monastic conditions: the monks had no running water, sanitary facilities, or even adequate food. The difference between income and expenditure, which in 1906 had been estimated at 87 percent,[21] had over the years been the object of either malversations or of speculation. The Coptic press, in particular *Misr*, printed pages galore of letters and telegrams supporting Senator Suryal. They were unsparing in their criticism of the clergy, and *Misr* went so far as to accuse them of being so busy selling lands, to pad their own pockets and those of their relatives, that they were serving the Devil rather than God.

The entry into the church of a reform-minded new generation of prelates, however, began to have an effect as early as the 1960s, when the bitter strife in the Monastery of St. Anthony's ended to the monk's satisfaction with the forcible removal of their abbot.[22] This occurred again in the mid-1970s in the Monastery of the Romans, where the petty feuding over discriminatory distribution of gifts of choice foods, money for machinery, and the like by the overseer (*Amin*) to his favorites had culminated in the burning down of his cell. Although five monks, considered the ring leaders, were expelled for this act, the abbot was replaced by a fair-minded and morally impeccable monk, who later became Bishop Arsanios of Minya.[23]

But the principal strategy of the reform-minded generation for combating corruption was not punitive but pre-emptive: socializing the youth in such a way that their criteria of achievement would no longer be western-style conspicuous consumption but the emulation of Egyptian church fathers like St. Anthony, who gave up his worldly possessions to live off honey and locusts in the desert. Such ancient saints were to be held up to them as models of frugality, discipline, and perseverance, and that would turn them not only into good churchmen but also into good citizens.

The extensive use of the hagiographies of the Egyptian church fathers of old, and recourse to the modern media, particularly video, to glamorize their image has succeeded in persuading a sizable contingent of youth to dedicate themselves to the church. These *khuddām* (laymen who devote themselves to church service) do so on a volunteer basis, part-time or full-time. In the latter case, they sacrifice better paying jobs and live on meager church wages, in tiny, overcrowded apartments which, at least to the western observer, sometimes appear to be situated in slums. Having myself visited a few of the apartments of Bishop Moses' church-servants in Cairo, I was left with the impression that only a high degree of motivation could deter their inhabitants from emigrating to the West. Their idealism is a far cry from the materialism that attracts thousands of Copts (and Muslims) to the consumer society of North America.

Obedience

Just as the vow of poverty serves a worldly purpose, once it has been transmuted into an ethic of frugality, so too does the vow of obedience. The word *obedience* uttered in the Egyptian monastic context immediately evokes two stories, to which every visitor to the Monastery of the Syrians is treated. One is about a novice who a long time ago was ordered by his abbot to go plant a stick in the field. The young man meekly took the stick and planted it, watering it dutifully day and night even though he knew, in his heart, that nothing would come of his effort. One day, after many months, God rewarded him for his perseverance and the stick began to bud. The result, the visitors are told, is the magnificent tamarind tree that, today adorns the monastic courtyard. In contrast to this the other story tells of the recent graduate of the faculty of agriculture, who was given an onion bulb and instructed by his superior how to plant it. This scion of Egypt's modern educational institution grasped immediately that his superior, Abbot Tewfilios was mistaken. He did not dare tell him that but merely took the bulb and planted it the correct way. When it yielded a harvest, pleased with himself, he reported it to him. Abbot Tewfilios shook his head at him: "Young man, you will no doubt make a fine agronomist one day, but you will never make a good monk."[24] And he dismissed him from the monastery.

This kind of obedience, which has as its prerequisite humility—the humility that enables a monk to prostrate himself before the abbot, touching the ground with his forehead, and accept without a murmur the unjust rebuke of a superior bent on breaking his pride—may not be thought conducive to the creation of the assertive personality needed for modern enterprise. What is productive, however, is obedience to the exigencies of the monastic schedules. For the real tyrant in an Egyptian monastery is not so much the abbot as the clock. One of the most important services rendered by the monastery is to introduce Egyptians, who are notoriously indifferent to its compulsions, to the notion that time is a precious commodity that should not be wasted. Without being subject to the rigors of monastic schedules, which begin at 3 AM, and to monastic work assignments, which grind their tireless course until midnight, it is doubtful that these men would have assimilated the modern concept of industry, which is a sister of punctuality. It is a lesson essential to the creation of leaders: bishops in Egypt have to be extremely parsimonious with their time. Otherwise they would not achieve half of their daily itinerary. Many of the bishops whom I got to know well, such as Bishops Bula and Bishoi, only slept three hours a night. An Orthodox bishop has, in addition to his administrative responsibilities, which resemble those of a governor of a state in the United States, a very heavy load of pastoral duties, such as is normally relegated to the priests in the Catholic Church.

It should be obvious that in the East as in the West, an ascetic way of life finds expression in the values of hard work, whether spiritual or physical, in a scrupulous observance of schedules, and in frugality. This so-called Protestant ethic is a feature of other radical religious movements as well. Saad Eddin Ibrahim, one of Egypt's foremost authorities on its Islamist groups, sums up their ethos as follows: "austerity, hard work, self-reliance."[25] These words could just as well describe the ethos of the reform-minded generation of the Orthodox community.

It was mainly the *khuddām* who were responsible for disciplining the Copts and integrating them into the reformed church by means of a new ideology, one that was based on the cult of the saints. For these middle-class laymen with a modern education realized that the affection that the common people had for their saints since time immemorial was a tremendous asset that should be capitalized on rather than devalued (as it had been in recent times by a secular upper class who considered it superstition). The stories of the church fathers of old were mined to yield the equivalent of a Protestant ethic, with the help of which the cultural renaissance and socioeconomic development of the Coptic community was to be achieved. That community was to be characterized by the virtues of punctuality, frugality, industriousness, truthfulness, and reliability, all of which ran against deeply ingrained Egyptian habits. The unflagging zeal and enthusiasm needed to sustain a commitment to this goal were to be aided by much prayer and prolonged fasts (the Orthodox fast over half of the calendar year).

Some of these *Khuddām* then went on to the monasteries, where they were hardened for the unremitting labor of the bishopric that awaited them. The authenticity with which these men sought virtue enabled them in turn to mobilize new constituencies and new leaders from among the faithful.

Why did this new moral discipline suit the needs of the rising middle class? Modern Orthodoxy offered young Egyptians what Walzer, in his study of radical Protestantism, has called an ideology of transition.[26] It was functional to the process of modernization in Egypt, because it tempered the frenetic mobility and the attendant anxiety of the postrevolutionary era, when one's place in society was determined not by one's birth but by how much money one was able to make. The moral discipline of the Sunday School generation, with its emphasis on methodical work and perseverance, was also excellent preparation for the kind of attention to detail and exactitude required by Egypt's newly modernized schools and commercial and industrial establishments.

5

Roots and Branches

Nāzir Jāyid versus Saad Aziz

Although the disappointment in the unfulfilled promise of equality made in the name of democracy gave it further impetus, the movement of church reform, known as the Sunday School Movement arose earlier, at the beginning of the twentieth century. The chief catalyst for change then was not Islamic militancy but the threat posed by western missionaries, particularly the enterprising Protestants, to the national Church of Egypt, the Egyptian-Orthodox Church. The latter was fiercely proud of its heritage and desirous of protecting itself from foreign inroads.

While the Protestants were the most active group of missionaries in Egypt in the nineteenth century—by 1878 the American Presbyterian church alone had opened thirty-five schools—they were not the first ones on the scene. That place belongs to the Catholics: the Franciscans arrived in the eighteenth century.[1] Their success was less spectacular than the Protestant one was to be, but by the nineteenth century, they had had their first illustrious convert in the person of Mualim Ghali, the ancestor of former U.N. secretary general Boutrous Ghālī. Mualim Ghālī served as chief secretary to the ruler, Muḥammad Ali. The opposition of the Orthodox Church to these conversions was so fierce that the Coptic Catholics were unable to establish an independent clerical body until the late nineteenth century. In 1895, they finally obtained a patriarch of their own, who was appointed by the Vatican. In time, they achieved independence from Rome, so that their patriarch was appointed by a local synod of bishops.

However much the Orthodox Church objected to the Catholics, their fiercest ire was reserved for the Protestants. The latter were far more aggressive in competing for converts and were scornful of Orthodox ritual, in a way that the more traditional Catholics were not.

Although the upper class's aim to redesign their church along western parliamentary lines, with the congregation having a real say in all decisions and in matters of clerical appointments, was sanctioned by Coptic tradition, the tradition lay dormant under the weight of an authoritarian culture. The reaffirmation of the will of the people in church affairs, in modern times, was largely influenced by the example of the American Presbyterian churches in Upper Egypt, which were run democratically. Furthermore, the sons of the rich Coptic landowners, who were the only ones able to afford the tuition fees of private missionary schools, began, toward the end of the nineteeth century, to seek to upgrade both the cultural and material level of their community. In this process, these dignitaries were also seeking to enhance their own status, which was degraded by association with it—not only in the eyes of their Muslim compatriots but for the Europeans as well. The British, who had occupied Egypt in 1882, were full of contempt for the Copts, whom they found unlettered by comparison to the Syro-Lebanese Christians.[2] Lord Cromer also accused the Copts of being deceitful, pathological liars and cowardly in their subservience.[3]

Paradoxically, if as a group the upper class sought to overcome this image of the Copts by taking over the leadership of the community from the clergy, as individuals they struggled to downplay their ethnic identity. Religion was losing its hold on them, because of the arrival from Europe of a new ideology, nationalism.

Unlike the upper class, the peasants were unreservedly committed to the meaning of the cross tattooed onto their wrists; it suited well their life of hardship and inexplicable misfortune. The women in particular, who were often subject to the double yoke of incessant toil and tyrannical husbands, could hardly have coped without the cross as both an identification and an outlet. But beyond their passionate attachment to Christ, their Savior, they were not sufficiently versed in the doctrinal fine points of the faith to care whether the prayer meetings they attended, the dispensaries they used, and the schools to which they sent their children were run by a Protestant or Orthodox church, even if at times they showed some vestige of loyalty to the mother church by reserving it for their weddings and baptisms. They suffered from neglect at the hands of ignorant and indifferent Orthodox priests, and they were only too happy to avail themselves of the welfare and medical services offered by the Catholic and Protestant missionaries, principally from the Franciscan order and the American Presbyterian Church.

If some were content to straddle across denominations in this way, there were also many outright converts. The Protestants themselves reported that while they had set out for Egypt in the nineteenth century to convert Muslims, they soon noticed that they were making very little headway in that area and switched to the conversion of Christians. In 1953, the American Presbyterian Church reported that it had nearly 100,000 Christian converts but only 100 Muslims.[4]

Orthodox youths irrespective of class, were also attracted to the more modern style of worship that prevailed in the Protestant churches. Not only the addition of the sermon and the shortened version of the Eucharist had considerable appeal (the Orthodox mass seemed to them to drone on for three interminable hours) but also the use of church hymns. The staunchly conservative Orthodox Church, which was proud of its endless Mass (as Bishop Moses once said to a youth who asked if the Orthodox Mass could not be shortened: "We have translated the mass for you from Coptic into Arabic, but don't ask us to tamper with its content"),[5] made do with the traditional Coptic chants. These were generally intoned by a blind cantor to the accompaniment of cymbals. Their low, dirgelike strains punctuated by loud wails could not compete with the cheery Protestant hymns. The missionaries sparked church reform by giving the example of energetic churchmanship.

The initiative for the reform of the Orthodox Church came from the lay members of the congregation, for whom the missionary activities were a sore reminder of the neglect characteristic of their own church (some of these laymen were later to take monastic or priestly vows). A foreign observer, Edward Waking, who noted that in Egypt of the late 1950s, unlike in the Christian West, the laity was more devoted to its church than the clergy, quotes one of these laymen: "We were very angry with the way things were. . . . The priests weren't preaching, they didn't visit people, they didn't keep records. We wanted to revive the function of deacon and to have him teach Sunday School, preach, assist priests, help the poor."[6]

Though these laymen-turned-deacons liked to think that they were inspired by the example of the catechistic school of third-century Alexandria, which they saw as the origin of their own Sunday School Movement, there can be no doubt that the catalyst for change was the example of the missionaries and the Orthodox Church's desire to keep its members within the fold. Thus, sermons were introduced when it was felt that Protestant sermons were attracting Orthodox youth away from the mother church, and the catechism classes on Sunday were inspired by the example of the Catholics, just as social work was a response to the work of the Franciscan nuns in the slums of Alexandria, which gained momentum after World War II, as well as in the shanty town that was developing in the Mokatam hills flanking Cairo. In contrast to the medical services offered by the Catholics in Upper Egypt, in and around Assiut, and by the Protestants in Middle Egypt, in and around Fayoum, semiliterate Coptic priests were still using the symbols of Christ, the cross and the candle, as instruments of primitive healing practices based more on superstition than on religion. For example, rabies would be treated by the manipulation of the magical number seven, whereby the patient would be made to eat seven morsels of bread followed by seven dates, which had been blessed by the priest, and infertility, with magical formulas from the *Book of the Seven Angels*. The cure administered for mental disturbance was exorcism, in which the evil spirit would be driven out of the body of the possessed by a priest, who came armed with a palm branch and jug. He waved the palm branch at the spirit, intoning prayers, and thereby drove it out of the body into the jug, which he then buried in the desert.[7]

The priest, who would otherwise not have been able to survive, received money for such services. For, as already discussed, the priests were recruited from the lower classes; no upper- or upper-middle-class family would have considered priesthood a vocation with sufficient social standing for its sons. Father Maximos of Shubra al-Kheima, who himself joined the profession because he could not find any other job, said to me: "Priests were looked down on as beggars who lived off the church collection dish, which was passed around after the Sunday Mass."[8] A vicious circle, therefore, came into being, whereby priests were scorned as social inferiors by the upper and upper middle classes; and because priesthood had so little prestige, it in turn attracted second-rate people. (The more educated opted for the traditional minority occupations, business and the professions.) The church then made matters worse by neglecting the education of priests and paying them low salaries. The priests' preoccupation with finding the wherewithal to feed and clothe their numerous children made them apt to sell their services to the rich and neglect the poor. If their devotion to their parish suffered as a result of their preoccupation with their own families, the quality of their theological scholarship is well captured by the story about the foreign visitor to Upper Egypt, who found the church he was longing to see locked. When its priest was found, he could not admit him, because the key was with the janitor and he had no idea where the janitor was. After the janitor was finally located and they had gained access to the church, the priest could not explain its history and had to send for a parishioner to narrate it.[9]

The Sunday School Movement had its official beginning in 1918, when the first general committee was formed with branches in the provinces. It was the brainchild of a pious layman by the name of Ḥabīb Jirjis, a clerk in the employ of the patriarchate, who may be considered a forerunner of the *mukaras* (a celibate layperson dedicating all his life to church service). Anxious to protect Orthodox children from the lures of the Catholic and Protestant missionary schools, where Christian teachings were presented in a more dynamic form, he began to collect them every Sunday in the Church of the Virgin, in the middle-class Cairene district of Fagalla, and to teach them the Bible as well as Coptic rites, the history of the Coptic Church, and the lives of the Egyptian saints and martyrs. (The practice of sending children to Sunday school, which began in the West, had not been adopted by the Orthodox Church as yet, although the Egyptian Protestant and Catholic Churches, which had come under the influence of foreign missionaries, had done so.) He also tried to enliven the lessons by distributing holy pictures and by adding illustrations to the religious books. His method of teaching, which used the question-answer form rather than the traditional lecture form—a method he popularized in his catechisms, which began to be published as early as in 1896 and which were later used for the Sunday schools—had been inspired by the catechism of the Catholic Missionary Schools. This modern approach, Christianity made comprehensible for the broad public, was further popularized in a magazine, *Karma*, which he launched in 1904. It may be considered the prototype of the Sunday school magazine *Majalat Madāris al-Aḥad*, launched in 1947, whose editor-in-chief was Nāzir Jāyid, later the monk Father Anthony and still later Pope Shenuda. (A new name, that of a saint or apostle, is given to the layman who takes monastic vows as part of the ceremony in which he sheds all ties to his family. If he becomes a bishop or a pope, he once more changes names. The names of the bishops in this study are mostly Greek names like Athanasios, Dimitrios, and so on, because the Greeks of Alexandria were the first converts to Christianity, in ancient times, hence the Greek Orthodox Church is the origin of the Egyptian Orthodox one. But some bishops have either the names of apostles or of local saints.

The initiative for the Sunday School Movement actually came from outside the church. It was essentially a lay movement. And unlike the Communal Council, which was dominated by the upper class until the 1952 revolution, the members of the Sunday school committee were solidly rooted in the middle class—a class that did not at that time speak foreign languages or vacation or study abroad and was therefore less likely to be influenced by western secular literature and contacts.

This lay movement was the product of the modern educational institutions established in Egypt since the nineteenth century. It is significant that the first Sunday school committee was formed in 1918, a year of intense anti-British agitation that was to culminate in the 1919 revolution and in the declaration of independence of 1922. One of the measures taken by the Egyptian government following independence, as we have seen, was to greatly increase the budget allotted for education. This in turn was to bring the first generation of university-educated leadership to the Church.

In the late 1930s, a group of Coptic students from Fouad University (then named after the king, later renamed Cairo University) began to hold regular meetings on Wednesday and Thursday evenings for university students, aimed at forming leadership cadres from among these newly educated and urbanized young men who would become agents of church reform. They, as well as the Nasserite junta that stemmed from the same lower middle class, were the beneficiaries of the vast expansion of education sponsored by the liberal nationalist government, once the British turned over to it the control of Egypt's educational system, after the 1922 declaration of independence. That same government opened up the military academy to the lower middle classes, just as it had done the schools. Nasser's group of free officers was the first group of humble origin to graduate from the military academy, in the 1930s. Previously, that institution had been an exclusive reserve for the dull and decadent sons of the aristocracy who, since the British saw to it that the army was reduced to a showcase, spent their time there learning to ride horses and play polo.

It was in the bosom of the Sunday schools that these university student leadership cadres, which included Pope Shenuda, grew up. By the time Shenuda reached manhood, in the early '40s, the Sunday School Movement had grown from its humble beginning in Fagalla in 1908, which was limited to a handful of students, to include an estimated 42,000 students spread across the country, all of whom shared a common curriculum.[10] Such a large, strongly centralized educational campaign could no longer be ignored by the papacy, and in March 1948 Pope Yusab officially took the movement under his wing. The name of the committee for Sunday Schools, which he now headed, was changed to *al-Lagnah al-Ulyah li-Madāris al-Aḥad* (the High Committee for Sunday school Education), and the pope appointed Ḥabīb Jirjis as its vice president.[11]

Pope Shenuda and his peers, who had throughout their adolescence dreamed of ridding the church of obscurantism and venality, seized their first opportunity after graduation to sweep away the old guard and replace it with an enlightened administration. The takeover of the church by this reform-minded generation was as radical a change as the revolution of 1952, which rid the country of the ancien régime and replaced it with a military junta. These devout Christian youngsters were propelled by the same forces that had spurred an entire generation to rebel against the backwardness and corruption of the country; like the junta, they wished to put an end to stagnation and corruption, and they resented foreign encroachments, albeit in the guise of Catholic and Protestant missionaries. Their hostility was greatest toward the Protestant missionaries, who did not believe in intercessors between humans and God, and therefore disapproved of the prayers offered daily in the Coptic Mass to the saints and to the Virgin Mary, as well as of the role of father confessor—a role of cardinal importance in the Orthodox Church. Most of all, they disapproved of the aura surrounding the priests and bishops: the kissing of the priests' hands and the prostrations before bishops by the faithful seemed to the missionaries mere eastern obsequiousness.

The label *Protestant* remains a damning epithet to this day in Orthodox circles. During one of Pope Shenuda's lectures, in a series for theological students that I attended on Tuesdays, he used the term *Protestant* thirteen times while showing a videotape of a sermon by Father Daniel to castigate the recently excommunicated priest. In the old days, that label was applied by Shenuda, as the layman Nāzir Jāyid, and by his like-minded peers, centered around the Church of St. Anthony in Shubra, Cairo's populous middle-class district, to their rivals led by Saad Aziz (later a monk by the name of Father Macari and still later Bishop Samuel) of the Church of Giza, a university district.

There were in the '40s at least four Sunday schools with established reputations in Cairo, similar to the Ivy League schools in America. And just as

Harvard might distinguish itself in political science, Yale in literature, and Princeton in the history of science, so too each of these Sunday schools excelled in a specific area. St. Anthony's school was intensely spiritual, the Giza school had more social consciousness, Geziret Badran was reputed for its intellectuality, and so on. St. Anthony's had its quarrels both with the Giza group, "the Protestants," and the Geziret Badran group, whose critical intellect was viewed as debilitating to the church, the opposite of what was needed—a reaffirmation of the faith. While the Geziret Badran group played a role of undoubted importance in the '40s and early '50s, they fall outside this study because their most prominent members made their mark thereafter not on church life but on secular life. (Some of the more renowned intellectuals of Geziret Badran Church are Mīlād Ḥannā, today a prominent member of Parliament, William Soliman Kīlādā, today a jurist, and Murad Wahba, today a professor of philosophy at Ain Shams University.)

My purposes primarly concern the opposing priorities of the St. Anthony and the Giza churches. Nāzir Jāyid's group, in the Church of St. Anthony, believed that the revitalization of the church depended on their digging for their spiritual roots, on looking backward and inward toward their own heritage, which had been largely lost over the centuries. The St. Anthony school of thought was principally interested in the resurrection of the Coptic language, in unearthing the century-old church hymns and dirges, which were no longer chanted, and in exhuming the stories of Egypt's saints and martyrs. The name of Yūsuf Iskandar (Joseph Alexander in Arabic) must be mentioned here, because he was a pioneer in the cultural field. While he was not officially a member of the Church of St. Anthony, since he was based in the Delta city of Damanhour, he was a colleague of Nāzir Jāyid and one of the first young enthusiasts to enter monastic life with him. Yūsuf Iskandar (later Abbot Matthew the Poor) was resolved to reintroduce the lives of Egypt's saints into the monasteries. To this end, he asked one of the church-servants, Yassa Ḥannā (Hannā is John in Arabic), to travel to England, to disinter some of the old manuscripts on Egypt's saints from the subterranean vaults of one of Oxford University's libraries.

It would be a mistake to regard St. Anthony's group as the traditionalists and the Giza group as the modernists. I prefer to refer to Nāzir Jāyid's group as the spiritual revivalists and to Saad Aziz's group as the social activists, for both groups were, in my opinion, modernists. The interest that the revivalists showed in their ancient heritage was itself a function of the modern system of education to which they had been exposed, as was the quality of scholarship they brought to ancient sources. More important, perhaps, the revitalization of the cult of the saints was a modern strategy of communication meant to reaffirm Orthodox Christian identity in the face of the omnipresent Islamic role models. This was to be accomplished by restoring a very popular form of worship, namely the veneration of the icons of saints and martyrs and of their relics, which had been devalued by the upper class in modern times because it was tainted with superstition.

There can be no doubt that, without this digging for its roots, the Orthodox Sunday School Movement would have been merely a mediocre imitation of the West's Protestant Sunday school. The lives of the ancient church fathers, unearthed by Yūsuf Iskandar, the rediscovery of old hymns by Rāghib Muftah, who has been collecting them indefatigably for the past forty years, and the resurrection of the Coptic language all gave the Sunday School Movement its autochtonic vitality.

If the St. Anthony enthusiasts were the roots of the movement, then the Giza enthusiasts were its branches, reaching out to the world beyond the church. And while in retrospect it is clear that both were needed to ensure the growth of the reform movement, in those days the Giza group referred contemptuously to their rivals as *Darāwish* (members of a mystical Muslim sect) and reproached them for their "monastic mentality" (their closed-minded dogmatism). The Anthonians returned the compliment by referring to the Giza group as *Kufār* (atheists), because they consorted with Protestants who were viewed as secular. So strong was this antipathy that when the Institute of Copic Studies opened in the fifties, the Anthonians objected to having "foreigners" (Protestants) hired to teach Hebrew and Greek.

They taught their youth to sing:

> Oh, Institute of Coptic Studies, I love you. . . . [Y]ou are Egypt's blessing. . . . [Y]ou are a rising sun. . . . I was born the day I enrolled in you, you taught me to speak my own language, in my own country, and to pray with joy, and to sing with joy. I live in your heart and you live in me, because God the merciful created you for me.[12]

But if the St. Anthony group believed that the way to prepare for pastoral care was through prayer, fasting, and meditation—and yet more fasting—the Giza group was convinced that the only way pastoral care could be learned was on the field. The story of the distribution of the three fish and five loaves of bread by Jesus accounted to them for the church's responsibility for the body as well as the soul.

Just as Nāzir Jāyid was the most outstanding member of St. Anthony's church, the most prominent member of the Giza church was Saad Aziz. Perhaps, because he had studied at the American University in Cairo, an institution founded by American Protestant missionaries, he was a pioneer in ecumenical relations; he took the Coptic Church out of its centuries-old isolation and made it a member of the World Council of Churches. He also established the first Coptic church abroad, in England, and sent another member of the Giza church, Salib Surial (later a prominent priest) to establish a second church in Germany, as well as a monastery. These travels, whose purpose was to extend pastoral care to Copts abroad, had the beneficial side effect of bringing in financial aid for developmental projects from them and from Christian organizations abroad. But the Giza church members were not viewed with favor by the St. Anthony group, which, according to the late Bishop Bimen of Mallawi, himself a former Giza church member (then known as Kamāl Ḥabīb), objected in no uncertain terms to travel to "Protestant lands."

The Giza church could not help but be aware of peasant misery, since it was situated on Cairo's wretched rural periphery. "You are eating baklava," Yassa Ḥannā, who had gone to collect money for blankets for the poor peasants, told the priest of a neighboring rich church, "while all we ask for is that you give us some bread for the poor."[13] If Protestant organizations like Brot und Leben were willing to help these peasants, Saad Aziz was not one to refuse.

Yassa Ḥannā did not take the peasants bread, he took them chocolates for Easter. He was appalled to discover that the peasants did not even realize it was the Feast of the Resurrection. Pastoral care was very poor at that time in the villages. The priests were often so by heredity, rather than by conviction: their fathers and grandfathers had been priests in that same village, and it was usually the dullest son who was chosen for the profession, the brighter siblings having gone off to the towns to further their education and seek out better job opportunities. As an example of the priests' lack of dedication, Ḥannā tells of the many times they had made a long trip to get to some village only to find the church closed. "The priest had ended the mass early, because he could not wait to get to his cigarette!"[14] Yuhannā al-Rāḥib (Johanna the Monk in Arabic), another member of the Giza group, also recalls his disappointment on finding the village churches empty: "Only old men attended. And it was not unusual to find a twelve-year-old child that had not even been baptized."[15]

To remedy this situation, the Giza enthusiasts began to travel regularly to the villages armed with something called a *Nota ruḥīyah* (spiritual notebook), a little chart on which they ticked off the number of times a child had prayed, had had Communion, read the Bible, and so on during the week. It was, in fact, the Giza group that began a practice that is now firmly entrenched throughout the church, *Iftiqād* (follow-up visits to members of the congregation), either merely as a show of support and encouragement or to check on someone who may have been slack in church attendance or have gotten into trouble. These trips to the villages, which began as ad hoc caravans to bring much-needed spiritual, material, and medical aid to the depressed rural areas of Egypt, soon became institutionalized in the form of permanent departments in the provinces. They were staffed with talented laymen turned *khuddām*. And talent was not lacking—at the graduation party hosted by King Farouk in 1944, 75 percent of the church servants had *jāyid jiddan* (high honors).[16]

But how could the Orthodox priesthood be revitalized by drawing on this new blood? In the late Bishop Bimen's words, "If our priests do not renew themselves people will become disgusted with the church. The priest has to know how to take confessions; it is not enough to say 'my son pray for your sins'; if he knew how to pray he wouldn't be in trouble in the first place!"[17]

The new strategy, therefore, as of the 1940s, was to try to recruit educated laymen to the clergy, rather than to consecrate as priests people for whom priesthood had always been a family vocation. All of the most outstanding members of the Giza group were offered the priesthood, but Saad Aziz had his heart set on becoming a monk and Yassa Ḥannā was ambivalent about leaving his family and hometown of Fayoum. Those who accepted, however, were made priests virtually overnight, which meant that a bride had to be found for them immediately because, as we have seen, unlike the Catholic priests who must remain celibate, marriage is mandatory for Orthodox priests so they can take the confessions of women. For example, Father Boulos Boulos (Paul), another distinguished member of the Giza group and the first university graduate to be consecrated for priesthood, was engaged on Thursday, married off on Saturday and consecrated on Sunday. Yassa Ḥannā recalls:

> We called a meeting at the home of one of the *khuddām* and nominated him for service in Damanhour, in the new Church of St. George which Yūsuf Iskandar had founded. So we had to find him a wife and one of the church servants present offered his sister. The next day they were married, despite her mother's protests that she did not want her daughter married without a wedding party.[18]

The next person to be consecrated was Father Salib Surial (Salib means a crucifix in Arabic), who was to become one of the Orthodox Church's most outstanding priests. He was to serve in the Giza Church, and Yuhanna al-Rāhib generously offered him his own sister in marriage. Finally, it was decided that Father Antonios Amīn (another one of Egypt's renowned priests) was to serve in Fayoum and for him, too, a bride was quickly found; yet another sister of a church-servant obliged.

The entrance of educated laymen into the ranks of priesthood brought about a change, in the method of spiritual service, that was as profound in its effects on adult members of the congregation, as the introduction of Sunday school had been on its children. To the Mass, which had ground its tireless three-hour course for centuries, was now added an innovation, the sermon. It drew on the insights of the social sciences, in the application of spiritual values to the solution of mundane problems. Despite the fact that the modernization of the spiritual service did not reduce the long liturgical part of the Mass, the introduction of a modern sermon, as well of lively hymns—another novelty—did much to swell the ranks of Orthodox churchgoers.

This new breed of educated laymen-turned-priests was bound to conflict, sooner or later, with the old guard. And indeed wherever they went, they clashed with their superiors. Father Salib Surial led the struggle, in the early '50s, to prevent Pope Yusab from consecrating one of the old guard as the bishops for the diocese of Giza. Like others who were the product of the Sunday School Movement, Father Salib favored the selection of Ḥabīb Jirjis for the post. William Kīlādā, a highly regarded intellectual, then a member of the Geziret Badran group, recalled in vivid language how he and his friends went to church early to capture the front seats at the consecration ceremony, and when Pope Yusab put his hand on the head of the bishop to be, they began to call out "no, no" and to hoot, until they were subdued by the deacons and forcibly dragged out of the church.[19] In subsequent years, Father Salib Surial suffered greatly at the hands of the new bishop, who never forgave him his opposition. Much the same fate awaited Father Antonios Amīn, in Fayoum. There the enormous popularity of this young, dynamic, university graduate did not sit well with the old bishop who, jealous of him, threw him out of the church.[20]

Father Boulos Boulos did not find life any easier in Damanhour, though the Communal Council proved the more formidable opponent, in this case, to his reform proposals. Father Boulos had been a deacon at the Giza church as well as overseer of church-servants *Amīn al-khidmah* during the ten years he spent in Cairo working for the government as an agronomist, before he was ordained a priest for Damanhour, in 1950. When he arrived in Damanhour, there was only one church. He very quickly made his mark as an energetic leader. In contrast to the older clergy, who contented themselves with the performance of the liturgy, he made it a practice to visit every single Christian family in the town of Damanhour at least three times a year. And he did not content himself with traditional endeavors like raising money to build more churches for the city. He tried to do innovative things that would attract the youth, such as acquire a movie camera to produce religious films in a small theater he had erected next to his church. It was small-scale projects like these, regarded as wildly extravagant in his time, that alienated the members of the Communal Council, who considered such expenditures wasteful. But in Father Boulos's eyes and in those of his like-minded peers turned priests, such money was well spent: they were convinced that an invigorated youth movement was the foundation of a church revival, and such a youth movement depended, in turn, on a rich and versatile Sunday school program.[21]

Another important step toward church reform was the creation of a *Bayt al-khilwah* (house of retreat), within the monasteries, to which adolescents came to live a holy life for a few days. Often, they hitched a ride up to the restaurant of the Cairo-Alexandria highway and then trekked across the desert on foot for three hours to reach the monasteries of the Natrun valley. Once they got there, they shared in the monastic discipline, which began at 3 AM with a communal prayer, followed by Mass, from 5 to 8, and a period of silent meditation, from 8:30 to 10:30. Then they participated in the manual work that went on in the monastery and, after the period set aside for lunch and rest, from 2 PM to 5 PM, they began a second round of activity with a communal prayer at 5 followed by conferences with the monks and readings from the Holy Bible and from the hagiographies of the Egyptian saints. The day ended at about midnight after they met privately with the monks, who talked to them about their lives, their sins, and their future. That future for many was to be a monastic vocation. But even those who did not have the stamina for the rigors of monastic life usually returned enchanted to their hometowns, where they testified to the virtue of the monks.[22]

The unquestioning acceptance of monasticism as a superior way of life by these youngsters, who had gone to the retreat homes to seek inner peace and acquire the strength to face their problems, did a great deal to restore the reputation of the monasteries, which had fallen into disrepute. They had been virtually abandoned, before, to a few pious old men and semiliterate peasants. The sight of the monks, in their soiled black habits, roaming about the cities in search of alms from the faithful or peddling talismans to cure ills, as a way of making a living, had lent credence to those who felt that, outside of a handful of true ascetics, most of those who joined the monastery were nothing more than beggars.

The chief architect of this *Bayt al-khilwah* for young boys was Father Anthony (previously Nāzir Jāyid),[23] who along with Father Matthew the Poor (previously Yūsuf Iskandar) and Father Macari (previously Saad Aziz) was one of the earliest recruits from amongst educated laymen to monastic life. The acquisition of this new generation of educated laymen by the monasteries had much the same beneficial effect on them as the acquisition of Fathers Boulos Boulos, Salib Surial, and Antonius Amīn had on the churches. At the time they entered the monastery, morale was very low. This was reflected not only in widespread desertions (when Pope Cyril VI ordered all monks to return to their monasteries and forbade them to ask for "personal contributions," it was estimated that nearly half of the monks were outside their monasteries),[24] but also in the endemic feuding within the monasteries over the discriminatory distribution of work assignments, gifts of food, allowances for machinery, and so on.

In conclusion, the Revolution of the Saints was marked by a strong commitment to the cause, an ardent zeal, and a stoical devotion, which helps explain why the Christian enthusiasts in Egypt succeeded where the secular nationalists failed.

Unlike the nationalist movement, which was bereft of any ideology other than that of ridding the country of British domination and of a corrupt monarchy, desert monasticism, having performed a critical role in the fourth and fifth century against an imperial church grown rich and decadent, remained a potent reforming myth for Shenuda's generation. The stories about Egypt's saints and martyrs, legendary local figures like the bandit Black Moses, and the boy-martyr Abanob, constituted the staple diet of all their growing years, and the sayings of the ancient church fathers collected in a book called *The Monks' Paradise* (*Bustan al-Rohban*), which was read to the monks aloud at mealtime in the refectories, inspired and shaped their manhood. The real ammunitions of the monasteries were not the arms, which they were accused in the '70s by the Islamic militants of harboring, it was the moral mettle they were forging.

Though Nasser and some of his co-conspirators were no doubt moved by a genuine concern for the country when they launched the 1952 revolution, and their dreams of reform were equally worthy, they were unable to inspire the rank and file with their own dedication. Hence their dream of a social revolution was aborted because, short of grassroots participation, the junta was forced to rely on a coercive machinery to see to the implementation of their projects. This inevitably led to abuses of power and corruption. The leaders of the movement for church reform, unlike those of the Free Officers Movement were able to call on a second rank of volunteers, devoted *khuddām* cadres, ready for self-sacrifice.

Given the rudimentary nature of transportation in the 1940s, spreading the word often meant having to trek across the countryside for miles on foot, under a punishing sun. But they were young and their enthusiasm was fueled by their prayer meetings, all-night affairs that lasted until morning Mass. In one account, Yuhannā al-Rāhib reported: "It was all very emotional, we often cried during mass. Our Church was for us a pillar of strength. It was always packed, even though many parents didn't want their sons to join us. They wanted them to spend more time at home, studying, and they didn't want them to fast during the school year."[25]

If money was needed, the church-servants would empty out their own pockets, in contrast to the men Nasser entrusted to carry out tasks, many of whom used their posts to pad their pockets. Thus, a story is told of how, when the Giza group built the first student hostel so that youngsters arriving for their studies from the provinces would reside in a place with a proper religious atmosphere, they began by taking up collections among themselves. One of the church-servants gave LE 100 (a considerable sum in those days). "Shortly thereafter," according to Yassa Hannah, "he died in a fire accident at Shell, where he worked as an engineer, and we discovered that he only had LE 103 left in his bank account."[26] In a similar fashion, Father Boulos Boulos, who was then still a church servant, gave half his salary every month to the Sunday schools so they could buy small prizes for the children: crosses, holy pictures, and the like. And the engineer Yassa Ḥannā tells the story that whenever they needed money they would go and dip into the cash register of one of the Church servants who owned a pharmacy. "He never minded." (The pharmacist was Yūsuf Iskandar, who took St. Anthony's example. In compliance with Jesus's message, "If thou will be perfect, sell all thou hast and give to the poor," St. Anthony sold his inherited 300 acres. Iskandar in turn sold his lucrative business, gave the money to the Church, and became the monk Matthew the Poor.)[27]

Thus, they were able to accomplish what the young officers who seized power were not. Both they and the Free Officers had had to face the thankless task of reforming a corrupt administration (two popes had been sent into exile in the twentieth century amid charges of corruption and abuses of church privileges) and of bringing to their people the benefits of a modern civilization. But the Free Officers naively believed that it was possible to develop the country by importing western science and technology, without its values and cultural underpinnings. This led the highly regarded Coptic writer Louis Awad to comment that the regime believed it could modernize Egypt by the mere transfer of boxes of machinery and technology from Europe "into heads very similar to boxes."[28] Even Nasser came very early on to realize that the infusion of the government bureaucracy with a vast number of engineers, scientists and agronomists did not ipso facto turn it into an effective instrument of modernization. Shortly after he had nationalized the commercial and industrial sector, in 1962, he complained: "We could not develop the government machinery to a revolutionary level. . . . [S]ometimes this machinery was unable to convey to the people the feeling of being a mere servant of its interest, but on the contrary the interests of the people seemed to have been exploited for the benefit of the government machinery."[29]

The same problems of venality and inefficiency attended its agricultural enterprises. Very early on, Nasser was forced to write off the Tahrir desert reclamation project, which had been featured in every school textbook as an emblem of the regime's accomplishments. In Nasser's words: "The problem is theft: everything gets stolen. There is a gang in the Tahrir province that I do not know how to arrest. The state spends and things get stolen. And, how can we arrest the gang, unless we arrest everybody and replace them with other people, and this is impossible."[30]

What the Sunday school enthusiasts did was precisely to try to change people. The story of this endeavor is the story of this book.

6

The Warring Founding Fathers

Bishop Shenuda, Bishop Samuel, and Abbot Matthew the Poor

The "revolution of the saints" in Egypt was replete with the kind of fierce infighting and bitter feuds that characterize worldly revolutions, for each one of its leading figures had his own burning vision of the Orthodox revival movement and went after it with single-minded, almost ruthless, determination.

When in 1959 the papal throne became vacant, the members of the Sunday School Movement felt that their turn had come. They decided to put forward the candidacy of a member of St. Anthony's Church, Father Anthony, and that of a member of the Giza church, Father Macari, as well as that of Father Matthew the Poor. In the words of another former member of the Giza church, Bishop Bimen, "We felt that if the pope was chosen from among members of the Sunday School Movement, he would be younger, more energetic, more dynamic, and more moral."[1] But the revolutionary ideas of this generation were suspect. The old guard quickly closed ranks against it, by influencing the Holy Synod to enact a law making ineligible any monk who had spent less than fifteen years in a monastery and who was under 40 years of age.[2]

Having been thus disbarred, the new generation cast about for someone who at the very least would not be hostile to their youthful dreams of church reform. They found him in the singular, somewhat unconventional figure of Father Mina the Solitary (so called because this monk had lived in total isolation for many years in an old mill on the Mokattam cliffs, until the British, who intended to mine the cliffs in preparation for World War II, evicted him). Many of the members of St. Anthony's and Giza's churches had first come to know Father Mina when they were no more than schoolboys. They would climb up the dark, rugged cliffs for the spiritual thrill of sitting at his feet at night, under an open sky, surrounded only by the ominously silent desert and by the invisible presences whom Father Mina invoked.[3] Later, in the early '50s, when they grew up to be young men whose critical intellect had made them unwelcome in their monastery, they had turned once more to Father Mina. He made a home for some of them in the abandoned Monastery of Samuel, in Upper Egypt, of which he was the nominal head.

Some of the old guard objected to the nomination of Father Mina for pope, regarding him, with skepticism, as a somewhat eccentric figure. He was rumored to practice sorcery, because he distributed talismans to his devotees. (Bishop Gregorios still had one in his possession. He showed me a yellow, tattered piece of paper on which Father Mina the Solitary had scribbled something mysteriously divine in the Coptic language.) They also believed that he was empowered to perform miracles.[4] There is a whole literature on his miracles edited by a group of his devotees, who call themselves the Sons of Pope Cyril VI.

But Father Mina's youthful fans remembered his help with gratitude and voted for him. He in turn, as Pope Cyril VI, was later to reward them: Finding no vacant diocesan bishoprics to give them, he created a new office, that of general bishop (a sort of minister without portfolio) in lieu of the traditional diocesan bishop and offered one of these bishoprics to each one of them. The Bishopric of Social Services went to Father Macari and another bishopric, the Bishopric of Higher Clerical Education, went to Father Anthony, while Father Matthew the Poor was made abbot of the Monastery of St. Macarios.[5]

Edward Wakin reported that a Coptic priest told him about Pope Shenuda's predecessor, Cyril: "The Patriarch is a very holy man. He is a saint. . . . There is much praying every day at the patriachate, but we need more than prayer. Prayer is not enough."[6] Wakin commented on this remark that it seemed that in Egypt, "Not only has a monk become a Patriarch, but the Patriarch has remained a monk."[7]

Nonetheless, the reign of Pope Cyril VI (1959–1971) marks the beginning of church modernization, because it made possible the cooptation of the reform-minded generation into the administration. By the time he took over, in 1959, the Sunday School Movement was fully institutionalized, with over four hundred branches in the provinces (900 town and 400 village centers and a central committee *al-Lagnah al-ʿUlyah li Madāris al-Aḥad*, the High Committee for Sunday Schools, was established that same year).[8] It was headed by the current archbishop of Damanhour, Bishop Pachomios, whose chief virtue seems to have been that though he had attended the Giza church ever since he arrived in Cairo for university studies, from his small town of Zagazig, he was on good terms with all the different and conflicting church groups.[9]

The Sunday School Movement was then at its apogee and its central committee rostrum read like a Who's Who of modern Orthodoxy: in addition to the

Giza group, people like the educational psychologist Salib Surial, the engineers Yuhannā al-Rāhib and Yassa Ḥannā, Kamāl Ḥabīb and Father Macari, both Princeton University graduates; it also contained two highly educated newcomers, Abd al-Messih Bishara, a professor of English literature who later, as Bishop Athanasios, ran a model diocese in Banī Suwayf, and Wahib Attalah, just back from London University with a Ph.D. For him, Pope Cyril VI created yet another general bishopric. He named him bishop of Advanced Coptic Research, thus carrying the process of institutionalization one step farther.

But the modern church structure, which Cyril VI had erected, in which the old and the new were meant to mesh in a unified whole, proved to be only plastered over. Soon cracks began to appear. The principal cause may be defined in broad terms as political. Shenuda's generation looked on the church as an all-embracing institution, which was there to deal with issues temporal as well as spiritual, whereas Pope Cyril's generation preferred to see the church as solely a spiritual body.

Even the more enlightened members of the older generation, who had welcomed the infusion of new blood into the church, thought of reform principally in terms of spiritual elevation. A man like the abbot of the Monastery of the Syrians, Tewfilios, the only one in 1954 willing to open his monastery to university graduates, soon ran afoul of some of his youthful recruits. Both Fathers Anthony and Matthew the Poor left him to have a free hand, in the remote and uninhabited Monastery of Samuel, to work out the principles of the godly commonwealth they intended to create. But like all true revolutionaries, they had different ideas about how the new order was to be founded. They soon quarreled with each other and one of them, Father Anthony, left and returned to the Monastery of the Syrians. Though this history graduate from Cairo University appropriately took on himself the duties of librarian for the monastery, he frequently interrupted his stay there for periods of isolation in a nearby cave cut into the sand stone in ancient times, where he reflected on the brave new world he hoped to found some day. Father Matthew the Poor, whose rugged independence of character was fortified by his three years of hermitage in a remote desert cave, would no doubt have clung to his solitary dream to the bitter end, had not illness, brought on by the absence of potable water in this monastery, which centuries of neglect had reduced to a ruin, compelled him to return to civilization.[10]

Pope Cyril VI versus Bishop Shenuda and Abbot Matthew the Poor

Pope Cyril VI, who had at first welcomed these two reform-minded monks into his administration, began to tire of them. For one thing, the pope, a man of mild disposition, did not care for Bishop Shenuda's confrontational style. (It is perhaps fitting that the fiery Father Anthony chose for himself, when he was consecrated bishop, the name of St. Shenoute. The latter was the glory of militant Egyptian Christianity in ancient times.) The strong-willed bishop had shown a tendency very early on to seek a centralization of power. Soon after he was consecrated bishop of Higher Clerical Education, in 1962, he tried to assert his control over the Coptic Institute, which brought him into conflict with its director, the highly regarded archeologist Dr. Sami Gabra. The Coptic Institute, one of the fruits of the Sunday School Movement, was principally a secular institution, for the study of the Coptic language, art, archeology, and history, as well as church dogma and canon law. It prided itself on its illustrious university professors and had heretofore maintained an autonomous existence under the protective umbrella of a lay communal council.

This conflict led to resignation of the director, Dr. Gabra, which was followed rapidly by that of his successor, the historian Aziz Aṭīyah, who left for the university of Utah, in the United States, where he produced a *Coptic Encyclopaedia*—but not before he had given Pope Cyril VI an earful about his "dictatorial" new bishop.[11] Shenuda also came into conflict with yet another venerable member of the institute, Bishop Gregorios, who had been appointed bishop the same year as Shenuda. Eventually, their animosity grew to a point where Gregorios withdrew in "disgust" from the clerical seminary he headed and immured himself at the top of a ramshackle old building that had once served his friend, Bishop Samuel, as headquarters. He devoted the rest of his life to the preparation of a new Arabic version of the Bible and to other scholarly pursuits.[12]

All these undercurrents of tension in the church were bound to perturb the noncombative Pope Cyril VI and to affect his relations with his bishop of Higher Clerical Education. Furthermore, Bishop Shenuda's Friday general meetings with their political undertones had begun to alarm the pope, whose enlightened ideas, which had led him to sponsor the entry of a new generation of educated young men into the church administration, stopped short of such a radical change to the traditional format and content of the homily. In addition, the pope was coming under pressure from Nasser's authoritarian regime to rein in his outspoken new bishop. Pope Cyril therefore ordered Bishop Shenuda to stop his Friday meetings and return to his monastery. But this move caused such furor among Bishop Shenuda's youthful devotees that the pope was compelled to invite him back to Cairo. Shortly thereafter, however, Shenuda found his lecture hall closed down, by papal edict, purportedly on grounds of safety (a crack in the ceiling!).[13]

Relations between the bishop and the pope soured to a point where, when a water stoppage occurred at Shenuda's residence at the Anba Ruweis Center, the bishop made it clear he suspected the pope of having given the orders for the water to be cut off, with the following pointed telegram: "We have been without water for thirteen days now, but God is on our side!" By then, each of the two men had their supporters and followers and tension had reached such a pitch that according to Bishop Gregorios, when a party of pro-Shenuda protestors directed themselves toward the old papal residence, in Clot Bey, Pope Cyril was sufficiently alarmed to have called in the national guard.[14]

The pope's disagreements were not limited to Bishop Shenuda. He also had his difficulties with another headstrong scion of the Sunday School Movement, Father Matthew the Poor. Like Shenuda, Matthew the Poor wanted to centralize power in his own hands and he could be blunt and sardonic when angered. During his term as the pope's vicar in Alexandria, Matthew had a number of clashes with the conservative lay notability that sat in the Communal Council. For this reason, Pope Cyril VI relieved him of his responsibilities there.

Having failed to make his mark in church administration, Matthew the Poor returned to the solitude of the desert, with a small band of some ten youngsters handpicked from the sizable following he had acquired among university students in Alexandria. He was soon thereafter to build an empire of his own around the trail of the abandoned monastery of St. Macarios in the Natrun valley. His redoubtable energy and money donated by West Germany transformed this neglected, impoverished monastery into a modern agricultural enterprise—too modern for the pope's taste. He is said to have greeted the report that Frisian cows were being shipped to the monastery with the quip that Matthew the Poor ought not to have been named "the Poor" (*miskin* in Arabic) but "the Possessed" (*maskūn*).[15]

We do not know what specific course of action eventually led to Matthew the Poor's expulsion from the monastery by Pope Cyril. Most likely it was an accumulation of irritations. Right from the start of his rein, Pope Cyril had objected to some of his innovations. An idea that had been all too new for the more traditionally inclined pope was Matthew's founding of a nonmonastic lay order, in 1958, that of *Mukharasin*. Its members were meant to live "as monks in the world," which is to say, remain celibate and devote their life to prayer, theological and hagiographic study, spiritual service, and religious education. These men lived communally, in the style introduced by St. Pachomios to Egypt's monasteries. It was he who established the basis for communal life in the monasteries as opposed to St. Anthony's individual hermitage. Matthew's *Mukharasin* differed only in job location—in the world rather than in the monastery itself. But they pooled their money to cover their basic needs, which were determined by a budget set for the entire group.[16]Among the small group of young men with whom he began this enterprise was Kamāl Ḥabīb, who was later to achieve reknown as the enlightened Bishop Bimen of Mallawi, a diocese in Upper Egypt.

After founding the first such house, called *Bayt al-Takris* (the home of the consecrated laymen), in an old palace in Helwan that had once belonged to an Egyptian princess, Matthew went on to support many other such groups throughout the country—without consulting the pope or waiting for a ruling from the Holy Synod of Bishops on whether the creation of a lay order such as the *Mukarasin* could be justified in terms of church tradition.[17]

At any rate, Pope Cyril eventually pardoned Matthew the Poor and allowed him to resume his role of abbot of the Monastery of St. Macarios, thanks to the mediation of the Vatican on Matthew's behalf.

Abbot Matthew the Poor versus Bishop Samuel and Bishop Shenuda

Such conflicts did not exist just between the older and the new generations. There was also considerable tension between the leading members of the reform movement themselves, Abbot Matthew the Poor, Bishop Shenuda, and Bishop Samuel, each of whom had his own ideas about what the reform movement should entail and his own group of devoted and overzealous followers.

Matthew the Poor was very progressive in the way he ran his own monastery. He strongly encouraged research and scholarship among his monks and built a major publishing house and a library unequaled, except for the pope's own collection. And his agricultural enterprise, based on modern technology and a fearsome work discipline, grew to encompass a major desert reclamation project, which created work for several hundred Copts, ranging from agronomists and agricultural engineers to manual laborers. He even employed some Muslims. In this, too, he was unconventional. He was as exacting in the standards that he imposed on the monks at work, as those by which he measured their industry in learning and their religious devotion. Two of the bishops who had been monks at the monastery of St. Macarios, Bishop Besanti, an agricultural engineer, and Bishop Johanna, an agronomist, complained about this draconian workload—one told me he had fallen ill from lack of sleep.[18] A third one, Bishop Sherubim, whose opinion I sought in the course of a visit I paid him in Kena, his diocese, did not harbor any such resentment but did describe Matthew as hard driving, both of himself and of others and, by Egyptian standards, inflexible in matters of discipline. "He never said *Ma 'alish*" ("it doesn't matter," a much-used Egyptian expression).[19]

Despite, this modern, Protestant-like profile, which makes him very definitely one of the founding fathers of the reformed church, there were significant differences in his outlook and that of Shenuda—or even Samuels. Matthew the Poor was very close, in his orientation, to what may be called the St. Anthony Church school of thought. The main emphasis of that school was, as we have seen, on looking inward at the foundations of the church of origin, the third-century Church of Alexandria. Bishop Samuel was very much a product of the Giza Church. The focus of the adherents to the Giza school of thought was less on a return to the dogmas and values of the church of origin and more on an adaptation of Christian values to the contemporary world. They looked outward toward the experiences of the western Christian world. Not only did that mean that Samuel's followers, during their travels abroad in the '50s, were in touch with the Protestant churches and their pastoral activities, but beginning in the nineteen sixties, they became very much involved in the Vatican II campaign of "the Church in the World." This campaign, which focused on the pastoral and social mission of the Catholic Church, was part of a strategy mapped out at the Vatican II Council with a view to winning back a modern world grown indifferent to—if not outright alienated from—the church.[20]

Western Christendom was also eager to improve its image in its former colonies through the forging of new fields of action in the Third World. Bishop Samuel was perceptive enough to take advantage of this new current of thought in the West by promoting the ecumenical movement in Egypt. This rapprochement of the Egyptian Orthodox Church to the other churches worldwide, after centuries of enmity and isolation, was possible precisely because in pastoral work he could find a common ground with the Catholics and Protestants that was not as full of polemics as the dialogues on the nature of Christ were.[21]

The main activity of Samuel's bishopric in this period, the 1960s, consisted of sending caravans out to the rural areas with church-servants entrusted with extending medical aid to the peasants; teaching the women about the importance of having their babies vaccinated and keeping their homes clean and launching adult literacy campaigns and offering vocational courses in plumbing, electrical work, and carpentry.

Bishop Samuel also inaugurated special training for what he called his "diaconal" groups, although these shared nothing, outside of their nomenclature, with the traditional deacons whose responsibilities were exclusively religious instruction and assisting with the performance of the Mass. For these courses in the new field of pastoral theology and practice, he recruited Protestant teachers since the Egyptian Protestants had a long-standing experience in that domain due to the influence of American Protestant missionaries. This had become institutionalized in the Coptic Evangelical Organization for Social Services (CEOSS). The cooperation between the Egyptian Orthodox and the Egyptian Protestant Churches, which was consistent with the new ecumenical spirit, was encouraged by the European donors to Samuel's various enterprises.[22]

Samuel went even farther by allowing Protestants to minister to Orthodox communities in the villages—to the outrage of the Shenuda camp, which bitterly remembered the days when the offer of such services was used to lure Orthodox peasants into the Protestant Church.

At first Pope Cyril, mindful of the tensions between Samuel and Shenuda's camps, named Samuel's bishopric *The Rural Diaconate* to emphasize that it was just a continuation of the social work already begun in the mid-nineteen forties in the rural areas by members of the Sunday School Movement. The name was meant to calm Shenuda's fears that it would trespass on of those carrying out the religio-cultural work, which, at the time, was chiefly centered in the urban areas. Whatever reservations Shenuda had about this, he could not impose his will over the Rural Diaconate in the same manner he had over the Coptic Institute, since the former was outside his jurisdiction. But he let it be known that he did not care for Samuel's manner of fund-raising;—his "gallivanting" around Europe with the Protestants (his chief donors).[23] And since both Shenuda and Samuel had their zealous devotees, there ensued a considerable amount of mudslinging between their respective partisans. As for Samuel himself, he offered the somewhat lame argument, in self-defense, that his ecumenical encounters did not influence the direction of the social work enterprises he had launched, but on the contrary enabled him to explain to the European prelates the way in which the pastoral work of his own church was modeled after that of the Egyptian church of origin.

By the time Pope Cyril's death intervened in 1971, barely a few months after President Nasser's own death, which empowered Shenuda, as the new pope, to hamper Samuel's activities, it was no longer possible to set back the clock. The expectations the average Copts had of their church had altered. The legitimacy of the church had come to rest in large part on the socioeconomic aid it provided to its parishioners. Bishop Samuel was, therefore, not only able to consolidate his gains, but to invade a terrain previously considered Bishop Shenuda's, the urban conglomerates. He began work in the two garbage collectors' areas of Cairo, Mukattam and Muʾtamidīyah (garbage collection is mainly a Christian occupation in Egypt because pigs are raised on the refuse). And he penetrated not only the physical space of his opponent but his field of operation as well, since along with the medical and nutritional services he brought to the garbage collectors came religion and pedagogy and vocational training.

Previously, the garbage collectors' zones, which were in remote residential areas, had been neglected by the Orthodox. To the extent that they received any spiritual and welfare services, the initiatives were taken by Catholic missionaries, under the leadership of a Franciscan nun, Sister Emanuel, who later worked in conjunction with the Egyptian Protestant social worker Mary Asʿad. It was Bishop Samuel who established an Orthodox presence in their midst.

Bishop Samuel also expanded his outreach program to include the middle-class Cairene districts of Shubra and Faggala, which are heavily Christian, bringing to them offerings like language and computer courses. Here, as elsewhere, the religio-cultural dimension was fused with the technical one, through a whole series of prayer services, homilies, and readings from hagiographies that accompanied these courses. Samuel did not content himself with the activities traditionally associated with the Sunday School Movement but launched new ventures in the urban areas such as homes for drug addicts, delinquents, the mentally handicapped, and girls pregnant out of wedlock. The latter were called *Beyout al-Rahma* (Homes of Mercy) and were the most radical of all his ventures, as such girls were previously not only thrown out into the street by their families but sometimes even killed by them in the small towns and villages of Upper Egypt to salvage the family honor.

Significantly, in addition to multiplying his initiatives, he changed the name of his bishopric from Rural Diaconate to the more encompassing Bishopric for

Public, Ecumenical, and Social Services to signal to Pope Shenuda the enhanced scope of his operations, which had by the mid-nineteen seventies grown to encompass the entire country. He had set up branches of this bishopric in all the provinces of Egypt, and his activities and enterprises were emulated by many of the diocesan bishops.

If Samuel's concern was with the adaptation of Egyptian Orthodoxy to modern Christianity, both Matthew the Poor and Shenuda were more interested in reviving the Coptic religious heritage. But their interpretations of what that entailed was at odds. For Shenuda the meaning of revival lay primarily in the use of the ancient church legends to reaffirm the Coptic identity of the community, while for Matthew it was a quest to recapture the basic values of early Christianity. So both tendencies, though fundamentalist, had very different political implications.

Very early on, in the 1960s, Matthew had parted ways with the revival current led by Shenuda, because he judged it to be too much in the social round—in a word, too public. He feared both the politicization of the church in its new role of communal spokesman and the instrumentalization of the monasteries through the growing recruitment of monks for presbytery, pedagogical, and social work throughout Egypt. To preserve their spirituality, he felt, the monks had to live out their vocation as simple believers within the monasteries, outside of the ambitious trappings of the clerical hierarchy. Otherwise, what was to prevent the faithful from looking on their entry to the monastery as a stepping stone to a bishopric?

This was no idle concern for a reform movement that aimed not just to enlightenment, but also to moral elevation. And while one no longer heard, as in the past, of monks who paid influential intermediaries commissions so they would recommend them to the pope for bishoprics, there was still a danger lurking that an ambitious *khadim* or *mukaras,* who had been zealous in the service of some bishop might look upon the monastery as the only way toward eventual emancipation from clerical tutelage. He might secretly nurture the hope that once he entered the monastery, his bishop would recommend him for a bishopric, which would give him prestige and power. One is not supposed to harbor such ambitions, when one joins a monastery; Bishop Bishoi told me he had hidden in the desert from the pope when he came to the monastery to recruit him for a bishopric, and bishop Bula said that he had actually cried at having to leave his monastery—stories I believe of these two intensely spiritual individuals—but the temptation nonetheless remains.

In writing about his monastery, in a work entitled *A Quick Look at the Monastery of St. Macarios and at Monastic Life in Egypt,* Matthew the Poor points out that St. Pachomios insisted on keeping the monks out of the religious polemics raging in his time over the single versus dual nature of Christ, and refused to preach when called upon by Pope Athanasios, because he felt that such an activity would interfere with his monastic vocation. Matthew the Poor himself followed his example by refusing to preach and by addressing the faithful only through his writings. For Matthew the contemporary movement of religious revival lost its bearings once it allowed itself to become involved in communal and political problems. In a work entitled *Articles between Politics and Religion*, he insists that the clergy was to serve as a model of virtue for others, to help them through prayer and persuade them to repent—and not to cater to their material interests or defend their political rights. All attachment to such worldly purposes was against the spirit of Christianity, in his view. A Christian community should not seek to increase its weight and power in this world, and above all not try to triumph over its enemies. Christians, he writes, should be prepared to lay down their own lives to defend their faith, but not to attack their opponents. Christ neither attacked his enemies nor fled from them. In his book Matthew writes that in defending the gospel one sacrifices oneself, but in attacking others one sacrifices the gospel for oneself.[24]

This is a very different viewpoint from that of Shenuda who, in *The Spiritual Wars*, writes that one can make this kind of choice out of a love of peace, if only one's individual rights are at stake. But in what concerns the collective rights of the entire community one has a duty to act to prevent the stronger party from devouring the weaker one.[25] In warning against the instrumentalization of Christianity for worldly purposes, as Shenuda and his followers were doing, Matthew invokes the fanaticism to which this can lead; he gives the example of the Crusaders and the Zionists.[26] And in one of the articles in the same book entitled *The Church and the Complex of Persecution*, he goes even farther, suggesting that the theme of Coptic persecution is principally evoked by Shenuda to mobilize the faithful toward ultrareligious (political) goals.[27]

Given such a frontal attack against the more politicized current of the Church Revival movement, it is no wonder President Sadat nurtured a very close relationship with Matthew—in contrast to his enmity with Shenuda. And Sadat is thought to have had, at the very least, Matthew's tacit support when he later sent Shenuda into exile. The relationship between Pope Shenuda and the abbot was so strained as a result, that when I began my fieldwork in 1992, I found Matthew the Poor living in self-imposed exile in the desert near Alexandria and not a single one of the persons I approached was willing to give me a letter of introduction to him. They all talked of their fear of the pope's reprisal if he should learn that they had acted as go-betweens. In the end, I myself succumbed to cowardice: I did not want to jeopardize my work for the sake of one man, no matter how important his contributions to the reform movement. I let myself be persuaded by one of the prominent intellectuals closest to him, William Kīlādā, to give up my attempts to meet a person who was anathema to the pope because "if His Holiness ever finds out, all the welcoming doors of the church will suddenly be closed to you."

I contented myself with visiting Matthew the Poor's monastery. I spoke to the old monks who were closest to Matthew the Poor. One of them, who asked not to be named, told me that the reason Matthew had left the monastery was that the pope had conducted an "unrelenting campaign of vilification" against him. He had even "intrigued" against him within his own monastery by "infiltrating it with his spies" (new novitiates, whose loyalty lay with the pope, not the abbot) and by "luring away" some of St. Macarios's monks with the offer of positions in the clerical hierarchy. Two of those, bishops Bisanti and Johanna, had become the pope's secretaries, positions of power, because they act as intermediaries for those seeking an audience with the pope. "In the end," this old monk said, "he got fed up and one day he told me, "If Shenuda wants to take over my monastery, let him have it!—and he left."[28]

But if we set aside this animosity, we will find that Matthew shared with Shenuda a stance that was rooted in the fundamentalism of the St. Anthony School of thought; namely, a profound distrust of the ecumenical movement that influenced and financed the social work within the Coptic community. Ecumenicists like Bishop Samuel were regarded as crypto-Protestants, because they were less concerned with the issue of a return to the origins of the Coptic Church and more with debates on poverty in the Third World that engaged the attention of western Christianity.[29] For them, the revalorization of the role and the influence of the church of origin seemed less pressing than the reintegration of the contemporary Coptic Church into mainstream Christianity.

All the leading proponents of social work, Bishop Samuel, Bishop Bimen of Mallawi, and Bishop Athanasios of Banī Suwayf, had indeed had some exposure to Anglo-Saxon culture. Bishop Samuel had studied at the American University in Cairo, and at the Princeton Theological Seminary, where he specialized in a subject new for Egypt, pastoral theology. Bishop Bimen had studied at Princeton University, where his fields were psychology and education, and Bishop Athanasios, though he had not studied in America or England, was a graduate of the faculty of English literature in Alexandria, which at the time he attended it was almost entirely staffed with English professors.[30] These bishops tended, therefore, to see modern Christianity—particularly in its Protestant guise—through Anglicized eyes, which is to say as progressive and rational. But for Shenuda and Matthew the reconstitution of the ancient Coptic heritage was a priority because, in their view, it served the current needs of the community by providing it with an important and valuable sense of capability.

Matthew also feared that Samuel's focus on socioeconomic projects would corrupt the relationship between the clergy and the faithful; the Copts would be lured into the church by the prospect of material assistance rather than spiritual fulfilment. He warned that loyalty toward those dispensing social services would degenerate into a form of patron-client relationship. The only obligation one should feel, according to him, was toward the Savior. In his book *al-Khidmah* (The Service), he wrote that the principal way of witnessing for Christ, should be to offer spiritual sustenance, not material assistance.[31] As opposed to the social work Bishop Samuel's *khuddām* engaged in, Matthew the Poor's *khuddām* offered only spiritual and pedagogical services to the community.

In contrast, for Samuel the spirit of Christianity must manifest itself first and foremost in the mutual aid of the Coptic community; love your neighbor as yourself was a precept that must be translated into charitable deeds. And it is, perhaps, because he set so much stock on deeds as a way of perpetuating the charity of Jesus that he wrote very little, as opposed to the prolificacy of both Shenuda and Matthew.

Faced with the question, What must Copts do to live as a good Christians? both Shenuda and Matthew would no doubt respond by saying that they must express their faith through spiritual work, work on themselves. To that end Shenuda and Matthew both published an impressive number of books. (Pope Shenuda told me he had written sixty-three books.) In two of them, *Milestones on the Path to Faith* and *Spiritual Awakening*,[32] he set out a number of spiritual exercises for the faithful to follow (exercises against egotism, vanity, lust, and so on). In works like *Spiritual Wars* and *Wars against Satan*,[33] he visualizes life as a perpetual combat against one's baser self—against Satan who is always at one's elbow. Other works are devoted to an exposition of Orthodoxy (such as *Orthodox Understanding of the Concept of Salvation*).[34] Loosely put, Matthew's *With Christ All the Way to the Cross*[35] would fall into the first category, while his *Importance of Tradition in the Christian Faith* would fall under the second.[36] The only difference between these two clerics is that in Matthew the Poor's writings the emphasis is not so much on combating negative elements within the self, as it is in helping one's intrinsically good nature surface through prayer and communion—and especially confession, which plays a vital role in Orthodoxy.

Undaunted by the literary outpouring of his peers, Bishop Samuel had only written two pamphlets *Family Planning from a Christian Point of View* and *With the Youth*. For him, life as a good Christian was not so much expressed through work on the self as through work with and for others—in a word, through social work. By ministering to the sick, teaching the children, and helping the poor financially, one realized one's Christian faith.[37] His work on family planning was not published by Dar al-Mahaba, the main Orthodox publisher, but by a Protestant press, Dar al-Thakafah al-Misriyyah. This is no mere coincidence; in one of the youth meetings I attended, bishop Moses, considered a paragon of progressive Orthodoxy, said that it was "selfish" for a young couple to decide to postpone procreation because they wanted a few years to study in peace or felt they had not saved enough money to support a family: They must have faith that "God will provide."[38]

However much Shenuda and Matthew—two strong personalities with differing views of what the church reform movement should entail—may have clashed, Shenuda's worst ire was reserved for Samuel. In a walk the pope and I took together on the grounds of the Monastery of Bishoi, he once referred to this bishop as "a very bad man" and described his assassination at the hands of the Islamic militants as an act of "divine justice" that had rid the church of a "scourge."[39] I never heard him refer to Matthew the Poor in this fashion; on those occasions when we discussed him, he went no farther than to describe him as headstrong, imperious, or arrogant.

To be sure, to understand the extent of the animosity between Shenuda and Samuel, one must look beyond the personal rivalry that bedeviled their relationship to their respective visions for the church. Nonetheless it remains true that their animosity was intensified by their personal rivalry. Samuel was more popular than Shenuda: It was Samuel, the amiable, easygoing fellow, not the stern, doctrinaire Matthew—Shenuda's other competitor for the papal throne—who garnered the most votes when all three men came up for the papal elections later in 1971. Only the rule that the selection among the three finalists is, in the end, determined by lottery, when a blindfolded boy is made to pick a name tag out of a silver bowl to allow the "Divine hand" a role, gave the election to Shenuda. (Shenuda's devotee, Archbishop Bishoi, a mathematical wizard who got his degree from Alexandria's faculty of engineering with the motion "Excellent," tried to demonstrate to me arithmetically how Bishop Samuel had obtained the greater number of votes by "cheating," But his computations were too complex for me to follow!.)[40]

Bishop Samuel also posed a greater doctrinal challenge to Orthodoxy than did Abbot Matthew the Poor. His ecumenicalism threatened the specificity of Coptic identity that was at the center of Pope Shenuda's crusade against the state, as well as the autonomy of Egyptian Orthodox dogma—the latter because any earnest effort at rapprochement with the Protestant and Catholic Churches was bound to entail some compromise over conflicting interpretations about the nature of Christ and of purgatory.

For a long time Samuel's advocacy of an ecumenical rapprochement remained popular with only a minority of the clergy, the majority of whom shared Shenuda's outlook, which saw in ecumenicalism a danger of western acculturation. They feared it would weaken the Coptic community by eroding the religious specificity at the core of its identity. This position was also held by many prominent members of the lay community.

It must be remembered that the decade of the 1960s corresponded with the height of the anticolonial ideological campaign, led by Egypt's revolutionary junta. Ecumenicalism was suspect, because of the historical link between cross and the sword in the founding of new colonies. This negative view of evangelists and their ties to the imperialist powers found a modern corollary, during the Nasser era, in the notion that the CIA contributed funds to the World Council of Churches. Distrust of the West was reflected in the writing of many Coptic intellectuals, chief among whom was William Kīlādā. In addition to his own book, *The Egyptian Church Confronts Imperialism and Zionism*, a number of articles by Copts attacking Bishop Samuel's ecumenical leanings began to appear in the press in the mid '60s. However, Bishop Samuel persevered in his pioneering efforts. Whereas until 1960 the Orthodox Church was not even a member of the World Council of Churches, under Bishop Samuel's direction it soon joined a whole gamut of such associations and participated in numerous religious conferences in Europe, South America, Africa, and the Middle East, where the focus on pastoral concerns made possible a dialogue free of the acrimony that discussions of different dogmas and church doctrines aroused.

This not only gave the church a chance to recover some of the universal stature it had had until the end of the fifth century, when Constantinople supplanted Alexandria as the main center of Christian learning and power in the Eastern Mediteranean, but also to gain international support for its political cause. By bringing the Copts into contact with Western Christianity, Samuel was making it more difficult for the Egyptian government to discriminate against them without repercussions. While the bulk of the church's urban middle-class constituency had benefited as much as did the Muslims from Nasser's socialist measures, which included the opening up of the universities on a tuition-free basis to people of modest means, better work conditions in public enterprises, and job guarantees for new university graduates in the bureaucracy, they were disquieted by his pan-Arabism. The majority of the Copts identified with their pharaonic heritage, regarding themselves as genetic descendants of the pharaohs, and they did not care to exchange their Egyptian specificity for a larger pan-Arab one—particularly one that had Islamic undertones. Such an entity would only further marginalize them as a community and, by reinforcing their minority status, exclude them from the nations' political life. These dark premonitions were warranted by the fact that under Nasser no Copt ever rose to political prominence. The only ministerial portfolios wielded by Copts during his two decades in power were inconsequential technical ones.

The Copts' new status of "persecuted minority" was bound to evoke a responsive chord in the heart of the Christian Churches in Europe and the United States. Some of the Christian evangelical groups in America rallied to their support.

Bishop Samuel's ecumenical initiatives, which took the Coptic Church out of the quarantine to which it had been confined since the fifth century, had the incremental benefit of making western funds available for Coptic social work projects. Although the bishops' accounts are well-guarded secrets in Egypt, if we are to accept the testimony of knowledgeable Christian and Muslims, these funds were considerable. Hassanein Heykal, the editor-in-chief of the main daily *al-Ahrām*, says that at his death in 1981 Samuel was discovered to have a sizable reserve of foreign currency in a Swiss bank account.[41] This was confirmed to me by Fakhri Abd al-Nur, a Coptic banker very close to Bishop Samuel, whom he accompanied to a number of meetings with European ecclesia and donors, and to whose projects he himself contributed generously.[42] Certainly, Samuel's developmental work bears out the magnitude of that aid, regardless of what the exact figures in his secret Swiss bank accounts may have been.

He raised money in Europe from Catholic foundations like Miserio and Protestant ones like World Christian Association and Brot und Leben for the improvement of Christian village infra-structures (roads, electricity, potable water, and irrigation networks).[43] An indefatigable and resourceful fund-raiser, he did not confine his efforts to overseas Christian foundations, approaching secular ones as well. He enlarged his network to include the Ford Foundation in the United States and the Friedrich Ebhardt Stiftung in Germany. He also mobilized Coptic resources by persuading the well-to-do Copts in the diaspora, who cherished the memory of their monasteries, to invest in the new monastic agricultural projects, such as the cultivation of mushrooms, a commodity only recently introduced to Egypt. Locally, he concentrated his efforts on persuading wealthy Christians, who had profited from the economic liberalization under President Sadat, to hire Copts in their firms, businesses, and tourist agencies. And, according to Fakhri Abd al-Nur, he also approached the Coptic financial magnates to find positions for Copts in the newly reopened foreign banks and foreign businesses and to subsidize the education of Copts of modest circumstances who needed training abroad.[44] He was also able to obtain a good number of scholarships for his church-servants to further their training in Europe as well as in North America, particularly in England and at the Coady International Institute in Nova Scotia, on the campus of St. Francis Xavier University.

Shenuda, by contrast, concentrated on a conquest of the public orbit, making numerous declarations to the press about inequality of access to the state-run sector of the economy and to the high rungs of the civil service. He also sponsored numerous conferences on the political and economic rights of the Copts, the most important of which was held in Alexandria in 1977. But Samuel professed to concentrate on social work as a basis for communal solidarity, rather than engage in the politics of identity. He made it clear that he considered the turn that the reform movement had taken under Shenuda to be the mobilization and domination of the Copts for political purposes. He was able to marshal international funds to create for the Copts an autonomous socioeconomic sphere and alternative avenues of mobility, within an increasingly discriminatory state. He encouraged the Copts to forget about the public sphere, which marginalized them, and to invest their energy and talents instead in education and in the private sector—in short, to view social promotion as a compensation for political losses.

Ironically, when Samuel was killed by Islamic militants in 1981, and Shenuda took over the control of the Bishopric of Public, Ecumenical, and Social Services, he made a virtue out of necessity by fraternizing with the very Protestants he had once disparaged—particularly the Germans and Swedes who were the bulwark of that bishopric's financial support. In 1994, he even surpassed Bishop Samuel by becoming the first Egyptian pope ever to preside over the World Council of Churches.

PART III

The Church as Political Spokesman

7

Dealing with the Muslim State

Pope Shenuda

President Nasser's Empowerment of the Church

Ironically, President Nasser's authoritarian regime unwittingly schooled the church for a political role, by weakening the Christian secular aristocracy as well as the liberal institutions like Parliament and the Communal Council in which they had played an important role. Even before it issued the decree banning the multiparty system, the new regime that had come to power as a result of the 1952 revolution had undermined the political power of the Coptic landed aristocracy by destroying, through the Agrarian Reform Act, their economic base.

Nasser was uncomfortable with private voluntary associations: he regarded them as potential centers of subversion. The Communal Council, an institution dominated by that same aristocracy, was not done away with in quite as blatant a manner as Parliament had been, but it was reduced to a shadow of its former self. The same republican decree that limited land holdings to 200 feddans authorized the Agrarian Reform Authority to confiscate all church holdings beyond that limit. At first sight it might appear that this decree weakened the church, since income from land offered as a legacy to the church, known as *wakf*, provided it with one of its chief sources of revenue. Contrary to appearances, however, this measure enhanced the power of the church by placing the administration of all remaining land in the hands of a new body, the Coptic Orthodox Wakf Organization, whose members were to be chosen by the pope, thereby depriving the Communal Council of its financial control. The Communal

Council had already been hurt when Nasser abolished the religious courts under its jurisdiction—a law that was meant to bring all Egyptian citizens, Muslims as well as Christians, under the jurisdiction of the secular courts. (He also abolished the Islamic courts.)

With the council emasculated in this fashion, it became easy for Pope Cyril VI to make short shrift of it with government connivance. He abolished this longtime rival for control of the church and its properties altogether.[1] Thus Nasser prepared the way for the expansion of the role of the church and the empowerment of its high prelates, by curtailing the role of the Communal Council and of Parliament (it was an open secret that anyone wishing to get into the single-party electoral body he had set up, the Liberation Rally, had to get the pope's blessing, because Nasser submitted the list of his electoral appointments to the pope for scrutiny).

It was not just Cyril VI's accommodating disposition which made it possible for the church to reach a modus vivendi with the new regime but also the circumstances of the 1950s. Having very narrowly missed an attempt on his life in 1954 at the hands of a member of the Muslim Brotherhood, Nasser cracked down on that organization and kept its members behind bars for the duration of his rule, an act that indirectly redounded to the benefit of the Christian community. At the very least, the government could not be faulted for failing to protect the Christians from murderous attacks by Islamic militants.

At the outset, Nasser's regime, which had come to power by means of a coup d'état, had little legitimacy and was therefore anxious to ensure stability by, among other things, avoiding sectarian strife. Nasser tried to cultivate good relations with the pope by authorizing the building of a new cathedral in Cairo's Abbasia district, which was to become the new papal headquarters, and promising that licenses for the building of twenty-five new churches would be issued every year.

The resurgence of Islamic militancy in the 1970s made possible in part by the greater political freedom under Nasser's successor, Anwar al-Sadat, was to strain the church-state relationship to the breaking point and to rekindle the bitter feuds and fierce animosities within the church that had bedeviled the Sunday School Movement in the 1940s and early 1950s, by opening an acrimonious debate on what was the best strategy for dealing with the state. Once more the line of division ran between the Shenuda and the Samuel camps, only this time Samuel was in the conservative trench. He favored playing the political game in the old-fashioned way, by using the good offices of the aristocratic secular elite. Shenuda, on the other hand, impatient with niceties of diplomacy, wanted the church to assert itself and step forward as the spokesman of the Coptic community.

In the ensuing fray between Shenuda and his supporters, who went to prison for him and considered the high prelates who cooperated with the government "traitors," and Bishop Samuel and his supporters, who feared that the militant stance adopted by the church under Shenuda would generate a Muslim backlash, the reformist movement was split in two—a breach that was never repaired. But in the final account, despite the enormous services rendered to the church by Bishop Samuel's pioneering efforts in the socioeconomic and ecumenical fields, it was Shenuda, a politically astute, ambitious, and highly intelligent man, who proved to be the right person for the hard times ahead of the Christians.

President Sadat and the Radicalization of the Church

Muḥammad Anwar al-Sadat, who succeeded Nasser in 1970, had none of his predecessor's charismatic appeal—he was, in fact, a virtual nonentity at his accession, and this lack of any personal legitimacy exposed him to the danger of an attempted coup within a year after he came to power. In casting about for an antidote to the leftist forces that had tried to unseat him in 1971, he found it politically expedient to lean on the religious forces. One of the unintended consequences of this marriage of convenience was the growth of the power of Islamic militants, of which not just the Christians but he himself was ultimately to be the victim.

Once Sadat had decided to veer back toward a capitalist mode of production, he had to allow the market mechanisms to resume their course; many of the state subsidies and amenities from which the poor had benefited under Nasser were bound to fall by the wayside. An attempt to remove food subsidies, to let the prices of certain utilities like electricity rise, to remove rent controls and the like entailed ipso facto the dissolution of the populist alliance of workers, peasants, impoverished students, and lower-middle-class government officials on meager incomes that had constituted Nasser's chief supporters. Sadat needed to build up a different social base of support, and Islam seemed the most suitable ideological tool for the mobilization of a new constituency that he hoped would cut across class lines.

The country was ready for it because there had been a tendency in the aftermath of the Six Day War of 1967 to attribute the defeat by Israel to the absence of any meaningful ideology in Egypt that would motivate its youth. In comparison, the Zionist ideological fervor, which infused Jewish soldiers with a passionate devotion to their country, was said to be the cause of Israel's victory. The different ideological themes that were used at various times to mobilize the Egyptians—liberal nationalism and socialism—had all failed, it was argued, because they were western imports imposed from above. By contrast, many felt that for the middle and lower classes, which comprised the vast majority of Egyptians, Islam constituted the only meaningful cultural referent—an important part of their identity. It would provide a solid moral grounding for the youth and infuse them with zeal in combat.

When Sadat began positioning himself as *al-Rais al-Mu'min* (the devout president), seated cross-legged on the prayer rug for photographers, he was not introducing anything new: he was merely riding the crest of a wave of popular enthusiasm for Islam that had been latent during the last years of Nasser's life. Once Nasser's massive reassuring presence, which had managed in the aftermath of the defeat to hold together the conflicting elements within Egyptian society and to make them keep to the old beaten track of Arab socialism, was removed, political Islam burst forth and filled the vacuum.

In an attempt to consolidate his rule, Sadat began to lend state support to the Islamic groups both within and without the universities and to their publications. By the mid 1970s, the religious students had come to dominate the student unions, which had previously been Nasserite enclaves. The takeover of the student unions by the religious youth was accompanied by a growing militancy that led to several clashes with the Christian students, and to an attempt to remove the "pulpit parrots" (the traditional Muslim preachers who were considered in league with the government) from the mosques and have them replaced by militant young preachers. The intimidating physical presence of militant youth in the mosques had reached alarming proportions by 1980. That year, during the religious feast of *Eid al-Adha*, they managed to take over several of the larger mosques in the capital, including the one opposite the presidential palace in Abdin Square, where they drew a crowd estimated at 400,000 people. As one observer noted, "Such a large crowd would never have been able to gather within eyesight of the presidential guard, had it not been for government connivance."[2]

Not only the pulpit came to be dominated by the strident new voice of Islam but the media as well. Numerous publications advanced the concept of Islamic hegemony. They intimated that the Coptic Church was responsible for preventing Egypt from becoming an Islamic state and they advocated the destruction of all institutions that stood between the citizen and Islam.[3] Nasser's Arab nationalism was derided as a secular ideology, propagated by the Arab Christians to divide the Arab nation. (The first proponents of Arab nationalism in the nineteenth century were indeed Syro-Lebanese Christians who felt comfortable with the idea of the nation-state with equality for all citizens. And the best known of the twentieth century Arab Christian nationalists was the Syrian Baath Party theoretician Michel Aflak.) By contrast, in the Islamic nation, the Christian minority would have the status of second-class citizens: *Dhimis*, or protected people, and if the Islamic law (*Sharia*) were applied to the Christians not only in general areas but in family law as well, as the Islamic militants advocate, it would most probably entail the fragmentation of the Christian family units and their eventual assimilation into the Islamic community.[4]

It should come as no surprise, therefore, that egged on by this Islamist propaganda, already in November 1972, barely two years after Sadat came to power, the first instance of sectarian strife occurred on the rural periphery of Cairo, in an urban village called Khanka. Fistfights broke out between Christians and Muslims, because the latter objected to the use of a private home as a chapel. The violence escalated and the chapel was burned down.

What was the pope to do about the burning of the chapel in Khanka? His predecessor Pope Cyril VI would in all likelihood have opted for registering a discreet, behind-the-scenes protest to the government, via the intermediary of a respected lay member of the Coptic community like Mirit Ghālī, the president of the Coptic Archeological Society. Pope Shenuda, however, adopted a militant stance. He sent a contingent of one hundred bishops and priests to keep a vigil at the site of the burned chapel, ordering them to hold their ground even if it meant being shot at.[5] This in turn triggered a Muslim backlash: Christian homes and stores in Khanka were torched and looted after the contingent of bishops and priests had left. Sadat did not take any punitive measures against the perpetrators of the arson: he contented himself with visiting the pope and the rector of al-Azhar University and with getting them both to issue a statement condemning the strife.

Two years later, in 1974, came the first attack by Islamic militants on the regime itself: a foiled attempt by a group calling itself Shabab Muhammad (the Youth of Muhammad) to take over by force the military academy. The plan had been to follow that up with an attack on Parliament, where the president and his ministers were assembled. Despite this, in July 1975 the president allowed the Muslim Brotherhood, many of whom had been released from prison on his assumption of power, to reissue their highly inflammatory periodical *al-Dawah* (The Mission).

Further evidence of the president's effort to win over the Islamist groups is apparent in the government sponsorship, in the mid 1970s, of the enactment of the Islamic penal law by the People's Assembly. Had the drafted law been passed, it would have meant among other things the application of the death penalty for apostasy—which the church was bound to oppose since it would not only deter Muslims from converting to Christianity but more importantly affect the far more numerous Christians who converted yearly to Islam, mostly to benefit from promotions at work and other state amenities or to obtain an easy divorce. The passage of the Islamic penal law would make it very difficult for them to reconsider later and return to their religion. (Conversion to Islam, which is known to be widely practiced though exact statistics are not available because such conversions are generally conducted secretly out of fear of family reprisal, is one of the biggest sources of concern to the church.) The pope therefore called on all Copts to join in a five-day fast to protest the drafting of the law. And the church was able, in a concerted effort with Coptic immigrant communities abroad, to convince the government to back down.[6]

Even though President Sadat had appeased the Islamic Militants, there was a fresh assault on the government in 1977. This time a new group calling itself *al-Takfir wa al-Higra* (Condemnation and Holy Flight) captured and executed the minister of Religious Endowments (Waqf). Sectarian trouble also flared up in the late 1970s in Upper and Middle Egypt, where there is a large Christian population. A number of churches were burned, priests were physically attacked, and there were clashes between Muslims and Christian students in Assiut and Minya. In 1977, a priest and a woman and child were killed in the village of Tewfikya in the diocese of Samalut, while in 1980 in the neighboring diocese of Minya homes were set on fire; plants, pharmacies, and confectioneries were ransacked and looted; and the Church of St. George was attacked in the small town of Fikria. This in turn triggered violent confrontations between Christian and Muslim students in the streets of Minya.[7]

In Lower Egypt also, the Church of Abu Zaabal in Cairo had been burned down in 1978 (some nine priests participated in a protest march). A year later, in 1979, the historic Church of the Virgin of al-Damshiriyya was torched in that same city. The eve of the Coptic Christmas, January 6, 1980, witnessed several church bombings in Alexandria.[8]

Though these atrocities perpetrated by Islamic militants were officially frowned upon, the evident lack of zeal with which the government investigated them and the failure to bring the culprits to trial had by then made the Copts feel like stepchildren of the country at best. In the face of government inaction, the pope decided once more to take a stand. In March 1980, he canceled the Christian Orthodox Easter celebration and withdrew with his bishops to the monastery. Since these celebrations were habitually attended by government representatives, this gesture refused their good wishes, embarrassing Sadat as it signaled to the outside world that things were not as fine and dandy for the Copts as Sadat, the hero of Camp David, would have the West believe.

But the government continued to appease the Islamic militants. Within a few months, in May 1980, Sadat proposed a constitutional amendment making the principles of the Sharia the basic source of legislation (rather than just one of the sources). Sadat did not wait for the church to organize opposition to this law, which would dash Christian aspirations for a pluralist country with religious and cultural diversity. In effect, if literally applied, the law would return the Copts to a status of Dhinus from which they had been emancipated in the nineteenth century. On May 14, 1980, Sadat launched an all-out offensive against the pope. Sadat, no doubt, along with other Muslim Egyptians, thought that it was only right and proper for the Copts to be ingratiating and self-effacing. He was flabbergasted by the impudence of this pope who had dared to chide him in public. On March 26, 1980, Shenuda had delivered a speech in which he angrily lashed out at the suggestion that the Sharia be made the basis for legislation and alledged that Islam was being used increasingly as a new form of nationalism in Egypt.[9]

Sadat had another reason to be annoyed with Shenuda. As a result of the normalization of relations between Israel and Egypt, following the Camp David agreement of 1978, there had been a very large flow of Israeli tourists to Egypt. The Israeli government was displeased that only a handful of Egyptians—mostly businessmen in search of opportunities—had gone to Israel since the peace treaty, and this put pressure on Sadat to encourage Egyptian tourism to Israel to transform a pro forma peace into a genuine one. Since most Muslim Egyptians did not want to get into the bad graces of the Arab governments, who had placed an embargo on Israel, Sadat decided to encourage Coptic pilgrimage to Jerusalem. Before the Six Day War, when Eastern Jerusalem, which encompassed a Coptic holy site, was still under Jordanian control, the church used to organize yearly excursions of several thousand pilgrims at Easter. However, Shenuda did not wish the Christians to be branded as traitors, so he turned down Sadat's proposal. He refused to lift the ban he had imposed on Coptic pilgrimage. He told Sadat defiantly that he would only go to Jerusalem hand in hand with Yasser Arafat, the leader of the Palestinians.[10]

Sadat also suspected the pope of orchestrating, from Egypt, the protest demonstrations of Copts that invariably greeted his visits to the United States. They embarrassed him in front of his friend "Jimmy" by distributing pamphlets outside the White House and the United Nations describing in highly charged language how their churches were being bombed, their priests were being assassinated and blinded, their sons were being beaten in the universities, their daughters were being raped and abducted, their homes were being ransacked, and their stores torched and looted. In his May address to Parliament, Sadat accused Shenuda of trying to become a political as well as religious leader and of wanting to set up a separatist Coptic state, with Assiut as its capital. "But the pope must understand that I am the Muslim president of a Muslim country," was his conclusion.[11]

The president's words contributed to the igniting of religious tensions, which culminated a year later, in June 1981, in the worst communal violence in Egypt in modern times. It began in a lower-middle-class district of Cairo called Zawya al-Hamra, when a billigerent Copt shot at a group of Muslim vigilantes who had settled on his land and declared their intention of building a mosque there to prevent him from building a church. The reluctance of the minister of the Interior to intervene was evident from the way the police milled around for three or four days, seemingly content to let the Muslims have their revenge, while apartments were torched—their doors barricaded to prevent their Christian residents from escaping—Christian children were thrown out of windows, Christian shop owners were disemboweled, and passerbys were gunned down. Zawya al-Hamra was one of the rare instances, perhaps the first one since the Coptic uprising against Muslim rule in 831, in which the Copts actually took up arms and Muslims were killed. In general, the Copts have accepted molestation at the hands of Muslims with a resignation that borders on fatalism. Thirteen centuries of oppression have developed in them the traits of prudence and fearfulness.[12]

The government once more blamed the sectarian strife on the pope.[13] But the pope could hardly be held accountable, unless it was for being an inspiring example of the more militant temper of the times. It seems more likely that if anyone had anything to gain from the diversion of national attention provided by these gruesome scenes, it was the president of the republic. He was by then under attack from most of the political forces in the country—even the more moderate Islamists like the Muslim Brotherhood had turned against him since Camp David. For Sadat, who had to deal with mounting criticism of both his domestic policies (corruption and profiteering) and his foreign policies (peace with Israel at the expense of the Palestinians), the sectarian strife in Zawya al-Hamra provided an excuse to crack down, shortly thereafter, not only on the church leaders but on all those who had criticized him—including the Islamists. (Within a few months, in October 1981, Sadat himself was to reap the consequences of having rounded up and imprisoned 1,536 opposition figures from all political persuasions. He was shot dead by a member of a militant Islamic group, Jihad.)

The pope had been sent into exile by Sadat to the Monastery of Bishoi in the Natrun valley, and 170 bishops and priests had been arrested and imprisoned. Following Shenuda's exile, Sadat, who had heretofore sought unsuccessfully to get the church to stick to the rule of using the traditional channels of communication with the government, looked for elements within the church who would be willing to work through the old elite. For it was not only the government that had been embarrassed by the public confrontations forced on it by the militant Shenuda—they had not sat well with the old aristocracy which had lost its prerogative as the unofficial conduit to government officials.

Very early on, when Sadat was first faced with a defiant Shenuda he realized the advantage of shoring up the ancient regime Coptic aristocracy as a counterweight to the church. Now, following Shenuda's exile, Sadat found elements within the church willing to accept the old elite as mediators—not only among members of the traditionalist wing of the church, who were still smarting at having been upstaged by Shenuda, but even among the reformers like the Abbot Matthew the Poor. While he had been pioneer in introducing both modern culture and modern technology to his monastery, he represented the strand in Christianity that believed in leaving to Caesar what is Caesar's.

In short, Sadat was able to build an alliance consisting of the Coptic upper class and of high church prelates drawn from both the traditionalists and a wing of the reformers, who feared that the Shenuda confrontational style would generate a Muslim backlash.

If we look at the committee of five bishops set up by Sadat in 1981 to rule in place of the exiled pope, we will see that it reflected both trends within the church. Three of its members were veterans of the Sunday School Movement: Bishop Samuel, a longtime rival of Shenuda, though thoroughly modern in education and outlook, believed, as we have seen that the church should concentrate on building up the economic power of the Coptic community and leave the game of politics to the old elite. He himself, unlike the fiery Shenuda, was soft-spoken, preferring quiet diplomacy in his dealings with state officials. Bishop Athanasios of Banī Suwayf, as a disciple and close friend of Bishop Samuel, shared his predilection. The third veteran member of the Sunday School Movement was Bishop Gregorios, whose differences with Shenuda, like Bishop Samuel's, went back to the period of the '60s when all three men were consecrated bishops. At the other end of the spectrum were Bishop Maximos of Benha and Bishop Johanna of Tanta, both of whom were apolitical and governed their dioceses in the traditional way, which entailed a very narrow definition of a bishop's responsibility, principally limiting it to the business of saving souls.

These bishops shared the viewpoint of the old elite that religion should not mix with politics, and many of them had close ties to the latter. For example, Bishop Samuel, as chief fund-raiser for the church, had formed a close friendship with banker and financier Fakhri Abd al-Nur. Bishop Samuel was also a friend of another wealthy Copt, Mirit Ghālī, a cousin of Boutrous Ghālī, at whose daughter's wedding he had officiated. Bishop Athanasios, as a disciple of Bishop Samuel, was introduced by the latter to Fakhri Abd al-Nur, who contributed funds to his diocese; the two men became and remained friends at that point.[14] Bishop Gregorios who shared certain scholarly interests with Magdi Wahba, the scion of another affluent ancien régime family, became friends with him. Wahba, who was the president of L'Institut d'Egypte, often invited him to lectures held there.

But the sympathies of the vast majority of the Coptic community, its middle classes, were unquestionably with the pope—the only one, they felt, with the courage to stand up to the president with their demands. As they saw it, his role as political representative was forced on him; there was no one else to fill that void. The alternative was Coptic technocrat-ministers appointed by the revolutionary junta, whom many of them viewed as sycophants, or scions of a landed aristocracy whose wealth and family names sheltered them from the disadvantages that their religious affiliation would otherwise have entailed and who hence were indifferent to the plight of the *petit peuple.*

Indeed, one cannot fault them for this view. I questioned Boutrous Ghālī, the grandson of the prime minister by the same name, on the difficulty Coptic candidates had in gaining admission to the foreign service, an elite corps. He replied that as one who had sat on the board of examiners of the foreign service for eleven years he could testify that there were very few qualified Christians. Besides, he added after a moment's reflection, the number of Christian ambassadors had been increased to four under Sadat. When I pointed out to him that none of them occupied the weightier posts, in North America or Europe, he tried in all earnestness to argue that an ambassadorial post in Addis Ababa was more important than one in Washington. He also said that Sadat had appointed three Coptic ministers to the cabinet. To my objection that these were merely token Copts, technocrats appointed to posts without any power, he retorted that if they had not been awarded any of the major portfolios, it was simply because they did not have the personalities for them.

"Name me ten Copts with personality!" he burst out, before my silent skepticism. And he clinched the argument by giving himself as an example of a Copt who had been assigned a significant post. It would have been untactful to mention that he was merely "minister of state" for foreign affairs, while the post of foreign minister, as such, was reserved for a Muslim. Everyone knew that he had been passed over three times for promotion to that post, despite his brilliance and savvy—not to mention his command of foreign languages—in favor of Muslim foreign ministers of inferior talents.

When I tried to steer away from this touchy subject to safer grounds and brought up the general situation of the Coptic minority, he dismissed their grievances with a disdainful wave of the hand: "Believe me, these are nothing but exaggerations. You have been listening to too many frightened, hostile Copts. Besides, instead of whining and lamenting they should do something about their problems. Let's face it, the Copts just don't have balls!"[15]

Another grandson of a prime minister, Magdi Wahba, who belonged to a world of intelligence and sensibility, listened patiently to these same grievances in his elegant penthouse on the Nile. This former vice minister of culture then commented in a tone of melancholy sobriety, "*Ya binti imshi gamb al-heit*" (My girl, it's safer to walk close to the wall).[16]

"Walk close to the wall" may be regarded as the leitmotif of the ancien régime Coptic upper class, who had everything to lose: money, influence, power. Fakhri Abd al-Nur, too, was concerned that the pope was rocking the boat. The son of the wealthy landlord and prominent ancien régime Wafdist parliamentarian by the same name put it in these terms: "Shenuda's way of presenting himself in public with crosses to the right and crosses to the left, it gets on people's nerves. The prime minister told me to give him a piece of advice, 'tell him not to do it.'"[17] Only in the privacy of his own salon does Fakhri Abd al-Nur feel free to display his priceless collection of ancient Coptic crosses and Coptic icons, his very original painting of the Last Supper in which Jesus, surrounded by his olive-skinned disciples, looks very much like a Copt with his large dark eyes that seem outlined in antimony and kohl, as well as pictures of Fakhri Abd al-Nur himself being congratulated by Pope Paul VI for his efforts to bring about a rapprochement between the Orthodox and Catholic Churches and other pictures of Abd al-Nur with his friend Bishop Samuel.

This same prudence was expressed by Amīn Fahim, yet another scion of the landed aristocracy of old and a convert from Orthodoxy to Catholicism as a result of the influence of his Jesuit French Lycée. He had set up a network of free schools in Upper Egypt, which helped haul some of the most deprived regions of the country out of the Middle Ages into modern times. Fahim expressed his reservations about the pope in terms of an Aesop fable: "Just imagine to yourself an earthenware jug knocking against a bronze vessel; which of the two do you think is going to get broken?"[18] Mirit Ghālī, another member of the lauded aristocracy, who headed the Coptic Archeological Society, also felt there was nothing to be gained by being "provocative"; he preferred diplomay. Yet his ample correspondence with President Sadat, filled with complaints of Coptic mistreatment and petitions for redress,[19] testifies to the strength of his perseverance in the face of what to others might appear as a dialogue with the deaf.

In view of this, it is not surprising that the disenfranchised Coptic masses, finding no one to champion their cause, called out to pope Shenuda as he was being driven off into exile "*Bi'l dam wa'l roh nafdik*" (With our blood and our souls, we will vindicate you).

Church and State: The Uneasy Alliance under President Mubarak

An appraisal of relations between the church and the state under President Mubarak has to begin not with his ascent to power in 1981, but with Shenuda's reinstatement as pope, which did not take place until January 1985. From the date of his first public meeting after his reinstatement, on the eve of the Coptic Christmas, January 1985, when the pope called for a reconciliation with Muslims, asking his followers to embrace them as "brothers," to the present, the pope's relationship with the new president has been cordial and his strategy has changed from the confrontational to the diplomatic.

The handful of influential individuals from the lay aristocracy who had acted as intermediaries under Sadat had largely been eliminated by the mid '80s. Mirit Ghālī and Magdi Wahba had both contacted to illnesses that were to claim their lives in 1991 and 1992, respectively, and by virtue of his appointment to the position of secretary general of the United Nations, in 1991, Boutrous Ghālī was no longer a go-between to the president. This left Fahkri Abd al-Nur, whose close association with Bishop Samuel made him anathema to Shenuda.

These aristocrats had never in any case been a realistic prop for the new regime in its struggle against the church, because as a class they had been destroyed by the very revolutionary junta that now sought them out as allies. The Ghālīs, Magdi Wahba, and Fakhri Abd al-Nur were a residue of a colonial Egypt in ruins, a unique cosmopolitan Egypt in which a multitude of nations and religions, Greeks, Italians, Armenians, Syro-Lebanese, Eastern Europeans, Christians, Muslims and Jews mingled like different cells lending vitality to an organism. The Egypt of today no longer spoke French as these people did, in their soft, trailing Mediterranean accents. It spoke in the strident voice of Arab nationalism, it belonged unequivocally to the world of Islam.

Relations with the state were by Mubarak's time entirely assumed by the pope himself and his private inner cabinet of most trusted bishops, whose base of support was not anchored in the upper class but in the middle class from which they stemmed. In addition to a series of tactics designed to foster good relations with the state, such as holding a massive Ramadan dinner for Muslim state officials, heads of professional syndicates, important journalists and lawyers, and religious dignitaries every year, receiving the Muslim ministers and religious dignitaries at Christmas and Easter time—social niceties replicated at the level of the diocese—specific problems were now dealt with by the pope himself, instead of any of the secular elite close to the president. Thus, the addition of Koranic verses and poems in praise of the prophet and of Ramadan to textbooks used by Christian students was communicated by the pope to the minister of education,[20] whereas in the case of physical attacks on Christians the pope addressed himself to the minister of the interior.

At the diocesan level, the complaint would be made by the bishop to the governor. In several instances, the bishop who had succeeded in cultivating good relations with the governor was able to obtain a redress of the grievance. For example, in one instance a man was arrested in Sohag, when the neighbors reported that he was giving private Bible lessons in his home. The amiable Bishop Bachum got on the phone to the governor and the man was instantly released.[21] In another case, in Tima, the security forces surrounded a priest's home and quarantined it, when someone reported that he was building a second floor to use as a chapel (in fact, he intended it as a place of rest for the diocesan bishop when he came to celebrate Mass in the village). Here, too, the intervention of Bishop Fam, a very personable man on good terms with the authorities, resolved the problem.[22] A similar outcome greeted the negotiations between bishop Tackla of Dishna and the governor, when sectarian strife broke out in Rahmania, a village of his diocese, due to a football tossed into the courtyard of a mosque by some Christian teenagers, which resulted in the arrest of the boys. After a considerable amount of give and take between Bishop Tackla and the governor, the boys were released.[23]

The question, then, is why the church tactics shifted from confrontation to conciliation.

Many people observed that a subdued Shenuda emerged from the gates of the Monastery of Bishoi, were he had been interned for five years. They hardly recognized in the man so cautious now in his dealing with the state, so careful of his every move, the youthful firebrand of yesteryear. First to notice how subdued the pope had become were Bishop Michael of Assiut, who had been labeled a traitor for having sent President Sadat a telegram of support at a time when he was conniving with the Islamic groups in their persecution of Copts, and Bishop Athanasios of Banī Suawyf, who had been much maligned for insisting on holding his usual annual banquet in honor of the governor in 1980, a year of repeated molestation of Christians in Upper Egypt and of the bombing of several churches in Alexandria. The pope now seemed to ooze charm in the presence of high officials.[24] A certain *Schadenfreude* was detectable in these observations. For members of the committee of five who had ruled during the pope's exile had paid a heavy price for their collaboration with the government.

Of the initial members of that infamous committee set up by Sadat to govern in place of Pope Shenuda, two were dead, Bishops Samuel and Johanna, and Bishop Maximos, considered an innocent, was beyond blame, but Bishop Athanasios paid for his collaboration with numerous public rebuffs from the pope, who henceforth made himself inaccessible to him.[25] Bishop Michael, though not on the committee, paid for the telegram of support he had sent Sadat by being virtually quarantined within his diocese. And the Abbot Matthew the Poor had likewise to suffer the indignity of having his books banned from the church libraries,[26] and his church funds sequestered by the pope, in addition to having to suffer a long war of attrition within his own monastery, with a good number of his monks defecting and joining the pope's monastery (the Monastery of Bishoi, was both his weekend retreat and a place where he held meetings and conferences); three of those monks were rewarded with bishoprics.[27]

But contrary to his foes' belief, the pope's change of tactics in his dealings with the government was not due to anxiety over his long term of exile and the uncertainty accompanying the first years following Mubarak's assumption of power as to when—if ever—he would be reinstated. Rather the fundamental change of circumstances that had allied the church and state because of enemies in common.

It was no longer possible in the 1990s for the president of the republic to deny the danger posed by the growing Islamic militancy to the regime in power. This in itself was advantageous to the church. For nothing had irked the pope more than Sadat's attempts to appease the Islamists by his silence despite outrages committed against the Christians, or by his notorious balancing posture (pretending to be fair by blaming victim and victimizer equally) or by his outright denial. An example of the latter is the way he handled the complaints by Christian parents whose daughters were being abducted by Islamic militants. One of the techniques of forced conversions in Upper Egypt was rape (which compelled the girl to marry her assailant or face lifelong shame in her community or possible death at the hands of her parents). "It was only a love affair between a girl and a boy," was Sadat's response to a query raised in Parliament about the police, when they failed to help a Christian father look for his abducted daughter, and forced him to sign a statement that she was at a relatives' house, thus eliminating the complaint from the record.[28]

From the first major incident involving Christians in Khanka in 1972, Sadat had looked for scapegoats to avoid confronting the Islamists. At that time, before the peace with Israel, he had accused the American imperialists and the Zionists of fomenting trouble between Muslims and Christians to weaken Egypt through internal dissension. In January 1980, the bombing of several churches in Alexandria had been attributed to an Iranian spy (the alleged spy was displayed on the government-controlled television network). A few months later, in May 1980, Sadat accused the pope of turning the Copts into a fifth column and of encouraging foreign animosities against Egypt (by implication, the Coptic imigrants in America damaged Egypt's public image with their complaints of mistreatment). But the most extreme accusation occurred in a speech by Sadat to the People's Assembly on September 5, 1981, four weeks before he was assassinated. The Coptic Church leadership was accused of scheming with the Lebanese Phalange to partition the Arab countries into religious entities: Copts, he alleged, were being trained for military operations by the Phalange to realize the Coptic goal of creating a Christian state in Upper Egypt—aided by donations from the CIA, West German intelligence, and the Christian Democratic Party in Germany. (This money was said to be funneled to the church by the World Council of Churches.) Similar accusations were echoed by the press right up to the day of President Sadat's assassination, despite the absurdity of Egypt's accusing its allies of fostering subversive activities. Presumably, the survival of the peace treaty with Israel, in which America and the West had a great deal at stake, depended on the stability of the Sadat regime. By then, America had set up monitoring stations in Sinai to ensure Israel's borders and Egypt was receiving a massive amount of financial aid from the United States and Germany, aid deemed essential to maintaining the Sadat regime in the face of growing economic difficulties and political opposition at home. Sadat manipulated the usual prejudices about minorities by referring in both his 1980 and 1981 speeches to the churches' links to foreign powers—just the sort of thing likely to further incite the Islamists, who were convinced there was a Christian conspiracy aimed at keeping Egypt from becoming an Islamic country.[29]

At first, the mere absence of inflammatory rhetoric from President Mubarak was a welcome change. Even if he did little to improve the plight of the Christians, the head of state had, at least, stopped harping on the foreign conspiracy theme and looking for scapegoats. The relationship between the church and the state was henceforth relatively cordial, despite the resumption of violent attacks on Christians in the mid '80s, after a lull that was presumably due to the decapitation of the Jihad group and to the widespread arrests that followed President Sadat's assassination. Time was needed for the militant groups to reorganize themselves and form new leadership cadres. But beginning with the town of Abu Qurkas in 1986 and the devastation of Christian homes, stores, and pharmacies, followed by an attack in 1988 by Islamic militants armed with swords on a baptismal ceremony in the Church of the Virgin in the provincial main town of Minya, there had been bloody incidents involving Christians almost yearly.[30] This situation persisted throughout the decade of the 1990s.

Despite diplomatic maneuvers by the pope and the local bishops of the dioceses to create bridges across the communities, formally and informally, not much progress was registered. The pope, for example, set up the Committee of National Unity to foster good relations with Muslims, which included some of his most trusted bishops: Bishop Moses, the Bishop of Youth, Bishop Bula of Tanta, and Bishop Besanti of Helwan—three members of what may be considered his inner cabinet. Their responsibility was to invite prominent Muslims to a dialogue over Coptic problems like the difficulty of obtaining licenses to build churches, biased school curricula, and job discrimination. The bishops also strove informally to create good relations through a series of lectures like the ones offered by Bishop Arsanios of Minya, at his local theological seminary, entitled *White Points in Muslim History*,[31] as well as through the question-answer sessions that followed their weekly general meetings with their diocesan constituency. In one such instance, a man stood up to ask Bishop Bula whether, as a Christian, he was morally obligated to donate blood to a Muslim.[32] In another instance, in Shubra al-Kheima, a man wanted to know whether it was all right to employ a Muslim worker in his plant.[33] In both instances the bishops replied affirmatively.

For all the efforts at cooperation exerted by the pope with the president, minister of interior, and minister of education—replicated at the diocesan level by the bishops with the governors and heads of security—the state offered the Christians little more than lip service until the '90s, and the attitude of the population at large ranged from indifference to actual hostility. It is fair to say that until then most Muslim Egyptians knew nothing, suspected nothing, and desired to know even less about the sorry plight of the Copts. They looked down on them from the height of their good conscience. What happened to change this?

The answer lies in the Islamic militants' change of strategy, which turned a large segment of the public against them. In the 1990s, their attacks were no longer solely directed at Christians, so that the rest of the population could feel safe in its indifference. They now targeted tourists,[34] to deprive the regime of one of its main sources of revenue, and the security forces—operations that inevitably caused the injuries and deaths of scores of innocent Egyptian bystanders. From then on, the newspaper columns began to read, "Extremism Campaign Targets Us All,"[35] and the press featured emotional accounts of these events, coupled with snapshots of the woefully black-veiled widows of the dead police officers and their pathetic orphaned children, to manipulate readers into viewing the police as victims rather than victimizers.[36]

The chronicle of events reveals a very definite pattern for the closing decade of this century. Beginning in August 1991, there was a series of attacks in the crowded Cairene lower-class neighborhoods of Imbaba and Boulak Dakrour. The pattern was always the same: two or three men would suddenly surge out of the crowd, Molotov cocktails would be hurled at a parked police patrol van or at one of the nightly road checkpoints, and then the attackers would disappear in a matter of seconds, down one of the narrow, dark alleys that crisscrossed these areas.[37] By the end of 1993, the killing of security officials had increased to an almost daily occurrence and the toll of casualties for that year numbered in the hundreds.[38] That same period witnessed an ever-increasing number of attacks on tourists, with several of them, such as the incident of March 1993 when a bomb was thrown into a coffee house, resulting in heavy civilian casualties.[39]

The broadening of the Islamist targets to include tourists, the security forces, and high officials and the state infrastructure,[40] created a bond between the state and the church. The state now realized that the danger posed by Islamic militants could not be dealt with merely by means of increased police vigilance. This new attitude was reflected in the parliamentary committee, which met in January 1993 to discuss ways in which the educational system and media programs could be revamped to meet the danger posed by the Islamists.[41] It was evident also in the press, which not only featured appeals by high officials to the citizens to join in combating "terrorists," like the appeal of the governor of Alexandria but, more important, voiced the opinions of the ordinary citizens on the growth of violence perpetrated in the name of religion. A very good example is the following column:

> A comprehensive look at the terrorist-infested areas will prove that the terrorists are not imported; rather, they are the outgrowth of a neglected soil. They have grown up under conditions of frustration and despair and have been fed by viruslike tides. So people cannot be won over under such conditions without a change of these conditions. The key is not bulldozers (slum-clearance projects) or hunting down unlicensed vendors or the jobless. Rather, the way out lies in launching small-scale projects to provide job opportunities.

"So let's get down to business and let the next cabinet meeting be held in Imbaba (the poor district where the police cracked down on Islamic militants). Let this meeting be devoted to devising urgent plans to develop the area socially, economically and culturally,"[42] the column concluded.

Shenuda did not organize a demonstration of clerics following the massacre of thirteen Christians in 1992 in the village of Sanabo, in the diocese of Dayrout in Upper Egypt.[43] Nor did he call on the Copts to fast in protest against the carnage in Tima that same year (in addition to the bombing of the Church of St. George in Tima, Christians' shops and pharmacies were torched, ransacked, and looted).[44] In coping with these attacks, as with the attack on pilgrims in Deir Mawas in 1992 (ten Copts were wounded when their bus was shot at, as they were returning from a visit to the Monasteries of Assiut and Sohag),[45] as well as with the bloody incidents in the small town of Abu Korkas in 1995 and the village of Kush in 1998 in Upper Egypt, and on the Churches of Minya and Cairo in 1988 the only recourse left to Pope Shenuda, now that the state was his ally, was diplomacy.

Pope Shenuda's strength, based on the ability to confront an enemy by exercising self-restraint, may not be as self-evident as his heroic self-assertion during the Sadat years. But this self-restraint was one of his most important assets in confronting the bloody incidents in Minya, Dayrout, Tima, Qusia, Deir Mawas, Assiut, and other areas in Egypt. Not only did it enable him to resist his own peoples' hysteria and to act sensibly in a crisis but also, amid the violent hatred aroused by these incidents, to communicate to his followers that those who could master themselves would achieve mastery over a hostile environment.

Pope Shenuda contributed to the moral character and capability of his coreligionists during the Mubarak years in two ways: first, by reenacting for his people, whenever they were tested by Islamic militancy, the cultural model of saintliness and martyrdom, one familiar to them from the stories of their ancient church fathers. In this way, he put the Christian ethic of turning the other cheek to modern political purposes. Second, by asserting the precept of a public ethic as opposed to private obligations to family and friends he ruled out the kind of vendettas between Christians and Muslims which were the bane of Upper Egypt. (The Sanabo massacre was triggered by a vendetta between two families, a Muslim and Christian one, which began when the son of the Christian family, Jirjis, was found lying dead with a knife in his chest on a street pavement in Assiut, while the Tima bloodshed began as a quarrel between a Muslim, who having married a Christian girl came to claim her dowry, and her father.) To that end, Pope Shenuda successfully created a kind of church network, with branches in the provinces headed by his bishops whose task it was to organize, finance, and publicize the message of national reconciliation.

Exercising control on the impulse to retaliate—in short, self-restraint as opposed to self-assertion—is a kind of courage very far removed from the western ideal of heroics in combat. It is a courage closely related to monastic asceticism, whether the one practiced by Egyptian monks or the Hindu *tapasva*, through which a person is believed to acquire special powers. And indeed, Shenuda's method of resistence during the Sadat years bears some resemblance to Gandhi's practice of *dharma* as embodied in his protests through fasts and the peaceful march he organized to the British-owned salt quarries, along with his injunction to his followers to stay put despite the blows raining on them. Witness Shenuda's call to the Coptic people for a fast until the government backed down on its intent to enact the Islamic penal law for apostasy, or his instructions to his priests and bishops to keep up the vigil at the site of the burned down chapel in Khanka and to stay put even if it meant being shot at.

If the ethic of turning the other cheek derived from the New Testament, Gandhi's derived from the Gita, to which we are told he turned whenever he felt he was losing the war against resentment, fear, and vexation.[46] In short the influence of Gandhi's techniques of public action may be indirectly felt in movements of resistence to discrimination as diverse as Martin Luther King's civil rights movement and the Egyptian Christian struggle for equality. We know that Gandhi's capacity to master a hostile environment was closely related to his confidence that he could do so. This self-confidence generated what social scientists would refer to as a charismatic leadership. To some extent, Shenuda's leadership provides us with yet another illustration of the dynamics of charisma to which, in his case, the signs of Grace endow a transcendental element.

Pope Shenuda's leadership, regardless of what one may think of his character, had important consequences not only because his bravado during the Sadat years helped repair wounds in self-esteem inflicted by centuries of subjection to Muslim rule but, even more important, because his administration was able to galvanize a community and restore potency to a people whom centuries of existence as a threatened minority had rendered not only timid—Muslims who haven't lived the Coptic experience see them as cowardly and cunning[47]—but also passive. As we will see in the following chapters, because of the ability of Pope Shenuda and his crew of bishops to communicate a founding myth in a historically relevant manner, they were able to mobilize resources within their community that they did not ordinarily command.

PART IV

The Church as Socioeconomic Entrepreneur

8

Centralizing the Church Administration

The battle Pope Shenuda had to fight was not only against the state: within the church itself, it was not possible for Shenuda to implement his socioeconomic reform project without causing an upheaval and generating many enemies, both among the clerics and the laymen who served the church. For one thing, such reforms threatened their position, because they necessitated a centralization of power. During his reign, the church ceased to be the loose conglomerate of self-governing units (dioceses) that it had been in the past.

The dioceses were pretty much autonomous quasi-feudal principalities before the reign of Shenuda, with the bishops paying pro forma homage to their overlord, the pope, while in fact regarding their dioceses as their own private fiefdoms. Even the selection of the bishops was far more decentralized. Often the pope was happy to leave the choice of the bishop up to the local notability, in whose interests it was to nominate someone pliable, whom they could control. Wakin gives a vivid description of the way bishops were selected, in the late 1950s, in the Upper Egyptian dioceses:

> When the See of Guergeh [Girga] . . . became vacant, he [Cyril VI] stunned the leading Coptic family in that area by depriving them of their usual prerogative of picking the bishop. . . . [T]he head of the family had called a public meeting at which he put the names of three monks in a box and selected one of them as the next bishop. Soon after the family head died, and his family visited the Patriarch to tell him of their choice for bishop. When the Patriarch demurred, the family threatened: "We will

> convert to Catholicism unless you take our man." They had miscalculated. . . . [H]e raised his voice: "No, no, no."[1]

Under Pope Shenuda, the papacy moved in the direction of centralizing power. Shenuda paved the way for a more modern administration by enforcing parity and uniformity on the dioceses, through the abolition of local privileges and regional separatism. He replaced a quasi-feudal system of patronage, based on clan loyalties, with one that ensured loyalty to his person, by placing his spiritual sons in key positions in the administration throughout the country. ("Spiritual sons" is used here in the sense of someone who came under the pope's influence at a young age and, largely as a result of that, took the monastic vows or; at the very least, of someone young enough to have been the pope's son and who owed his position as bishop to him.)

Centralization became for the pope more than just a policy designed to introduce a new moral tone into the church administration, by reducing the influence of money. Even more important, it was for Shenuda a means of controlling the economic and cultural development of the Coptic community at large.

Aided by the vast improvement in technology and transportation that had reached Egypt, by the 1970s the new pope was able to bring the bishoprics of Upper Egypt, which had previously been left up to their own devices, firmly under his control. Powerful Mercedes vehicles and the newly macadamized roads enabled the bishops of the small dioceses of Upper Egypt to shuttle back and forth between the provinces and the capital at his bidding. In this way, he tried to ensure not only that the provinces would be more efficiently administered, by being cut down to size, but also that his cultural and socioeconomic programs would be uniformly implemented throughout Egypt. Though he left the day-to-day administration up to the discretion of the diocesan bishop and his team of local church-servants, the programs themselves were, for the most part, designed at the papal headquarters by the Bishopric of Social Service and the Bishopric of Youth that it housed.

The Bishoprics

Once he became pope, Shenuda managed to implement his vision of a reformed church, by dismantling its conservative power structure. To succeed in this, he subdivided and thereby vastly increased the number of dioceses in Egypt, and he appointed young, reform-minded clerics to govern them. In accordance with church law, a pope has to await the death of a bishop to subdivide his diocese, but Pope Shenuda sometimes managed to bring about this change during the lifetime of the incumbent bishop, when the boundaries of his diocese were fuzzy so that part of his area merged into a kind of no man's land or if he had no clear mandate over an area he governed. Thus, he was able to take some of the land that was under the jurisdiction of the aging bishop of Girga in Upper Egypt, Bishop Mina, and to turn it over to a young protégé, fresh from the Monastery of the Syrians. He created out of it and out of some additional land taken from the dioceses of Luxor and Kena a new diocese, that of Naga Hammadi. Though Bishop Mina withdrew in protest to the monastery, railing at what he considered to be a gross infringement on his prerogative, he eventually gave in to papal power and returned to govern his truncated diocese, after having had a chance to weigh, during four long years of self-imposed exile, the advantages of a life of active service over one of isolation in the desert.[2]

Although he never forgave the pope, old age compelled Mina in later years to accept from him the gift of a Trojan horse in the form of the reform-minded assistant Bishop Daniel, a doctor who had studied public health in France. In this way, if he could not take over Girga outright until the death of Bishop Mina, the pope could at the very least influence it from within, by implanting into it one of his own men. But for the most part his tactic was to surround a member of the old guard with his young protégés, ringing and isolating him in his diocese with the new dioceses he created for them. A good example of this is the pope's adversary Bishop Michael of Assiut, at the time of this writing in his mid-eighties, whom the pope surrounded on every side with his own creations: the dioceses of Qusia, Abnub, Tima, and Tahta—all of them governed by his devoted young disciples.

In the course of a reign spanning more than three decades, the pope had the opportunity to appoint over sixty-four bishops, thereby quadrupling the number of bishops that ruled at his accession. The extent to which the growth in the number of bishops is linked to the assumption of secular tasks by the church, in modern times, may be judged by the fact that, according to the list of dioceses published by the Coptic Archeological Society, the number of dioceses was only thirteen in 1933[3] (a year that marks the beginning of the organized activities of the Sunday School Movement members in the universities).

Pope Shenuda has subdivided the dioceses as follows: In Lower Egypt, he cut up the huge diocese of Gharbia, which spanned across three provinces—Gharbia, Behera, and Kafr al-Sheikh—into three distinct units. Then he severed the town of Damanhour from the province of Gharbia, and he further subdivided the province into two parts, centering around the towns of Tanta and Mehalla al-Kubra, while the new diocese of Beheira encompassed the port towns of Rosetta and Marsa Matruh. Damietta, another port town, was made part of a third diocese, Kafr al-Sheikh.

Thus, he created three dioceses out of one. Two of the provincial towns, the agricultural town of Damanhour and the mercantile town of Tanta, were endowed with bishops of outstanding intellectual and moral caliber, who contributed much toward turning their dioceses into a thriving nexus of activities. Closer to the capital, the pope severed Shubra al-Kheima, an industrial town, from the rest of the diocese, which was further subdivided into three units. Shubra al

Kheima received one of the most enterprising young bishops, Bishop Murqus (Mark), who had initially been sent by him to assist the aging, benign, but largely ineffectual Bishop Maximos. After his death, in 1993, Murqus took over the bishopric. He is another example of a Trojan horse offered as a gift by the pope to energize the previously slumbering diocese, until the pope could take it in hand, subdivide it, and reform it, following the death of its incumbent.

Major changes also occurred in the Suez Canal Zone during Pope Shenuda's reign. That zone, together with the province of Sharkia, initially constituted one diocese. Here too, the pope created several dioceses out of one: Sharkia and three more dioceses, centered around the major port cities of Port Said, Ismailia, and Suez. The new dioceses of Suez and Port Said were allocated to two enlightened and dynamic young bishops. In the case of Ismailia, the pope tried to energize his old friend, Bishop Agathon, by sending him a young assistant, Bishop Boutros (Peter), who was known to favor transforming the church into an agency of social change and economic development. To this end, he set up a joint board of development with the bishop of Port Said, Bishop Tadros, a doctor who had spent seven years as an émigré to the United States, which imbued him with many progressive notions, as well as with the Bishop of Shubra al-Kheima, Bishop Murqus, considered a dynamic asset.

In dealing with Middle Egypt, the pope was able to bring about social change by applying some of the same tactics. Minya, a wealthy diocese, was divided into three units by the pope: Minya, Samalut, and Mallawi. Both Minya and Mallawi were fortunate to receive very talented and hardworking bishops, Bishop Arsanios and the late Bishop Bimen (the former an engineer, the latter an educational psychologist), who put their resources to good use. In the same region of Middle Egypt, Dairut was separated from Qusia, which received a personable and devoted young bishop, Bishop Thomas, who had previously made his reputation as a popular Orthodox missionary in Kenya.

In Upper Egypt the pope's tactics of lopping off inert lumps of land and injecting them with new blood has really paid off. In this less developed part of the country, where the newly appointed bishops started off with a virtual tabula rasa, the change is dramatically, almost palpably evident. Virtually all the dioceses of Upper Egypt had been subdivided by Pope Shenuda, by the time this study began, with the exception of Girga and Assiut. And for the most part the result seemed felicitous. Abnub was severed from the diocese of Manfalut and it received young Bishop Lukas (Luke), savvy with experience gained from his work in the Gulf oil states. Tima and Tahta were severed from the diocese of Abu Tig, and both of them received energetic bishops dedicated to social change. The diocese of Kena was subdivided into four units: Kena, Dishna, Qus, and the Red Sea area—all four choices of bishops proved to be fortuitous—and Aswan was severed from the diocese of Luxor. A very high-caliber bishop, Bishop Hidra, took over Aswan.

On the whole, the subdivision of the dioceses into smaller units has been an effective strategy of change, with the possible exception of the severance of the Upper Egyptian town of Akhmim from Sohag—two towns connected by a bridge, which resulted in a brain flow (and consequent money flow) from Akhmim to Sohag, the provincial capital, leaving the newly instated bishop of Akhmim, Bishop Besada, with very few resources for development.

As a result of the manner in which the bishops are selected, the new dioceses that emerge out of the subdivision of a large unit have no guarantee that they will get bishops committed to economic and cultural projects. They may, as in the case of Damietta, Mallawi, Akhmim, and Luxor, in this sample, turn out to see the role of the church mainly in terms of canticles and jeremiads. Nonetheless, the mere fact of subdivision ensures them, at the very least, that a bishop who previously could not possibly have given a large share of his attention to the more remote towns and villages of his diocese can now reach every nook and cranny. For if some of the bishops in my sample lacked vision, none could be faulted for a lack of moral dedication and zeal.

A sense of just how necessary it was to subdivide the dioceses, to ensure, at the very least, a modicum of responsiveness to local needs, may be seen from the case of Tima, Tahta, and Abu Tig—three dioceses where I did fieldwork—which until 1976 formed a single giant entity. Bishop Tackla, of the Dishna diocese, who in 1993 was at age 29 the youngest bishop in Egypt, told me that before his appointment the people of Dishna only got to see their bishop once every second year. Bishop Fam corroborated this, by telling me that his predecessor, who resided in Abut Tig, only visited Tima once a year for a period of three days.[4]

The pope also reaped political capital from the subdivision of large dioceses into small units, and the consequent multiplication of the number of bishoprics. For he was able to people them, and consequently the Holy Synod, with his spiritual sons and protégés. Thus he could outnumber and overrule the few weighty high prelates of his own generation, by creating within the Holy Synod a majority of young bishops, who were ordained by him and hence beholden to him. Thereby he virtually ensured their support in instances of conflict between him and his peers over what punitive measures to adopt against bishops, priests, or monk-priests, as in the case of Father Daniel, or canonical issues such as whether or not the church should liberalize the divorce laws, a measure advocated by some bishops out of fear that if it does not Copts will convert to Protestantism or even Islam to obtain a quick divorce.[5] The pope, reflecting the fundamentalism of the St. Anthony school of thought, has adopted an extremely conservative stance, with his insistence on reverting to a literal biblical interpretation in matters of divorce and remarriage, because he believes that the Coptic family unit is the rock on which the community stands. It has enabled it to weather periods of adversity and withstand pressures to convert to Islam throughout the ages. Efforts to liberalize the laws of divorce, such as those undertaken in the first half of the twentieth century by one of his predecessors Pope Macarios, under the influence of the secular upper class that sat in the Communal Council, would, Shenuda fears, result in the community's disintegration.

The Monastic Order

Similarly, the pope centralized the administration of the monasteries, which play a major role in the reform project because the leading cadres of the church are formed there. Traditionally, the monasteries were pro forma directed by the diocesan bishops, but in fact they led an autonomous existence. Pope Shenuda transferred the overall responsibility for the monasteries to the papacy, incorporating the abbots of the monasteries into the Holy Synod to keep an eye on their activities.

The importance the pope assigns to the monasteries in his reform project is evidenced by the renowned examples of the Monastery of St. Anthony, the Monastery of the Holy Family, the Monastery of the Syrians, and the Monastery of the Romans, where he elevated the heads of these monasteries from abbot to bishop. To these monasteries, he added a large number of new ones by renovating those in disrepair. He also institutionalized them. Whereas before they were supervised by a priest sent out from time to time by the diocesan bishop in their vicinity, the pope appointed abbots (*komos*) to take permanent charge of them.

The centralization of the direction of the monasteries has been interpreted by the monks of the monastery of St. Macarios as a reaction against Matthew the Poor, designed to prevent autonomous monastic currents from resurfacing in the future.

The Priests

Shenuda has also tried to push his reform project across diocesan boundaries by opening up the debate on clerical reform to the public in the newspaper *al-Kirāzah* and by expanding and invigorating the network of church committees (*Majlis al-kanīsah*). In his call for *Mushārakat al-sha'b al-Qibṭī* (the participation of the Coptic people),[6] one cannot fail to detect an attempt to centralize church affairs by relying on the surveillance network inherent in popular control, in the name of the participatory nature of the church of origin.

It is a sign of the importance this reforming pope assigns to the media that he set himself up as editor-in-chief of *al-Kirāzah* newspaper, and he takes time out of his busy schedule to meet weekly with its reporters, who write about everything from the trips of church dignitaries abroad, to communal affairs, to the newly discovered benefits of garlic for one's health. According to one of the reporters, Dr. Nabila, he spends hours in a weekly session with the editorial staff, going over every single word of the forthcoming issue.

Two significant new columns have been created in *al-Kirāzah*, during Shenuda's reign, designed to encourage the public to engage in a scrutiny of clerical conduct. One, is entitled *Aftār ra'awīyah* (Pastoral Notebooks), is filled with criticisms of the conduct of priests, the allocation or misallocation of church budgets, and the like, and the other, *Ṣafaḥāt al-Ābā'* (The Father's Papers), is dedicated to newly ordained priests and meant to solicit grassroots recommendations for the improvement of pastoral services. It often serves as both a guide for future conduct and a warning to priests not to repeat the errors of their predecessors.[7] (From what I have observed, the ordination ceremonies of new priests generate considerable excitement among the parishioners and, by drawing huge crowds, provide the pope with yet another platform to publicize his new ideas.)

The pope has also made great efforts to raise the educational level of his priests, by recruiting university graduates and young professionals. To attract them, he has tried to raise the standard of living of the priests. Under his auspices, the Communal Council spent the better part of a year working out a plan for higher salaries and decent living accommodations for priests, as well as a pension scheme, loans for health emergencies, and so on.[8] The standard of living of the priests can be appalling in the remoter parts of the country. I once visited a priest in the Upper Egyptian diocese of Abu Tig, who lived with his family, including numerous children, in a one-room hovel, without any facilities, which he shared with his goat and chicken.[9] Some of the more progressive bishops, like Bishop Fam of neighboring Tima, do understand that if they want to attract educated young men from Cairo to serve as priests in the provinces, they must afford them a minimal standard of living—and indeed the homes of his priests, Fathers Wisa and Joseph, which I visited, were reasonably well furnished.[10] In many other areas of upper Egypt that I visited, the situation was very much like that in Abu Tig.

The pope, who once in a Wednesday meeting said within my hearing that the wives of the church-servants were often responsible for dissuading them from accepting an offer of consecration as priests, because they don't want their husbands to suffer a salary reduction, makes sure that special meetings are organized for the wives of recently ordained priests to boost their motivation and inform them of their new duties to the community. He himself often presides over such meetings; on one occasion he assembled seventy wives at his weekend retreat, at the Monastery of Bishoi.[11]

Another inducement for young talent to enter the priesthood has been the prospect of an eventual appointment to a diaspora congregation in North America, Australia, or Europe. In this way, Shenuda hopes to accomplish two goals: 1) to improve the quality of the local priests, by giving them a chance to learn foreign languages and gain exposure to western culture, which makes them more innovative and enterprising in their service, more tolerant of a diversity of opinions and more broad-minded on the subject of women; and 2) to keep the diaspora, whose material resources he needs for his developmental projects, tied to its community back home and to prevent its children from being assimilated into the mainstream cultures of their new Western homelands and, eventually, of disappearing from the Coptic flock through intermarriage. In my conversations with both visiting priests from the diaspora and returnees, which took place in the antechambers of the papal headquarters where they sometimes waited for hours to be received by the pope, I was invariably struck by these qualities in them, which set them apart from most of the local clergy I had come to know.

The Church-Servants

The pope could not rely on a relatively small group of bishops and priests to extend new religio-cultural and socioeconomic programs to a population of approximately 10 million Copts. He had to recruit laymen on a large scale into this service. He once told me, "I know some people accuse me of having ambitions. I have none. My only ambition is to integrate the Copts—every single one of them—into the church." In this endeavor he has largely succeeded, by bringing many people who had previously served the church only on an ad hoc basis into regular service. Laymen have been granted ecclesiastical titles like *shamas* (deacon), *mukaras* (consecrated layperson), and *khudām* (church-servant) as a way of strengthening their bond with the church. These tens of thousands of church-servants are the bulwark of the modern church. By integrating them into the lower echelons of the church, the pope has acquired invaluable expertise and team leaders for his reform projects.

But not just the church benefits from the mass recruitment of laypeople into its service. The church provides a purpose to the average Copt's life, beyond the scramble for everyday existence, through its numerous activities: devotional, cultural, educational, and economic, as well as its many feasts (celebrations of the saints). These brighten the drab hard lives of the faithful. The church also provides them with an alternative status system that compensates them for being deprived of a promotion or of some opportunity of economic betterment in the public sphere. It enables someone of humble birth to accede to highest office and be privy to hand-kissing and prostration to the ground. Bishop Bimen of Nagada's father, for example, was a landless peasant, who owed his ability to feed his large brood to the 1952 revolution, which allotted his father five feddans, after the passage of the Agrarian Reform Act. For his twelve children who slept out on the fields, the open sky often provided the only relief from their cramped and stifling hovel.[12] Though very few bishops orignated, like him, in the lower class, most have lower-middle-class roots. Their fathers were lower rank civil servants, telephone operators, electricians, railroad employees, accountants, and petty salesmen. It is not only those bishops, but all those church-servants who draw their status from the privilege of having access to them, for whom the church is a vehicle of social ascension.

Without this compensatory means to fulfillment offered by the church, the already-bloated queues of people waiting to receive immigrant visas at the U.S. consulates in Cairo would swell even more.

The Diaconal Corps

The pope has encouraged the clericalization of the church-servants to bind them more tightly to the church. It had been customary to casually call on a church-servant or on any lay male church devotee to assist with the liturgy. Now the pope insists on their consecration as deacons if they wish to assist the priest at the celebration of Mass. And he has sought to hierarchise that order, through the revivification of ancient Coptic titles like *ipoudiacon* (assistant deacon, who is in charge of the sanctuary and of the entrance doors), *aganosthos* (reader of the Holy Texts), *absalomos* (cantor), and so forth—with different prayers of consecration for each of these. Over the centuries, much of this practice had fallen into abeyance; the gradations were reduced to deacon, who assisted the priest with the ritual, and archdeacon, who assisted the pope with his ceremonial functions.

This canonical review, by the Holy Synod, of the order of deacons, is meant at one and the same time to revalorize the status of the deacon and to integrate the church-servant more fully into the church by emphasizing his clerical identity. As former deacons themselves, the pope and many of the bishops of his generation attach an enormous importance to this order, which is the principal link between the laity and the church. The late bishop of Mallawi, Bishop Bimen, expressed it this way: "[T]he beard can be intimidating."[13] He was referring to the long beard traditionally worn by the Orthodox priests and suggesting that a deacon could frequently be more effective than a priest at getting through to laypeople.

The bishops often remember their own frustration as young deacons with the limited traditional roles allowed them by the old-fashioned bishops they served. They tend, for the most part, to be sympathetic to the aspirations of the young generation of deacons for a broader scope of service. They are also more inclined than the priests, who compete with the deacons, to grant them autonomy in their service.

The church-servants in general tend to be more modern in their viewpoints than the priests, although lately the pope and the bishops have made a considerable effort to recruit educated priests into the service. Many of the most accomplished church-servants I talked to, like Samir Murqus of the bishopric of Youth, who once served in Damanhour, and Raef Hinawi of Minya, who once served in Cairo, complained to me about their difficulty in communicating their priorities to the priests, who are uninterested in projects other than those involving church repair or restoration or who want to control everything without the requisite know-how. Even at the lower level of university students acting as part-time church-servants in Cairo, I have often heard complaints that the priests were too authoritarian (*Mutaḥākim* is the Arabic term they used). They said that the priest interfered in everything they did, down to the most trivial detail, such as what hymns they had chosen to teach the children on a particular day in Sunday school or whom they had chosen to devote a special home visit to for counseling (known as *iftiqād*). Often the priests forbade them a particular visit, because they felt antipathy toward a family and insisted they go to someone else. The church-servants claimed that such choices are supposed to be left up to their judgment; that only the "hard cases," such as an imminent conversion to Islam or a recurrent problem of child abuse or drugs, should be referred to the priest.[14]

The pope has tried to compensate for the fact that the richer districts like Garden City, Heliopolis, and Zamalek, and some of the heavily Coptic-populated middle-class districts, like Shubra, might have more educated and liberal priests than the poorer districts, by introducing a system of rotation for church-servants. The priests have been asked to choose exceptionally dedicated and capable church-servants within their congregations and to send them for training to the headquarters of the Bishoprics of Youth and Social Services in Cairo. After their training is complete, they are meant to work in the underprivileged neighborhood churches, including those in the shantytown areas of Mu'tamidiīya and the Mokatam Hills. Occasionally, they are attached to the Bishoprics of Youth and Social Services as salaried church-servants who oversee the implementation of policies nationwide.[15] Some of them are laypeople who have taken a vow of celibacy, which may or may not lead them one day to the monastery (they are known in Arabic as *diacon ingili*), while others are married (known as *diacon rasaili*).

Even those attached to the headquarters are sent to serve diverse areas of Egypt, where they may carry out tasks very different from the ones entrusted to them at the headquarters. I was surprised one day during my fieldwork in Minya to find Shafik al-Hout, whose class for adults on the Old Testament, which he offered as part of his service in the bishopric of Youth in Cairo, I had visited, lecturing high schoolers during their midsemester break. On another occasion, when I was traveling to the Monastery of Bishoi with a group of students from the church-run university student hostel of Giza for a meeting with the bishop of Tahta (these students were from there), I observed that a high-ranking church-servant from the Bishopric of Youth was the vocal leader of a program of church hymns selected for singing in the bus.[16]

Shenuda's policy of rotation achieves two goals: it transfers the church servants' primary loyalties from their local church priest or bishop to the pope himself, and it standardizes the quality of service nationwide. It is also a way for the pope to get his reform projects across diocesan borders, regardless of the predilection of the particular reining bishop. Beyond serving the more remote areas of the country, the church servants' mission is to attract other talented youngsters into the service. The model they offer is that of Ḥabīb Jirjis, the founder of the Sunday School Movement, a simple deacon who transformed the church by raising its educational level, through the introduction of catechism classes for children and seminaries for adults.

Most of what Jirjis hoped to achieve, through the revival of a diaconal corps dedicated to the service of the community, has been achieved under Shenuda. But Jirjis's ultimate vision, to establish the diaconal corps as a partner in decision making, thereby not only rejuvenating but democratizing the church, is not yet reality. Shenuda, in the throes of a centralizing effort, has been more interested in using the deacons to achieve community cohesion, through the promotion of religious culture, than in power sharing.

But at the diocesan level, in certain instances, Jirgis's vision of power sharing has begun to take place. As Arsani, a deacon-church servant, once said of his bishop, Bishop Arsanios of Minya: "Saidna (our Lord) is very good about it. Although we often seek his counsel, he does not interfere in our work. He understands that just as his generation played a part in revolutionizing this church, now we, the young, want to do our bit."[17]

The Church Committees

Another important medium for communicating reform schemes across diocesan boundaries is the church committee (*Majlis al-kanīsah*). The pope thus has a considerable stake in seeing to it that the right people—meaning reform-minded laymen—are appointed.

The church committees are not Shenuda's creation. They were in fact set up at the beginning of the twentieth century by the secular upper class that controlled the Communal Council, as part of its effort to rid the churches of corruption. These committees have, however, been considerably democratized and invigorated through mass participation. They no longer consist of just the local dignitaries and some priests.

When operating on the neutral terrain of dioceses run by his spiritual sons or in dioceses that fall under his own jurisdiction, like Cairo and Alexandria, the pope often ensures an even tighter control, by putting one of the bishops closest to him, like Archbishop Bishoi of Damietta or Bishop Besanti, formerly the papal secretary, in charge of the committees of the most important churches. Conversely, the efficacy of the committees in solving the problems of their congregation and in meeting their demands for services (church-run daycare centers, video centers for the young, buses for church-sponsored family excursions, centers for family recreation, assistance to the needy, and so on) are often a direct function of the degree of closeness, and therefore access, of key members of the church committees to the pope.

The Communal Council

In 1973, shortly after Shenuda assumed the reins of power, President Sadat pushed for the revival of the Communal Council (*Majlis Milli*), which had been abolished by his predecessor. This was in the interest of the state, he thought, because it would constitute an alternative interlocutor to the militant church leadership. He had miscalculated, however. In the two decades since the 1952 revolution, the composition of the Coptic elite had changed radically. As the 1973 elections to the Communal Council showed, the old landed aristocracy and propertied class no longer dominated that body. Rather, the new profile of the Communal Council showed a predominance of middle-class professionals: physicians, pharmacists, engineers, lawyers, university professors, to which the 1985 elections were to add a new class of nouveau riche: real estate people, dealers in spare parts, businesspeople and industrialists who had profited from Sadat's policy of economic liberalization. These people, for the most part, hailed from the same modest social origins as did the clergy. Their families or they themselves were often rural migrants or came from the small towns of Upper Egypt; hence, they were churchgoers accustomed to venerating the clergy. It was therefore natural for them to take their directives from the church. They were not inclined to cooperate with Sadat.

Shenuda was justified in congratulating himself at the celebration of his twentieth anniversary, in the Monastery of Bishoi, in November 1991. He asked me to attend and placed me at the table reserved for the dignitaries of the Communal Council, which was flanking his own. Halfway through the meal, he stood up and toasted them with these words: "Behold, all of you here, who would have believed that one day we were enemies? Now we are the best of friends."[18]

After dinner, he took his nightly walk across the grounds, as a remedy for his ailing back, and I joined him (he had invited me to spend the night in one of the guest cottages he had had built for visiting church dignitaries, like the Greek patriarch whom he was then hosting). He told me that his predecessor, Pope Cyril VI, was not a "democratic" man. He had treated the Communal Council highhandedly, which had alienated it from him. And then he had conspired with President Nasser to have the council suspended altogether—contrary to church tradition, which was rooted in the participation of the Coptic people. "It was a very stupid thing to do," the pope added. "He was not a very clever man,"[19] I had to agree, for who was I to gainsay the pope? And, on that happy note of agreement, he blessed me and bade me good-night, turning in the direction of his own dwelling.

The extent to which the pope had succeeded in integrating the Communal Council into the church was made clear to the authorities during Shenuda's exile, in 1981. When Sadat took advantage of his absence to try to shore up the authority of the Communal Council, to use it as a rubber stamp for changes he wished to make, he found that in every instance it was enough for Shenuda to express his disapproval of a government proposal from his monastery for the Communal Council to oppose it. And after Shenuda's release, in 1985, not a single candidate who was known to have the government's support managed to get himself elected to the Communal Council, in the elections held that year. Nor can there be any doubt that in all the elections that followed, Shenuda succeeded in keeping out of the Communal Council candidates whose loyalty to the church or to his person were in question. He had a very succinct way of making known which candidates he wished to see elected, by publicizing, in the papal mouthpiece *Kirasa* his audiences with the laymen he favored.[20]

Once word of the pope's support for a candidate got around, as Jirjis Azer, himself a former member of the Communal Council, put it: "[T]hey always win, but the pope doesn't even look to the council for approval of his decisions."[21]

This picture of the transformation of the Communal Council into an appendage of the papal institution does not mean that it is totally ineffective. Judging from the heated discussions between the pope, who presides over it, and the council over questions of budget allocations for different projects and appropriations and misappropriations of religious endowments, it does act, if not as a countervailing power, at the very least as a check on the clergy (this is even more true of its branches in the provinces). And there are times, as in the case of the pope's nephew, who was forced to resign over allegations of corruption, when even this timid body shows extraordinary temerity. But on the whole the Communal Council is but a shadow of its former self, and its dissenting voice is rarely heard nowadays above a whimper.

In conclusion, the centralization of power did more than just consolidate Shenuda's hold over the Ecclesia; it enabled him to push his socioeconomic reform project across diocesan boundaries. The pope's centralizing thrust extended even to the philanthropic Coptic associations that he tried to bring under his control. The purported aim was to render them more efficient and responsible in the dispensation of welfare services to the community.[22] The unintended consequence was to increase the weight of the church vis-à-vis the state. The head of the state no longer had to deal merely with one of Egypt's spiritual dignitaries, but with the institutional representative of a large, well-organized and unified religious community.

9

Ḥaraka wa Barakah

Arsanios, a Model Bishop

While Bishop Samuel's idea of church-administered socio-economic programs, as opposed to a mere meting out of alms, was in itself a revolutionary idea for the Orthodox Church, it has by now been superseded by the realization that opening up literacy classes, family planning units, women's centers, and vocational schools, in an ad hoc fashion in response to arising needs, is not enough. There should be an overall plan for the development of the dioceses, with institutions to ensure the continuity of projects beyond the lifetime of the sponsoring bishop. Investments must be made in profitable enterprises that will generate local funds for welfare programs. And training institutes must be created for church-servants, some of whom will have to specialize in the writing of project proposals for submission to western foundations and nongovernmental organizations (NGOs)—a know-how that is vital for small dioceses, which do not have a stratum of rich professionals, merchants, and businesspeople to provide funding for major development projects. Though virtually everyone in my sample advocated this kind of comprehensive development program, it is still in a fledgling stage in most dioceses, outside of Minya, despite their bishop's good intentions and monumental energy.

The diocese of Banī Suwayf was generally held up to foreign researchers as a model of development, because its bishop, the late Bishop Athanasios, who was a close friend of Bishop Samuel, was the first one to put Samuel's ideas into practice on a systematic basis, back in the 1960s, when the term *development* had not yet become a staple of every church father's vocabulary. Athanasios's manual for church-servants, *Faith and Development*, was groundbreaking, a far cry from the authoritarianism of the old church guard. It couched some of the classic insights of the social sciences in religious terms, emphasizing the importance of letting the community determine its own needs. To demonstrate the value of holding a dialogue with the people one was trying to help, Bishop Athanasios offered the example of how God engaged in a dialogue with Abraham over his plan to destroy Sodom and Gomorah. And he admonished his church-servants to submit themselves to the criticism of their congregations, calling on the example of Jesus who always asked his disciples, portrayed as social workers, what was being said about him. In short, Athanasios introduced maxims that opposed Egypt's autocratic traditions.[1]

The problem that I determined was a gap between these notions—very advanced for their time and place—and their implementation, because the bishop did not have at his command a sufficient number of motivated and qualified church-servants to form leadership cadres. The reason is primarily demographic: Banī Suwayf is not a university town like Cairo and Minya, and its Christian population, which does not exceed 25,000 as compared to at least half a million in Cairo and roughly 350,000—400,000 in Minya, is scattered throughout a very large diocese.[2] Hence, Banī Suwayf does not act as a cultural and professional center, the way Minya and Cairo do, with experts in various fields readily available, offering their services to the bishop free of charge.

Athanasios had been able, by virtue of his engaging personality, to persuade some of the more gifted young men from major university towns to come work for him (for example, in the past, before he was consecrated bishop of Youth, Bishop Moses and the current director of Banī Suwayf development projects, Nabil Murqus, from Cairo). But on the whole, Athanasios's way of making up for the dearth of qualified personnel to whom he could delegate responsibility has been to rely on a cadre of working nuns. (Though this in itself was unprecedented in the Orthodox Church where, contrary to the Catholic Church, nuns have been solely cloistered and contemplative.) This new order of working nuns, founded in Banī Suwayf in the 1960s was called *Banat Mariam* (Daughters of Mary).

Bishop Athanasios's pioneering efforts succeeded in endowing his diocese with a female labor force, whom I found remarkably talented and dedicated,[3] and with many beneficial developmental projects—projects spanning the cultural as well as economic fields—such as the creation of a first-rate school and a large library (over 25,000 volumes of scientific, sociological, psychological, historic, and religious texts). This library was unequaled in any diocese not only in volume but in the genre of literature, which included books banned by the church establishment such as the works of the excommunicated monk Father Daniel and those of another persona non grata, Abbot Matthew the Poor (the removal of whose books from the shelves of a Cairene church library, at the command of visiting Bishop Bisante, I once witnessed). A highly stimulating Friday bible class modeled after Protestant Bible circles was taught by the bishop himself. And he had built a very large sporting club where toddlers were shown videos of local apostolic church fathers, children played ping-pong and dominoes while, in the soccer field, teenagers channeled their energies into rowdy games.[4] Yet his lifework still falls within a traditional pattern.

For a crucial measure of modernization is the extent to which social work is institutionalized. Though Bishop Athaniasios was radically innovative in the context of the Orthodox Church, he had tended to assign tasks to the nuns in his entourage in an ad hoc fashion, rather than to foster institutions for the training of a body of church-servants in the overall planning and administration of projects, which would ensure the continuity of his social work beyond his lifetime.

Not only the diocese of Banī Suwayf, but also the diocese of Damanhour lacked a department of development such as the Bishopric of Social Services in Cairo and the Community Development Center in Minya, with a professional cadre of church-servants. Damanhour, like Banī Suwayf, is a very large diocese, with a medium-sized (approximately 65,000) and scattered Christian population. It has a good resource base due to its rich agricultural hinterland, as well as an input of foreign contributions from the Copts working in neighboring Libya, who are under Bishop Pachomios's jurisdiction, and from the Copts working in Kuwait, whom he once served as a monk-priest. Damanhour's bishop, though a decade younger than Bishop Athanasios, was in his sixties when this study was underway—just old enough to have been part of the intellectual ferment and reform activism of the Sunday School generation.

The city of Damanhour itself boasts a substantial number of social services in the form of nurseries and orphanages, homes for abused women, and sanctuaries for girls pregnant out of wedlock, in addition to developmental enterprises like clinics, student hostels, and health awareness programs, as well as first-rate cultural programs for youth, run by Father Theodoros, a monk-priest, and even an unusually dynamic and pedagogically modern Bible study class for girls, taught by Father Andrawes, a church-servant turned priest.

Bishop Pachomios, like Bishop Athanasios, is an energetic, open-minded bishop who has worked indefatigably to bring culture to the numerous villages under his administration. He opened more than fifty literacy classes in the villages of his diocese, many of which, at the beginning, he taught by himself due to the lack of trained personnel.[5] He also collected, at considerable effort, the sizable sum of money needed to build a summer vacation club for village children. Every summer the children are brought in groups to Damanhour from their respective villages for a week of spiritual education, medical checkups, and entertainment. In the morning, during my stay as a participant observer, groups of seven year olds clustered around a church *khādim* to earnestly discuss the issues of carnal sin and repentance in St. Augustine's life, while in the afternoons they played basketball with the bishop. On Sunday, he made them laugh during the church service with his funny pantomimes of people's bad habits and sinful ways. At night, they were shown video films about the lives of local saints like the brave Abu Seifein (father of two swords), a warrior who was martyred for his faith. And, to make sure none of this is forgotten, the children were sent home at the end of the week with a small souvenir, a Coptic cross tattooed on their wrist.[6]

Like Bishop Athanasios of Banī Suwayf, however, Bishop Bachomios tends to run everything in the diocese himself with the help of his monk-priests, priests, consecrated laywomen, *mukarasat*, to whom he assigns responsibilities for this or that task or enterprise at random, without any necessary connection between their expertise and the task at hand. In short, piety, not ability, is the chief criterion for selection. There is no cadre of trained church-servants or any building to house them; and hardly any church-servants figure on the Committee of Development, which consists almost exclusively of the bishop and his priests and one consecrated woman. In short, all initiatives and ideas stem from the bishop himself, with the priests there mainly to carry out his commands. The longevity of any project or activity therefore depends on the bishop's good will, and no activity will survive the bishop, if his successor is less enlightened.[7]

The Institutionalization of Church

In Minya, more than in any other diocese, one can detect a movement toward what, in Weberian terms, would be described as a legal-rational bureaucracy. Minya is ahead of all other dioceses in overall planning and institutionalization. Its bishop, Arsanios, has sought to ensure the continuity of his reforms, not only by creating a bureaucracy of *khuddām* with a vested interest in the perpetuation of its activities but also by opening up bank accounts earmarked specifically for each project, instead of digging into the pockets of his habit, whenever funds are called for.

Arsanios may be considered one of the founding fathers of the reformed church, inasmuch as at sixty-five he belongs to the same generation as the pope, whom he met over forty years ago when they were both young church-servants in shabby flannel suits. They shared their dreams of Orthodox renaissance over modest repasts of falafel sandwiches, and sometimes, when proselytizing in small towns and villages, they even shared the same bed.[8]

Bishops who have been church-servants for a long time, prefer to rely on a cadre of church-servants and consecrated laymen to manage their developmental projects; they tend to relegate to the priests to matters of the soul. This is as true of Bishop Arsanios, who was a church-servant himself for 30 years, from 1946 to 1975, as it is of the outstanding bishop of Youth, Bishop Moses, and of the stellar late Bishop Bimen who, when he was first appointed bishop in 1976, the same year as Bishop Arsanios, also had nearly three decades of church service behind him as a *khādim* and later as a *mukaras*.

If Bishop Arsanios has succeeded in transcending the mental horizons of monasticism, despite the fact that he was the abbot of the Monastery of the Romans for many years, the reason is that he brought to his religious grounding the practical experience of twenty-four years as a mechanical engineer in Cairo, Alexandria, Tanta, Benha, Mahalla al-Kubra, Beba, Fayum, Ismailia, Port Said, and Hurghada. At the summit of his career, he reached the post of director general of the public works of Minya itself, dealing there with iron and steel plants, textile plants, cotton gins, water pumping and drainage stations, the laying out of pipelines, as well as with architectural planning and construction works. This wide exposure both to different areas of the country and to different types of work and people he translated into the skills necessary to develop his diocese and, before this, the Monastery of the Romans.

When the pope first put this monastery in his charge, it was so poor that squabbles actually erupted over the distribution of food received as gifts to the monastery.[9] Bishop Arsanios not only succeeded in creating a harmonious community out of a mutinous one, but he raised money, principally from Protestant German foundations, that enabled him to turn a neglected monastery into a prosperous one. He built paved roads, latrines, and other badly needed facilities for the monks' cells (there had formerly been no running water) and also developed the monastery's ability to support itself through land reclamation projects and food plants for pickling olives and other such marketable products.[10]

Arsanios is one of the few bishops who has erected office buildings for his church-servants complete with kitchens for those who work late, conference rooms, and audiovisual rooms in which they lead a separate and autonomous existence. Even though the bishop confers with them every Monday (much as Bishop Serapion, the head of the Bishopric of Social Services in Cairo did with his church-servants, once a week on that same day), the separate offices of the Community Development Center of Minya symbolize in a concrete form the differentiation and specificity of functions that characterize it. Each church-servant within it has his own responsibility. For some it is village social work, for others urban development, for others spiritual and cultural programs, and for still others loan programs for the setting up of small etnerprises, the unemployed, and so forth.

The program director in Minya, Raef Hinawi, was a highly qualified young man who was trained in Canada at the Coady International Institute, where many of the top cadres of Cairo's church-servants are sent for training by the Bishopric of Social Services and of Youth. Though raised in Minya, Hinawi began his apprenticeship in Cairo in the Bishopric of Social Services, but he soon quit because he felt things were too centralized, with all initiatives and directives for social welfare programs issuing from the capital. One of the lessons he had been taught in Canada was, precisely, that locals have a better sense of their own needs and priorities.[11] He and a number of other talented youth formed a core leadership cadre for Minya's Community Development Center, which today rivals Cairo's, and to which church-servants, and even bishops, from all over Upper Egypt come for consultation.[12]

Another thing that distinguishes the development plans of Bishop Arsanios from those of most other bishops is his understanding of the concept of community development as all-encompassing. And indeed, villages like Tihna al-Gabal, where I did my fieldwork, Nazlit Ebeid, and Nazlit Faragallah have comprehensive programs, which take a village child from preschool through to reading, writing, and arithmetic classes to vocational training for adolescents, and which include health awareness programs, family planning, youth meetings, women's meetings, and so on. The most commendable feature of these programs is that Bishop Arsanios has his church-servants, both men and women, live on the premises five days a week so that they may share in village life.[13] They thereby gain the trust of the peasants and are able to conduct effective follow-up home visits. Bishop Arsanios's programs are way ahead of other efforts to help the villagers, which are usually conducted in caravan style, with church-servants from the city circling the villages in minibuses, each taking his turn on a different day of the week.

In addition, local village leaders are brought over every summer from their villages to Minya for an intensive training program, which focuses on spiritual, pedagogical, agricultural, and medical concerns. In the one I attended, a physician, the wife of Program Director Raef Hinawi, was in charge of the health awareness courses, which included gynecological courses for women; a school teacher had been put in charge of those training for the adult literacy campaign; an agronomist lectured about the introduction of new seedlings; and the bishop gave homilies.[14]

In this regard, too, Minya has surpassed the other dioceses, which still rely on the Bishopric of Social Services in Cairo to invite them to send down their youth for training to Cairo or to Helwan, an industrial suburb of Cairo, or to the summer training courses in Abu Talat, a seaside resort near Alexandria. Minya has in fact developed its own "Abu Talat," which is presided over by Bishop Arsanios, who lends moral support, but which is independently and effectively run by his church-servants.

The Church as Fund-Raiser

The bishop of Minya must cope, as indeed all bishops must, with the rising expectations of the Copts. Therefore, in any one fiscal year Bishop Arsanios is engaged in a series of projects meant to create jobs, such as setting up a multipurpose school that would function as a foreign language school in the daytime, and double up, in the evening, as a vocational training center for the reorientation of unemployed university graduates toward new careers.[15] Other projects in the period under study were cattle breeding[16] and a leather factory for the unemployed urban youths.[17]

The cattle breeding farm was launched after Bishop Arsanios raised the substantial sum of two million deutsche marks from a German Protestant foundation.[18] The multipurpose school, to which Minya's affluent Coptic community donated their land, money, and architectural and engineering skills, was built after a long delay due to the governor's refusal to allow a Christian school to be built. This problem was only resolved when a particularly bloody attack on Christians by Islamic militants compelled the governor to lift the ban on building, as a gesture of good will.[19] For Minya has been the scene of more incidents of violent attacks on Christians by Islamic militants than any other diocese[20] (although the other dioceses of Upper Egypt have not been spared; in the course of my fieldwork in 1992, thirteen Christian peasants were mowed down by machine guns in the village of Sanabo, and four Christians were axed to death in the small town of Tima).

Bishop Arsanios believes that the stagnant economies of Upper Egypt and resulting unemployment are largely responsible for the tension among the young and hence for sectarian strife. His projects are therefore more than merely income-generating enterprises; they are informed by a moral vision. The school is open to Muslim students as well, with a view toward raising a new generation of Muslims and Christians who will become accustomed to living in harmony with one another during their childhood and a new, multireligious local elite. (The bishop conceived of this idea following a number of violent attacks on Christian churches, shops, and pharmacies at the hands of Islamic militants in the late 1980s.)[21]

Just as the school is meant to teach people of different faiths to tolerate of one another, the leather factory, whose workforce was to be chosen from among families that could not survive without church alms, was meant to inculcate a sense of community into a sector of the city's Christian population plagued by anomie and antagonism. To teach them the value of cooperation, the bishop drew up a plan in which the 600 poorest families in the city (the total number of Christian families that live below the subsistence level is estimated at 7,000)[22] would obtain shares of the factory as loans. He hoped thereby to subvert the rules of the jungle, characteristic of Fourth World cultures, in which people, even if they are of the same ethnic and religious background, seem prepared to kill each other in their fierce competition for a morsel of bread. Through joint ownership, an attempt was being made to show them that one person's gain is everyone's gain.

To launch such an expensive enterprise, the diocese, which holds the rest of the shares, had to persuade one of the wealthiest families of Minya to become co-owner of the shares. As for the 600 poor shareholders, it was projected that if one of their sons earns a regular income, they should be able to repay the shares in installments, within a period of one hundred months.[23]

In any one calendar year, a bishop tries to launch a diversity of such new enterprises, and hence he needs access to an ever-widening pool of funds and to new constituencies. Generally, people who have once made a large contribution feel they have done enough to ensure for themselves a place in heaven and are not moved again to similar largesse. Hence the perpetual need for new contributors.

In just one example of the efficacy of good public relations, in one year, 1994, Bishop Arsanios managed to persuade a member of a rich landowning family from Minya to cede to him land that he needed for his cow-breeding project, and a well-to-do doctor from Minya to let him have an apartment, rent-free, in Cairo for seven years, the time it would take for the owners' son to graduate from medical school and use the apartment as a clinic and Bishop Arsanios to acquire the necessary funds to buy a building in Cairo to relocate his Center of Hope for the Terminally Ill, so the poor people of his diocese afflicted with cancer, kidney failure, Alzheimer's disease, and other such illnesses could stay at the center, when they traveled to Cairo for consultations with physicians and for treatment.[24] In 1993 he managed to persuade the representative of Siemens, a rich entrepreneur originally from Minya, to install a modern telephone switchboard in the bishop's residence that would connect it to all the church premises.[25] And he persuaded the Mercedes representative to give him a Mercedes minibus, free of charge, for village service in Minya.[26] (Some of the wealthy Coptic industrialists, like the Suryal family, have even created a specialized department, within one of the firms, for dealing with the clergy's petitions for funds.)

This kind of public relations work is even more necessary in the stagnant economies of the Upper Egyptian small towns. Bishops who have been allotted areas severed from provincial capitals are the worst off, because the bishop who is lucky enough to be allotted the provincial capital inherits along with it a considerable amount of property, both in land and buildings, which Christians willed to the church (*Waqf*). So he at least begins his term with a minimum of funds at his disposal. But the others, who have received nothing but some thankless plot of land and the dirt poor population that comes with it, must link up with the town notables, if they wish to mobilize all the resources of their diocese for development purposes.

The bishop must therefore be a public relations man in the mold of an American fund-raiser. He is the first to realize this. Bishop Bimen of Nagada who, ever since a Muslim fundamentalist regime hostile to Egypt's regime came to power in the Sudan, faced an economic crisis because that country was the chief importer of Nagada's textiles, told me of the textile dying project for which he hoped to raise money, "It is too soon for me to ask people to make contributions [he had been in office a little over three years then, having been consecrated in 1989], but after I have officiated at the wedding ceremonies of a few of their daughters and visited them when they are sick, then will be the time to ask."[27] Just how important, in a traditional society like Egypt's, the cultivation of such personal relationships is may be judged from a meeting of members of a church committee (*Majlis al-kanīsah*) which I attended at Bishop Murqus's residence in Shubra al-Kheima. One of the elderly dignitaries inaugurated the meeting by reproaching the bishop, in no uncertain terms, for not having come to pay condolences on a death in the family. Bishop Murqus sought to excuse himself. He said he had not seen the obituary in the newspaper, he had been so busy of late he had not had a chance to look at a paper in three days. But the irate old man would not let the matter rest and berated him for ten minutes claiming this was the first time in generations that his family had been so slighted.[28]

However, even a rich diocese like Minya, whose income is 200 times greater than that of a small diocese like Dishna[29] (Bishop Arsanios received individual contributions ranging from LE 2,000 [$588] to LE 10,000 [$2,940] when I was in Minya,[30] in contrast to the small Upper Egyptian dioceses where the contribution of a well-to-do person was more in the order of LE 500 to 1,000 [$150 to $300]), cannot rely solely on local funds for major projects.[31] Half of the yearly budget comes from the contributions of overseas foundations. Bishop Murqus of Shubra al-Kheima also knew a number of well-to-do Coptic industrialists from whom he has received contributions of anywhere from LE 5,000 ($1,470) to LE 10,000 ($2,940) (an industrialist once contributed LE 30,000 [$8,923] for the building of the clinic in his residential compound).[32] But despite the presence of rich local contributors, Bishop Murqus has been compelled to turn to a number of overseas religious foundations, such as the EZE, a foundation connected to the German Evangelical Church, and Miserio, a foundation connected to the Catholic Church of Germany, as well as Protestant foundations like ECHO in Holland, and WCA in Britain, to help him set up a theater for youths, a language lab, and a hospital that cost him LE 8 million pounds ($242,000).[33]

It is fair to say that none of the small Upper Egyptian dioceses have such possibilities. Their church-servants have no notion of how to write project proposals and no foreign language skills. Bishop Thomas of Qusia wanted to build a foreign language school, which by catering to the children of the well-to-do in his area, would generate funds for development purposes. But this school would cost LE 1 million ($350,000) and could therefore only be built with the help of foreign donors. He did not, however, have in his diocese church-servants who could write project proposals and had therefore to turn to Minya's Community Development Center for help.[34]

The difference between Minya and other dioceses is that all of Minya's financial enterprises, large and small, have succeeded because they have a body of qualified church-servants able to conduct reliable feasibility studies. The feasibility study for the leatherwork factory, for example, was prepared with the greatest care, and the grounds for building it were very sound; namely, that there was in the whole area from Giza in Lower Egypt to Minya in Upper Egypt not a single leather goods factory, that Minya had the necessary expertise, because it was home to some of the country's most famous leather dealers, and that it was a product that was easily marketable—people would always need wallets, handbags, belts, and the like, and such merchandise was relatively modest in price and well within the reach of the average Egyptian.[35]

Unlike some of the other bishops, for whom development projects are often nothing more than new gadgets, Bishop Arsanios has never introduced anything into his diocese merely to keep up with appearances. For example, he considered but in the end rejected the idea of creating a fancy multimillion-pound hospital similar to the one Bishop Bivnotios, a physician, had built in the neighboring diocese of Samalut with the contributions of Coptic immigrants to the United States. This, despite the fact that Minya has both a large number of Christian doctors, medical personnel and paramedics, as well as rich donors to ensure the success of such a project. Rather than an $8 million hospital for the well-to-do, he felt that the large investment this enterprise called for would be better placed in a number of basic hospitals for the poor, like the one he built in the village of Banī Ahmad al-Sharkia, in 1993.[36] (To be fair to Bishop Bivnotios, though the hospital caters to the well-to-do, it is meant to generate a profit that can be used to fund welfare services.) Bishop Arsanios's attitude stands in sharp contrast to that of some of the other bishops, for whom securing a new item for their diocese is often a matter of prestige. For example, the bishop of a tiny provincial diocese in Upper Egypt, a real backwater, having heard that Bishop Bivnotios was acquiring dialysis equipment for his hospital, asked me to find out for him the name of American foundations that funded medical equipment, so that he, too, could acquire it.[37] He did not stop to consider that he had neither the professional staff in his diocese to handle such machines, nor a proper hospital to house them.

Yet another consideration that influences Bishop Arsanios to invest in small-scale plants and enterprises is political caution. He told me that modest ventures were less likely to arouse envy and resentment. He said he had come to that conclusion after two largescale and prosperous Christian-owned firms, the BTM clothing factory in the 10th of Ramadan industrial zone near Cairo and a blanket factory in Cairo, were burned down by suspected Islamic militants.

The Bishop as Investor

In addition to raising money abroad, a bishop is forced to become a modern entrepreneur, investing in local money-making enterprises whose profits can be used to support welfare projects. Examples of such projects are the summer resort hostel Bishop Arsanios was building at the seaside of Abu Talat, whose profits he planned to use to set up the "Center of Hope for the Terminally Ill" discussed earlier. In a similar vein, the multipurpose school project, referred to earlier, with its foreign-language program, was meant to attract well-to-do, upper-middle-class children. Fees collected from them would be channeled toward opening up the school, free of charge, for nightly vocational training for the underprivileged.[38]

Money-making projects such as Minya's call for relatively large investments, which are not within the means of the smaller Upper Egyptian dioceses. Minya, which is believed to have one of the largest Christian populations, and among them a stratum of well-to-do landowners, merchants, jewelers, and Cairo-based industrialists, can afford the expensive audiovisual equipment, which a modern foreign-language school requires, and the machinery imported from Milan, for a leather-work factory. Both the school and the leather factory are expensive projects, requiring an initial investment of LE 500,000 (roughly $150,000) and LE 800,000 ($236,000), respectively. The cattle-breeding farm project is equally ambitions, requiring an initial investment of LE 500,000 ($150,000) and the building of a summer resort hostel requires roughly the same amount.[39] Such projects are clearly not within the reach of a small bishopric like Dishna, in Upper Egypt, whose total yearly budget does not exceed LE 10,000 ($3,000), as opposed to an approximate LE 2 million ($590,000) in Minya, a ratio of 1/200).[40]

The bishop of the smaller diocese could, it is true, qualify for financial aid from the Bishopric of Social Services in Cairo. But Bishop Serapion's policy was, in general, to limit his aid to basic necessities, such as family planning units, health awareness units, women's centers, literacy classes, vocational training centers, and clinics.[41] The bishops of the small, impoverished diocese had therefore to turn elsewhere for the funding of their pet projects; namely, to small-scale money-making enterprises whose investment they could afford, like textile workshops, automobile repair shops, silk screen printeries, and carpentries. The young bishop of Dishna, a recent graduate of the faculty of commerce at Cairo University with a good head for business, thought of two profitable ventures. They called for relatively modest investments of LE 7,000 ($3,000) and LE 3,000 ($1,000), respectively, and were safe investments, inasmuch as they were products purchased by the average consumer. One was a small plant that would convert plastic powder into garbage bags, and the other was an ice cream plant, which was bound to find customers in the sweltering heat of Upper Egypt.[42]

Similarly, Bishop Fam, of the small diocese of Tima, in Upper Egypt, needed a minibus to transport his church-servants to the poverty-stricken villages under his jurisdiction. Some of these villages were beyond the reach of public transportation. Tasoni ("Sister," in Coptic) Imtisal, the consecrated young woman in charge of the village of Naga Ghadas, whom I accompanied as a participant observer, had to walk a kilometer under a scorching-hot sun, from the bus stop, carrying heavy bundles of clothes, medicines and provisions for the poverty-stricken homes she visited.[43]

Like Bishop Tackla, Bishop Fam's request for funds to purchase a minibus was turned down by the Bishopric of Social Services. So Bishop Fam, too, had to turn to small enterprises to generate money for this purchase, a chocolate plant and a textiles workshop. In both cases, he was able to set these up with the help of *Muḥibīn*, (literally, "people who love one"), friends he had made from among the ordinary people, who had come to congratulate him when he was released from prison, after the death of Sadat, in 1981.[44] (Bishop Fam had been one of bishops imprisoned by Sadat during the mass arrests of September 1981.)

Muḥibīn from the neighboring town of Sohag, who own confectioneries, provide a market for his chocolates, while Christians in the textile industry in Cairo ship out the raw materials for the production of T-shirts and place orders.[45]

This is a mutually advantageous arrangement: as much as western industries can offer lower prices for their products by branching out into the cheap labor markets of Asia, so too the workforce is considerably cheaper in the impoverished regions of Upper Egypt than it is in the main industrial regions of Lower Egypt, centered around Cairo and Alexandria. (The teenage girls employed by Bishop Fam were paid 10 piasters an hour, about 3 cents.)[46]

In a diocese like Tima, with a mostly subsistence level rural population numbering some 25,000 Christians and without any significant commercial, industrial, or professional strata, any profits Bishop Fam was able to glean from his small productive units had to be channeled toward the maintenance of some 3,000 families in the heart the small town of Tima itself, who lived in filthy mud hovels without electricity or running water or sanitary facilities, because the head of the household was either dead, chronically ill, or too old to work with a young wife burdened by a clutch of small children that she could not feed without a monthly stipend from the church.[47] As in other Third World countries, where women are less valued than men, it is not uncommon for a small-town man or villager in his sixties to marry an 18-year-old wife. Recently, the church tried to limit such marriages to a 15-year age difference, but this has been left to the bishops to enforce, and they have in general been very lax about it. I witnessed a typical example of such laxity in Minya. An old man and a girl, who looked 15—though she claimed to be 18—were brought before the bishop for a marriage dispensation. He contented himself with asking her if she was sure she wanted him—never mind that the girl would in all likelihood have been beaten by her father if she demurred.

It is self-evident, in considering the Upper Egyptian regions, that those bishops who have been fortunate enough to receive the governorship of the dioceses with big towns have more funds at their disposal for socioeconomic and cultural programs. In this study, this would include towns like Luxor and Aswan, the principal tourist sites of Egypt; Naga Hammadi, an industrial town; Girga, a mercantile town; and Sohag, a provincial capital.

However, if a bishop is enterprising, he can often partially surmount the problem of scarce resources. A comparison between Bishop Fam of Tima and Bishop Besada of Akhmim illustrates this. Both of these dioceses are rural, small, and poor. Akhmim used to be a famous textile center in the nineteenth century, known as the Manchester of Egypt, but the introduction of big mechanized textile plants in Cairo in the 1920s destroyed the market for Akhmim's Textiles, which was based on artisanal work and hand looms, and as a result the economy stagnated. Thereafter, the town gradually sank into oblivion.

In 1980, Bishop Besada, the bishop of Akhmim, was sworn into a diocese that had been divided off from a larger area encompassing Sohag, the rich provincial capital. Though pastoral care was improved in Akhmim, in that the bishop could now cover the entire area, the proximity of Akhmim to Sohag—only a bridge across the Nile separates them—meant that any professional with the slightest prospect moved to Sohag. In this way, Akhmim was deprived of the young and well-to-do professionals whose tithes (*'ushur*) and donations would have been invaluable to the bishop's treasury. Akhmim had no rich inhabitants of its own; it was mainly a diocese of low-paid government employees, school teachers, and peasants. Therefore, it could not afford to offer its population many services. And, indeed, the only social services in the entire diocese, when I did my fieldwork, were a nursery, in the town of Akhmim itself, and the literacy classes offered by the churches in some of the adjacent villages. Even such a small project as a vocational school for plumbers and electricians ran aground for lack of money. According to bishop Besada, the Bishopric of Social Services turned down his request for money; it would only agree to enough funds for one *khādim* to offer a literacy class.[48] Aside from that one allocation, it limited its help to doling out money for books and clothes to poor students from Akhmim, who studied in the university of the neighboring provincial capital of Sohag.[49] Likewise, medical aid in Akhmim had not evolved, when I was there, beyond the age-old custom of sending a poor person off with a note from the parish priest to a sympathetic local Christian doctor or pharmacist to receive free treatment or medicines.

But much of this had to do with the bishop's own conservative disposition, which disinclined him to exercise initiative to find alternative sources of funds. When I asked him why he did not try to attract tourists to the numerous monasteries and beautiful old churches of Akhmim by establishing a hotel, so that instead of just passing through for the day, visitors might stay a while, get to know the bishop, and become acquainted with his projects and possibly contribute to them, he said that such fund-raising would distract him from his spiritual work.[50] He added that he had tried to help his people in small ways, like giving money for vegetable carts, which cost about LE 200 ($60), and for felafel stands, but his resources were few. He claimed that in the whole diocese, he had not more than one or two physicians and he believed that his was the only privately owned car.[51] When I asked what he did to get more money, he said he relied first of all on God, then on his Cairene *muhibīn*. But of the projects he mentioned to me for which he had collected money from his friends, not a single one had developmental import—aside from a hostel he built for girls from Akhmim studying in Sohag. The other projects he cited were painting a church, fixing a church fence, and buying a chandelier for a church. Similarly, when asked why he did not try to emulate the European Catholic missionaries, who had set up a renowned school for weaving for girls and sold their products in Cairo, he replied that he had indeed established such a workshop, for about sixty girls. But he could not picture himself trying to market their products outside of Akhmim, because that would require him to call upon embassies and cultural centers in Cairo to advertise his exhibitions, and find suitable exhibit halls, for which he had neither the time nor the inclination.[52]

In part, the dearth of developmental and cultural activities can also be attributed to the bishop's own interests, which center primarily on liturgical studies and the resuscitation of the Coptic language. To that end, he opened a small theological seminary in his diocese, which he himself goes to the trouble of teaching. In contrast, he rarely attends the youth meetings; these are run by priests in the traditional style. It is significant that all activities are in the hands of priests rather than laypeople (khuddām), and though the bishop holds Friday meetings with the community at large, no questions are taken from the audience. Rather, following his homily, he comments on a clause of religious law, such as, when I attended, the prohibition of a priest taking a second wife if the first one dies.

But part of the reason for Bishop Besada's laconic response is that unlike Bishop Arsanios, he does not have the experience to raise money or to direct projects. After graduating from Assiut University, Bishop Besada worked for the government for only three months before he was called up, in 1968, for army duty. Since this was the period immediately following Egypt's defeat at the hands of Israel in the Six-Day War of 1967, he was compelled to serve for six years, after which he immediately entered the monastery. Thus, his only experience, outside of prayer, before he became a bishop was in helping erect the two-story building that now houses Pope Shenuda during his visits to the Monastery of Bishoi.

The Social Work Movement as a Socializing Tool

Social work was not just meant to compensate for a discriminatory state which, as the pie shrank in relation to an exponential growth in population, denied the Christian minority its fair share. It was also meant to provide a complete framework, parallel to the state structure, for an Egyptian Christian's life. Although Bishop Samuel was a pioneer in the field of social services at a time when Shenuda was still following a narrow spiritual track within the confines of the Church of St. Anthony, the imperatives of office compelled Shenuda to look upon social work, which he had previously considered a detractor from the spiritual strength of Orthodoxy, as a vital tool of socialization—a way of mobilizing the entire Coptic community behind the church.

Church-sponsored social work projects must therefore be judged not only in terms of their success in improving the material circumstances of the Coptic community, but also in terms of the changes in attitude and motivation they strove to bring about. In part, this meant steering the youth away from materialistic values and teaching them to substitute moral introspection for the pursuit of trivial pleasures in their spare time; in part it meant socializing a new generation in the values of thoroughness and reliability required of modern industry. The cultivation of moral introspection, under church tutelage, was intended to imbue the people with strength and dignity in the face of the deprivation experienced in a Third World country like Egypt, under conditions of sustained, unrenumerative labor. It was to free them from the anxiety-ridden quest for material wealth, which led so many of the church's sons to emigrate.

Bishop Arsanios himself acts as a role model for the hard-pressed youth in his diocese by denying himself every comfort. Though the ruler of the wealthiest diocese in Egypt, with ample money at his command, he lived in the most dilapidated building of any bishop I visited, full of fissures in the walls, cracks in the ceiling, and potholes in the floors. He ate the same unsavory vegetable stew as his janitor did. I know this because I have been invited on more than one occasion to share his humble repast.

The church also teaches its sons that the discipline of unremitting labor is a sine qua non for the attainment of virtue—even saintliness. The bishops themselves, under the aegis of the Sunday School Movement, had gone to the monasteries to learn the kind of self-control and repression the new work ethic entailed, one that shielded them from slipping into disorderly, dissolute conduct in the big cities to which they had migrated in search of a university education.

The Sunday School Movement's effectiveness in socializing a new generation was evidenced at a graduation ceremony I attended, at a vocational school in Minya. Bishop Arsanios said that the point was not for the graduates to learn a trade and acquire a machine to take home to their villages, but to acquire *a new outlook, new motivations.* Uppermost in their mind should be how they can improve what they have already achieved, both professionally and spiritually. Professionally, they should think of learning as a lifelong process and should constantly look for new ideas. This might mean starting out with a manual machine, he told them, then moving on to an electrical one, and eventually, to one with special features; or it might mean changing one's line of work altogether. Here, the bishop gave the example of an industrial exhibit he had just visited, in Cairo, which featured a machine that converted plastic powder into shoes. As a mechanical engineer, he remarked that he had found that process most interesting. The secret of success in any profession is perseverance, he said, and he hoped that they would not just shelve the machines they were receiving as graduation gifts at the first obstacle encountered.[53]

Even more valuable than their new professional know-how, he told them, were the *relationships* with their fellow students and with their teachers (church-servants). He hoped these relationships would be maintained on a lifelong basis, so that they would remain firmly committed to the church. Bishop Arsanios concluded that one of the most pleasing things he had noted was that several of the trainees had asked that, instead of being allotted the same machines, they be given different machines that complemented each other so that they could collaborate in the same workshops. This was the sort of Christian community he was trying to build.[54]

On another occasion, at a high-level meeting with the leaders of the church-servants (*umanā' al-khidmah*), the bishop stressed the theme of responsible citizenship. Picking on characteristic Egyptian shortcomings, the bishop said that just as the church-servants had an obligation to come to their Sunday school lecture well prepared and on time, the students had an obligation to be punctual at work and to perform their tasks with meticulous attention to detail—not to say, as Egyptians are wont to do, that the poor efforts they invest are commensurate with their poor salaries. Likewise, they should not litter the sidewalk, on the pretext that everybody else does. And they should not use that same rationale to disregard traffic regulations. The disciplined and responsible behavior required of them by the church, in the observation of Orthodox fasts, prayers, communions, and confessions, should be applied as well to their study, work, and everyday life.[55]

Bishop Arsanios's homily against carelessness, unpunctuality, and slovenliness well exemplifies the way social work is used as an instrument of character transformation. And in this context, it has a radical, even revolutionary thrust. What Lenin had to say about the "primitive" Russia he so despised might well apply to Egypt. For him the Bolshevik revolution was as much an internal struggle against the Russian "slovenliness . . . carelessness, unpunctuality" and "the tendency to substitute talk for work and the inclination to undertake to do everything under the sun without ever finishing anything"[56] as it was an external struggle against an exploitative and decadent ruling class.

By suffusing all his relationships with an earnest moral tone, Bishop Arsanios has provided just the right antidote to a culture that allows unreliability and untruthfulness, as well as breaches of promises and appointments. *Maʾalish*, "never mind," is the most used word in the Egyptian vocabulary. The bishop's pastoral staff, as one interviewer put it, has had to function as much as a rod as an emblem of the loving shepherd.[57]

Bishop Bachum, of the diocese of Sohag, once confided to me that at his ordination ceremony Pope Shenuda had said to him, "In the past a bishop had only to be a *Barakah* (blessing) to his people, but now he must be both *Barakah wa Ḥaraka* (blessing and motion)."[58]

It is this combination of a dynamic motive force propelling his people forward and a stabilizing moral presence providing his imperiled community with a sense of security in their traditional anchorage that I perceived in the bishop of Minya, where I did extensive fieldwork over a three-year period. Because of the discipline and moral rigor he tenaciously strove to inculcate in his followers, the work-muscle of church-sponsored endeavors in Minya, if not quite up to the standards of the Calvinist ethic, was nonetheless in far better shape than that of government agencies and the secular philanthropic associations engaged in similar developmental efforts in Minya.

Indeed, Bishop Arsanios is a model bishop, one whom other bishops seek to emulate. And the development in his diocese forcasts the direction of other dioceses in the future.

10

The Recruitment of Bishops

The reason for the rapid spread of developmental programs throughout the dioceses is not just that modern times have brought about a considerable expansion of the bishops' social consciences, but also, that the downtrodden Egyptian masses are far more vociferous in their demands today than they were before the 1952 revolution. They have been fed a lot of unfilled promises almost daily, on television and in the newspapers. Thus the church experiences, in much the same way as the state does, a crisis generated by the inability of living standards to catch up with rising expectations. In the case of the Christians, these demands are pressed upon the church, not the state, from which, as second class citizens, they have come to expect very little.

In most dioceses, the relationship between individual and church is not just pastoral but resembles a citizen-state relationship. Even though his relationship to his church does not carry with it the same element of compulsion as does the state-citizen counterpart, the demands made by a Copt on his church are similar. He expects it to not only cater to his spiritual needs but also to help him with educational, occupational, housing, and medical problems.

This new generation of teachers, medical doctors, engineers, and pharmacists, whose childhood and adolescence corresponded to the decades of the nineteen sixties and seventies—Egypt's first television generation—has grown up among images of western plenty. Nasser may not have been able to deliver on all his promises of material plenty, but his was without question a revolution of expectations. His slogan *Irfaʾ raʾsak, yā akhī* (Raise up your head, brother) encouraged the kind of ambitions that made even the most abject slum dweller dream of the day his son would be an engineer with a Mercedes parked in front of his doorway and a VCR at home.

Consequently, the new generation is not patient. Very few of its members would be prepared to say, as the popular member of parliament Mīlād Ḥannā did, in reply to my suggestion that he found a Coptic party to fight for equality for Copts:

> This is the American way of thinking. The Egyptian way is the patient way. I, for example, had to wait ten years longer than my Muslim colleague for tenure at the university, and I know I will never be a dean, just as surely as I will never be Speaker of the House. Mubarak, himself, told me he would have liked to appoint me speaker, but he cannot do it because the Muslim fundamentalists would never stand for it. But so what! So I won't be Speaker of the House. I will survive. We Copts even survived the dark ages, because we know how to be patient.[1]

But today's generation is not prepared to wait indefinitely. Unless the church caters to the demands of the youth, they will seek their salvation in the "promised lands." For the bishops, coping with the rising expectations of the youth within their dioceses has, not surprisingly, become a matter of great concern. This problem was vividly put to me by Bishop Lukas of Abnub, in Upper Egypt: "Every day young people come to me clamoring for clubs, libraries, theaters, sporting facilities. In a small town like this the youth get restive, because there is nothing to do. If the church does not respond to their needs they will emigrate to America, but where am I to get the money?"[2]

The problem of how to provide badly needed recreation facilities for the small-town youths was also uppermost on the mind of Bishop Tackla of Dishna, in Upper Egypt, when I visited him there. He had been recently consecrated bishop and one of the first things he did on assuming office, he told me, was to solicit contributions for the purchase of a second-hand bus that could be used to take youngsters on excursions to Luxor and the monasteries in its vicinity. But he was only able to raise LE 20,000 out of the required LE 50,000 and the Bishopric of Social Services refused to contribute the rest.[3]

The Problem of Recruitment: The Bishops

The question whether the Orthodox Church, as an institution, has been successfully modernized is of interest primarily because it cannot be an effective agent of development for its community unless it itself is capable of reform. Among the challenges faced by the Orthodox Church at the end of the twentieth century was how best to create effective leadership cadres that would be able to steer the Copts toward a brighter future.

Since bishops in the Orthodox Church cannot be chosen from among priests but must be monks and the pope cannot possibly know all the monks in the monasteries throughout Egypt, he relies on the recommendation of either the abbots of these monasteries or diocesan bishops. In certain cases, the bishops recommend people on the basis of their record of service, as laymen, to the community. And the choice tends to be propitious. Such, in the sample under study, was the case of Bishop Tackla of Dishna. He was recommended by Bishop Benjamin, of the diocese of Menufia in Lower Egypt, on the basis of his work as a church-servant in that province, before he joined the monastic order. Such is also the case of Bishop Thomas of Qusia, who was recommended by Bishop Anthonios-Murqus of Kenya, on the basis of his distinguished record as a missionary for the Orthodox Church in Kenya.[4]

However, if the bishop recommending the monk himself shares the viewpoint of the old guard that a holy man should not be a man of action but a man of prayer, and that all investiture of energy in development projects is at the expense of one's spirituality, the monk he recommends for a bishopric is likely to lack enterprise. Such, for example, is the case of Bishop Dimitrios, who was chosen on the recommendation of Bishop Bishoi—himself of the old school of thought—and of Bishop Amonios, who was chosen on the recommendation of his abbot.[5] Bishop Dimitrios's predecessor, Bishop Bimen of Malawi, was one of the most outstanding personalities within the church—a pioneer in the field of socioeconomic development and in the emancipation of women, who, especially in Upper Egypt, were often totally subjugated by despotic fathers, older brothers, and husbands. And he had the further merit of not only trying to emancipate the village women of his own diocese, in whose oppression he saw his priests conniving,[6] but of trying to carve out a role for women in church service. Having worked closely with women in his ten years as a church-servant affiliated to one of the vanguard churches within the Sunday School Movement, the church of Giza, he did not share the fear of women characteristic of bishops who have no experience outside of the monastic order. (Some bishops are candid in their admission of this fear. In a taped interview conducted with Bishop Bimen, in Naga Hammadi in 1992, I asked him if he had ever thought of recruiting young women into the service of his diocese. "No," replied the bishop. "You don't like girls?" I asked, tongue in cheek. "I fear them," was his response.)

It was the late Bishop Bimen of Mallawi who created the role of *Mukharasa* (consecrated laywoman), sending many young women who joined that order abroad for study[7]—an example widely followed at present. But, with his premature death of sclerosis of the liver and the succession of Bishop Dimitrios, much of the socioeconomic development in his diocese came to a standstill. The more intelligent and dynamic of his consecrated men and women, feeling unused and unwanted, left the diocese altogether to enter the service of more progressive bishops, like Bishop Moses, the bishop of Youth, and Bishop Serapion, the bishop of Social Services, in Cairo.[8] Today Mallawi, which was a model of development in the '70s and early '80s is overshadowed by neighboring Minya.

Similarly, Luxor lags behind Aswan, despite its greater resources for development, as the number one tourist destination of Egypt, because its bishop, Bishop Amonios, lived in the world, when I did my fieldwork, as though he were still in the monastery, insulating himself from the economic and political pressures faced by his community. His time was spent in prayer, and after prayer he vanished into the labyrinthine underground passages of the church, where no one dared approach him. So fearful were the priests of him that once he remained missing for three days, until he was discovered lying in a coma in his subterranean vault (he suffered from extreme low blood pressure).[9] Aside from his regimen of prayer, Bishop Amonios had few activities. His sole contact with his constituency were the twenty minutes or so after Mass, when he received petitioners and complainants. He rarely left the church, except to visit the abandoned monasteries, which he had populated with consecrated women. Though he was not personally corrupt, he had nothing to show for the huge donations he received, other than church buildings and restored monasteries. He actually boasted to another bishop that a Coptic immigrant to the United States sent him a check for $2,000 along with a request that he be told where the money would be invested, because he wanted it to be earmarked for developmental projects. The bishop raged at his impudence and sent it back with a note saying that he did not need the money. He could get as much, in one day, from his church collection boxes.[10]

The cavalier manner in which Bishop Amonios turned down money on which an average Christian family in Luxor could have lived for five years (at the rate of LE 100 a month—the income of a family of modest means in that region) typifies the way in which, traditionally, the bishop considered the diocese his own personal fiefdom. This attitude is further illustrated by the experience of two bishops who paid visits to Bishop Amonios's diocese. In one case, Bishop Domadios of Giza, though paralyzed from a stroke, had traveled all the way up to Luxor in a wheelchair to celebrate a mass for a friend, only to discover that he had made the journey in vain because Bishop Amonios would not allow him to officiate in any of his churches. (Bishop Amonios had had a falling out with the town dignitary for whom the Mass was to be held.)[11] Bishop Domadios was, therefore, forced to conduct the service in the chapel of a monastery near Luxor, outside of Bishop Amonios's jurisdiction. In another instance, Bishop Fam, who was stranded on the West Bank of Luxor because of low tides, was denied overnight shelter in a monastery. The consecrated woman who guarded the gate of the monastery would not admit him without a written permission for fear of incurring Bishop Amonios's displeasure.[12] So many complaints about Bishop Amonios reached the pope's ear that in the end he was forced to take action. He asked Bishop Amonios to take a "temporary" leave of absence in a monastery and leave the administration of Luxor to a consortium of bishops from the neighboring dioceses. Fortunately for everyone concerned, Amonios complied with the pope's wishes, as the pope would not have had the authority to forcibly remove him from his diocese or replace him before his death because, as noted earlier, a bishop is considered "married" to his diocese and can only be removed for womanizing, corruption, or insanity. Neither Bishop Amonios nor Bishop Dimitrios had any notable experience as laymen in social work. While they no doubt would have been suited to be abbots of monasteries, they were clearly not cut out to deal with the temporal day-to-day problems of their community.

Cases of ineptitude or autocracy raise the question among the faithful of whether the entry of the church into the twenty-first century and the problems facing the Coptic community at large do not call for a drastic revision of the criteria for the selection of bishops—as indeed of the selection of the pope himself—so that the choice of bishop does not depend on the whims and vagaries of the particular bishop or abbot recommending a monk for the office. The vigor and discipline of monastic life is still considered crucial to the formation of the strong personalities that are needed for the thankless job of bishop, with its excruciatingly long work hours and the comfortless "cells" that serve as the bishop's abode. (A bishop's abode is referred to in Arabic as a cell, *alayah.*) But many leading Copts close to the church feel that a new criterion must be set, which also takes into account his prior experience as a church-servant in charge of organizing activities and leading people.[13] For a bishop, as for a pope, a superlative monastic track record is no longer considered a sufficient criterion of selection. There is a growing demand, voiced by an opposition front that has formed in recent years to push for church reform, that priests and bishops be elected according to criteria beyond mere piety.[14] Traditionally, priests and bishops are appointed by papal decree. After a candidate has been recommended to him, the pope takes the opinion of the notables of the diocese where the bishop will serve but he is the final arbiter in the selection process.

If the sample of twenty-six bishops in this study demonstrates anything, it is that a bishop's experience before consecration is more important than any other factor such as age, class, or education in determining his performance. Lack of experience can prove a handicap, even to an enterprising bishop and to one with great resources, as the case of Bishop Besada's neighbor, Bishop Backhum, shows.

Bishop Backhum was appointed bishop in 1986 at the age of thirty-three. He had both the funds and the charm to induce virtually any church-servant to join his clerical corps. He chose his priests judiciously; he did not confine his appointments to people of his own generation, like Father David, formerly a dynamic church-servant in charge of youth programs, and Father Joseph, a talented doctor, but chose a number of older men as well, so that he would not be accused of trying to launch a revolution of Young Turks. And, in fact, he was careful to include in his development committee some retired citizens; he put them in charge of his vocational training program, his model nursery, and other ventures. In this way, he has deflected criticism of radical innovations and reforms and has progressed without opposition since the beginning of his term as bishop.[15]

However, the mere availability of expert personnel is not sufficient if the bishop lacks the experience with which to build and direct an administrative cadre. Sohag is a university town and there are plenty of educated young men, eager to volunteer their services, in Bishop Backhum's entourage. But, while Bishop Backhum has a winning personality that would make anyone happy to work for him, he lacks experience in the administration of finances and personnel, having spent only one year as a lab technician in Aswan before cloistering himself in the monastery. Consequently, the young church-servants, including bankers, accountants, engineers, and doctors, seemed to me to float about his court, acting more as his personal attendants than as an organized bureaucracy with clearly delineated functions and responsibilities, such as existed in Minya within the Community Development Center.[16]

And, though Backhum is energetic, open-minded, and accessible to anyone with a new idea, and he has managed to launch a number of successful small-scale enterprises such as a model nursery, a flourishing audiovisual center, a vocational school, and a silk print workshop, his development committee consists of a few affable old gentlemen, whose chief quality seemed to me that they have taken this charming young bishop to heart. They did not have the experience necessary to conduct feasibility studies and write project-proposals, a sine qua non for raising the sums needed to develop the villages under Bishop Backhum's jurisdiction.

A bishop's particular field and interests may influence his pattern of investment. It is not altogether an accident that Bishop Bivnotios of Samulut, a physician, chose to invest in a hospital, while his neighbor Bishop Arsanios, an engineer, chose to invest in a leather factory. Or that Bishop Thomas, formerly a missionary in Kenya, an English-speaking country, chose to invest in an English language school. But neither a bishop's specialization nor his educational level have a determining impact. It is prior experience that counts the most. Of two bishops of the same generation and field, veterinary medicine (Bishop Thomas of Qusia and Bishop Amonios of Luxor), one is very eager to invest in the cultural and socioeconomic growth of his diocese, while the other is not. Nor can one attribute this to the fact that the former, Bishop Thomas, was born in Cairo, a city with a relatively high level of culture and considerable interaction with Westerners, while the latter was born in Upper Egypt. For it is possible to demonstrate that other bishops born and bred in Upper Egypt such as Bishop Fam, who grew up in Kena, Bishop Backhum, who grew up in Luxor, and Bishop Bimen, who grew up on a small farm near Manfalut, are far more progressive than Bishops Besada and Adrawes who grew up in Cairo—not to mention that one of the most enlightened bishops of the central administration, Bishop Serapion of the Bishopric of Social Services, is Upper Egyptian born and raised. (Though both the pope and Bishop Moses, who shares his progressive orientation, were born in Upper Egypt, I have not mentioned them as examples because their youth was spent in Cairo.)

Just as place of birth does not to determine whether a bishop will be more or less progressive, neither does level of education. Because Egypt is a developing country, the sciences tend to be more highly prized than the humanities and social sciences, and the choice of field is not left up to the individual student as it is in the United States, but is determined by a central government bureau (*Maktab Tansīq*) in accordance with grade point averages in the final secondary school examinations. In this way, the government has, since the 1952 revolution, channeled the brightest students into medicine and engineering, followed by the natural sciences, followed by the other technical fields such as geology and agronomy, followed by commerce and the social sciences (except for the Faculty of Economics and Political Science, which requires a high grade point average as a preparation for the diplomatic corps and the ministries of finance and planning). Presumably, the duller students end up in law and the humanities. In this way, an elite of technocrats advanced to the ministerial ranks, replacing the ancien régime elite, trained mostly in the French-language law schools of Egypt and Paris, and to a lesser extent in the humanities. The same thing happened in the church: among the older members of the church reform movement, many, such as the pope, Bishop Athanasios, Bishop Gregorios, Bishop Samuel, were trained in the humanities. When we move beyond that first generation of founders, born in the decade that spans the mid 1920s to mid 1930s, we find not a single bishop trained in the humanities.

Most of the second-generation bishops in my sample, the pope's spiritual sons born in the decades of the 1950s to 1960s, divide about evenly between the sciences (physicians and engineers) and the technical fields (agronomists, economists). Given the postrevolutionary prestige scale, Bishop Bishoi, a graduate with distinction from the faculty of engineering, would be considered of superior intellectual merit to Bishop Backhum, a graduate of an institute for laboratory technicians, and Bishop Besada, also an engineer, would weigh more than Bishop Lukas, graduate of the faculty of commerce. Even Bishop Amonios, though somewhat lower down on the scale, as a graduate of a veterinary school of medicine, would weigh considerably more than the latter. Yet, as we have seen, Bishops Bishoi, Besada, and Amonios have virtually no economic developmental programs and cultural activities in their dioceses, while Bishops Backhum and Lukas do.

If neither the level of education nor the subject matter determines bishops' accomplishments, their social class does not seem to have a bearing either. The bishops come overwhelmingly from the same class, the middle class. None comes from the ancien régime upper class or even the upper middle class: the "grande bourgeoisie" of financiers, bankers, industrialists, and owners of large department stores or transport vehicles. A few of those in my sample come from the lower middle class. Bishop Murqus's father was an electrician, and Bishop Backhum's father was a tailor. None come from the lower class except for Bishop Bimen, who may be considered from the upper stratum of the lower class inasmuch as his father was not a landless laborer but a small, hard-pressed tenant.[17]

The bishops stem from a traditional milieu, which means religious and native. They spoke Arabic at home, read local authors, watched local movies, and ate native food, in contrast to the ancien régime upper class that was westernized, spoke foreign languages, read foreign books, watched foreign movies, and ate foreign cuisine. They are therefore solidly rooted in Egyptian mores and values.

While the kind of experience a bishop has had prior to the monastery has a lot to do with how he performs later on, one cannot entirely discount personality factors, which may predispose him toward a conservative or progressive stance. Here, a note of caution is in order; for lack of better terminology, this study has had to distinguish between progressive and conservative bishops, the conservative ones being heir to the revivalists' school of thought of St. Anthony Church, whose primary concern was unearthing their spiritual roots (the life and sayings of the ancient church fathers), and the progressive ones being heirs to the activist school of thought of the Giza Church, which was for a church engaged in social work. However, we must be careful not to equate conservative with reactionary. Some of the conservative bishops like Bishop Andrawes of Abu Tig and Bishop Isaiah of Tahta, are open to changes that will benefit their communities and are both zealous and energetic in pursuing such changes, even if their choice of projects falls into the more traditional realm of philanthropy rather than that of development.

For example, Bishop Andrawes, of Abu Tig in Upper Egypt, was a pioneer in bringing spiritual services to the deaf and tried to learn their language himself to be able to communicate with them. He goes to the trouble of collecting them once a week by minibus from all over his diocese and brings them to the hall of his residential compound, where he has a first-rate church-servant instruct them, and often attends their meetings himself.[18] He also has a very well developed Orthodox Brothers of Jesus program with all sorts of services for the poor, and he has built a clinic for the poor and was, when I did my fieldwork, developing an orphanage for them.[19]

Likewise, Bishop Isaiah of neighboring Tahta has managed to build up, step by step, one of the best Orthodox Brothers of Jesus associations. Bishop Isaiah's role model is one of the saints from his hometown, Fayoum, the late Bishop Abraham whose picture is prominently displayed in the entrance to Bishop Isaiah's residence. His charity is legendary. A story has it that he took off his black cashmere mantle, a gift from a town dignitary who had traveled to Great Britain, and gave it to a beggar. A few days later, that same man spotted it on the beggar and bought it back for the bishop.[20]

Bishop Isaiah has all the poorest of the city of Tahta to lunch at the bishop's residence four times a week (he told me he began with once a week and was hoping by the end of the decade to be able to afford to have them daily). He has also shown considerable concern for the poverty stricken physically handicapped.[21]

This is in sharp contrast to Bishop Fam, who discontinued a lunch program for the poor on the grounds that it would be better to invest the money to help the poor raise the poultry than to feed it to them.[22] Not surprisingly, Bishop Isaiah is not one of his admirers and though they are neighbors, some twenty minutes apart by car, I noticed when I visited him that Bishop Fam's picture did not feature among the many pictures of bishops in his reception room.

Not to say that Bishop Isaiah and Bishop Andrawes have no developmental activities whatsoever. As spiritual sons of Pope Shenuda, both of them have had to open the doors of the dioceses to the socioeconomic programs originating from Cairo. Andrawes created developmental centers in the villages, with the help of the Bishopric of Social Services, as has Isaiah, who tried to bring the peasants such amenities as summer clubs for the village youth and better sanitary and health awareness. (Although the first such joint venture failed because Bishop Isaiah could not tolerate a situation of divided authority, wherein the church-servants sent from Cairo to instruct the locals looked to the capital for instructions. Nor, for that matter, did he care for what he considered the effrontery of these city people, who dared to smoke cigarettes.) Under pressure from the urban youth, Bishop Isaiah even collected money from his former Coptic parishioners in Australia, where he served as a monk-priest, for a computer and video center in the town of Tahta.[23]

In short, there is no implication here that a bishop who is absorbed in matters of the soul is ipso facto closed to the world and hence has no interest in development, as long as he is not single-mindedly obsessed with the liturgy as was the case with Bishop Amonios of Luxor. For example, Bishop Bula of Tanta, an intensely spiritual person whose entire life was a single track between his abode and the church until the day he entered the monastery (virtually his only outing throughout childhood was the Sunday Mass, because he had rheumatic fever),[24] and who to this day stays up for nights on end before the religious feasts to personally wrap the blankets and clothes that are gifts for the poor[25] is, nonetheless, open to suggestions that are not, strictly speaking, philanthropic.

What remains true, however, is that, in addition to being mostly interested in philanthropic projects, such bishops shy away from moneymaking endeavors that could sustain large-scale growth in the welfare sector.

Furthermore, one should not necessarily equate conservative with autocratic and progressive with democratic, for there is no 100 percent correlation. Even if, on the whole, the sample in this study has shown a near perfect correlation between development-oriented bishops and democratic ones. The development-oriented bishops need to tap local resources for their projects, both in terms of donations and expertise, which of necessity makes them listen to people's suggestions and criticisms. But there are some exceptions to this rule. Bishop Isaiah's diocese best exemplifies the possibility of development under an autocratic regime, such as we have seen in certain countries of Asia and Latin America. The priests in his diocese are so afraid of incurring his displeasure that they abstain from any initiative. Several of his priests complained to me of being rebuked or publicly humiliated by him for not consulting him on some small matter or other, and others told me they had left the diocese altogether because of mistreatment. The priest in charge of the diocesan headquarters of Shubra al-Kheima, at the time I did my fieldwork there, had fled the enlightened despotism of Bishop Isaiah of Tahta for the liberal administration of Bishop Murqus.

The extent to which the priests fear Bishop Isaiah became evident to me as soon as I arrived in Tahta. I found Bishop Isaiah was not back from the village, where he was celebrating Mass and I asked the priest if he could show me the church-run carpentry on the premises, while we were waiting for the bishop to return. But he declined, saying he could not show me *anything* without the bishop's express permission. Therefore, I decided to spend the time strolling through the town until the bishop returned. But he ran after me, stopping me at the gate to tell me that I could not leave the premises without the bishop's permission. When I showed him that I could and, later, meandered into a church in the center of town, it was the church janitor's turn to run after me, saying no visitor was allowed into a church in Tahta without the bishop's permission.

I had much the same experience as a guest of Bishop Bishoi in the Christian rural precinct of St. Dimiana, which houses a nunnery and a consecration home for laywomen. On arrival in the reception room, I felt myself cringe with embarassment at the sight of a tottering old priest, his long white beard literally brushing the floor, crawling at the bishop's feet begging his forgiveness. And when, after a number of days there, I tried to leave the bishop's compound, my car was stopped at the gate and my chauffeur informed by the guard that no one was allowed to leave St. Dimiana without the bishop's permission. Since the bishop was napping, this entailed a long delay. (In this case, there was a correlation between the autocratic predisposition of the bishop and the lack of development I observed in his diocese.)

By contrast, in most of the development-oriented dioceses, such as among others those of Bishops Arsanios and Fam where I did extensive fieldwork, I went and came as I pleased and spoke to whomever I chose, without any interference from the bishop.

The Problem of Recruitment: The Priests

Aside from access to a big town's industrial, mercantile, or tourist revenues, a bishop has a great advantage if his jurisdiction is over a university town or one adjacent to a university, because he can easily recruit educated church-servants and priests. For example, Qusia is a small rural diocese, but because it is near

Assiut, the provincial capital, Bishop Thomas was able at the time I did my fieldwork to ordain nine priests with university degrees: a medical doctor, a lawyer, three agricultural engineers, a geologist, and three teachers.[26] They acted as antidotes to the veteran priests who opposed his reform plans.[27] He was also able to recruit ten first-rank church-servants to assist him in his developmental activities (five medical doctors, two agricultural engineers, a geologist, and two teachers).[28]

The need to infuse the villages with new blood in the form of educated church-servants turned priests was particularly pressing in Upper Egypt, because the priests in that area were frequently both ignorant and, if not corrupt, at the very least mercenary, catering to the rich and neglecting the poor. Even if the priest was not illiterate or dishonest, he might, particularly if he was an older man, simply resist on conservative grounds any change that a young *khādim*, or bishop, was trying to introduce—especially if that priest was not going to be in charge of its implementation. In one case under study, for instance, the priest was only willing to encourage people to make use of a clinic newly set up by the Bishopric of Social Services in his village if his brother was put in charge of it. The peasants often covered long distances on foot to get to the clinic only to find that it was closed, because the priest's brother was late or failed to appear. When they became discouraged and stopped coming, Dr. Maurice, the program director at the Bishopric of Social Services, tried to persuade a volunteer physician to take over its management. But the priest would not hear of it.[29] (Often, in small villages the priest's family controls most of the church activities. Thus, the priest's cousin may be on the church committee, a son may be in charge of Sunday school, his wife might be head of the nursery, a nephew might be in charge of the vocational program, and so on.) Although in theory the priests are supposed to obey the bishop regardless of his age, in fact, older priests often look down on thirty-year-old bishops. Bishop Thomas, who was appointed bishop in 1989 at the age of thirty-three over the diocese of Qusia, ran into stiff opposition from two veteran priests who were old enough to remember having taught the pope theology when he was still a youngster.[30]

Much the same welcome greeted Bishop Bula, who was appointed bishop of Tanta at the age of thirty-seven. The priests of Tanta, who were used to dealing with his septuagenarian predecessor, the autocratic Bishop Johanna, paid scant attention at their first meeting to his declaration of intentions, which included a number of sweeping cultural reforms. These new ideas, which they dismissed as youthful impetuousness, would soon be dropped, or so they hoped. But at the next meeting, they learned that they had underestimated the resolve and the mettle of this soft-spoken, smiling young bishop, and that he had every intention of pushing ahead with his planned reforms, over and above their protests against sponsoring activities for mixed groups of boys and girls, which they believed would court disaster.[31]

Often, even if a priest does not express his opposition vocally at a meeting with the bishop, his passive non-cooperation is enough to ensure the failure of a venture, because he may be the chief authority figure and role model in the village, or his church may be the only place large enough to accommodate an assembly of people for any communal activity. Examples of non-cooperation I encountered were a priest who would not open the church for a church-servant to offer a literacy course, because he objected to the hanging of posters such as "Learning is Light" on the church walls. He thought a church should be reserved for pictures of the Virgin and the saints.[32] In another case, people found that they were often barred from access to the church library in the evenings, because the priest was making money renting this space to wedding parties.[33] In a third case, the priest refused to support a campaign to encourage parents to allow their daughters to attend church-sponsored activities for girls because, as he said, he did not approve of girls leaving their homes other than for purposes of Communion.[34]

The success of any new venture, therefore, whether it be a women's conference, a church-run clinic or a church library, often depends on the priest's participation, because the peasants, who are themselves illiterate, may not teach reading to their children, fathers may not allow their daughters to set foot outside the house, a man with a recurrent kidney pain may prefer to put a talisman under his pillow than to see a doctor, and an infertile woman may go to a priest to put his hand on her stomach and recite a prayer, instead of seeking help from a gynecologist. The late Bishop Bimen, who had he lived would have been today, alongside Bishop Arsanios, a beacon of the social work endeavor, recalled that when one day he announced before mass that no one would be given Communion who was wearing a charm or harboring a talisman, he collected over 320 such items from the churchyard.[35] In another instance I witnessed, in the Upper Egyptian diocese of Abu Tig, a woman came up to the *mukarasa*, who had just held a mass meeting for the subsistence level families receiving a monthly allowance from the Orthodox Brothers of Jesus Association (*Ikhwāt al-Rabb*) that I attended, and told her that even though she had had the priest pray for her daughter, the girl was still sickly with a chronic fever. When the *mukarasa* suggested that she bring her to the church-run clinic, the mother answered that she would first have her undergo a clitorectomy; maybe that would help. The *mukarasa* did not try to dissuade the woman or suggest she would be better off bringing her to the clinic, even though the church, officially, is against clitorectomy. She just smiled at her benignly, as one might at a foolish child, and walked away.[36]

There is not much the bishop can do if a priest is unenthusiastic about his reform proposals and will not exert himself on their behalf. Although in theory a bishop can punish an obstructionist priest by defrocking him (a sanction known as *ḥurman*), it is a weapon he resorts to only in extreme cases, such as corruption or womanizing (Orthodox priests are considered "wed" to their churches, just as the bishops are to their dioceses.) Some of the bishops, like Bishop Lukas of Abnub, whose avant guardism owes much to the influence of

Bishop Bimen's writings that crowd his bookshelves, tries to use his weekly meetings with the priests to socialize them and to persuade them to support his reform plans. He himself travels the villages indefatigably to lecture on the dangers of belief in sorcery and the magical power of amulets, which people commonly carry about with bits of scroll written out by the priests in the Coptic language. He has also instructed his church-servants to discuss social issues, not just spiritual ones, in their meetings with the peasants. Under the influence of the late Bishop Bimen, who devotes a central part of his book, *The Village and Development* (*al-Khidmah fī al-qarya*), to the plight of girls in the villages and the connivance of village priests in instances of forced marriages, Bishop Lukas has encouraged girls to participate in church activities. He instituted mixed youth meetings, which he presided over himself for the first two years, so the parents would have no objections to allowing their daughters to attend.[37] (To this day, in most villages of Upper Egypt, youth meetings tend to mean boys' meetings; even the idea of sending girls to an all-girls meeting is not yet fully accepted.)[38]

However, rather than trying to reeducate the older retrograde priests, in Upper Egypt, most bishops resort to a procedure known as doubling, which amounts to leaving the old priests in their churches but confining them to celebrating Mass. The socioeconomic and cultural development of the villages is entrusted to priests newly graduated from Cairo's theological seminary or to monk-priests or to church-servants with university degrees recently recruited to the priesthood.

One of the chief concerns of bishops is to keep a sharp lookout for outstanding church-servants in Cairo, in their own diocese, and in their neighbor's backyard and to try to persuade them to take the priestly vows. In the course of this study, for instance, Bishop Fam succeeded in inducing two outstanding church-servants to leave Cairo and join his staff as priests in Tima. Father Abraham, who as a laymen had been a longtime volunteer in the Bishopric of Social Services, was placed in charge of developmental activities and Father Wisa, a graduate of Cairo's Theological Seminary, was entrusted with youth programs. He was actively campaigning, while I was doing fieldwork in Tima, to persuade a third church-servant, Mīlād Murqus, in charge of youth programs in Tima, to take his vows. As is often the case, resistance to the offer came from Murqus's wife, who according to what he told me, did not want him to give up his comfortable pay at the bank for the minimal wage that the church offered him as a priest.[39] Meanwhile, in Qusia, Bishop Thomas informed me that he had just lost his best church-servant, the director of his youth programs, to the neighboring diocese of Manfalut. Bishop Antonios of Manfalut had managed to lure him away and ordain him as a priest, because he could afford to offer him a decent salary while Bishop Thomas, who was in financial difficulty at the time, could not.[40] Bishop Thomas's small rural diocese was so poor that he was forced to sell his own car to raise the LE 30,000 (a little under $10,000) owed a property owner who was threatening the church with eviction from a building he was renting out as a church-run nursery.[41]

To sum up, having ruled out age, level of education, field of study, and social class as determining factors in a bishop's orientation and performance, one is forced to return to my original premise, that the single most important variable is experience. A bishop who had considerable experience as a layperson makes both a better governor of people and administrator of projects than does one with little or no experience. This holds as much for the oldest generation of bishops who, at the time of this study, were in their sixties (for example, Bishop Arsanios and bishop Athamasios) as for the second generation who were in their forties (for example, Bishop Fam, who had considerable experience as a mining engineer in Kenya in charge of Muslim miners), as for the third generation in its thirties, such as Bishop Tackla, who had wide exposure as a church-servant administering the village of Birket al-Tira in Menufia governorate. These experiences taught them how to move men to do their bidding in democratic ways, by listening to them and learning from their criticisms.

PART V

The Church as Cultural Agent

II

Culture and Hegemony

"Islam Is the Solution"

To observe the gradual eclipse in Egypt of the Coptic cultural orbit by Islam, we have to backtrack to the middle of the twentieth century.

President Nasser, 1952–1970: Islamizing the Schools

The revolutionary junta that came to power in 1952 was drawn from the lower middle class, whose cultural mooring was religious, hence Islamic. The leading cadres of the conspiratorial movement of the Free Officers did not feature a single Christian (possibly because of the underrepresentation of religious and ethnic minorities in the Egyptian military academy).[1] Unlike members of the old regime, not a single member of the junta had studied in the West, and few spoke a foreign language. Thus, they had not come into contact with western secular thinkers or with the notion of the separation of church and state. And though Nasser himself was not wed to any particular ideology when he first came to power (he had ties at different times to a variety of political groupings), other members of the junta had had close ties with the Muslim Brotherhood. One of them, Kamāl al-Din Hussein, came to head the Ministry of Education, which played a key role in determining a person's life chances in the new revolutionary era. Henceforth, one's position was no longer merely a function of family connections and wealth but also of merit: Nasser had opened up the universities to the lower-middle and lower classes, by making them tuition-free, and launched an intensive indoctrination campaign aimed at persuading ordinary

Egyptians to realize that higher education was the panacea for their ills and for Egypt's. The new regime's emphasis on rapid economic development, which generated a need for technical expertise, lent the sciences prestige at the expense of the humanities and law, fields that had been highly prized by the ancien régime—particularly the latter. (Engineering and medicine did not have as much aura before the revolution of 1952, since they were traditionally middle-class professions). The competition centering around the faculty to which one was admitted became fierce, because the sons of electricians, plumbers, railroad workers, petty merchants, school teachers, and accountants were no longer content to follow their fathers' trades: they wanted to be medical doctors and engineers.

It was therefore not only an issue of getting one's children into university but of getting them into the right faculties. Nasser did try to ensure fair admission to universities, by setting up a national board of examiners for grading papers and a department for channeling examinees to faculties in accordance with grade point averages. But loopholes in the system fanned religious prejudice. One example was the grants for study abroad, important because these grantees became the better paid professionals following their return home. The grants were handled by the Ministry of Education, headed by a minister with biases acquired through his close association with the Muslim Brotherhood before the revolution. Since at each stage between applications and selections for study abroad the candidate had to face a Muslim-dominated screening committee, it is very easy to see how the final list could be biased in favor of the Muslims.

Officially, grant funds were allotted in accordance with the needs of the country and the amount of money from external and internal sources at the disposal of the Egyptian government. Each student was expected to repay the government by working for it for approximately twice the number of his grant years. But it is clear that these were not the sole criteria and that religious bias influenced in the selection process. A Coptic medical student who had graduated with the grade "very good" was bypassed in favor of two Muslims with grades of "good." When this student appealed to the government for redress, he was told that all the grant money had been used up and that he should try again the following year.[2]

At the university level prejudice against the Copts began to be evident at the level of appointments to the position of lecturer (*muid*), a position that in the past was given to graduating students who excelled, irrespective of religious affiliation. Attempts were also made to limit the number of Christian students admitted to certain faculties, like gynecology, because it was thought to be improper for a Christian to see a Muslim woman's private parts. The same policy applied to instructions of Arabic, on the grounds that a sound knowledge of Arabic only came through a mastery of the Koran.

The inequality of opportunities for all citizens was perhaps less damaging than the tampering with the educational curriculum. Nasser himself had no interest in religion per se. His Arabization of the schools was a nationalistic reaction to the cultural imperialism of the British occupying power. Prior to the revolution of 1952, it was not uncommon for members of the upper classes who were fluent in more than one foreign language not to be able to read and write their own properly, because the private British and French schools they attended did not deign to teach Arabic. French was the medium of polite conversation in the ancien régime; Arabic was relegated to discourse with one's servants. Not only was the paperwork in all the banks and commercial enterprises carried out in French, but even some official government correspondence up until the 1940s.

But Islam had a definite hold on Nasser's minister of Education, Kamāl al-Din Hussein, who revealed his attitude from the start by modifying the school curriculum to have extracts of the Koran and poems in praise of the prophet Muhammad, as well as sections on Islamic history, incorporated into the textbooks. Despite the protest of Christian parents, Hussein would not back down until a confrontation arose over a required textbook, written by a converted Christian, that advocated the supremacy of Islam over all other religions. The minister himself had written a foreword to it, in which he praised the book as "a brick in the foundation of spiritual unity, uniting our people in a common faith in Allah, the One."[3] In face of the outrage of Christians, who considered the author of the book, Nazmi Luka, a traitor, the minister was forced to rescind the order that this book be a required text. It nonetheless remained on the official textbook list.

The nationalization of the economy also meant that the biases of the state bureaucrats, who ran the state enterprises, could affect the career opportunities of the new generation of Christian graduates to a far greater extent than before, when Christian and Jewish minorities had occupational niches in the private sector. It is true that Nasser had passed a new law in the 1960s guaranteeing all university graduates government employment. Christians, like Muslims—the sons and daughters of the lower-middle and upper-lower classes—were to benefit from this law, just as they had from free university education. But, though they had equal access to government jobs, their chances of promotion within the state-run enterprises were not equal. There was an unwritten rule that a Copt could progress to the rank of vice president of a company or business enterprise and no farther. Outside of the one or two token Copts, much the same rule applied to governmental departments and ministries.

When Amīn Fikri was director of the Bank of Egypt, in the '60s, Nasser opposed his decision to appoint a Copt to the bank's board of administration. Fikri's persistence in openly and defiantly championing the Copt is one of the factors that led to his ouster from this bank. Promotions within the nationalized banks were a particularly controversial issue in those days, because prior to the revolution the Copts had figured prominently among the senior staff and directors of banks. Their competence in money matters was rooted in their historical experience of accounting, tax assessment, and moneylending—pursuits that had been left to the Copts as well as to other minorities until the late nineteenth century—so that on the eve of the revolution they were vastly overrepresented in the Ministry of Finance. Once Nasser opened up the universities to the middle classes, their skill with figures became evident in the large enrollment of Copts in the faculty of engineering. The new regime had, therefore, to overturn the normal considerations of experience, seniority, and performance to place Muslims in positions habitually occupied by Copts.[4]

As a colonial country Egypt had been dominated economically by a foreign bourgeoisie most of whose members emigrated soon after the king's overthrow. In their absence the role of investment fell by default to the state. While it had been possible before the revolution for a Copt and other members of Egypt's religious and ethnic minorities to live their entire life outside of the political orbit, this new dependence on the state for jobs meant that henceforth equal access to economic resources hinged on equal access to political power. Thus, for Christians who wished to ensure their own livelihood and their children's, it was important whether or not they had access to power. And it became increasingly evident over time that the Christians were being squeezed out of most influential government posts.

Another institution that suffered because of Egypt's pan-Arab direction was the Foreign Ministry, which showed a marked deterioration in the ratio of Christians to Muslims. A comparison between the 1952 Egyptian directory, the last one to be compiled before the revolution, and the 1959 directory shows that in 1952 there were ten Christians and seventy-seven Muslims employed in the higher echelons of the Foreign Ministry in Cairo. That number had dropped to five Christians by 1959 even though the number of Muslims working in the Foreign Ministry had tripled, to 226. The ratio of Christians assigned to embassies, legations, and consulates had also deteriorated, dropping from seven Christians to 231 Muslims to five Christians (three of whom were appointed back in the reign of King Farouk) to 378 Muslims.[5]

In over two decades of rule, Nasser appointed only two Christians to ambassadorships, both to small countries (Burma and Nepal). This may not have been due to any particular prejudice on his part against the Christians or to a conscious desire to deny them equal participation in the state, but rather to his increasing realization that Egypt was compelled to seek political alliances with the Arab states. The extent to which he needed the support of these states had been dramatically demonstrated to him shortly after he came to power. He had seen the Arab oil embargo used effectively to stymie the tripartite invasion of Egypt by Britain, France, and Israel that followed his nationalization of the Suez Canal in 1956. Ever since, his priority became to instill in Egypt's predominately Muslim masses a commitment to Arab unity. If in the process it meant raising the slogan of a common faith and pushing the Christians to the sideline—so be it. Presumably it was a regrettable but a necessary price to pay: The problems of minorities were clearly not his primary concern.

President Sadat, 1970–1981: Islamizing the Media

If Islamic themes began to permeate the school curriculum during the Nasser years, it was under Sadat that they captured the media. The Islamic programs were allotted thirty hours on the radio, which was government-controlled, as opposed to the mere half hour allotted to the Christian programs—the broadcast of the liturgy on Sunday. Islam also made rapid inroads into television programming. In addition to the Friday sermon, which was televised live and followed by the popular commentary and question-answer series with the flamboyant Sheikh Sha'rawi, there were a plethora of Islamic religious programs. (This trend was to continue under Mubarak, with programs ranging from theological series such as that of Sheikh Omar 'Abd al-Kāfi entitled *Judgment Day*, to films about the prophet and his military campaigns, such as one shown during the Ramadan fast in 1993 entitled *Prophet of Islam*, and to the series for children called *Sons of Islam*.)[6]

Sadat no doubt calculated that granting the Islamists more airtime was a cheap way to buy their favor—and perhaps simultaneously a way to pull the rug out from underneath their feet by having the state show an interest in Islam. That his conscience was not much troubled by the concept of equal time is evident from the fact that a Christian program was allowed to be featured on television only once a year, during the Orthodox Christmas (January 7), when the pope's address was televised. The Copts had a highly regarded representative on the committee of the media in the person of the vice minister of Culture, Magdi Wahba, who voiced their demands that their pope receive greater coverage—they wanted his receptions for local state dignitaries as well as his visits to the United States, Australia, and Europe covered—and that they be given one full time radio station such as that given to Muslims entitled *The Holy Koran*. But even their more modest request, put forward by Magdi Wahba, that the time allotted for the radio broadcasting of the Sunday liturgy be increased from half an hour to one full hour had fallen on deaf ears, despite the personal regard that Sadat held for Magdi Wahba[7] (Wahba was a professor of English literature at Cairo University who had sat on the examining committee of Sadat's wife, Jihan).

President Mubarak's Losing Battle against Islamic Militancy

By the end of the century, Islam was everywhere in the day-to-day life of Egyptians—including that of the new upper middle class of businessmen, real estate agents, merchants, dealers in spare parts, professionals, and government officials, all of whom had profited greatly from the economic aperture under Sadat. Being themselves upwardly mobile members of the middle and lower middle class, they were far more attuned to the religiosity of the lower orders.

The new wave of popular enthusiasm for Islam could be seen in the construction of special reserved areas for prayer called *Zawiyyah* in many of the posh new buildings, in the proliferation of privately built mosques and of fund-raisers in the streets for such purposes, and in the work stoppages in the government bureaucracy and on worksites during the call to prayer (five times a day) and the gathering of prayer groups in the corridors of all such public buildings.

Sleep stoppages were also in order, as the minarets blared out their call on loudspeakers at dawn, in every nook and cranny of the city, wrenching its somnolent citizens, willi-nilly, out of their beds. Even such exclusive preserves as the island of Zamalek, once considered a bastion of privilege and secularism, was no longer immune. The invading nouveau riche had brought with them their veils and their minarets to its very heart, the Gezira Sporting club.

Moreover, all the newsbriefs on the government-run television are now interrupted during the call to prayer and the nightly closure of televised programs consists in a reading from the Koran. Religious programs on television continue to multiply, including daily lessons at 3:30 PM, given by the Ulema from al-Azhar University, and the very popular Tuesday night program *Science and Religion* (*al-Ilm wa al-Iman*), in addition to the standard fare of sermons and ensuing commentary on Friday at 11 AM and at 2:30 PM.

Member of Parliament Dr. Rifʿat Said pointed out the subtle ways in which children are indoctrinated. When he was a schoolboy, his civics book, which was printed by the Ministry of Education, exhorted the pupils to wash their hands before and after eating. Today, the phrase has been altered to read: "A *good Muslim* washes his hands before and after eating." Are Christian children supposed to deduce from that that they, as inferior beings, are not expected to wash their hands, he asked?[8]

In other areas, the media emphasize the superiority of being a Muslim[9] by inviting European converts to Islam, like French philosopher Roger Garaudi, to extol its virtues,[10] or by publishing articles like "Western Women Take the Veil," as well as by discussing the repentance and return to Islam of secular celebrities like the movie star Shadia (as many as twenty-seven movie stars "repented" and took the veil in the decade spanning the mid-'80s to mid-'90s). This figure takes on additional significance if one considers that, for the average Egyptian, the fact that a movie star allows herself to be kissed and fondled by the male lead makes her only one notch above a prostitute.[11]

President Sadat's successor, Hosni Mubarak, who took over the government after his assassination in 1981, was aware of the danger posed to his regime by the forces it had nurtured. But by the time the government in the 1990s concluded that brutal force alone would not quell Islamic militancy, and Mubarak's minister of Education tried a new approach, a whole generation had grown up on Islamist propaganda in their schools and mosques, and on radio and television. The announcement of the minister of Culture that he had asked the media, in its covering of events, to differentiate between the correct principles of Islam and "terrorist" interpretations[12] seemed a gesture that was too little to late. (It was sufficiently provocative however to the Islamic militants to warrant an attempt on his life.)

The government's efforts to exercise tighter control over the mosques was another response to the extremist threat.[13] Security forces under President Mubarak clamped down on previously tolerated religious activities by militant city youth and, in certain cases, as in November 1992, they even cordoned off a mosque in the Upper Egyptian city of Assiut that was a hotbed of Islamic militancy, to prevent a weekly meeting. But it was as unrealistic to think that the government would take over and control some 70,000 private mosques in Egypt as it was to think that the media could undo overnight the damage of three decades. As the parliamentarian Dr. Rifʿat Said once pointed out, by providing practically unlimited airtime on government-controlled television to sheikhs with narrow-minded notions of Islam, the government had invited the problems it was experiencing. Said said that he could provide a long list of imams who preached hatred against the country's Christian minority.[14]

Extremism is evident also in an anonymous broadsheet that was widely distributed in Minya in 1988, at the time of the attack on the Church of St. Mary:

> Know you crusaders that you are the primary cause for all of Egypt's problems and of those of Minia. You are responsible for the corruption and decay of morals. . . . [Y]ou deal in drugs and in sex, and in pornographic films, and in underground video clubs. You encourage social intercourse between the males and females in our universities, and it is you who betray the activities of the Islamic groups to the government and to the security forces, persuading them that these activities are harmful to national unity. The result is that your churches are protected and our mosques are laid siege to.[15]

To be sure, President Mubarak tried to counter these ideas by publicizing the moderate voices in the government-controlled religious institutions. One of the tenets of the Islamic militants that the government tried to combat was the notion that it was *ḥalal* (a good deed) to loot Christian jewelery stores to finance their groups' activities. Although this pattern of looting was initially confined to the Upper Egyptian regions (such as the incident in Abu Korkas in 1986), it soon spread to Lower Egypt, where Jihad members attacked a jewelery store in Shubra al-Kheima in February 1991, following that up with another attack on a store in Heliopolis two months later.[16] Even small stores, like the one in the village of Khusus in the province of al-Qalyubia, were not spared. The government encouraged the formation of a committee of respected Islamic scholars to refute extremist ideas—particularly that any property or money owned by Christians is fair game.[17]

It also tried to avail itself of the moderate voice of the mufti (supreme religious leader) Dr. Muhammad Sayed Tantawi to challenge the arguments used by Islamic militants to justify their armed attacks on atheists and apostates. Dr. Tantawi maintained that, contrary to the Islamic militants' arguments, the prophet Muḥammad's injunctions as quoted in the Hadith (the prophet's sayings), "Whoever of you sees an evil action, let him change it with his hand, and if he is not able to do so then with his tongue, and if he is not able to do so then with his heart" does not give all Muslims the right to set themselves up as judges over others and to prosecute and punish them on the grounds that this constitutes justice.[18]

However, Sheikh Tantawi was put on the Islamic militant's hit list, and their attempt to assassinate the minister of Information was meant to signal their opposition to the new policy he advocated for the media and to warn the various media networks against any plan to join the government-sponsored anti-Islamist campaign. The fact that the government did not have recourse to any of these state-affiliated Islamic establishment figures—the mufti, the Sheik of al-Azhar, the Islamic University, and the minister of Property in Mortmain—when it needed go-betweens to the Jihad and al-jamā ʿa al-Islāmiyya groups underscores the irrelevance of their support of the regime (all three of these religious high officials were on a hit list of the Islamic militant groups, according to police sources).[19]

But the more pertinent question is how significant the difference is between the moderates and the extremists. Is it true, as parliamentarian Dr. Rifʿat Said said, that no more than a hairline separated the two and that regardless of whether the moderates or the extremists came to power the result would be the same—the execution of persons opposed to their views?[20] The trial of the alleged assassin of secular journalist and writer Farag Foda lends some credence to this view. Foda, who was shot down in October 1992 by the Jihad, had infuriated the Islamists with his critical articles and books. One of these, *The Trick*, exposed the malpractices of the Islamic banks, which robbed thousands of Egyptians of their savings, and another, *The Absent Duty*, attacked the idea of an Islamic state. Just before he was killed, he had publicly made fun of the Islamists for wanting among other things to ban satellite television. Foda had remarked sarcastically that they would soon ban on the consumption of zucchini and eggplant on account of their suggestive shapes.[21]

He stood out among the silent liberals as a courageous man, who did not hesitate to take on fundamentalist audiences of several hundred angry and abusive men. Though a Muslim, he was committed to the cause of equal rights for Christians and tried to raise the money to found a party called *al-Mustakbal* (The Future) jointly with Christians, which would fight for the principle of a secular Egypt. But his party was unable to gather enough supporters in the increasingly antagonistic climate.[22]

Sheikh al-Ghazālī, considered a moderate, who was called upon to testify before the civil court that was trying Foda's alleged assassin, said that the presence of an apostate inside the community constituted a threat to the nation: someone who kills an apostate may be committing a crime before the state, he said, but he was not committing a sin against God. He added that he himself favored life imprisonment for an apostate: "[H]e should be given a chance to repent, but if he does not he should be killed."[23] These remarks infuriated the supporters of Foda, who felt that the victim Foda had been put on trial, not the murderer. They objected to the way al Gazali was arrogating to himself the right to accuse others of atheism, saying it only aided those who sought to achieve political power through terror.[24]

Fahmy Howeidi, a moderate Islamist writer who defended Sheikh Ghazālī's stand during the Foda trial, declared that a person was an apostate if he seceded from Islam[25] or if he defamed it by openly insulting its laws, respected figures, or teachings. Herein lies the significance of the opposition to the passage of the law of apostasy, which was championed by Sadat. For had he succeeded in getting the draft law passed, it would have meant than anyone who disagreed with the Islamists could be branded an atheist and therefore be put up for execution. Indeed, shortly after the Foda trial, an Egyptian novelist/playwright was sentenced to prison on the grounds of his "atheism."

Not only people are eliminated if their views are considered offensive, but also their works. The weekly magazine *Rūz al Yūsef* reported in January 1993 that the head of the Egyptian Organization for Human Rights sent a secret letter to the director of the Egyptian Book Organization inquiring about the complaints of writers whose books had disappeared from the bookstores and libraries.[26] These books include the complete works of the assassinated writer Farag Foda, a novel by Edward al-Kharat, *Creatures of Flying Passion,* and an anthology by the poet Hasan Teleb, the *Sura J* (al-Kharat, along with literary critic Ghālī Shukri, both of whom are Christian, have been accused by the Islamists of being missionaries who portray Egyptian society in a Christian way and seek to implant a Christian culture in a Muslim country).

Al-Azhar University's self-appointed censorship committee claims it confines its role to scrutinizing and reviewing books related to Islam. Yet this public stand is contradicted by the mysterious silence it maintained on the subject of banned books. The authors of these books were in a Kafkaesque situation in which they were not told who was passing judgment on them, nor where they might seek redress. The banning of films by al-Azhar was likewise shrouded in mystery; sometimes that ban was publicly declared but sometimes it was known only by chance. Some writers felt that once their films were submitted to al-Azhar for scrutiny, they were confiscated and irretrievably lost. The gifted scriptwriter Salah Abu Seif sought in vain for some eighteen years to obtain a license for his film *Marry and Live Happily,* because al-Azhar did not approve its focus on the sexual apathy of a man. Only when Abu Seif submitted a revised script, in which he added some koranic verses and a religious figure, was he able to obtain al-Azhar's approval. The same fate awaited another film entitled *A Lady's Threshold,* which dealt with a barren woman who went to a sorcerer. She hypnotized her and impregnated her by means of a piece of cotton soaked in sperm.[27]

In 1992, just before the yearly international book festival was due to open—a big event in Egypt where books published in the West are often hard to get or in short supply—Sheikh Muḥammad Khalifa Abdullah led the book-banning campaign. He confiscated four books by state councillor Said al-Ashmawi, a secularist: *The Islamic Caliphate, Political Islam, Usury and Interest,* and *Aspects of the Sharia.* Also banned were *Behind the Veil,* by female social scientist Sanā' al-Maṣrī, *Bombs and Holy Books,* by ʿAdel Ḥamuda, and *The Naked,* by Ibrāhim ʿĪsā.

The same fate even befell government publications. For example, the government tried to combat the ideas of the extremists by having the General Book Organization publish a series entitled *Confrontation,* which reintroduced the moderate nineteenth- and early-twentieth-century religious thinkers like Gamal al-Din al-Afghani and Muḥammad ʿAbdu, as well as liberal writers from the same period, to the reading public. Sheikh ʿAbd al-Mutajallī, a member of al-Azhar's Fatwa Council (the Islamic University's legal council), demanded that the government-sponsored series be banned since the series contained two books that called for a secular state, one of which was a reissue of a book by ʿAlī Abd al-Rāziq that had been banned by al Azhar when it was first published in 1925.[28]

Although the opinions of al-Azhar's board of censorship are not binding on the government, it has had considerable influence. For example, the series on "terrorism," *Confrontation,* disappeared from the bookstands after al-Azhar publicized its disapproval.[29]

Whatever the ultimate outcome of the contest of wills between the government and al-Azhar, it is certain that if al-Azhar were ever to obtain the legal right to ban books, then these books could come to be regarded by the public as blasphemous or at the very least against Islam. This, as the Administrative Court Justice Said al-Ashmawi warned, would justify the execution of their writers as apostates.[30]

Al-Azhar, however, feels confident of widespread popular support of its role as the defender of Islam by virtue of the upsurge of religiosity. For example, the best-selling books in fin de siècle Egypt were not the novels of Nobel Prize laureate Nagib Mahfuz—or any works of fiction, for that matter—but the *Tafsirs* (commentary on the Koran) of Sheikh Shaʿrawi, the prime-time television preacher, whose program on Fridays, the Muslim day off, is avidly watched by millions of viewers. Sheikh Shaʿrawi, who was chosen by Mubarak as a man acceptable to the Muslim militants to mediate between them and the government, drew upon himself the wrath of the Egyptian Orthodox Church more than once for ridiculing in public the concept of the Virgin Birth and the trinity and for his insinuations that Jesus *knew* Mary Magdalene in the biblical sense of the term.[31]

The works of two other sheikhs are very popular: those of Sheikh Muḥammad al-Ghazālī, considered, like Sheikh Shaʿrawi, a moderate acceptable to the regime, and that of Said Kotb, who was imprisoned by Nasser after an assassination attempt on him by the Muslim Brotherhood. Kotb's books were smuggled out of his prison cell, printed, and distributed clandestinely, and they are known to be among the writings that inspired the Jihad group in its assassination of President Sadat. No books sell as well as these, outside of the Koran itself which is a popular gift item—particularly in its paperback desk edition and its mini pocket edition. Outside of books, fiery preachers like Shaʿrawi and Omar Abd al-Kafi do a thriving business selling their tapes, which are full of anti-Christian allusions and oblique attacks on the secular regime.[32]

The taste for this kind of material was cultivated by the school system and the media. Islam, as we have seen, began, under Nasser, to be injected into the textbooks of Arabic language, history, and civics in ever greater doses (on top of the religious instruction per se which became mandatory for every child). Though Christian children had their own religious instruction, they were bound to study and be examined in the extracts from the Koran, which came to replace the modern Arabic poetry that was in fashion before the revolution. Instead of memorizing, as in the past, verses of the romantic poet Ahmad Shawki, a Christian child would henceforth have to memorize and recite the liturgical introduction to the Koran or verses extolling the noble exploits of the prophet Muhammad for his Arabic language class.

Witness the occlusion of Christianity by Islam in the Egyptian cultural orbit as reflected in this extract from a secondary school reading and comprehension textbook:

> You are the best people amongst mankind. Proclaim the Holy Message, prevent all that is sinful and believe in God. [By implication the Muslims are a chosen *Ummah*, or community.][33]

Or this text on moral purity, which asks why Muslim morality has not been upheld and concludes:

> The affliction which now besets us comes from the winds of the West. We have fallen a powerless nation under the influence of foreign powers, whose ways of behavior conflict with ours as Muslims.[34]

And what is one to make of the fact that only 4 out of 240 pages are allotted to the four centuries of Christian Egypt? In short, the only form of civilization which Coptic students are introduced to in school is Islamic civilization.

The cultural hegemony of Islam, the foundations of which had been laid by Nasser, was consolidated by Sadat at the outset of his rule in 1971, when he stipulated that not only was Islam to be part the school core curriculum but that a religious exam was henceforth to be a requirement for admission to university. With this background, one can better understand the odds that Mubarak's minister of education was up against when, in March 1992, he resolved to reform the teacher-training colleges and the national curriculum to combat religious extremism. For example, he was much criticized when, in an attempt to inculcate tolerance toward people of different faiths, he removed an account of the prophet Muhammad's victories over the Jews from the school curriculum. The pro Islamist paper *al-Sha'b* editorialized:

> It would seem that this tampering with the educational curriculum is a way of silencing the opposition to the normalisation of relations with Israel, to the World Bank's funding of the Educational Development Center in Egypt, and to the American funding of its schools. . . . In Israel children study the Old Testament with all of its religious wars. Yet here we are removing prophet Muhammad's encounters with the Jews. . . . [M]eanwhile there is material about birth control and living abroad in the new textbook for teenagers, *Egypt Is My Country*. This should be taken out, not the chronicles of prophet Muhammad.[35]

This sort of criticism was replicated in other papers.

The problem for the minister of education was that while it might have been possible to purge the textbooks, it was not possible to change the mentality of those who explained the textbooks, at least not overnight. As the minister himself put it, some of the educational faculties had "turned into nothing but labs graduating teachers supporting terrorist ideas."[36] He further intimated that some teachers were deliberately planted in the educational institutions to proselytize the ideas of the Islamic groups, which in turn provoked a scathing attack from the heads of the clubs of the teaching staff.[37] That there was not terribly much the minister could do about the teachers is evidenced by his attempt to have a teacher removed from school for playing an inflammatory tape of Sheikh Abd al-Hamid Kishk on the suffering that sinners (by implication, the Christians) would be exposed to after their death. After the minister of Education transferred the teacher from the province of Qalyubia in Lower Egypt to Kena in Upper Egypt (a less desirable location, because Upper Egypt is considered a backwater) and expelled four girls involved in introducing the tape to the school, there was a furious popular backlash against the town's Christians. The local governor, anxious to appease the mobs, issued an invitation over the mosques' loudspeakers for the expelled girls to return to their school, thereby overruling the minister. When the minister went on television on March 13, 1993, to reassert the expulsion order, the mobs firebombed the local church. An emergency session of the ministerial cabinet was hastily convened, and the minister of education was compelled to readmit the girls. As for the teacher, she was said to be on "temporary sick leave"; the minister was forced to concede that he would consider her reapplication when she recovered. Thus on March 15, the voice of the people defeated the liberal minister.[38]

In this case, the tape was brought to the minister of education's attention by a Christian schoolgirl's complaint. The complainants however are not only Christians. In November 1992, a Muslim girl complained to a local weekly magazine that the headmistress slapped her across the face when she arrived at school without her veil. The headmistress in question, of a secondary school in Mansura (Lower Egypt), a stronghold of the Muslim fundamentalists, when criticized for her policy of compelling all girls attending her school to wear the veil, said in her self-defense that the council of parents (equivalent to the American PTA) had recently met and approved her decision. Here again, although the minister of education announced that the "veil is not compulsory, it is not part of the school uniform," adding that the wearing of the veil should be at the girl's and her family's discretion and that no one could prevent a girl from entering a school because she did not wear a veil, he could not prevail.[39] The headmasters and headmistresses continue to make their own rules, as evidenced by the ruling of the headmaster of the Shagaret al-Dur secondary school for girls that no girl would be allowed to enter the school without a veil. A similar controversy broke out in a secondary school at Helwan (on Cairo's periphery) when a headmaster ruled that all girls in school, including Christians, must wear the veil. He justified this by saying that the veil was the traditional head-scarf of the region—one had to respect people's customs and mores.[40]

The Islamic stranglehold over the universities, where Islamist professors had recourse to verbal intimidation of their secular colleagues, was also apparent. Islamists had become such an intellectual force in the universities that in 1993 they succeeded in denying tenure to a professor, Nasser Abu Zeid, by branding him an atheist. Even as a student, Professor Abu Zeid had shown a decided tendency toward controversial issues by choosing to write about an Islamic tradition that upheld an alternative authority to the Koran and Hadith. He wrote about the ninth-century Muslim theologians, the Muʾtazila, who believed that since God's revelation is rational, reason could be brought into the service of revelation. But what cost him his tenure, and his marriage, was that he dared to question the reliability of the transmission of the Koran, in a historical work published during his term as assistant professor at Cairo University. He tried to demonstrate that at first various tribes had different versions of the Koran, but that in the seventh century the Caliph Uthman compiled the divergent versions into one, that of the Meccan tribe of Quraish, to which both he and the prophet belonged, and ordered all other versions burnt. (Abu Zeid's thesis caused an outcry, because it is an item of faith in Islam that each and every word in the Koran was a direct revelation to the prophet Muhammad from God.) Abu Zeid was immediately accused of heresy; and not content with having succeeded in denying him tenure, they sought a court ruling declaring his marriage to fellow professor Ebtehag Younis null and void, on the grounds that Islamic law prohibited the marriage of an apostate to a believer.

The same pressures were brought to bear, at the student level, on secular students (liberals and Marxists) by Islamic vigilantes. Prayer time was particularly charged with tension, because some of the Muslim students made it a practice to knock on the doors of students who had failed to appear when the *Azan* (the call to prayer from the minaret) sounded.

In the late '70s, there was also considerable tension between Islamic and Christian students: Islamic vigilantes attacked and beat up Christian students in a number of universities. By 1979, the clashes had reached such a pitch that after a number of violent incidents at the Universities of Alexandria, Ein Shams (Heliopolis), Minya and Assiut even Sadat, who had at first encouraged the take-over of the student unions by the Islamists, as a way of edging the Nasserites and leftists out of their predominant position, felt compelled to make a series of tough speeches full of dire warnings directed at the troublemakers.[41]

12

"The Glorious and the Sacred"

Bishop Moses and the Socialization of the Young

The growing presence of militant Islamic groups within the universities and the growing friction between them and the Christian students caused the latter to turn increasingly to the church for support. Previously, the Coptic university groupings known as *Usar jāmiʿīyah Qibṭīyyah* (Coptic university families) had led a fairly autonomous existence. They were created in the fifties by the Sunday School generation. Their founder, Dr. Shafik Abd al-Malik, had grounded them in Cairo's faculty of medicine. He had encouraged the organization of Christian students there, for the purposes of excursions and collective prayers, but also for mutual aid in saving front seats in the crowded university lecture halls, assembling study groups for review before exams, and for photocopying and distributing learning materials. This kind of solidarity and this model of organization had then been transplanted to the other faculties and university towns, thanks to the efforts of the Sunday School generation.[1]

With the changing climate of the '70s, it became increasingly difficult for Christian students to hold meetings. The reason they were disliked, I was told by Muslim students at Cairo's faculty of engineering, is that they did not try to mix with Muslim students; they were clannish. This argument had an ominously familiar ring. By the mid '70s, Christian students felt sufficiently uncomfortable to seek the protection of the church. They were faced in essence with two choices: to meet clandestinely or to try to merge their "university families" into a larger family, the Orthodox Church family, to be less vulnerable to attacks by Islamic militants.

And so they began to lose their autonomy: From the mid '70s on, the church increasingly took over their role in organizing proctors for the review of study material before exams, photocopying facilities, rooms for study-groups to meet, as well as in planning their leisure time activities, at hobby centers, sport fields, and summer camps.

The tighter incorporation of the "university families" into the church also enabled it to exercise better control over the young generation. In the past, the youths tended to take initiatives in the course of their pastoral service without consulting their "spiritual fathers." They were also a little too free with their opinions, criticizing issues that "were none of their business," and sometimes even taking issue with certain of the pope's actions.[2]

The first decade of Pope Shenuda's reign had been a schismatic one, due to his conflicts with Bishop Samuel, and there had been many cases of youth being banned from their churches, of their clandestinely distributing material discrediting the pope and his "clique," and of a mushrooming of secretly consecrated churches in private homes in the Cairene districts of Heliopolis and Helwan, and in Gezr al-Suez.[3] The latter was interpreted by the pope as a motion of censure against the high clergy and a rejection of the direction of the Coptic Orthodox Church. (This phenomenon resurfaced once more in the 1990s with the excommunication of Father Daniel. Many of his young devotees continued to attend his Masses in private homes, after he was prevented from preaching, and they even received the Eucharist in the private chapels set up in these homes.)

What the pope aimed for, through a tighter incorporation of the university student groups into the church, was more than just the loyalty of the young people. He wanted to achieve their total assimilation into the clerical space. It was with this in mind that he created the Bishopric of Youth in 1980.

To the doctor and church-servant who was consecrated bishop of Youth, Bishop Moses, fell the task of keeping the young within the fold, by offering them a forum that in appearance was alluringly modern, with its colloquium on mundane problems, its secular visiting lecturers from the ranks of academia, journalism, and the professions, and its publications inspired by American sociology and psychology. In substance, however, it remained staunchly conservative, upholding traditional Orthodox values and lifestyles.

Like the pope, Bishop Moses hails from a well-to-do farming family in Upper Egypt—his father was the mayor of the village in which President Nasser was born. Bishop Moses grew up in a typically large middle-class family of nine children, most of whom were born late enough in the century to benefit from the vast expansion of university education initiated by Nasser. An example of the dramatic new social mobility after the 1952 revolution is evident among most of the bishops' families. Whereas Bishop Moses' oldest brother was a petty railroad employee, the four youngest children, including Bishop Moses himself, became medical doctors. Likewise, in Bishop Arsanios's family, the three older brothers were a telephone operator, a shoe salesman, and a bookkeeper, while the two younger ones, including himself, were university graduates.[4]

Bishop Moses was sent to an American missionary school in the Upper Egyptian provincial town of Assiut and, later, to Cairo for his medical studies, where he came into contact with Bishop Samuel, who was then a monk-priest by the name of Father Macari serving in the Butrusia church near Bishop Moses' home. Samuel, undoubtedly one of the most enlightened church men of his time, became his father-confessor. At eighteen, therefore, Bishop Moses was exposed to Samuel's ideas of church reform,[5] in much the same way as another member of his generation, Bishop Murqus of the diocese of Shubra el Kheima, was exposed to the pope's progressive ideas: Pope Shenuda, then the monk-priest Father Anthony, had approached Murqus when he was a mere boy of sixteen and asked him if he would like to confess. After taking his confessions, he became his spiritual father.[6]

Bishop Moses had become actively involved in church service during his university years, first as a church-servant *khādim*, and after making his mark, as an overseer of church-servants, *Amīn al-khidmah*. Following his graduation, his first appointment as a medical doctor in government service was to the diocese of Banī Suwayf. (In Egypt doctors were sent during the Nasser regime to the provincial small towns and villages for a year of compulsory medical service after their graduation as part of an effort to improve the health services of the less developed parts of the country.) In Banī Suwayf Bishop Moses, then a church-servant called Emile, was to come under the influence of yet another enlightened mentor, Bishop Athanasios, a disciple of Bishop Samuel's. Emile so distinguished himself during his twelve years of service as a church-servant in Banī Suwayf, that he was invited to give talks all over the country. Like Bishop Arsanios of Minya, he gained considerable firsthand experience in public relations and in the organization of work teams from his service in the towns of Alexandria, Damanhour, Zagazig, Shebin al-Kom, Tanta, Benha and Shubra al-Kheima. It was in the course of one of those visits—this time to the Upper Egyptian town of Assiut with its large concentration of Christians—that he was to recruit one of the prize students for the church, the future Bishop Serapion of the Bishopric of Social Services, who was then a student in the faculty of medicine at the University of Assiut.[7]

During his term as *Amīn al-khidmah* in Banī Suwayf, Emile had frequently invited Shenuda, then the bishop of Higher Clerical Education, to give talks to the youth, and the two men had come to form a close bond—so much so that when Emile decided to cloister himself in the distant monastery of Samuel, to remove himself from visits by his many teenage fans, Shenuda, who had since become pope, traveled in person to Upper Egypt to persuade him to seek his spiritual calling in a monastery closer to his own monastic weekend retreat in the Natrun valley. Emile therefore moved down to the Monastry of the Romans where, under the pope's watchful eye, he was consecrated monk within two months (the normal period of novitiate is two years) and within three years he had risen to the rank of bishop of Youth.[8]

For Bishop Moses, as for the pope, winning the loyalty of the youthful constituency is cardinal: both men realize that once a youngster has been firmly planted in the church, he will remain a lifelong servant of the church, a lifelong donor of his time and money. One key element in a successful bonding of the young to their church is the formation of a cadre of church servants who identify primarily with the church and only secondarily with their family, social milieu, and residential neighborhood. Such a body of *khuddām*, which are a dependable linkage between the church and the young generation, result from a process of selection at the level of their local churches and special formation at the papal headquarters where they are sent for training. Sometimes they go on to further training in the West.

The Bishopric of Youth, under Bishop Moses, has systematically attempted to penetrate the private space of the young. The most important instrument developed for that purpose is the *Iftiqād*, or home visit, which has gained considerable momentum since it was introduced by the Sunday School generation in the 1940s. This practice of sending young church servants, deacons, and priests to check on the families to make sure the children's attendance in Mass is regular and, if not, to talk over with them the problems that may be preventing them from attending, has spread to the point where today such church emissaries cover every Christian residence in Egypt in a systematic fashion, town by town, village by village, district by district, living quarter by living quarter, house by house.

In my many interviews with middle-class Coptic families, I have rarely heard resentment at this intrusion. Occasionally, someone, usually a youngster, expresses his annoyance that the local priest could barge into his home at any time without notice, because when this happened he had to interrupt the football game he was watching on TV or give up his planned get-together with friends. But for the most part, my impression was that the average Copt was flattered by this attention. Not only did the call for his participation give him a sense of importance, which compensated for his lack of stature in the public sphere, but reminding him that he was part of a larger collectivity made him feel secure. This feeling was confirmed by the insistence of the church emissaries that the entire family participate in all church activities, not just Mass. Parents were encouraged to attend the general meetings; adolescents to participate in the youth meetings, church-sponsored choral groups, art and photo exhibits, biblical quizzes, summer camps, and the like; children to join the Sunday school programs and to take part with their parents in the excursions to the monasteries, as well as to encourage their friends to sign up for them. There Coptic families found a part of their identity that added much to their self-esteem. Beyond the sense of belonging to a larger collectivity of the living, they now discovered a glorious ancestry of heroes and martyrs.

Often I was told by young people that their interest in the church dated back to the first visits of "Abuna" (Father, meaning "the priest"). The goal the church has set for the young priest or deacon is to turn the family itself into a small church. Ideally, if he has a winning personality, he will be able to engage with them in a discussion of their problems—the father's inability to make ends meet, the nervousness of the overworked mother, the failure of a child at school, the bad habit of an older son, the rupture of a daughter's engagement or lack of a suitable suitor or dowry. He will try to persuade the father who previously felt he was too busy for church meetings to attend, the daughter to help her overworked mother with house chores, the son who previously wasted his time loafing about the city to take charge of a church-sponsored photo exhibit, and so forth. After he has soothed the family tensions, he will conclude his visit by inviting them all to join him in a collective singing of Agape canticles.

This sketch may seem too idyllic, but it corresponds to reality. I have witnessed it time and time again during my three years of fieldwork. A group of church-servants, deacons, or a lone priest or monk-priest targets a family and succeeds by sheer perseverance in captivating it, but, to be sure not always. Some cases they must write off as "*nās qulubuhum ma'fulah*" (people whose hearts are irremediably closed), which could mean that the father pretended to be out of the house when in fact he was having his siesta, the teenage son was always at the sporting club or the daughter at the Bon Appetit coffee house with her girlfriends, and other cases, which I witnessed, of recidivism into "bad habits" once the follow-up visits ceased. But often times, even after the regular visits had ceased, the family continued to seek the counsel of the church-servant or priest, whenever issues of importance or problems arose. This was especially true in the case of tension between a newlywed couple or between children and their parents. Sometimes, when I interviewed a priest or monk-priest in Cairo, Minya, and Tima, I had to wait over two hours beyond the appointed time, because the line of young people queuing to talk to their favorite priest or monk-priest resembled a long cinema queue in New York.

It is primarily to church-servants, who are generally chosen on the basis of their abundance of energy and seemingly inexhaustible stock of enthusiasm for the cause, that the task falls of looking for the lost sheep and bringing them back to the flock. Bishop Moses once narrated, to a group of youth leaders (*Umana' al-Khidmah*) how a priest, who keeps a register in his church, had complained to him that out of approximately eight hundred university students in his district only about one hundred came regularly to the youth meetings, while the others came irregularly or not at all. It was the job of the church-servant, Bishop Moses enjoined, to reach out to those who did not come. At that same meeting, he assured his church-servants that in some of the Cairene districts if all the families came to church—assuming they were at a minimum composed of four members—there would be 20,000 Christians to a church, more than any church could hold. "God is going to ask you about those others who did not come to church and you will say I was busy, I was a university student, I had a lot of homework, or I had to work afternoons to earn money for my schooling.

But He will say: Why did you not try to enlist others with you? If others participated in the church service, instead of visiting ten people a week, you would have visited ten hundred."[9]

Moses advises his church-servants not to knock at people's doors with the stern face of a prosecutor and shake their heads at the boy who, when asked, can't quite remember the number of times a day he prays. Rather let them go with the smiling face of a friend, who comes with an offer of unconditional love and support. Moses recalled, from his own experience as a church-servant, visiting a boy whose first question to him was whether he had read Mustafa Maḥmud (a popular left-wing Egyptian author at the time). Why shouldn't I read him? was his reply. To which the boy retorted that when the priest, who had visited him the day before, noticed that he was reading one of his books he exclaimed, "Leave off this nonsense!" and advised him to read the Bible instead. As a result, the boy could not wait for him to finish his tea, so that he could politely show him to the door. But Moses, on the contrary, engaged him in a long discussion of Marxism and Buddhism, the two fashionable ideologies in the 1960s, at the end of which the boy was forced to admit that, even if he did not agree with him on all points, he liked him because of that sense of self-assurance and inner peace that he conveyed.[10]

Aside from showing his church-servants the right approach to winning over people, Bishop Moses tries teach them two very alien values: Discipline and moral rigor. He teaches his church-servants such basics as how to sit at the door, notebook in hand, to keep a record of attendance rather than to content themselves with passing a piece of paper around for people to sign during the meeting, which involves whispering and other disturbances—not to mention the fact that the paper gets stashed away and often times forgotten in the pocket of one of the church-servants: "Whereas, by keeping a register at the door, you can spot the youngster who absented himself the previous week and ask him why he did not come, which will show him that he is important to you. In order to make him feel he matters to you, you should also visit him at home, if he has a problem at school, falls sick or has a death in the family."[11]

In addition, Bishop Moses primes his church-servants in the art of attracting youngsters by choosing "in" topics like drugs, sex, emigration, and job anxiety. He also urges them to print out schedules of church meetings on the back of pictures of saints, so that the recipient of these schedules would be reticent to toss them into the wastepaper basket and just might, after sticking them into the corner of some mirror or windowpane later, take a second look at them. He recommends organizing big conferences from time to time to keep the youth involved in the church, a tactic he deems essential in the summer, when children prefer to go to the beach rather than to church.[12] For this purpose, Bishop Moses himself has organized a nationwide yearly competition in church hymns, dramatic presentations of biblical themes, the arts and crafts, quizzes on the Old and New Testament, and the like, in the scenic oasis of Fayoum with its many lakes and its tropical flora. He has also set up a very popular summer camp in the beach resort of Abu Talat.

Outside of these methods, which for Egypt constitute pedagogical innovations, Bishop Moses targets the teenagers with his very up-to-date magazine called *Risālat al-Shabāb al-Kanasī* (The Mission of the Church Youth) which makes *Majallat al-Aḥad* (The Sunday School Magazine), a radical innovation in the 1950s, appear old fashioned. If we pick up a *Sunday School Magazine* created by the Sunday School generation, we will find the cover story "A Message from His Holiness." The next item is about the sayings of Saint John, then there is a story about angels and another about the missionary role of the Egyptian Orthodox church in sub-Saharan Africa, and finally an article with social relevance on "How to Extend Pastoral and Social Care to Families."[13] In contrast, in Bishop Moses' *The Mission of Church Youth*, only about 20 percent of the coverage concerns the religious matters, while the bulk of the magazine addresses itself to the problems of modern life. If we examine some of the issues, we will see at a glance why this magazine is considered a radical, even impious, innovation by some of the more conservative church prelates. The cover of the January 1993 issue features, in place of the Virgin cradling Baby Jesus on her lap, a picture of astronauts, video-cameras, and other electronic gadgets. Its stories span such topics as "The Psychological Symptoms of This Age" by psychologist Magdi Isaac, a discussion of how a youth can cope with his aggressive instincts and depressive moods; "Youth Torn between the East and West," by family counselor Dr. ʿAdil Ḥalim; "What One Can Learn from British Ways," by Magdi Makram, a *mukaras* sent by Bishop Moses to England for training; and finally an article on the problems of unemployment by Bishop Serapion, of the Bishopric of Social Services; an extremely progressive bishop.[14] It is no wonder that this magazine is suspect in conservative church circles. A man like Bishop Bishoi, the self-appointed guardian of Orthodox purity, has expressed his misgivings about it on more than one occasion,[15] despite the fact that Bishop Moses is very conservative in sexual matters.

To this same middle-class youth who may have to wait as much as a decade from the time he graduates from university to save enough money to buy a flat, without which he cannot hope to marry (in Egypt it is the bridegroom's obligation to provide the flat, just as it is the bride's to provide the dowry) Bishop Moses enjoins a life of chastity (*tahara*, or "purity" in the church parlance).

The inability to marry preys on the mind of every would-be suitor in Egypt. At a youth meeting I attended, the young men were asked, tongue in cheek, by one of Bishop Moses's church-servants, psychologist Magdi Isaac, what would be the three questions they would have to confront when they went to propose. In response, they chanted derisively:

> How much money do you make?
> Do you own a flat?
> What are your family's circumstances?

The church is aware that chastity may be difficult to observe in a country where it is common for a man to be unable to marry before he is in his late thirties. The girls are not the object of the churches' solicitude since, in a male-dominated culture, it is assumed that they are without sexual desire. But to the young men the bishop has this to say: "If you are full of God you can resist sexual desire. If you fall it's because you don't pray and fast enough, so the devil is constantly at your elbow tempting you with a passing girl, with a foul joke that you overhear, with a dirty magazine one of your friends shows you."[16]

The fundamentalism of St. Anthony's school of thought predominates in the cultural discourse of the Bishopric of Youth, which frowns on the viewing of films in movie theaters or on television, characterizes pop music as "devilish," prohibits the consumption of alcoholic beverages except for the Eucharistic wine, castigates disco dancing as "indecency" and dating as "immorality."[17] Bishop Moses went even farther in a joint newspaper interview conducted with Bishop Gregorios in November 1992. Both of them expressed their approval of the veils worn by Egyptian Muslim women, as a highly commendable "modest" attire. (The consecrated women in the church entourage, though dressed in ordinary clothes, wore head-scarves.)[18] Bishop Gregorios, the bishop of Advanced Theological Research, said that "the divine order calls on women to cover their heads—it is a sign of modesty, politeness and submission to God."[19] Bishop Moses added that it was proof of a women's respect for her husband and that a woman insults her husband in public when she walks with her head uncovered: she seems to be announcing that she is not content with him. Expressing a traditional viewpoint of Eve as the seductress, he further asserted that "she often uses it (her hair) as a vehicle to lure and infatuate men and to hinder them psychologically and spiritually."[20]

Bishop Moses shares the monastic belief that sexual activity drains vital energy, which is better used in study, work, and worship. Sublimation of this sexual drive is therefore the answer. And it is the responsibility of the church-servants to see to it that this sublimation takes place by putting the boys' souls, minds, and bodies to hard work. (Bishop Moses seized on that particular occasion to congratulate the church-servants for having successfully raised money for a workout machine.)[21]

That Bishop Moses is not the only one to believe in the success of such a regimen for adolescents may be judged by the words of Bishop Tackla of Dishna, who at twenty-eight was the youngest bishop in the sample I studied, and hence presumably the one who belonged to the more permissively raised generation. He told me: "I never felt particularly attracted to a girl during my adolescence and I never had wet dreams. We have a very religious climate here, which enables us to satiate ourselves with church service, excursions, choir practice, club activities—all of this uses up our thoughts, energy and time. It transforms our sexual urges into spiritual strivings."

Although Bishop Moses' book *al-Shabāb wa-ḥayāt al-ṭahārah* (Youth and Purity) still reads to a westerner like a quaint Victorian manual—he says that masturbation can be avoided if one refrains from eating spicy foods, wearing tight clothes, and sleeping on one's tummy and that homosexuality is a "disease" attributed to glandular disorders—the mere fact of discussing sex openly in a country where sex education is still not part of the school curriculum in itself constitutes a revolution.

It is not only Bishop Moses' magazine that has raised some eyebrows, but also his encouragement of the production of taped church hymns, which are immensely popular with the young. In contrast to the traditional Coptic chants of the church deacons, their tunes are often borrowed from pop music, and even their words are sometimes thinly disguised adaptations of romantic songs—with the object of adoration being transmuted into the Christ figure. This "cultural pollution" of the Coptic heritage has been decried by many bishops, led by Bishop Hidra of Aswan, who devoted a whole book to this theme.

But even though the Bishopric of Youth concentrates its efforts on the adolescent years, when it feels that a person's loyalty to the church may be secured for life or irretrievably lost, it realizes that socialization must begin in infancy. Witness, for example, a magazine called *al-Malāʾikah* (the angels), which behind conventional cover art, with Jesus seated with a small child on his lap or the prophet Moses holding up the tablet of the Ten Commandments, features homilies disguised as Donald Duck and Superman cartoons, alongside role-models such as the story of the daughter of a Roman emperor who was martyred for her faith.[22] The children's parents are also the targets of moral enlightenment in a magazine entitled *Dunyā al-Ṭifl* (A Child's World), which contains such articles as "The Exemplary Mother," "How to Talk to Your Child about God," "Your Child and Television," and "How to Prepare an Excursion for Your Child," as well as entries on childhood diseases written by health specialists.

The editor of the magazine itself is a pedagogical expert, a church-servant named George Nagib.[23] He, also, was sent for training to England and was afterward put in charge of transforming the church nurseries, which heretofore were merely any room in a church compound where a working mother left her child to be cared for by an adult, into model nurseries. There the children learn languages and acquire reading and arithmetic skills, in addition to engaging in a number of games meant to strengthen their imaginative faculties and their powers of association. Nagib is a leading proponent of the transformation of traditional nurseries into western-style, head-start schools.[24]

The reformed church is not content with a Christian who is merely versed in liturgy. As Bishop Moses once told his church-servants: "We want someone who not only has read the Bible but has read Camus. Once you've read the Bible well, you will be immune to the poison of atheism."[25] In a Third World country like Egypt, where the universities are at best capable of turning out well-trained technocrats versed in the skills of surgically removing kidney stones or powering a hydraulic engine, but devoid of culture—culture is considered a frill that a developing country can't afford—the church must try to compensate by imparting to its constituency a modicum of general knowledge. That the emphasis here is on *modicum* can be judged from a youth meeting I attended, in which Bishop Moses recounted a telephone call the pope received from Israeli Foreign Minister Shimon Perez, asking him why he did not permit Egyptian Christians to come to Jerusalem. Not a single person in the audience knew who Shimon Peres was, much to Bishop Moses' amusement.[26]

Even their knowledge of the Bible is rudimentary; they shy away from the Old Testament, looking upon it as too dense and complex for comprehension. Bishop Moses' efforts to encourage them to tackle it ranges from verbal support to the notion that the Old Testament should be considered required reading for anyone attending his lectures to sponsoring a series of lectures on the Old Testament, which he entrusts to one of his church-servants, an engineer by the name of Mamdouh Shafik. It is given in the papal headquarters immediately following the bishop's own youth meetings on Sundays, to take advantage of an already captive audience.

Bishop Moses' own pedagogical efforts date back to the late '60s, when he was a mere church-servant in Banī Suwayf. There he instituted what came to be known as the shoe-box library; he set up a young man at the entrance of the room where he held his lecture with a dozen or so Bata shoe-boxes filled with small booklets, so that each person coming to his lecture could sign up for a booklet and return the one he had previously borrowed.[27] By the time he became bishop of Youth, Bishop Moses had at his disposal a vast arsenal in his battle against ignorance, which included a publishing network, and a chain of libraries in the churches throughout the country—some of which, like those of Banī Suwayf and Tanta, were most impressive in the range of subjects covered—both secular and religious. The problem of poverty as a hindrance to learning persisted, however, despite the passage of two decades. Witness, for example, a note scribbled to Moses at the end of the a youth meeting I attended in the papal headquarters in 1992:

> Beloved bishop, you urge us to read. But where is the time? (I have to work at two jobs to make ends meet.) And where is *rawaaet al-bal* [peace of mind]? And where is the money to buy the books?[28]

Bishop Moses' efforts to educate the youth included educating the educators because, as he told his church-servants, times had changed: "Today you should expect to get questions about new planets and organ transplants, which you must be able to answer. I myself am ashamed when I see these children around me who are all computer wizards, while I don't know how to use one."[29] Therefore Bishop Moses spares no effort to enlighten his church-servants by calling in all kinds of experts: medical doctors, scientists, psychologists, sociologists, and educators to lecture to them on the fashionable topics of the day: the effect of drugs and smoking, computers, housing problems, depression, anxiety about job prospects, sex in contemporary society.

The church not only wants a knowledgeable person, but one who is socially and politically engaged. In a lecture series entitled "The Characteristics of Orthodoxy," Bishop Moses emphasized that the church wanted a person not only to have good relations with the clerics but also with his family and his neighbors and his Muslim colleagues at work—in short, with society at large. "We aim at the formation of a young man who is different from the world, set aside by his saintly ways, a *mukharas*, yet a sociable person, one who bears witness to Christ within the world."[30] Bishop Moses continued that "a social personality is useful to the church, he is the one who organizes conferences, exhibitions, competitions, excursions, he is the one who prods the church to move in the direction of a dialogue with the Muslims." Some people looked on Christianity as an otherworldly religion, he said; they accused the church of lacking a sense of social obligation. This was true of some of the churches in the past: "We know that the Russian church was insensitive to the needs of the poor, which caused Marx to say that religion was an opium doled out by the clerics, with the encouragement of the ruling classes, to the poor, so they would be patient under suffering. But Jesus Christ did not neglect the need of man for food; when he saw that the people were hungry he performed the miracle of the fish."[31]

The importance Bishop Moses attaches to the youth is shared by most of the bishops in the dioceses under study. Bishop Bachum of Sohag, in Upper Egypt, makes a point of going on excursions to the monasteries and to the pharaonic sites with the young boys and girls of his diocese; he disdains the comforts of his own Mercedes, preferring to sit with them in the bus, and he shares their modest accommodations. Thus, a seven-day trip to St. Catherine's Monastery in the Sinai affords him a chance to get to know his youthful constituency. Every evening at sundown, the youth form a circle around him on the sand, and they engage in a free give-and-take with their bishop on matters personal, social, and political until the wee hours of the morning.[32] Bishop Thomas, of neighboring Qusia, himself presides over a debating club, to which he invites some of the best known national figures, such as the Coptic journalist Majid Aṭīyah, member of Parliament Mīlād Ḥannā and others to engage the youths of his diocese in discussions on such controversial topics as the role of Parliament in Egypt and Christian-Muslim relations.[33] Bishop Bula of Tanta, in Lower Egypt, has done a great deal to encourage artistic endeavors among the youth of his diocese. He attends their theatrical rehearsals himself, taking copious notes during performances and criticizing them afterward to prove that he was paying attention. In one funny instance that I witnessed, Bishop Bula remarked to the male lead that he had read the English letter he received from right to left, the way one reads Arabic script, when in fact his eyes should have scanned the page in the opposite direction.[34] We have seen that in the diocese of Damanhour, in

Lower Egypt, Bishop Bachomios, though past sixty, joins in games of basketball and soccer in the summer camp he has established for the village poor and performs hilarious pantomimes—social satires of bad habits and sinful ways of his congregation, for Sunday school children.[35] Bishop Murqus of the Lower Egyptian diocese of Shubra al-Kheima, though by any measure one of the busiest bishops in Egypt, allots as much time to discussions with schoolboys and to the confessions of eight-year-old girls as he does to his meetings with western project funders, the representatives of the World Council of Churches, or the church committees of his diocese.[36] Even conservative figures like Bishop Bishoi, the pope's vicar, will take time from a hectic schedule to sit up nights in the Christian village of St. Dimiana, in his diocese in Lower Egypt, to sing church hymns with young girls.[37]

Most bishops make pedagogy and entertainment for the young one of their top priorities in drawing up their annual budgets. This holds as true for relatively well-to-do dioceses like Minya, as it does for some of the poorest and small dioceses in Upper Egypt like Dishna. Just as youth projects receive a generous share of the budget in every diocese, they are allotted the most outstanding personalities at the bishop's disposal as youth leaders. Though Cairo has a richer pool from which to draw, the other dioceses are not lacking. Each diocese I visited had at least one outstanding individual who had been put in charge of the youth program. This may be a charismatic monk-priest such as Father Daniel of Minya, before his excommunication, or Father Dioscoros, who serviced some of the Upper Egyptian dioceses, moving from one to another, and attracting large crowds of teenagers wherever he went. These popular monk-priests tend to draw young people from outside of their diocese as well, who often travel great distances to hear the homilies. Or the bishop may appoint outstanding church-servants, who have been persuaded to take the priestly vows (such was the case for Father Wisa in Tima and Father David in Sohag). Finally, the bishop may call on laymen to devote their time after work to the service of youth (such was the case for Atef Abd al-Messih and Mīlād Murqus of Tima, the former a schoolteacher the latter a banker).

What sort of young person is the church trying to fashion through its publications—its books on the early church history, the history of the Coptic Saints, the national heroism of the Copts, the Orthodox moral vision on such subjects as sex, smoking, alcohol, and artificial insemination—through its extensive production of tapes and videotapes of sermons and homilies, which include the pope's widely attended Wednesday-afternoon sessions, through its videotaped film series on the lives of the saints and martyrs, through its hymns, through its weekly meetings for university students, secondary school students, newlywed couples, workers, and the like, through its prolific output of posters, banners, and calendars with pictures of the pope, the bishops and the Egyptian saints?

The primary aim of the church is to build up a youth's self-esteem, against the daily onslaught of propaganda at school and at home by the media, which unrelentingly drum into their heads the message that their Muslim peers are superior as well as to fortify them against a possible encounter with prejudice. I myself twice experienced this: in one instance when I was strolling with a *mukharasa* in the market in Port Said, a passerby spat at her cross and, in another instance, when I accompanied a Muslim woman to a clinic in Cairo, she tweaked her nose, as we entered, as if there were a bad smell. When I gave her a puzzled look, she winked and nodded in the direction of a black-robed clergyman who was exiting. The efforts of the church to fashion a new generation of outspoken, self-assertive individuals, by holding up to them heroic models drawn from their "glorious and sacred history," bears some resemblance to the efforts by the pioneers in Israel to fashion a new generation of tough Sabras, in contrast to the supposedly weak and craven diaspora Jews, by invoking heroes from the legendary eras of the First and Second Temple.

The strength of the young generation of Copts, who are meant to shed forever the self-effacing, fearful image of earlier generation of Copts, is to be derived from the solidarity of a community firmly rooted in its church. That church is portrayed by Bishop Moses as a body, with Christ as its head, in which the members are both equal and interdependent. Equality, however, does not entail the concept of the priesthood of all believers, he insists, as it does in Protestantism; rather it means that the foot needs the eye to show it the way and the lungs cannot function properly without a sound liver. The saints and martyrs are a very important part of the Orthodox Church family. Bishop Moses constantly urges the youths to read a work called *Siyar al-Ābā'*; which consists of the life-histories of the local saints and martyrs "You have to get to know the rest of the family who are now in heaven" he once told a group of youth in my hearing; "they are our past, present and future."[38]

Siyar al-Ābā' is thus the cornerstone of the educational program set up by Bishop Moses for Cairo and the dioceses. As he himself once said in a youth meeting, its perusal is essential because "a nation without roots can easily be destroyed."[39] And, in another instance, he told them:

> Say your grandfather had been the mayor of a village, you would have been proud of him. You would have wanted to hear all about him, even though your farm did not exist anymore. Well you have to get to know the saints, because they too are part of your family: They are your brothers and sisters in heaven. Each one of them has his own special virtue and you should take them as your models. You will come to admire Saint Bishoi for his diligence in study—he used to tie his long hair with a cord and string it up on a nail on his cell wall, so that if he happened to nod off in the midst of his readings he would be jerked awake—and Saint Arsanios for his unpretensiousness. You will discover how much the West is indebted to Saint Anthony, who sold all his belongings to found monasticism in the Egyptian desert, and to

> our missionaries like St. Moritz, after whom the famous Swiss mountain resort is named, and St. Verena who taught the Swiss cleanliness. Today, Alas! it is they who teach us cleanliness."[40]

The reformed church is seeking not only to build a model community firmly rooted in the church but also one that remains firmly rooted in Egypt. The survival of the Copts as a nation with its distinct religio-cultural heritage anchored in Egypt is predicated on prevention of mass Christian emigration. To that end the church leaders try to teach the youth values which will enable them to better cope with the difficulty of life in a Third World country.

In his address to a group of fresh university graduates, Bishop Moses, who must have been aware of how dim employment prospects were—very few openings in the small private sector and a seven-year wait for a guaranteed government job—told them that they were going out into a materialistic world in which their meager earnings were bound to make them appear lightweight. But he assured them that even though they might end up earning only LE 200 a month (approximately $60) and see others earning double or triple that, they were the richer ones because they had the Lord's blessing. And Bishop Moses proceeded to give them the example of an old friend, "now in heaven," who told him that when he was first married he earned only LE 20 a month while his upstairs neighbor, a police officer, earned LE 200. Yet, at the end of every month, his neighbor's wife would come downstairs to borrow money from his own wife. She did not have enough left to hold out until her husband's next paycheck, he said, because there was no *baraka* (blessing) in their home.[41]

Psychologist Magdi Isaac also addressed himself to the problem of poverty, in a series of lectures entitled *Christianity and Psychology*, which is meant to boost the morale of the underprivileged. His principal message to the university graduates is:

> When you look at yourself in the mirror in the morning before going out to work, you should not let your eyes dwell on your dowdy coat or threadbare shirt, rather you should see yourself in the image of Christ and you should venture forth into the world happy in the knowledge that Christ will not fail you. His love does not depend on how rich or how famous you are, it is unconditional.[42]

Dr. Isaac reminded his audience that God often chooses the poorest and the humblest for his great work: men like Jesus Christ, born to a mere carpenter, and his disciples, some of whom were illiterate fishermen.[43]

To this youthful constituency whose role-models during childhood were a mother weighed down and prematurely aged by all the cooking, washing, and cleaning she had to do for her large brood and a father in a shabby brown suit and frayed collar, washed out and irritable at the end of his double work-shift, Bishop Moses' message must of necessity be, "Do not try to break out of your hard-pressed, humdrum existence through graft or theft." In a cultural context where all kinds of graft from taking bribes to outright theft are commonly accepted ways of padding meager pocket-books, Bishop Moses tells the youth that even if all around them dishonesty is a way of life, they as Christians must be a "light" to others;[44] they must never forget that they are Christ's emissaries on earth.

In a youth meeting I attended, he gave them the example of a friend, the chief accountant in a luxury hotel in Cairo that was government-owned: One day he was visited by the hotel manager, who told him that there was half a million pounds left over from the money allotted for renovation that had to "disappear" or else it would have to be returned to the Ministry of Tourism by the end of the budget year. The manager offered him a generous share of the money for falsifying the records. But the accountant refused, and he held fast to his resolution, even after the manager warned him that if he did not cooperate he would ask to have him transferred to another hotel, which might mean that he would end up in the provinces. The accountant lost his job. But Bishop Moses assured his audience that the Lord stood by him and eventually he landed in a better paying job in a five-star hotel in Cairo.[45]

The church recognizes that one of the principal problems of Egyptian youth is anxiety about their future. Hence, one of the commonly discussed topics at youth meetings throughout the country is *al-Shabāb wa-al-mustaqbal* (Youth and the Future). This basically functions as a career counseling session, in which the bishop discusses the jobs of the future—where they will be and how to go after them—and gives out practical tips to career changers or to people with diplomas who cannot find jobs short of emigration. Many bishops have also opened vocational training centers to teach the unemployed, among whom figure many university graduates, carpentry, plumbing, electrical work, refrigeration, car mechanics, sewing, and silk-screen painting. Although the largest and most successful centers are to be found in Lower and Middle Egypt, where the funds of foreign donors are more readily available—particularly in Cairo, Banī Suwayf, and Minya—caravans with makeshift workshops are dispatched by the Bishopric of Social Services to Upper Egypt and offer six-month courses in all the major Christian population centers. The church has now become a firm believer in the Chinese maxim that it is better to teach a man to fish than to give him a fish.

Emigration is but one response to the financial difficulties of middle-class Copts and to their estrangement from Islamic Egypt; cooptation within the church hierarchy is another. Shenuda's critics have leveled the following accusation at him: "[T]he Pope has in-gathered Orthodox Christians into his own state within a state. Copts defer participation in city councils for participation in church councils, and refer their problems to bishops rather than governors."[46]

It is not, however, Pope Shenuda's encouragement of Coptic withdrawal from civil society that has created this situation, as some people like the prominent Coptic civil rights activist Marlene Tadros believe. In her words: "Now Copts are living in a cocoon. They're not interested in society. They are either interested in making money or in emigrating."[47] Rather, it is the reverse: Discrimination resulted in voter apathy (out of approximately 80,000 potential voters in the heavily Christian Cairene district of Shubra, only 6,000 were registered to vote in 1994). The church, on the contrary, has been encouraging the Copts to vote, out of a concern to prevent the kind of alienation from the Egyptian national scene that would lead to mass emigration. Thus, Tadros's statement, while perfectly true, must be taken within the context of the year it was made, 1994, when there was not a single Christian governor, ambassadors, or elected member of Parliament. The only Christians in the People's Assembly were the five presidential appointees and those in the cabinet held two powerless ministries.

Not only was access to leading positions in civil society blocked, but the realistic possibility for average Copts to improve their chances of promotion in the government-owned sector, which remains to this day the largest employer of Christians as well as Muslims. The only chance for average Copts to improve their lives would have been to take a high-profile position in the government-backed National Democratic Party, as well as in the leading opposition party, the leftwing Tagamu'. But in the absence of a system of proportional representation, the parties had little incentive to woo the Christian minority. And beyond this, as the then-leading Coptic parliamentarian Mīlād Ḥannā perceptively observed: "You can't create interest in public life unless there is a real possibility of turnover in the political system."[48]

In the absence of political channels to combat discrimination in employment (there was not a single Coptic university president or dean among Egypt's thirteen universities when I undertook this study) and other sectors of public life, the Copts have turned to the church. By giving all Copts a role to play from their early teens on, the church has provided them with a compensatory status system and a chance of upward mobility outside of civil society.

PART VI

The Politics of Identity

13

Coptic Cultural Nationalism

One of the hypotheses informing this work is that the church under Pope Shenuda has capitalized on the great value placed on religious identity in fin de siècle Egypt, to outbid the state for the loyalty of its beleaguered Christian citizens. It has done so by organizing a plethora of communal activities, by clericalizing laymen on a massive scale and above all by nurturing a potent religious culture. The numerous religio-cultural activities of the Bishopric of Youth aim, in part, to imbue the faithful with the conviction that the church is the social space where one receives one's true identity and that spaces that exclude it are a negation of the Coptic patrimony.

The cultural space that was created, under Pope Shenuda, and was meant to be complementary to the place of worship, was not destined only for the young. He created many forums, other than the Sunday schools, where adults, who felt excluded from Egyptian public life and from the informal social networks that sprang up among Muslims in the workplaces and in their residential neighborhoods, could get together with their co-religionists. In these forums, all subjects were discussed, from ethics and canonic law, the history of local saints and martyrs, to the contemporary problems facing the Copts.

Explaining the fundamentals of the revived faith in his book *Hayat al-Iman* (A Life of Faith), Shenuda writes that it is no longer sufficient for Copts to maintain their links to the mother church merely by attending a weekly prayer session; they must familiarize themselves with their religious patrimony as well, through the study of theological and canonical issues specific to the Orthodox Church:

It is their "duty," he insists, to enter into a series of "apprenticeships," which will enable them to graduate to ever higher levels of faith[1]—levels once attainable only by those with a priestly or monastic vocation. For this new discipline, the pope stresses that perseverance is key. And indeed the seminaries, not so long ago limited to priest-hopefuls or would-be monks, are overflowing with laymen who sometimes (as in the case of the theological seminary in Minya, which I attended) travel long distances by train, just to get this *Kulturbuildung*.

This kind of socialization "from the cradle to the grave" is in its pedagogical guise an entirely new phenomenon, one that was viewed negatively by previous generations of Orthodox clerics, who considered it a form of secularization—a "Protestant deformation" of the Coptic religious patrimony. Indeed, it is without question a venture in religious modernization, which equips the church not only to take on Muslim supremacists but also to hold its own against the Egyptian Catholic and Protestant churches, which looked down on it in the past as archaic.

The church has sponsored all kinds of groups, including Bible, hagiography, Coptic archeology study groups, as well as groups for the study of Coptic canticles. Musicologists familiar with the history of the canticles have been placed in charge of modern laboratories for the work of recapturing the old tunes and of creating archives for them, as well as of recording them for sale.

Coptic liturgical music is among the oldest in the world. The chants existed as part of an oral tradition going back to ancient times. They were passed on by one generation of cantors to another. Dr. Rāghīb Muftaḥ, the head of the music and hymns department of the Institute of Higher Coptic Studies, resolved to save this Coptic musical heritage from oblivion, by recording and transcribing it into a western notation system—an endeavor that began seven decades prior to my research. In 1927, when he was still a young agricultural engineer active in the Sunday School Movement, Muftaḥ met a British ethnomusicologist, Earnest Newlandsmith, who had stopped in Egypt on his way back from Palestine. Newlandsmith was himself a Protestant clergyman's son with strong monastic proclivities (he used to refer to himself as the "hermit of Mt. Carmel").[2] The two young men, who shared a common interest in Coptic music, became friendly and Muftaḥ invited Newlandsmith to share his accommodations in his boathouse on the Nile. Muftaḥ spent nine winters, sitting cross-legged on the floor with the Englishman, learning, under his guidance, the western system of musical notation. Since there were no recordings as yet of Coptic liturgical music, they had to hire singers to come to the boathouse and chant the scores for them. Day in and day out, the Englishman went on laboriously scribbling down the chants of the blind master cantor Mualim Michael Jirjis al-Batanuni, while Muftaḥ tried to record them on the old-fashioned reels of tape that Newlandsmith had brought him from England. Together, they went on to transcribe enough music to fill the sixteen volumes of text, which have recently been acquired by the Library of Congress.[3]

The culmination of Muftaḥ's lifework was the publication in 1998 of a 1,200-page manuscript containing the complete musical scores of the liturgy of St. Basil and its accompanying words, translated from the Coptic into English and Arabic. When I met him when he was 94, he was still working, on the liturgical music of St. Cyril, which had almost been lost half of century earlier, due to the death of the last surviving cantor who knew the music.

This lifework, begun seventy-one years ago, required a singleness of purpose that was nothing short of monastic asceticism. Like the celibate founder of the Sunday School Movement, Ḥabīb Jirjis, Muftaḥ gave himself up entirely to it: he lived as "a monk in the world," though later, in old age, he sought out a female companion; his marriage was, by his own admission, "never consummated." He himself declared that he had married because he began to feel the weight of his age "I just needed someone to look after me"[4]—a statement that in the context of Egypt's male chauvinist culture shocked no one.

Taped canticles along with the taped hymns and the videos of the lives of church heroes—the Egyptian saints and martyrs—have been very successfully commercialized during the reign of Pope Shenuda. Their sale provides the many churches throughout Egypt with a considerable revenue.[5]

The formation of new song repertoires in Coptic, which are often used at the inaugural ceremonies, such as welcoming canticles for visiting bishops,[6] is a very good example of the usefulness of religious ritual for cultural nationalism. A traditional practice, the singing of church canticles at the beginning of Mass, is modified, ritualized, and institutionalized for a new purpose, namely, to mobilize the Coptic masses. By generating a sense of pride in their ancient heritage, it creates an esprit de corps. These are new songs, using the same idioms as the old canticles, often composed by professors at the Coptic Institute and then transferred via musicologists to a choral repertoire. Sung in unison at inaugural meetings, they have become a tradition of great symbolic force. The songs, which reflect the historical background and culture of the Coptic people, are for them what "The Star-Spangled Banner" is for Americans. They not only proclaim their religious identity, but also extol the sovereignty of their church, which has fought a fierce battle, since time immemorial, to maintain its independence from western Christendom.

The videotaped legends of the saints and martyrs have also become a potent cultural agent linking the different age groups and generations. I have seen children barely out of kindergarten, solemnly watching together with their parents and toothless grandparents a video about Barsum the Naked, the Egyptian hermit who lived alone in a cave with a snake he had tamed, and whose only clothes were his long hair and beard.[7]

In many of the families with whom I stayed during my fieldwork in the different dioceses, the only music the children were allowed to listen to up until the age of eighteen, when they finished high school and went off to universities in the big towns, were the canticles and hymns. The only films they were allowed to watch on television were these dramatized epics of the local saints and martyrs.[8]

Mention must also be made of the multiplicity of small church-sponsored printing workshops. The plethora of new religious publications is not just the product of big institutions. Aside from the papacy and the Department of Youth and all the diocesan bishoprics, which have acquired their own publishing houses, as have many of the churches and monasteries, many small groups like the diaconal groups, the groups of consecrated laymen and woman (*mukarasin*), the Sunday school groups and all manner of church-related voluntary groups have their own publications. These church-sponsored printing workshops have, since the advent of Shenuda, produced thousands of new publications that explain in simple language designed for mass consumption the historical roots of certain ritual practices, the stories of the ancient monastic church fathers and of the Egyptian martyrs, who gave their life for the survival of the church at the time of Roman persecution, as well as emphasizing the importance of regular participation in prayer—all of which are designed to turn religion into the predominate referent of identity for Copts.

But, of all the church-sponsored cultural groups, perhaps none are more important than the ones that have been put in charge of the resurrection of the Coptic language. It is part of the genius of the Sunday School Movement that it grasped the intimate connection between a private-property language and a sense of belonging to a nation. By 1961, it had succeeded in getting the education committee of the Communal Council to make the instruction of the Coptic language mandatory for all Sunday schools throughout the country.[9] And it is as a nation that the Coptic clergy thinks of the Coptic community—even though, unlike the Maronites in Mount Lebanon, they do not aspire to separate statehood, because it is realistically impossible to achieve. The Copts, unlike the Maronites, are not concentrated in one geographic area, nor do they even have a majority in any single city (in Assiut and Minya, they form no more than approximately 30 percent of the inhabitants). In referring to the Copts, in their conversations with me, the clergy either talked about *Sha'bina* (our people) or *al-Ummah al-Qibṭiyah* (the Coptic nation).

This sense of the Copts as a distinct entity is antagonistic to the view of Christianity as solely a religion, held by the ancien régime upper class. Indeed, its members even object to the terms *community* or *minority*. On several occasions when I, out of habit, slipped into such usage, to explain what I had come to study, I was sharply upbraided by one or the other of my interviewees, who insisted that the Copts were not a community distinguishable from their Muslim compatriots: both were Egyptian—different only, through one of those contingencies of birth, in religion; just as some Americans, they would add, worshiped in a synagogue and others in a church.[10]

In encouraging Coptic etymologists, philologists, grammarians, and lexicographers to work on the reconstruction, by scientific reasoning, of what was in effect a protolanguage, Pharaonic written with the help of a Greek Alphabet, the church was engaging in activities central to the political identity of the Copts. Some of the Sunday School visionaries had gone all the way to the great libraries of Europe, where they devoted their best years to the compilation of word lists for monolingual dictionaries and to the study of the etymology of Coptic words. Bishop Gregorios, had, in his youth, gone to the University of London to write a 538-page doctoral dissertation—in an old-fashioned copperplate handwriting—on the etymology of Greek words in the Coptic language. To complete such a monumental task, he must have been moved by great passion, the kind of passion that sustains revolutionary activities. Later, as the bishop of Advanced Coptic Research, he devoted himself to the translation of ancient Coptic texts, transliterating the words into Roman script and tracing their etymology to the Greek and demotic languages.[11]

The importance the church attaches to the resurrection and transmission of the ancient Coptic language is evidenced by the diocesan bishops, with fantastically busy schedules, who take time out to teach Coptic themselves (I attended such courses in both Akhmim and Minya), and that Archbishop Bishoi, who is probably the bishop with the heaviest load of responsibilities, because he doubles up as the pope's vicar in most domestic matters, drives up all the way from the port town of Damietta to Cairo to teach a lesson once a week at the papal seminary. In one of those lessons, which I attended, professors, like Dr. Emile, although far more versed in the subject matter than the bishop, sat humbly at his feet, while he spent over an hour on a ponderous explanation of a single sentence.

Coptic was never successfully vernacularized the way Hebrew was by the indomitable pioneers who came to Palestine in the 1920s (Ben Yehuda, the father of vernacular Hebrew, is said to have refused to exchange a single word of Russian with his visiting old mother, even though she was not conversant in any other tongue). Nonetheless, or perhaps because of this, Coptic is potent as a tool of solidarity. The fact that even the high clergy have only a rudimentary grasp of that language and that their legions of church-servants have succeeded in passing on no more than a few words to the Sunday school children is unimportant, because it suffices for the community to use sacral words—many of them Greek words incorporated into the Coptic language—like *Kyrie Eleison* (Lord, have mercy), which is repeated forty-one times in the course of a single prayer—or to refer to their bishops as *Anba* (a change introduced by the Sunday School generation, from the previous use of the Hebrew word *Abba*), together with the reintroduction of ancient Coptic titles like *absalomos, aganostos,* and so on for the male deacons, and of ancient names of Greek derivation, like Phoebe, Anastasia, and so on for the female *mukarasat,* or to greet each other, over the telephone, with the word *Agape,* or on Easter Sunday with *Christos Anesti* (Christ is risen)—Greek words unintelligible to their Muslim compatriots—to maintain a sense of distinctiveness from the Other. This is their revenge against the

Muslims, who exclude them from their social networks in the workplace, the universities, and the residential neighborhoods.

The fact that Coptic is reserved mainly for canticles, hymns, and a few prayers, particularly those used in the week of the Passion, only consolidates the astonishing power of the Orthodox clergy in Egypt: through their superior knowledge of a sacral language, they are looked up to by the faithful—not just as mediators between the Arabic vernacular, into which the mass has been translated, and Coptic, but as mediators between heaven and earth.

It is presumably for this reason that the Sunday School Movement in the 1940s and '50s succeeded in interesting the Copts in their language, while the secular nationalistic *al-Ummah al-Qibṭīyah* movement did not. The community's confidence in the sacredness of their language is tied to the conception of their church as cosmically central to Christianity in its role as the church of origin. Secular nationalists, like the lawyer and founder of *al-Ummah al-Qibṭīyah*, Ibrahim Hilal, could not compete with those who are linked to a supraterrestial order through the medium of a sacred language.

Coptic cultural nationalism remained a powerful current at the end of the twentieth century and its political ramifications may be gauged by the way the government and the local press reacted to a church-sponsored project to build a Coptic university in Egypt. Shenuda's meetings, in his papal headquarters, with a number of well-to-do Copts from the diaspora, to discuss the financing of such an institution as well as the possibility of recruiting Coptic expatriate professors "to help educate their younger brothers at home" were lambasted in the press as a "seditious" scheme. Predictably, the government was able to enlist the support of a Coptic member of Parliament, Gamal Asʿad, who described it as a "dangerous" project that threatened to ignite sectarian conflict in Egypt.[12]

The question whether the Copts are to be allowed to set up such a privately endowed institution remains unresolved, despite the many compromises offered by the supporters of the project—down to the very name of the university, Coptic-Egyptian University, from which they were willing to delete the word *Coptic*. All of this failed to win government acquiescence, even though the Muslims have a similar institution in the Islamic university, al-Azhar, and even though the government itself insists on religious labeling on personal identification cards—a practice that works to the detriment of the Christian minority.[13]

The church is not merely reacting to the exclusivism of the Muslims by creating a compensatory private space for Christians. It is trying to reverse the secularizing trend of the first half of the twentieth century, which had made possible the political integration of the Copts. Secularism is a danger to the Coptic patrimony, in its view, almost as great as Islam. The church's attempt to mobilize the Coptic masses around a religio-cultural platform may be read, therefore, as a defeat of the secular upper class, whose disdain for all forms of religiosity is well captured by a statement the late Magdi Wahba made to me:

"Tout les deux sont des bandes d'abruties" (Both of them [the religious Muslims and Copts] are a bunch of morons).

It is a sign of the growing prestige of the church that toward the end of the century, even the secular ancien régime aristocracy had felt compelled to pay homage to the pope. For example, Magdi Wahba described to me a meeting with the pope, to which he had been invited as a member of the Coptic Archeological society, on some matter relating to the preservation of Coptic Church antiquities. He had brought along his oldest son, Murad, and had had to pinch him, he told me laughingly, to get him to kiss the pope's hand. The young man, in whose hearing this was said, winked at me and jestingly remarked: "Je ne suis pas un lache comme mon pere!" (I am not a coward like my father). Similarly, shortly after his appointment to the post of secretary general of the United Nations was announced, Boutrous Boutrous Ghālī felt compelled to visit the papacy, ostensibly to obtain the pope's blessing for his new mission. Such a show of humility by the upper class would have been unimaginable prior to the advent of Shenuda to the papal throne. These two men, whom I knew well since they were friends of my parents, are both agnostics. They married outside the church—an abomination in the eyes of the Orthodox clergy—and both to Jews at that, a worse abomination. (The Egyptian Orthodox Church still holds to the traditional view of the culpability of the Jews in the killing of Jesus.)

Someone who marries outside the church is considered to be engaged in fornication (*zena*) and is an outcast, as evident in the story told to me by a Greek-Egyptian friend, Lela Petrides. Soon after her marriage, her husband, a Coptic physician of the Orthodox faith, was killed in an automobile accident on the desert road to Alexandria. When the police bearing his bloodied corpse woke her up at seven in the morning, she ran in tears to the neighboring papal headquarters to ask for their help. But the church refused to bury him, because he had married outside his faith (even though she was Greek-Orthodox, she would have had to convert to Egyptian Orthodoxy to be married in the Egyptian Orthodox church, which she refused to do on principle). So she turned in her despair to her own church, which at the beginning also refused to bury him, since he was not Greek, but finally gave in to her tears and put him to rest in the Greek cemetery.

The church has also spared no effort to catch the new upper middle class of successful, well-to-do physicians, engineers, businessmen, travel agents, real estate people, and the like, who have replaced the ancien régime aristocracy and are too preoccupied with advancing their careers to have time for religion, even if they consider the church a nice place to send their wives to on Sundays with the children. These grandees do not deign to mingle with the ordinary people in the general meetings of their local churches. So special meetings, accompanied by prayers and sermons, have been designed for them, both at the diocesan and papal level. The meetings with the pope, which take place both at the patriarchatal and in the Monastery of Bishoi, his weekend retreat, are often organized by profession: groups of prominent journalists, medical doctors, university professors, engineers, and the like are invited in turn.

In one such meeting with a group of well-known Coptic doctors, which a doctor friend of mine, ʿAkil Yūsuf, described to me, the pope at the end of the meeting asked each one to write down what he was prepared to do for the church. Some offered to contribute money, others volunteered their time in church-run clinics, and he himself put down "technical help only"—and indeed he treats bishops, priests, and monks for free in his private practice at the Anglo-American hospital.

All in all, the pope has succeeded in gaining the support of this new upper middle class, because, with a few exceptions such as Akil Yūsuf, whose grandfather was minister of Defense during the heyday of liberal nationalism in Egypt, they are nouveau riche of humble social origins and therefore share the same religio-cultural idiom as the clergy.

14

The Church as Battleground

Under Pope Shenuda the church is a rallying place for Copts, where they can reaffirm their collective identity. The mass has become for them what it was in the early Christian era, a kind of communal affirmation of survival in the face of persecution. Its strength derives from the awareness of every single individual Copt hurrying to his local church on his day off that millions of Copts throughout the country are doing the same thing. A feeling of power results from the knowledge of this simultaneity, one that is reinforced at the end of the Mass when each member of the congregation clasps the hand of his neighbor to the right and the left, in front of him and behind him in a symbolic gesture of communal unity. Similarily, the common practice of baptizing large groups of babies together on auspicious days, such as the feasts of the saints, is an act of affirmation by a community ever conscious of its minority status. As the babies are carried in their white baptismal gowns by their mothers in procession around the church, the communal rejoicing at this visible blessing of fertility resembles the pride ultra-Orthodox Jews take in their large clutches, which they look upon as a triumph over the Holocaust.

The restrictions on church building was one of the sorest contentions between Christians and Muslims when I undertook this study. Licenses to build or even expand or renovate churches were obtained with the utmost difficulty. Bishop Michael of Assiut was unable to obtain government permission for the building of an awning, within the church complex, underneath which the children could play while their parents attended Mass.[1] Bishop Arsanios of Minya was not allowed to tear down a church wall that served as partition between it and its adjoining church-run youth center to expand the seating capacity of the church.[2] And a case actually exists of a priest being imprisoned for having dared build a latrine for his church without a license.[3] Churches dating back to the third century AD, with priceless old shrines like the Church of St. Abigoue in Minya and the Church of Saint Fam in Tima were being gradually reduced to rubble, because the government would not issue permits for their restoration.[4] The government's attitude was seen by many Copts as a deliberate attempt to obliterate the historical memory of Christendom in Egypt.

The law stipulates that churches must be built at least 100 meters away from mosques, while no such restriction applies to the building of mosques in the vicinity of churches. Nor is there any limitation to the number of mosques built—on the contrary, citizens are encouraged, by means of tax exemptions, to build as many mosques as they can finance. In Minya a hole still remains in the ground today on the site where Bishop Arsanios's predecessor, Bishop Suweires, tried to erect a cathedral. The construction was halted when a Muslim headmistress objected to having a church close to her school.[5] Whenever a new church is built, local residents often hastily erect a mosque next to it. This was the case in several of the dioceses under study, where the appearance of a new church was invariably greeted by a Mosque, planted in such close proximity that the priests' sermon was drowned out by the deafening sound of the neighboring minaret's loudspeaker.[6] Naga Hammadi's Bishop Kyrilos incurred the governor's displeasure when some members of his own community, partisans of Bishop Mina of Girga, who had been their bishop before part of the diocese was reapportioned, betrayed Kyrilos's plan to secretly build a church. The authorities encouraged the erection of the makeshift mosque which now flanks his residence. It blares its message day and night straight into his cell.[7]

By redoubling its services, holding the Masses in shifts, the Coptic Church has been able to get around the ban on the building of new churches and the restoration of old ones, while the faithful, for whom these services are destined, are made to feel that it is their moral duty to attend—not simply on grounds of piety but as an act of defiance against a government that seeks to blot out their heritage.

A very rigorous discipline of daily prayer is mandatory for the Copts. Their daily prayer manual, the *Agbeya* ("Hours"; each hour commemorates a major event in Jesus's life), contains long prayers and psalms designed for them to recite five times a day. In addition, they take part in a very long liturgy (three to five hours) during the Sunday Mass, for which they have to fast a preparatory twelve hours; this fast may not be broken until after Communion, which is generally not given until noon. It therefore entails considerable discomfort during the long hot seasons, because no water can be drunk. Pope Shenuda once stated categorically at a Wednesday meeting that not even the aged or pregnant women could have a single sip of water before Communion. The majority of the Copts have never questioned their duty to engage in such an intense spiritual life: The fact that they may not live up to their intention of fasting 200 days out of the year or that they may not have the stamina to pray all the prayers enjoined on them only fills them with humility and admiration before those more fully committed to spirituality. Their feeling of inadequacy and guilt at failing to carry out their religious obligations in full makes them submit all the more readily to the moral authority of those who have been able to live up to the monastic ideal.

Why does the average Copt not revolt against such onerous strictures? No one has put it more succinctly than the Benedictine Monk Mark Gruber: "[T]he demands of rigorous religious observance, intense communal dynamics, and an elaborated and complex liturgy, catechism and hagiography are exactly the counterweight of spiritual and communal integration the Copts need in face of their national alienation."[8]

Church attendance has gained enormously during the Shenuda administration: The Sunday Mass has been replicated on Friday (the official day off in Egypt), for the benefit of Coptic government employees, who must work on Sunday, and another day, Wednesday (a day of fasting for the Orthodox because it commemorates Judas's betrayal of Jesus), has been added to it. The number of services has also been multiplied to meet everyone's schedule: the government employees, who have to be at work by 9, have a 7 o'clock Mass. This is followed by a second one at 10 for the housewives, and there is a 6 PM Mass for students who are at school or university during the day.[9] (Although a Friday Mass had already been in existence for some time in some of the churches of the big cities like Cairo and Alexandria it did not become generalized to the churches throughout the country until the advent of Pope Shenuda.)

It should be obvious that these new prayer schedules would not have been maintained if the churches had remained empty; the success of Shenuda's mobilization campaign has guaranteed the churches a full house.

Collective prayers came into practice first among the church servants, to inaugurate their own weekly meetings, as well as at the gatherings of the choir groups, of seminarians, members of the Coptic Institute, and members of the church councils. They were later generalized to encompass all gatherings and activities within the Coptic community. So, too, collective fasts became, under Pope Shenuda, a way of mobilizing the population at large. While this practice may appear traditional, it is for laypeople, unlike individual fasts, a new phenomena.

The majority of the middle and lower class, who were more traditional than the upper-class Copts, tended to observe the Wednesday and Friday fasts (commemorating, respectively, Jesus' betrayal by Judas and his crucifixion), as well as the special fasts (3 days to mark the period Jonah spent in the stomach of the whale, symbolic of the 3 days Jesus spent in his grave, 15 days to commemorate the assumption of the Virgin Mary, 21 days to commemorate the feast of the Apostles, 43 days before Christmas to commemorate the Good News of Jesus' birth (analogous to the 40 days fasted by Moses in preparation for the reception of the tablets with the Ten Commandments, because Jesus is considered by Christians the Word of God made flesh), and 55 days at Lent. But the practice of setting aside days for collective fasts that involve the total abstention from food or drink (*inkita'i*)—as opposed to the usual abstention from meats, fish, and dairy products—was adhered to mainly by the monastic community. The monastic discipline involved in a total abstention from food became generalized, under Shenuda, to the faithful at large, both as a means of hardening the mettle of the members of the heavenly commonwealth that the Sunday School Movement was trying to create on earth, and as a mode of civil disobedience.

The method of passive resistance so long practiced by the monks in their battle against sin could also be used to resist the persecuting state. Shenuda, as we saw, first called for a collective fast in January 1977 to protest the imminent passage of the law of apostasy, then a second time on Easter day of 1980 to protest against the inaction of the state after the bombings of the churches in Alexandria. By 1981, this practice had become so deeply ingrained in the community that, when Shenuda was exiled by Sadat, a grassroots, nationwide collective fast was organized to express popular indignation.

In his book *The Life of Faith,* Shenuda puts forward the notion that *inkita'i* fasts are a crucial component of the spiritual discipline necessary to achieve higher levels of faith, to which the Copts should, by degree, be able to ascend.[10] By mobilizing the community to embrace fasts, as both a test of its endurance and a way of honing its capabilities, Shenuda was also countering the frenetic mobilization that precedes the yearly Muslim fast of Ramadan; promotional songs, films, theatrical productions, and sales promotions on television make Ramadan an impatiently awaited, enthusiastically embraced time of year resembling the month between Thanksgiving weekend and Christmas day in the United States. Collective fasts, in particular, because of the sociability entailed in joint prayers, Bible readings, and a shared sense of sacrifice, keep the lone Copt in an office of ubiquitous veiled female employees from feeling marginalized.

Like the Jews, who for most of their history were not permitted secular self-government and depended heavily on their rabbinic leaders for community cohesion, Coptic monasticism from its very beginnings bears the stamp of a people who have had, in the absence of self-government, to rely on a spiritual consensus rooted in the leadership role of the monastic elite.

The adaptation of an age-old monastic tradition for modern political purposes must be seen as a step beyond the radical innovation of the 1940s and 1950s under Bishop Samuel of endowing the church with the secular role of social welfare agency (in Vatican II parlance, "the Church in the World"). It is not simply a pastoral initiative, but rather an ambitious venture on the part of Shenuda to incorporate the lay community into the church, by making religious values relevant not simply to a good afterlife but to the here and now.

But it is not only that the faithful have been brought to the church; the church has come to the faithful. The Sunday School Movement has been successful in its attempt to convince the majority of the Copts that all activities and social gatherings should be preceded by a prayer. It has accomplished this by habituating them from childhood to recite a collective prayer before beginning any church-sponsored activity, pedagogical or social. Teams pray when they meet on the football fields, families before setting out on excursions, students before sitting down to their exams.

For the majority of the hard-pressed middle class, church-sponsored summer resorts, both in and near Alexandria and in the Red Sea area, as well as church-sponsored and subsidized excursions to the Pharaonic sites and to the monasteries, are the only ones parents can afford for their children. In this sense, it ensures the church a captive audience. And the church hostels, which I visited in Abu Talat near Alexandria, where the pope himself has a summer home, resemble palaces by comparison with many of their own homes. They are also a testimony to the success of Shenuda's mobilization campaign, because they cost millions of pounds to build—money each bishop has to raise from contributions within his own diocese. In one instance, when I asked an architect who was supervising some construction work how much had been invested so far in the building, he said over LE 1 million (a little over $330,000), but it was far from finished.[11] And this is just the cost of the materials and blue-collar workers—the professional cadres in charge of the construction often donate their time. For instance, my electrician, Osta Nasif, who made big money in the posh district of Zamalek, told me he and his son gave their labor for free to both church summer camps and monasteries as a form of *'ushur* (a tithe paid by Christians to the church). In another instance, I heard Bishop Moses, during a week of talks devoted to the blue-collar workers, in the church of the Virgin in Shubra, say that it was every worker's duty to offer part of his time for church repairs and church sponsored constructions, "even if it was just to put up light fixtures."[12] In this way, every member of the community with technical skills, big or small, is mobilized. On the construction site of the summer resort being built for the diocese of Minya, I saw the vice minister of Housing, engineer Fahmi Basili, himself, donating his time. But, clearly, it is not just these posh buildings, but the programs, which include many spiritual offerings, that make these church-sponsored resorts popular with the young, who welcome this chance for clean fun.

Another method used by Pope Shenuda to toughen the mettle of the Copts, in their struggle for survival in an increasingly hostile and dangerous environment, has been a massive campaign of church-organized and subsidized excursions to the monasteries. These are for the faithful memorable occasions, which imprint in their hearts the picture of the great sacrifices of the martyrs. The visitors are meant to live out their life thereafter in total subservience to these heroic figures, whose example is to serve them in the difficult times ahead.

Whenever I participated in these pilgrimages, I was struck by the complex feelings the passengers on the bus expressed, which combined a sense of inferiority before their invincible faith and of pride in their martyrdom. Many of the Coptic families I visited, displayed, with visible pride, their cherished pictures of the cadavers, discovered in a recent dig in Fayoum, with smashed skulls, broken and mutilated fingers, and feet nailed to a piece of wood—presumed to be Christian martyrs.[13]

The Orthodox Church leaders are aware of the enormous capital to be gained from a public show of devotion to the martyrs and saints; hence the pope's efforts to persuade the Italians to yield the relics of Saint Mark for reburial in Saint Mark's Cathedral in Alexandria and the much publicized pictures of him dotingly holding up the skull of a martyr, exhumed on the site of the Monastery of the Martyrs near Akhmim, which features an eyesocket pierced by a stick. This is not to say that the church leaders merely invoke these relics for manipulative reasons: The bishops themselves are fervent believers in the saints' powers of mediation; each of them has his own patron saint, and many of them believe they have personally experienced miracles or visions. Bishop Tackla of Dishna told me that a woman to whom he had given a bit of the ointment scraped off Black Moses' coffin, at the Monastery of the Romans, had consequently been healed of kidney stones diagnosed as needing surgical intervention.[14] Likewise, Bishop Tadros of Port Said told me of a woman with terminal breast cancer who was cured through an apparition of the Virgin.[15] Bishop Moses related, at a youth meeting I attended, the case of a woman professor he had met in the United States, with a malignant brain tumor, who on the night of her operation placed a picture of the boy-saint Abanob in the pocket of her pajamas. She was visited by him in her sleep and the next morning, when she was wheeled into the operating theater, the doctors could not find the slightest trace of tumor.[16]

The bishops also believe in the power of demons and evil spirits: Bishop Arsanios described to me an exorcism he had attended. The priest had raised a cross and a candle in the face of the man who was possessed and threatened to burn the demon if he did not leave the body he was inhabiting, and the demon was driven out. (Bishop Arsanios actually heard the dialogue between the priest and his interlocutor, the demon, who was called Mustafa, an Islamic name!)[17] Some of the priests, like Father Samaan of Cairo, have acquired such a reputation for their ability to exorcise demons and evil spirits that I once witnessed the arrival of a Muslim woman, with her mentally disturbed daughter, who had traveled all the way from Syria to seek his aid.[18] Likewise my servant, a devout Muslim, noticing that I was receiving a cleric at home for interviews connected to my research, asked me if I could arrange an exorcism session for his newly wed daughter, who had run away from her husband due to the influence of evil spirits. When I suggested that it was more likely because this sixteen-year-old had been raped by him on her wedding night and repeatedly beaten, he would not hear of it and kept after me until I gave in. Unfortunately despite this priest's legendary powers, no marital harmony ensued and soon after the girl, who had been forced by her father to return to her husband, committed suicide by means of her gas oven.

The shrines of saints are believed to provide protection against demons and evil spirits. Hence, newborn children are often brought to them to be protected against the evil eye. It is common in Egypt to demonize human relations by attributing trouble to the evil eye (*al-Ein*) or to some magical malevolent deed, commonly referred to as *ʿamal* (a deed). A young woman who haunted the patriarchal headquarters in Cairo told me how her first two pregnancies had ended in miscarriages, despite the fact that in her second pregnancy she had gone to the priest of her church who had given her holy water to sprinkle all over her house to drive out the evil spirit. Finally, in despair, she had gone to Pope Shenuda. She related to him her belief that the series of miscarriages she had suffered was due to an *ʿamal* carried out by a woman rival, who had desired her husband for herself, and the pope, she said, had performed a miracle by placing his hand on her stomach and praying for her. This miracle was incarnate in her son, whom she named Abanob after the very popular child martyr.[19]

Demons do not just belong to popular belief; they form a very real experience in monastic life, where the struggle between the angels and the demons is but a reflection of the wider ranging struggle between the forces of good and evil. St. Anthony's long exegeses about demons and their tricks in his Life and Saint Shenute's report "A fight with the Devil on the Ninth of the Month of Tybi" constitute two gems of Coptic literature, not to be outdone by any horror story written in modern times.[20]

This very real sense of the demons and angels hovering in the air all around us is not something restricted to ancient times. Once Bishop Moses described to a youth meeting I attended how he had seen on videotape a small transparent hand, that of an angel, appear during Mass at the exact moment when the Bishop of Girga, Bishop Makarios, collapsed dead with a heart attack while celebrating the Eucharist. The hand snatched up the consecrated bread, so that it would not touch the ground.[21] As Gruber perceptively noted:

> Coptic life is permeated with all manner of transcendental presence. Angel guardians, archangel, heavenly hosts, patron saints, saint intercessors, saint occasional-defenders, and the Virgin Mary round out the constellation of divinely commissioned agents of God who pervade Coptic society. . . . The category of secularity has collapsed under the weight of heaven. Hence the Copts are available to experiences of visions, locutions, inspired dreams, mystical apparitions, miracles and revelations. . . . The Copts need their heavenly friends since their counterpoint—earthly enemies with religious zeal—abound.[22]

I myself have been struck by the number of times in casual conversations with Coptic friends I was told of success in an endeavor thanks to the intercession of this or that saint or certainty of success in some improbable venture (such as winning the lottery for U.S. immigration) because the patron-saint never failed. I have heard Copts hold long soliloquies out loud at home to their favorite saints, chatting with them with a familiarity they would use for old friends and sometimes even quarreling with them. Thus, I witnessed a friend of mine, who had been very upset when St. Barsum failed to respond to his entreaties that his son obtain a waiver from conscription in the army (most Egyptians hate to serve in the army and try to get out of it by any means possible), knock vigorously with his fists on the picture of the saint demanding that he come to his aid and rebuking him for not being responsive to his calls. A few days later he called me to report "a miracle"; his son had been sent home with a note that his medical tests had revealed him to have bilharzia, which made him ineligible for service.

The shrines of the saints are also believed to have healing powers: People bring to them their ailing infants, their infertile wives, and their invalid old parents to seek miracles. (Many solicitors accompany their prayers with a vow of fast, called *som el nadr*, in fulfillment of their request.) Thus, the doctrine of supernatural intervention by saints and angels is unquestionably accepted by believers from the illiterate peasant all the way up to the pope himself. The number of miracles performed by Pope Shenuda's predecessor, Pope Cyril VI, by the time I began this study, were apparently sufficient to fill eight volumes entitled *The Miracles of Pope Cyril the Sixth*.[23] (Currently they have reached thirteen.)

The opening up of the monasteries to mass visits, the building of guest houses and hospices, and the furnishing of accommodations within the monasteries and churches themselves to accommodate large numbers is a relatively new phenomenon begun in the 1950s with the Sunday School Movement. In the past, mass visits were mainly limited to special occasions, mostly to the feast of the monastery's patron saint known as *Mouled*. The central event, then, would be the collective prayer offered as eulogy to the saint in question, followed by the religious procession with his effigy. These celebrations could last anywhere from one to three days. Some of the most popular monasteries were the Monastery of the Romans, believed to harbor the remains of Black Moses, the Monastery of the Holy Family, where the Virgin is believed to have sojourned with Baby Jesus and Joseph during her flight from Judah, the Monastery of St. Dimiana (St. Catherine), who was murdered along with the twelve virgins by the Romans, and the Monastery of St. Mina, where the camel bearing the remains of this saintly warrior is supposed to have stopped, during its trek across the desert, thus determining his burial site. On the anniversary of the latter two saints, their monasteries would be mobbed for several days of commemorative masses and religious processions.

Mouleds have retained their popularity, and certain sites such as the sacred mountain at Dronka near Assiut and the banks of the Nile at Biba are surrounded by a veritable sea of colorful tents at pilgrimage times, as peasants from the surrounding villages camp out in these makeshift accommodations. Not only the peasants come, trekking across long distances on foot or the more affluent among them on donkey-back, but also the urban middle classes. The newly macadamized roads and modern buses have made the trek more comfortable for them, and the Sunday School Movement has enhanced their awareness of their history and their desire to become acquainted with their religious geography. The urbanites are more demanding in terms of hygiene and comfort and it is to attract them that the church has built pilgrimage guest-houses. These accommodations, which offer amenities like toilets and refrigerators, separate them from the poor peasant tent dwellers, but the classes mingle at the fairs.

These fairs have not changed very much from medieval times, offering the crowds of pilgrims all sorts of stalls with games, firing ranges, sweets, pious objects and the like, platforms with various tricks on display, and even a slaughterhouse, for Copts like the Muslims distribute meat to the poor during religious feasts. The pilgrimages for the Copts are not just occasions for a display of piety but for entertainment as well, and some of the fairs, like the one at Rizikat, near Luxor, which attracts tens of thousands of pilgrims from all over the country in November for the feast of St. George, and the one in August at Dronka for the feast of the Virgin, resemble mammoth playgrounds swarming with small children, groups of friends, and young men in search of a good times. This is not only the occasion to buy a toy for a child or some ointment scraped off the relics of a saint for an arthritic elderly aunt who could not make the trip, but also to have one's babies baptized, one's little boys circumcised and often one's girls excised, as well as the demons exorcised by the local priests from one's disturbed family members.

In dwelling on the colorful particularities of these Mouleds, the intention is not just to evoke atmosphere, but to show the way in which the age-old Christian traditions of Egypt are perpetuated and reinvigorated to bond together different social classes, levels of education, and rural and urban backgrounds. For the Mouleds have become for many urbanites primarily acts of communal affirmation. Not only have the Mouleds grown in popularity among these classes in recent years, but new pilgrimage sites have been informally added to the old, such as the one in Zeitun, a district in Cairo where the Virgin is said to have appeared in 1968, and at the Monastery of St. Anthony, where a very popular monk, Father Justus, died in 1976. There is also the Monastery of St. Mina where, in addition to the ancient warrior-saint Mina, Pope Cyril VI, who died in 1971, is now buried and his grave-site has become another cult object.

Formerly, on regular days, virtually the only visitors to be seen were a few devout young men who came for a period of retreat (*Khulwa*). Now nearly every church in Egypt sponsors trips for its congregation. Both families and youngsters are taken in groups to spend a few days in the guest quarters of their favorite monastery (which is often the one that harbors the remains of their favorite saint), sharing in the monks' routine of prayers, nights of adoration (*Tasbiha*), and fasts. In return the visitors support the monastery, stuffing their collection boxes with money and offering gifts of sugar, tea, vegetables, fruits, and cereals—and, during the feasts, water buffaloes and sheep.[24]

The visitors make it a point to arrive at 3 AM to participate in the morning prayers which, when I attended them at St. Anthony's Monastery, began at 4 AM. After that, they tour all its chapels, to look at the murals, relics, and sarcophagus and visit the libraries, containing what remains of the priceless collections of ancient books and parchments (those fortunately left behind by the scavenging European missionaries and scholars who carried off many of them in the eighteenth and nineteenth centuries, when the ignorant monks were indifferent to them). Then, they settle down to a collective breakfast with the monk in charge of visitors, or some of them may have meals in private chambers with their monk friends or monk relatives. Often, at the end of their visit, the abbot meets them in person and gives a small talk about a saint or martyr associated with the monastery.

Monasteries are also growing in popularity as places to hold wedding ceremonies and baptisms. When I was in Luxor I heard this from a local Coptic dignitary who owned Hotel Emile, where I stayed. His daughter (who had just been engaged to a pharmacist) was to be wed in the nearby monastery; he planned to donate two water buffalos to the monks.[25]

Most of the old guard, and even some members of the Sunday School generation like Abbot Matthew the Poor, do not care for such collective visits, which they feel disrupt the solitude needed by monks to sustain their spirituality. Even as late as the 1960s, the monasteries held out against the attempt of the Sunday School Movement to assimilate them into the larger corpus of the church. They wanted to safeguard their distinctiveness as a place of devotion to Christ, as opposed to the pedagogical centers in which the Sunday School generation was transforming them.

But by now the Sunday School generation has succeeded in turning the monasteries into schools for the socialization of the faithful. Mass visits have not only become a favorite family outing for the average Coptic family but a place of pilgrimage for nostalgic émigrés visiting from the diaspora. They also serve as a place of worship for young university graduates in search of jobs, newly engaged couples, and high school examination candidates, who come to solicit their favorite saint, often accompanied by a vow (*Nadr*) in case of fulfillment of their demands, which they scribble on little bits of paper and stuff into a slot in the glass casement containing the saint's coffin, after prostrating themselves before him. This gesture of reverence is accorded the saint even by bishops, and presumably the pope, who rank below the saints and martyrs. I once witnessed a bishop touch the ground with his forehead three times, before Black Moses' coffin, though his age and his corpulence made that difficult. Another time, I accompanied Bishop Tackla of Dishna, who had driven with his mother all the way from upper Egypt, during the sultry month of July on the occasion of his twenty-ninth birthday, to visit these same relics. He performed the same prostrations.[26]

In addition, busloads of schoolchildren, accompanied by a priest, are routinely brought to the monasteries, the way they are taken to the science and art museums in America, not only as a cultural experience but to develop in them an appreciation of the enormous sacrifices and acts of stoicism of the monastic fathers. The monks act the part of big brother to the children, reading stories to them from the hagiographies about the stoicism of the monks of old, who ate the barest minimum essential for survival and gave up all bodily comforts. Instead of snuggling under their warm bed covers at night, the children are told, they would stand for hours on end with outstretched arms in their cells or leave the warmth of their beds to deliberately expose their blanketless bodies to the bitterly cold winter desert winds all through the night. In the summer, they trekked for days under the blazing desert sun, at the risk of dying of dehydration, in search of isolated caves where they could live an even more intense spiritual life as hermits. The children are encouraged to emulate these edifying examples of self-discipline and asceticism by hearing such examples: specifically, St. Shenute who began fasting all day when he was a mere boy-shepard; and Baraksia, who when she visited a convent at the age of nine refused to leave it. They are also told stories about the heroism of child martyrs like the eight-year-old Dollasham, who chose to die rather than worship Roman gods, and the three-year-old Qirakius, who called on his mother to die with him for the sake of their Christian faith. Nor is the very popular Abanob forgotten. The mothers are encouraged to take their children to visit the church recently built in the Delta region to honor this martyr, a site that has since become a center for pilgrimage. There, they are themselves taught heroic examples of mothers who welcomed martyrdom with their children like Um Dullagi and her five sons and Um Rifqa and her five children.

The children's visit was usually rounded off by a demonstration of things of particular interest to them, such as the old wells that until recently constituted the monasteries' only source of water and the windmills the monks used for grinding wheat. The monks patiently answered all the children's questions. Then they would be given small souvenirs, like fountain pens with the picture of His Holiness and keychains that depict Saint Barsum taming a snake.

During a number of such visits, I would take advantage of the availability of the monks, who would otherwise flee at the mere sight of a woman or be afraid to antagonize a superior by talking to one without a written permission from the abbot to add my own questions to those of the children. On the walk back to the monastery, after we had waved good-bye to the children in the bus, I would ask him what habit had been the hardest to give up or what he missed the most in his first two years as a novice in the monastery. The answer was never sex, which most of them had never fully experienced anyway. Out of the seventy-eight monks I was able to talk to in the course of a three-year stay, only 30 percent said that they had a hard time kicking the "secret habit" or that they sometimes fantasized a naked women lying in their cell-bed. Fifty eight percent thought the hardest thing was giving up their tea, a real addiction in Egypt. (Monks are not allowed tea or coffee, which is considered addictive; they are served a brew of guava leaves instead.)[27] Ten percent said they yearned for cigarettes, and the remainder either mentioned their morning newspaper or their mother's cooking.

It is not only for the young that the monastic example has become an important referent for everyday life. The practice of *khulwa* had gained enormously in popularity among adults—even among people who were never particularly close to the church. They seem to find in the few days they spend with the monks, sharing their prayers and moments of meditation, a welcome feeling of historical anchorage in a country that increasingly marginalizes them. As Gruber beautifully expressed this, "The nation has orphaned them, but God hems them in."[28]

15

The Church as Amphitheater

The General Meetings, which the Coptic canticles inaugurate, well examplify the way in which the new and old mesh to create traditions. Pope Shenuda first called these meetings "*Dars*" (Lesson). This at one and the same time underlined their innovative character, by distinguishing them from the religious sermon, and created a tradition, by emphasizing their continuity with the pedagogical mission of the founder of the Sunday School Movement, the by then "resting" Ḥabīb Jirjis. (Pious Copts never use the word *dead*; they say *itnayah*, "he rested.") Thus, we can see how new traditions are fashioned, as the rapid transformation of society weakens the social patterns for which the "old" traditions had been designed. The sermon itself was at one time an innovation for the Coptic Church. Prior to its adoption, by the Sunday School generation in the 1940s, the Coptic Church was limited to the celebration of mass. But the growing Islamization of the state after the 1952 revolution and particularly, as we have seen, of the educational system under junta member Kamāl al-Din Hussein required a new "tradition" that would deal not just with the battered self-image of the Copts, through a revalorization of their past, but also with their day-to-day mundane problems. This was what Shenuda's "Lesson" was designed to accomplish, by reformulating the sermon into a freewheeling give-and-take between the preacher and his audience. Both the nomenclature and form of these meetings was in fact borrowed from the Protestants, and first used in the 1940s, when Shenuda's generation were still deacons and seminarians, to apply to their own meetings. In short, the church revival and reformation, which took place in the twentieth century, involved a series of adaptations of old models for new political and social purposes.

Notwithstanding the attempt of Pope Shenuda and other members of the Sunday School Movement to legitimize these changes by drawing on analogies with the church of origin, there can be no doubt that his meetings were a distinctly modern form of organization. By expanding what was once restricted to deacons and church-servants to include the laymen, Pope Shenuda increased the mobilizational potential of the church. (It is estimated that anywhere from 5,000 to 8,000 people crowd into the Anba Ruweis Cathedral to listen to him on any given Wednesday.)[1]

Hence, it is not surprising that when Shenuda, as bishop of Higher Clerical Education, first began to hold these meetings, the authorities became very disquieted by the kind of mobilization it entailed and asked Pope Cyril to reign in his new bishop. A number of other bishops and priests, across the country, who were emboldened by Shenuda's example and had begun to imitate him, were placed under surveillance by the secret police. Pope Shenuda told me about one priest, Father Zakaria, who had to be put on a plane and spirited out of the country to Australia to elude his captors.[2] The secret police were after him because his church meetings had gained so much in popularity that they had begun to attract Muslims, some of whom he was rumored to have converted.

The political potential of Pope Shenuda's "lessons" was not just noted by the authorities. Many of Egypt's foremost intellectuals, including the former editor-in-chief of al-Ahrām, Hassanein Heykal, underlined the political potential of Shenuda's lessons by pointing out that at its inception, in the 1930s, the Muslim fundamentalist movement also began as a series of weekly "lessons" by its leader Hassan al-Banna.[3]

Later, Pope Shenuda changed the name from "Lesson" to "General Meeting" (Ijtima' 'Am), a name meant to highlight the popular nature of the meeting and its element of social cohesion, by implying the assemblage of the entire community.

The change in nomenclature did not in any way mean a change of substance. The "Lesson" was drawn from either the reading of an episode in the bible or from a hagiography; in the former case, it was often meant to supply a social ethic that would help Copts cope with contemporary problems, while in the latter it was mostly meant to impress upon them their inferiority vis-à-vis the saints and martyrs who sacrificed their lives rather than deny their faith. The implicit message was, today's Copts must be prepared to endure any hardships to safeguard their patrimony. This put an onus on anyone tempted to convert to Islam to enhance his chances of promotion in the public sector (as Bishop Arsanios once put it to me, "There is no one baser than he who betrays his religion").[4] It was also meant to comfort the one who has lost a family member to an Islamic militant's bullet, by providing the bereaved family with a saint-martyr as role model.

Shenuda soon moved the day of the General Meeting from Friday to Wednesday, to enable the diocesan bishops, who had themselves begun to hold similar meetings on Friday, to attend his own. Some of them, like the bishop of the neighboring diocese of Shubra al-Kheima, Bishop Murqus, were regulars, while others, who had to travel long distances to get there, generally came when a choir from their own diocese was scheduled to sing the opening canticles and hymns. This was considered a big event, widely attended by accompanying parents and friends and reproduced on videos for mass consumption back home. To encourage the singing of such hymns, the bishop of Youth, Bishop Moses, holds competitions every summer: The winning choir brings prestige to its diocese comparable to the honor a local Egyptian soccer team brings to its club or town.[5]

Thus we can see how a practice like the "Lesson" became formalized and ritualized, and turned into a tradition—if only through repetition. As a young bishop, Shenuda had built up his reputation on his ability to personify and popularize the biblical heroes and legendary personas of the hagiographies in such a way as to make his "Lesson" draw larger audiences than did the soccer stadiums in Egypt. Later, when he became pope, he was able to magnify the impact of his Friday meetings a thousandfold, because cassette tape players had by then succeeded transistor radios in the low-income households. Soon the diocesan bishops, following Pope Shenuda's example, themselves began to hold General Meetings on Fridays.

As many as 300,000 tapes of Pope Shenuda's address at the General Meeting were sold each week when I was doing my research.[6] It has become common for people to kill time in the course of their tortuous drive through the congested Cairene streets by listening to his homilies. Recordings of his latest talks are also often offered as gifts to elderly relatives, who are unable to attend his meetings, as well as listened to together with the children, before an event like a birthday party. Both the vernacular Arabic he uses and his humorous allusions make them intelligible to old and young, educated and uneducated alike.[7]

The ambiance of Pope Shenuda's General Meetings is festive, with its phosphorescent lights and loudspeakers, its red carpets and incense, its processions of deacons and choristers. It is once again an example of the "invention" of a tradition through the creation of an alloy of old ritual practices and modern techniques of organization, such as one encounters in a political podium, and is meant to impart to the Copts a triumphal feeling of "power and glory."[8]

Even before the meeting starts, a Copt on his way to the papal headquaters is swept up by a feeling of tumultuous excitement at the sight of the long lines of cars inching their way forward, with big crosses dangling from their mirrors, pictures of the Virgin on their windshields, and occasionally an effigy of the pope placed by the rearwindow. All of these indicate that at last the Copt is leaving hostile Muslim territory and entering his own domain where he holds sway, if only for a few hours. This feeling is reinforced by the host of watchful young deacons at the gates, whose task is to detect individuals suspected of being Muslims and check their identification cards.

Arriving an hour ahead of time, and on special occasions several hours, to ensure a good seat in a packed house is by no means unusual. Latecomers may have to content themselves with standing room at the back or near the jammed doorways, in this vast hall with a seating capacity of several thousands, which only adds to the smug satisfaction of those fortunate enough to have gotten seats. (The loudspeakers, which will bellow out the pope's "Lesson" into the courtyard, ensure that those who did not find places in the cathedral can follow his speech.) Half an hour before the pope's arrival, the jostling crowds lend the cathedral the air of a bazaar in which the question of who's to get what seat is being negotiated (loud and heated arguments can be heard over someone's refusal to cede a seat to a foreign reporter, a visitor from the diaspora, or an "important" member of the community). The attempt of the church-servants, who act as ushers, to discipline the unruly crowds, by shouting them down, only adds to the pandemonium.

Some of these church-servants, who have been assigned to the pope as "public relations men," are people of outstanding caliber and dedication, while others are little more than petty bullies with the manners of street thugs. On one summer evening when it was too hot to wait for the pope's arrival to the General Meeting inside the cathedral, I spotted Bishop Murqus seated by the side entrance on the lawn, surrounded by a group of church-servants. Since I knew him well and liked him, I waved at him from a distance and pulled up a chair to his side. But just as I was about to sit down, a squat grey-haired church-servant called George swiftly pulled the chair away from underneath me, causing me to fall on my back. The fact that I could have been seriously injured did not seem to trouble him. It was the bishop who felt compelled to make amends. He said I should excuse him, he was a Saidi (an Upper Egyptian) who was not used to seeing a woman seat herself next to a bishop. Another time, when I climbed, for one moment onto the podium to take a picture of the pope during a Coptic New Year celebration, a church-servant pounced on me and wrenched me off it so violently that I fell and sprained an ankle. (Having recently begun my research on the church, I was not yet aware of the double standards by which male photographers were allowed on the podium but women photographers were not.) Nor was this to be the last time I would be manhandled by church-servants. Once Bishop Tackla took me along to the summer camp of Abu Talat, where he was scheduled to give a talk in the evening. As soon as the bishop arrived he went upstairs to nap, leaving me to my own resources. So I sat down to rest in the shade by the water basin near the entrance. The monk in charge of the camp, arrived on the scene soon thereafter and, apparently not pleased to have a woman visitor, ordered me to leave. When I said I had just traveled three and a half hours from Cairo to hear the bishop's talk and that I would only leave if the bishop himself asked me to, the monk beckoned to his church-servants to get rid of me. Four young men rushed at me, tore my camera out of my hands, threw it in the basin, and forcefully pushed me out of the gate. This time too, it was the bishops, Tackla and Moses, who felt compelled to offer excuses when they later learned what had happened.

But this kind of boorish conduct does not trouble the Egyptians, who have grown up in an authoritarian environment where orders are not questioned—especially by women. On the contrary, they seem to approve of these representatives of clerical authority, whose behavior does not differ significantly from that of some of the priests who will interrupt the service to scream *Uskut* (shut up) at someone in the congregation or scold someone as though he were a child, A'ib kidah! Kifāyah dawshā! (Shame on you! Enough noise!). And perhaps they recognize in this manhandling by church servants a need to compensate, by a show of power, for the frustrations of being trapped in the genteel fringes of Cairo's slums.

Finally, when everyone is seated, the papal Mercedes arrives. The pope always makes his audience wait a long time, which only seems to increase their pleasurable anticipation. As soon as he steps out of his Mercedes, hangers on at the doorway rush at him, some only to touch his habit in veneration, others to prostrate themselves at his feet, still others to whisper their solicitations to him or to thrust their ailing baby at him for a blessing. By that time, the church-servants have given up any hope of enforcing order by means of their strong-armed tactics, and the pope, unflustered by the commotion, navigates through the teeming multitudes the way a U.S. presidential candidate might in a primary, smiling at this one, giving a word of advice to the troubled youth, patting the cheek of a child. When the pope feels he has been sufficiently obliging, he disengages himself by calling out in a peremptory tone "Bas! uwʿa inta wa-huwwa" (Enough! Make way, you and him). Then he picks up the hem of his black cape with the embroidered golden crosses and thrusts himself upon the stage to the general euphoria of the waiting spectators, who stand up and roar their appreciation.

But he silences them with a regal gesture. The church music begins to envelop them, and the sound of the children's choir appeases them and reinforces their awed sense of being a linkage in a great chain of being that stretches across the generations. At that moment the church becomes the custodian of their ancient identity. And this feeling increases, as the pope invokes the supernatural world of saints and martyrs, in his opening prayer known as *al-Da'wah*, which encompasses the entire Ecclesia from the dead to the living gathered that day, beginning this awesome chain of being with the apostle Mark, considered the founder of the Coptic Church, in Alexandria.

As the 117th successor to the See of the Church of Alexandria, the pope then starts his lesson, which consists of a back-and-forth movement between a biblical narrative and direct interlocutions with members of the audience. The idea is to demonstrate that there is an analogy between the combats of the Copts against the devil (their own weakness, lust, envy, egotism, material greed, and so on) and against their external adversaries (currently the Muslims) inasmuch as if they cultivate the strength of character needed to defeat their own shortcoming, they will be able to stand up to the Muslim adversary.

Unlike Abbot Matthew the Poor, the pope does not dwell too long on the relative inferiority of the faithful today in comparison with yesterday's martyrs. Such a course of action seems to him too disheartening. Rather, he tries to encourage them to adopt religious values by personifying for them the victorious biblical heroes in a simple manner and by showing them that hardly any of the great biblical figures even Jesus himself, was not tempted by the Devil and did not weaken at some fateful moment. The internal adversary, this Devil, has the same goal in mind as the external adversary, the Muslim supremacist: To erode the spiritual strength and fortitude of the Copts. Hence, it becomes the duty of every Copt to engage in a spiritual combat against the Devil (*harb Rūḥiyya*) to preserve his or her religious patrimony, which is depicted as superior to all others, including those of the other Christian denominations.

The examples he selects usually have the miraculous happy endings one encounters in fairy tales, which permits the audience to identify with the trials of these saintly figures without losing heart. The purpose of this exercise, as far as the pope is concerned, is not to impart "scientific knowledge" of the Bible or the canon laws or church dogma, after the manner of the bishop of Advanced Research, Gregorios, nor to inculcate the humility befitting a Christian before the "sacred and glorious" history of the Egyptian church fathers and martyrs, as Abbot Matthew the Poor would have done, but to convey to the faithful a sense of belonging to a universe of their own, governed by its own values, that has its roots in the immemorial past—a universe it is the duty of each and every one to perpetuate. Beyond that, he strives to give them a feeling that they have the support of the church in their daily trials.

In telling these biblical stories, the pope does not adopt the stern tone of a preacher but rather poses as a casual raconteur at a family gathering. He looks like a jolly, portly grandfather, and his tone is full of humor. He uses the Arabic vernacular rather than literary Arabic, and he often sidetracks into personal anecdotal material. He creates the illusion of being on the same plane as his listener, by frequently using the *we* or *us* form (*iḥnā*), and by seasoning his remarks with expressions like *Yā ḥabībī* (love) in addressing someone in the audience—all of which his predecessor, the formal, gaunt, ethereal Cyril VI would have found horrifying. In short, Pope Shenuda uses a thoroughly modern idiom, which appeals to the young.

At the end of his talk, the convivial pope takes questions (an unprecedented practice). He assumes an even more intimate role of pater familias, and the level of his discourse plummets from the sublime to the profane. A married woman wants to know if the church objects to her having a child at age forty. The pope asks, in a sarcastic tone, why this idea has not dawned on her earlier, and without waiting for her reply says that it is "unnatural" for a woman of "advanced" age to have a child. Crushed, the woman falls silent. He then turns to his next questioner. A father complains that his son engages in the "secret habit" (he found out from the tell-tale sheets) and asks what he can do about it. The pope gives the standard litany about all the horrible things that will happen to the boy if he persists: loss of ability to concentrate on his studies, fatal exhaustion, disease—even madness. (Such questions are often addressed also to the bishops during their youth meetings; the fact that they themselves have had very little sexual experience—if any at all—does not inhibit them from giving advice freely on sexual and marital questions or deter the faithful from seeking their "expert" council.) Another man wants to know if it is all right for him to savor his food when he is fasting, to which the pope replies that if God has blessed him with a wife who cooks well, there is still no excuse for gluttony on such a solemn occasion. Finally, a man announces that his wife sees reason only when he beats her, and he adds that she is in the audience and agrees with him (the audience roars with laughter). Fortunately, the pope expresses disapproval. And a boy wants to know if his sin of slipping unnoticed into the subways without paying can be washed clean, if he donates the equivalent to the church.

After a number of such questions and answers, the pope stands up and turns his back on the audience, to face the East. He intones a prayer in Coptic, followed by the Lord's Prayer in Arabic. And once more he recites the Daʾwah, which blesses the entire Ecclesia, living and dead. Then he sweeps off of the podium, flanked by a flutter of black habits.

But long after the pope has made his dramatic exit, followed by his devotees, who scramble after him, hoping to get one last grasp of his sleeve, the faithful linger in this intoxicating world that excludes the Muslims. They try to make the magic last, by surrounding the bishops and priests, by exchanging precious bits of gossip among themselves, by strolling arm in arm along the many stalls set up at the gateway, which sell banners with gaily embroidered Coptic crosses, necklaces, and rings depicting the Virgin, key chains depicting the Egyptian saints, recordings of Pope Shenuda's latest talks, and paintings of Pope Cyril VI with "natural" white hair glued on for his beard. (When I met the newlywed son of Bishop Arsanios's brother Tewfik, whom the bishop was visiting to bless his new apartment by sprinkling it with Holy Water, his nephew showed me with great pride a large portrait of Pope Cyril VI, with a long "natural" beard that he had received as a wedding present. In his bathroom, he had another picture of Pope Cyril, this time taken when he was a young recluse in the Napoleonic windmill, on the Mokatam Hills. In that picture, he looked very much like an American hippie in the 1960s.)

For all of these reasons, Shenuda's "Lesson" cannot be regarded in the same light as the late Ḥabīb Jirjis's pedagogical efforts to preserve and pass on the religious heritage—or even compared with the precepts of present-day followers of Jirjis, like Abbot Matthew the Poor or the Bishop of Advanced Coptic

Research, Gregorios. Shenuda is engaged not just in an effort to revalorize the heritage for its own sake, but in one that is intended as an affirmation of the self. Through the knowledge and appreciation of their heritage, the faithful will acquire the self-confidence to be more assertive in taking on the Muslim supremacists.

It is this instrumentalization of religious knowledge that men like Matthew the Poor oppose. They systematically denounce this attempt to analyze the day-to-day problems of the faithful by means of analogies to the trials of the saints and martyrs. Nor do they care for the freewheeling give-and-take with the congregation at the end of the "General Meeting." They look upon it with the same distaste as the establishment press in America feels for Baptist fundamentalist talk shows. The job of the preacher, as they see it, is to deal not with the here and now, but with the hereafter. Excessive concern with contemporary problems is for them a form of modern egotism, an inability of the Copts to love unconditionally and to sacrifice themselves unquestioningly to their faith.

PART VII

Three Questions for the Twenty-First Century

16

Toward a More Democratic Church?

We have seen that the bishops of the Sunday School generation, as rulers of dioceses, were driven by the nature of their worldly commitments to create a modern administration. The growing complexities of economic development compelled them to withdraw from day-to-day administration and separated the ruler's household from the administrative apparatus. This led to the growth of a bureaucracy of church-servants with specialized tasks and to institutions with their own budgets, office buildings, and staff. Even if, as has been argued, this process is more advanced in Cairo and Minya than in some of the other dioceses, the movement toward a legal-rational bureaucracy is unmistakable.

In much the same manner, it brought about a separation of the ruler's purse from the developmental budgets. Things are no longer run as they were in the old days, with various priests or church-servants approaching the bishop with a suggestion for some new activity or enterprise and the bishop digging into the pocket of his habit to give him some cash, along with his blessing. Rather, projects are submitted to outside donors for funding and, once they are funded, they have their own accounts in the bank, which helps ensure them some measure of continuity—even beyond a bishop's lifetime. This marks the beginning of a divorce between politics and administration, which up until then were fused; it means that even if a bishop's successor does not share his own progressive orientation the administration of the project will continue.

A further result is the beginning of the dissolution of personal government. To the extent that the bishops needed to rely on the expertise of their church-servants, not only in administration but in developmental planning and in fund raising, the church-servants—at least at the high level of *Umana' al-Khidmah* (those entrusted with the supervision of other church-servants and the coordination of activities in the various church premises, districts, small towns, and villages)—were in effect no longer merely servants. They had become more like consultants for a corporation, whose advice the bishop had to heed and whom the bishop had to court, because expertise is scarce in Egypt and each diocese depends for its development on a handful of key men whose loss could prove disastrous. Unless the church-servants maintain a good working relationship with their bishop, they can bolt to another diocese or move to Cairo, where their services are much sought after by the Bishoprics of Youth and of Social Services.

Not only has the enormous expansion of the bishop's workload brought about the beginning of an end of personal government, by compelling the bishop to delegate responsibilities to a cadre of qualified church-servants but he also needs to win over his lay constituency to acquire the necessary funds and free expertise for his development projects. The bishop must therefore be as responsive to the laity as he is to those within the high ranks of the church hierarchy.

Thus, we may conclude there is some connection between development and democracy. The bishops now need to court not only the rich dignitaries but also the rank and file to ensure the adoption or the success of their pet projects. For example when Bishop Tackla of Dishna tried to launch developmental activities, a youth club, a clinic, and a sewing workshop for a village in his diocese, the village priest opposed it because these activities were to be managed by lay church-servants. Bishop Tackla, who told me he had learned the art of lobbying for popular support from the pope, managed to outmaneuver the priest by calling a meeting of the village youth and pretending to ask them what *they* would like to have in their village. They immediately came up with the suggestion of a youth club. The bishop pretended to treat their suggestion with skepticism but led them on by suggesting that he would go along with their idea, if they managed to sell it to their priest, thus placing the priest in the predicament of having to appear the villain if he refused. Once the youth club proved a success, Bishop Tackla had no trouble getting his other two projects adopted.[1]

Originally mostly the rich dignitaries, who write a regular, generous monthly check to the bishopric referred to as a "subscription," *Ishtirak*, were admitted to private audiences with the bishop. Bishop Bula of Tanta recounted to me how one of the first things he had done, following his consecration as bishop, was to have the office in the bishop's abode moved down to the ground floor so he would be accessible to *all* people. His predecessor, the late Bishop Johanna, he said, had sat upstairs in his second floor office and entrusted to his janitor the task of separating out the unimportant people who presented themselves at the door and ushering in only the town dignitaries (*al-kiyadat*).[2]

Thus behind its seemingly unaltered autocratic facade, the church has been undergoing profound changes. It could not remain impervious to the spirit of modern times. The difference between the old-style bishops—remote, revered figures who, if they gave their people any time at all, gave them only as much time as it took to allow them to kiss their hands—and the new-style bishops, who resemble baby-kissing American presidential candidates on a campaign trail, is in part what this study is about. Whereas in the past the majority of the people only got to see their bishop during Mass, now they have his undivided attention.

In exchange for this reciprocity, the bishops are able to tap their peoples' resources for developmental purposes. In this regard it does not make any difference whether a member of the Sunday School generation of bishops is more formal in style, like Bishop Arsanios of Minya, or whether he has a more casual manner, as Bishop Athanasios of Banī Suwayf did. Bishop Athanasios was apt to pull his hand away from anyone who tried to kiss it,[3] and he disdained the traditional monastic style of dress: he sported instead a western-style frayed tweed coat that matched the color of his beat-up old jalopy (bishops customarily drive in shiny Mercedes).[4] Bishop Arsanios, on the other hand, who takes very seriously the notion that a bishop must project the image of Christ's vicar on earth, would never dream of appearing in public without the black turban worn on top of a cowl with golden crosses and the traditional black cape, and he is prepared to suffer the hand kissing and prostration. But behind his intimidating facade, he is every bit as accessible as Bishop Athanasios. I once saw the latter approached by a grimy peasant, who, seizing the bishop by his big, wooden, pectoral cross, vociferously rebuked him for not coming to bless his cow at her calving. He claimed this had caused her to fall sick and die.[5] Another time, in my presence, the bishop turned down an invitation to a banquet prepared by the village dignitaries to sit down on the floor with a peasant family to a meal of pickled turnips and bread, in a malodorous mud hovel.[6] Even in the privacy of his own abode, he spurned the pomp and aura of his station; once, after he had invited me to lunch, I saw him withdraw to a tiny bedroom for his afternoon siesta and, in answer to my query about why he did not sleep in the spacious, adjacent bedroom, he said he had turned it over some years back to his church-servant Emile (Bishop Moses), so he would be more comfortable. He refrained from moving back into it after Emile left his service, so Emile would feel free to visit anytime[7] (Bishop Moses' youthful book collection was still on the shelf, as well as his poster of Jesus with a crown of thorns).

Paradoxically, at the same time that the diocesan units, which previously resembled feudal principalities, have moved in the direction of decentralized decision making and a more liberal form of government, the papacy has, as we have seen, moved toward centralized power, resembling the enlightened absolutism of eighteenth-century monarchies. In much the same way as the benevolent despots of eighteenth-century Europe cleared the way for democracy by replacing a feudal system of patronage with one that ensured loyalty to their persons, by enforcing parity and uniformity on the different regions of their countries, Pope Shenuda has paved the way for a more modern administration as well as, inadvertantly, for a more democratic one.

The unit of central administration at the papal level, which functions as the pope's "Privy Council," is an inner cabinet consisting at the time of this study of five of his most trusted spiritual sons: Bishops Bishoi, Serapion, Moses, Benjamin, Bisante, and Bula—though the first three had considerably more influence with the pope than did the latter three. It is not only that these men had the ruler's ear and acted as his advisors but they had unlimited access to him, a sine qua non for getting things done in a system where everything has to be sanctioned from above. The other bishops, who had less favored status, could not simply ride up the elevator to the third floor of the papal residence but had to be admitted by the pope's secretary, which entailed hour-long, sometimes day-long waits, and sometimes vain waits, in the antechamber on the first floor of the residence.[8]

The hallway of the papal headquarters is always buzzing with the petitioners and complainants, who have been waiting for hours to corner the pope on his way out of his office to toss a few hastily whispered words or a tiny piece of paper at him, as he hastens toward the elevator that will put him out of their reach.[9] (Once when I was standing near that same elevator waiting in hopeful anticipation of the pope's appearance, I saw Bishop Serapion emerge and shut the door behind him. Just as I was about to leave disappointed, he reopened the door and beckoned to the still invisible pope to step out, telling him it was only me!) The notes that the pope stuffs into the pockets of his habit are not only requests and pleas, but also complaints about other priests and bishops. The pope tolerates this form of intrigue, and even encourages it, because it keeps him informed about what is going on in the church and helps him to exercise control. It may be a grievance justified or otherwise against the bishop of a diocese divided into warring clans, as is that of Naga Hammadi, part of whose land once belonged to Bishop Mina of Girga, so that the partisans of Bishop Mina remain hostile and distrustful to this day of the pope's protégé, young Bishop Kyrilos. Or it may be a complaint against a bishop, like Bishop Besada of Akhmim, for expelling the novices of the Monastery of the Martyrs without sufficient proof that they had participated in the pilfering of the collection boxes. Or it may be complaints about a bishop such as Bishop Bishoi, whom the pope dispatches on missions all the time, that he spends too much time outside his own diocese,[10] or against a priest that he is corrupt, or even pettier level intrigues against a lay person who seems to have the pope's favor and whom others wish to dethrone.[11]

Even if at times these rivalries exasperate him and frustrate his objectives, they never threaten the pope's position. But they can threaten the position of a priest, and even of a bishop, against whom accusations are made without his knowledge or chance to defend himself. Although, unlike a priest, a bishop cannot be relieved of his functions through *ḥurman*, he can nonetheless find himself "dethroned" overnight: from one of the privileged few with access to the pope, to the object of disfavor and rebuff.

This happened to Bishop Arsanios, originally one of the high prelates closest to the pope, when Bishop Arsanios chose to stand by the monk-priest, Father Daniel, whom the pope and his inner cabinet of powerful bishops wished to excommunicate. Since bishops do not have a veto power within the Holy Synod, and most bishops who disagreed with the pope, like Bishop Athanasios, were afraid to openly take a stand against him, the excommunication measure was pushed through.[12]

Long after Father Daniel had been excommunicated for his "Protestant" excesses,[13] the pope's envoys, Bishops Moses and Tadros, continued to pressure Bishop Arsanios to change his mind and add his signature to those of the others, to give the document the appearance of unanimity.[14] It is to his credit that he held out, despite this intense pressure and ostracism by the pope and his devotees among the young bishops, until the matter resolved itself. This happened when Father Daniel, who was denied the right to pray in Orthodox churches and even in the Catholic ones, because the Catholic Church, which was in throes of an ecumenical rapprochement with the Orthodox Church, did not wish to incur the pope's displeasure, finally left the Orthodox church altogether. He in effect became a Protestant preacher and took a wife. (When, after his excommunication, Father Daniel first came to my house secretly, since I feared the pope's wrath if he found out I was receiving him, he was still dressed in the black habit traditionally worn by Orthodox clergy, although he had stopped wearing the cowl with the golden crosses distinctive to monks. It was a Wednesday, so I offered a vegetarian fare. But he announced that he had stopped fasting the Orthodox fasts. Those made sense, he explained, only if one was part of that community, but he had just been expelled from it. A year later, in 1993, when I visited him, under cover of night, in the house of one of his youthful fans in Heliopolis, he was dressed in jeans and a T-shirt.)

The resolve shown by the pope not to tolerate any dissent within the Holy Synod over Father Daniel's excommunication shows that he is still far more than just *primus inter pares*. Nonetheless, this system of personal government is being undermined by some of the very forces unleashed by Pope Shenuda himself. In the first place, the increase in responsibilities, far beyond the capacity of the principal members of the pope's inner cabinet to handle, pushes the administration farther along the path toward institutionalization and decentralization. The creation of the Bishopric of Youth, under Shenuda, was the first step in that direction. More recently, the emergence of a Bishopric of Immigration and the consecration of bishops for two of the areas with the densest population of Coptic immigrants, namely England and the United States, showed the beginning of a recognition that the doubling up of Bishops Serapion and Moses as the pope's all-purpose emissaries to the West, as well as the pope's representatives in any domestic crisis, was bound to take a toll on the Bishoprics of Social Services and of Youth. Much the same thing is true of the dioceses, which were bound to suffer from neglect if a diocesan bishop like Bishop Bishoi, considered the eminence grise of the papacy, was put in charge of just about every committee, from the one to try priests for misdemeanors, to the ecumenical committee, to the one on personal status—a committee he was recently compelled, out of sheer lack of time, to turn over to his son in confession Bishop Bula.

Young Bishop Bula of the diocese of Tanta, a rising power in the inner cabinet, who in addition to the aforementioned committee has been placed by the pope on the Committee on National Unity (in charge of fostering good relations with the Muslims), manages to cater to the needs of his own diocese as well as to be at the pope's beck and call only by sleeping less than three hours, by his own admission to me, on any given night and, consequently, walking around with terrible headaches during the day.[15] And I have on more than one occasion observed Bishop Bishoi, who is terribly over worked, nodding off at a public meeting. As the problems associated with socioeconomic development and with attacks by Islamic militants keep increasing and the number of the committees departments and bishoprics set up to deal with them multiply, the trend away from the method employed by the pope of entrusting new tasks to his favorite spiritual sons on an ad hoc basis toward further institutionalization and decentralization of power is bound to continue.

In addition, the populist style of Shenuda's General Meetings, which encompassed a freewheeling give-and-take with the common people, helped spread the notion among his peers that good government depended on the leaders linking up with the grassroot population. As evidence of this, one has only to observe the rapid spread among diocesan bishops, of the practice of holding general meetings. But, perhaps more important, this semblance of a dialogue based on parity encouraged the people themselves to demand a greater say in church affairs.

Some of Shenuda's critics feel that the democratization of the church is only one of form, that Shenuda has adopted an informal style to cater to modern tastes but that the substance of the way the Coptic community is governed remains unchanged.[16] But I would argue that while the final say is the pope's (or bishop's), he must now govern in consultation—not just with a body of clerics but with the laymen who make up the Coptic community. Since the Sunday School Movement seized control of the church, this has come to mean not merely the lay leadership, on whose financial support the church depends, but the educated middle class, whose professional skills the church needs for developmental purposes.

The Egyptian Orthodox Church has a populist tradition. From time immemorial, it has seen, despite its authoritarian hierarchic structure, an inordinate amount of lay involvement in church affairs. The ferocity with which laymen have fought one another during papal elections to obtain the candidate of their choice (in the first half of the twentieth century, the acrimony over the unsuitability of a candidate for the papacy reached such a pitch that on more than one occasion the government was asked by the conflicting parties to come to their aid); the protest movements, whether sit-ins in church to prevent the consecration of a bishop deemed unsuitable, as in the case of the Giza bishop in the 1950s, or the demonstrations and petition campaign to remove the bishop of Minya in that same period—as well as the great excitement and heavy turnout for consecration ceremonies for new bishops—all bear witness to the laymens passionate involvement in church affairs. As Wakin, observing the scene in the late '50s, put it, "The Coptic Church is probably the only Christian church whose laity in the twentieth century has been more dedicated than its clergy."[17]

Once appointed to a diocese, an Orthodox bishop in turn, even a traditional one, is in much closer touch with his lay constituency than is his Catholic counterpart. It is both the strength and weakness of Orthodoxy that the bishop is a man of all trades. He not only meets important foreign delegations of donors, as well as state officials, and adjudicates in disputes between the people and their priests, the priests and each other, the priests and the layboard of church management, and so on, as a Catholic bishop might but, in addition, he spends a considerable amount of time celebrating early-morning Mass and participating in the nocturnal hymns in praise of the Lord (*Tasbiha*), ministering to the sick, hearing confessions (a role relegated to priests in the Catholic Church), and listening to the problems of married couples, siblings quarreling over a legacy, girls pregnant out of wedlock, and husbands distraught because they discovered on their wedding night that their wife was not a virgin. A bishop, who asked not to be named, told me while I was doing fieldwork in his diocese about such a case. He was awakened from his sleep at 5 AM by an outraged bridegroom, an engineer, who had come with his bride in tow, after their wedding night, to ask for a divorce on the grounds that she had not bled. He would not listen to reason, until the bishop called in a gynecologist, who proved to him by getting him to prod the hymen with his finger that it was still intact. It had simply been too sturdy to yield to his first assault!

Such challenges constitute the strength of Egyptian Orthodoxy, keeping the prelates very close to the simple folk from whom they stem. But as the responsibilities of the bishops for cultural and socioeconomic endeavors continue to expand, this grueling schedule from dawn to past midnight every day takes an increasingly heavy toll on their health. Some have suggested that it would be a good idea to delegate part of their spiritual work to priests, as the Catholic Church does, for example, by limiting themselves to the celebration of Mass to high holidays and letting the priests take over the daily masses, the condolence visits, and the confessions and visits to the sick. Such a course seems to be inevitable, but it remains to be seen whether this is possible without a loss of the grassroots connection that makes the Orthodox Church, despite appearances to the contrary, more populist than the Catholic Church.

The pope also, though not as accessible as the bishop, is nonetheless involved in the day-to-day problems of his people to a considerable degree—although the circle of people who have access to him tends to be restricted to the families known for their service to the church. For example, Bishop Arsanios told me that when he decided at age 20 to become a monk, his father, who was so enraged by his refusal to leave the monastery that he took out a lighter and set fire to his beard, had recourse to Pope Cyril VI. Pope Cyril, who was used to receiving appeals from parents opposed to their sons decision to cloister themselves, was persuaded by the father's argument that the son was needed at home because his mother was chronically ill. He called the young novitiate, whose name at that time was Amīn, and ordered him to leave the monastery, comforting him with the words, "You can live as a monk in the world." Later, when Amīn came to the attention of his diocesan bishop, because he was a model of both chastity and energetic church service, and the bishop wished to make of him a priest, it was Amīn's turn to seek the counsel of Pope Cyril. The pope told him they must pray together for three days in a row, after which he would pronounce himself. At the end of the third day of prayer, he was inspired to the thought that marriage, which was mandatory for priests, was a snare where unforeseen dangers lurked for the young Amīn: he had best keep out of trouble by remaining celibate. Accordingly, the young man turned down his bishop's offer. In another instance, when I was doing fieldwork in Tanta, a consecrated woman (*Mukharasa*) told me that when her father was going to forcibly marry her to a man she abhorred, she ran off to see the pope who, after a similar prayer session, told her to go back home and not to worry. Three days later, a "miracle" intervened: the obnoxious suitor withdrew, after a quarrel with her father over the dowry.

At least in principle, the Orthodox Church requires that a pope have the consent of the people for his selection of bishop. In the consecration ceremony, which takes place before an assemblage of several thousand laymen and laywomen, the pope asks the question; "Is anyone of you opposed to the investiture of this man with holy office? Let him speak up now or forever keep his peace." In the past, this question was often merely rhetorical, as in the instance of Giza, described earlier, wherein Pope Yusab responded to the protests of William Soliman and other members of the Sunday School generation against his choice of bishop by having them forcibly removed from the church premises. Currently this no longer happens. Pope Shenuda's relationship to his people, whatever its limitations is governed by an acceptance of their right to choose their leaders. In that regard, at least it does represent a change of substance as well as of style.

On two occasions I witnessed this: the first, the ordination of a new priest and the second, the consecration of a bishop. The pope engaged in a spirited discussion, at the end of a Tuesday clerical seminary I attended, with two groups, each of which pressed upon him the choice of their pet candidate for a post that had fallen vacant, in the church they attended in common, as a result of the death of one of their priests. When he could not get them to agree, the pope announced in an exasperated voice that he would appoint no one until there was a consensus. But he did not overrule either of the groups.[18] In another instance, the pope locked himself up in the reception room of his Anba Ruweis residence with a delegation from the Red Sea region, in an attempt to persuade them to accept his choice of bishop, his personal secretary Bishop Johanna, for their diocese. After an hour or so, the pope emerged redfaced and visibly irritated, having failed in his endeavor. (The delegation had its heart set on former assistant-Bishop of Minya, who had fallen out with Bishop Arsanios over his support of Father Daniel and withdrawn in protest to the patriarchal headquarters.) Here again, the pope did not force his choice upon them.[19] Eventually, the matter was settled with a compromise. While the Red Sea folks did not receive their first choice they were offered an acceptable alternative to Bishop Johanna in the person of a young monk-priest who had distinguished himself during his service of the Coptic immigrant community in Paris.

Another way Pope Shenuda has heralded the democratization of the church is by launching the practice, during the difficult Sadat years, of inviting in the media to broaden his support against the government beyond the narrow circle of his co-religionists. He inadvertently gave his Coptic critics, in later years, a national platform from which to vent their grievances against him. For, by playing up to public opinion, and projecting himself, through his boldness and wit, as a media superstar, whose opinion was subsequently sought by the press on everything from the national debt crisis to soccer,[20] he inadvertently enhanced its interest in church affairs in general.

In June 1994, for example, the national press raised a storm over the summary dismissal of Father Agathon, a monk-priest, from the historic church of Abu Seifein in old Cairo. Father Agathon, whom the pope banished to his monastery, had been in charge of the restoration of this ancient church with the help of a UNESCO grant of $2 million. Shenuda cited as the reason for his decision the monk-priest's failure to consult him during the restoration work.[21] But others claimed that the tension between these two men had been building up for some time, because Father Agathon, who hailed from Matthew the Poor's monastery, known to harbor opinions on church reform divergent from the church establishment's, had often criticized the pope.[22] Furthermore, Father Agathon had a large number of supporters.

When even the *Sunday School Magazine* criticized the pope's decision, he retaliated by prohibiting its entire editorial staff, both the church-servants and deacons, from serving in the church until they had issued an official apology. This brought to a head the whole matter of arbitrary punishment and how to prevent abuse of power by the high prelates. As the fired editor, Kamāl Zakher, put it after he had been punished in this manner by the pope for siding with Father Agathon: "We need greater democracy and greater accountability."[23]

Another priest, Father Abd al-Sayed, who had been summarily dismissed after officiating for thirteen years in Cairo's St. George's Church, put it even more bluntly: "He [the pope] is a dictator. He listens to no one and no one can criticize his decisions without being punished."[24]

The number of monks, monk-priests, and priests who have been banned from their churches or monasteries during Shenuda's papacy, and in some cases, if they were advocating ideas considered heretical, even denied Communion and church rites after their death, was by the time this study was concluded at a minimum of twenty-seven (by the pope's own reckoning) and, by the reckoning of his critics, as many as sixty-seven.[25] And while some of them undoubtedly deserved it because of their corruption, others—when they were not mere victims of personal intrigue due to jealousy—were guilty only of engaging independently in some course of action or of holding opinions different from the pope's.

An example of the penalty for not submitting to the will of the pope is evident in the case of Father Angelios, a monk on whose behalf I once tried to intercede with Pope Shenuda. Father Angelios, who was from the Monastery of Samuel in Upper Egypt, lived in disgrace in his sister's apartment, at the time of our encounter, in the heavily Christian, middle-class Cairene district of Fagalla. I visited him at the request of a dignitary of Tima in Upper Egypt where I had done fieldwork. Knowing I had easy access to the pope, he asked me to go to him and plead for mercy on Father Angelios's behalf.[26] When I conferred with the monk himself, I found out that his only crime had been to seek treatment in America for his kidney failure. He had been traumatized the previous year by the loss of his best friend in the monastery—a young monk's death that he felt was caused by the neglect of the monastic authorities. And Father Angelios's fear of a similar fate grew as the months passed, and his condition worsened to the point where it became life-threatening. Yet the pope persisted in his refusal to let him go for a consultation to the United States, claiming that he could be cared for just as well in Egypt. Finally, faced by his rapidly deteriorating condition and the continued inaction of the papacy, he decided to take matters into his own hands and simply left for the United States, without papal authorization. (His brother, an immigrant to the US, covered his expenses.) For this act of disobedience, he was punished on his return by being banned from his monastery.[27]

His story sounded to me perfectly credible, because I had been involved a few months before I visited him in a similar case, concerning another monk, Father Mitias, from the Monastery of the Romans. Father Mitias suffered excruciating pains due to a spinal deformity that pressured his dorsal nerves—pains that had been increasing after he had dug out his own cave during a period of hermitage away from the monastery. But when I went on his behalf to persuade the pope to send him to America for an operation, he told me that his own Orthopedic physician, Dr. Farouk Nessim, had examined Father Mitias and did not think it necessary for the surgery to be done abroad. The monk, however, who knew that if the neural surgery were improperly done paralysis could result, refused to consider medical treatment in Egypt.[28]

In this case, I was more successful, because I was able to bring an American friend of mine, Dr. Martin Albert, to examine the monk—the same doctor I had taken to the Monastery of Bishoi to examine the pope himself. He succeeded in persuading the pope that the case was very different from his own (the pope only suffered from chronic lower back pain) and that indeed it required a very complex operation, which warranted a trip abroad. In the end, Father Mitias was allowed to leave for California, where Bishop Tadros of the diocese of Port Said, whose brother was an immigrant doctor in the United States, made the arrangements for the neural surgery. But, as for Father Angelios, the pope clung stubbornly to his original position, namely, that "as a monk he should have obeyed me,"[29] waving aside my pleas for mercy with an impatient motion of the hand.

I did not find him any more open to discussion concerning another bishop to whom I felt an injustice was being done. I had gone on my own initiative to speak to the pope on behalf of Bishop Arsanios, after I witnessed the humiliating treatment he was suffering because his support of the excommunicated Father Daniel. This bishop, who governed the most populous and richest diocese in Egypt, had been reduced to tears in my presence by the pope's continued refusal to receive him after a daylong wait in the reception room.[30] (It was a familiar scene: I had once observed Bishop Athanasios, whose support of President Sadat the pope had never forgotten, being rebuffed in the same demeaning way in the papal headquarters.)

The ostracism of Bishop Arsanios by the high prelates as well—even by those the bishop himself had ordained as monks when he was abbot of the monastery of the Romans (a position from which the pope had forced him to resign after the dispute over Father Daniel)—was deeply hurtful to him. As he told me once when Bishop Bula was unduly curt with him, "I can't believe it of them, my own sons. [He was referring to Bishop Moses as well]. When they first came to me, they were still in *effendi* suits [gray flannel suits denoting the white collar class in Egypt]."[31]

So I went, unnanounced, to see the pope during his weekend retreat at the Monastery of Bishoi, where I knew I could always obtain an audience with him if he was not locked into some meeting. I felt it was better to raise this sensitive issue far away from the malevolent eyes and wagging tongues of the petitioners who haunt the patriarchy. But although the pope received me very graciously on the terraced entrance to his residence and generously offered to share his dish of raw bean pods with me, I came away from the meeting feeling he had not budged: He kept wagging his head and saying, "You just don't understand, my girl, it's not a matter of my being understanding, it's a matter of defending Orthodox church dogma," and he added, "I cannot tolerate a bishop who shelters a heretic: Father Daniel is a heretic and Bishop Arsanios was making a home for him in his diocese. To this day he continues to stick up for him. There is no forgiveness for heresy, unless the heretic recants."[32]

If the bishops have gotten off with ostracism, the priests have often had to pay a higher price. Besides Father Daniel's excommunication—despite the fact that he upheld the doctrines of the Orthodox church in his writings[33]—Father Zakaria of Alexandria was summarily dealt with for having published a book in which he considered the possibility of instant salvation upon repentance—a Protestant belief contrary to Orthodox dogma. He was labeled a heretic and an edict of *ḥurman* (suspension of the right to preach) was issued against him, which was annulled only after he publicly recanted.[34] The threat of being labeled a heretic and suspended from church service is as effective in silencing divergent theological interpretations within the church today as it was of old.

To this must be added the strong corporatism of the Orthodox Church, which makes it very risky for a member to stand out by excelling. The enormous popularity of Fathers Zakaria and Daniel, each one of whom had a devoted coterie of youthful followers (as well as Muslim converts) who were prepared to leave the church if their spiritual mentor was expelled was at least as responsible for the fate they suffered as were their differences of opinion and style. The Orthodox prelates have always been jealous of outstanding members. Back in the '60s, when he was no more than a church-servant, Bishop Arsanios was expelled from the Church of Amir Tadros in Minya, because Father Sidrak, the priest in charge of the church, was jealous of him.[35] The stellar Father Anthonios Amīn had suffered a similar fate, in Fayoum earlier, because the aging diocesan bishop was threatened by his popularity.[36]

Currently, the chief complaint of the monks and priests who have suffered retribution is the lack of due process. As Zakher, at one time a press counselor to the papal headquarters, put it, after he and others who had been active in the *Sunday School Magazine* were banned by Pope Shenuda from church service because of their support of Father Agathon, "He punished us without giving us any chance to defend ourselves."[37] In a press release in the Coptic newspaper *Misr*, Father Agathon challenged the pope to reopen his case and put him on trial. Likewise, Father Abd al-Sayed claimed that he had never been told what the charges against him were nor brought face to face with a complainant before he was put on "forced vacation."[38]

It is impossible to know whether Father Abd al-Sayed is innocent or not, because the clerical corps headed by the draconian Bishop Bishoi that sits in judgment over priests shrouds its charges and proceedings in secrecy to safeguard the reputation of the Orthodox Church. What cannot be doubted, however, is the lack of due process. Father Agathon is right in saying that "there are no written rules as to what constitutes an error and what the punishments should be."[39]

The problems caused by this low institutional level of church legal proceedings are compounded by the absence of a lay jury to which derelict clergy could appeal, despite the fact that the Communal Council had initially been set up to monitor such proceedings. Although the 1887 decree calling for the establishment of such a council stated that one of its principal functions was to supervise the comportment of priests, it listed no specific procedures for disciplining the clergy. Neither did any of the subsequent amendments to that document, made in the twentieth century. As Jirjis Hilmi Azer, himself a former member of the Communal Council, says: "There is an absence of regulations and law in the church administration. . . . The pope does not even look to the council for approval of his decisions." [40] This is confirmed by the pope's own account of how he handled the Agathon case by decree, without referring to the council.

One of the chief goals of the reformers, therefore, is to wrest from the pope a greater say for the Communal Council. In his struggle to bring the formerly independent-minded council under his thumb, the pope has so far successfully negotiated a trade off: a hands-off policy in matters related to the inner workings of the church, in exchange for some say in the administration of its properties and land holdings—another prerogative granted to the council by the 1887 decree. However, even in the question of monies, the power of the Communal Council is limited at best. The main complaint voiced by Ḥannā Yūsuf Ḥannā, a member of the Coptic Committee for Properties in Mortmain is, "There is no accounting system at all for patriarchal funds. I have requested that one be set up, many times, but it is always refused."[41]

The pope's insistence on keeping these accounts secret—much as the bishops keep their diocesan revenues secret and the abbots their monastic ones—is being increasingly questioned by an opposition movement made up of a number of disparate groups, among which the most vocal is the Front for Church Reform, which demands control of the church budget.[42]

Revenues from church property in Mortmain are audited, since Nasser took power in 1952, by the national Central Auditing Agency, and the World Council of Churches maintains the right to review the books to keep track of its own donations, which are earmarked for specific development projects and amount to approximately $2.3 million a year.[43] But the third major source of revenue for the Orthodox Church, the contributions of well-to-do Copts, is not subject to any such external auditing system. These monies have grown exponentially since the massive increase in Christian emigration to the West beginning in the mid 1970s. (The pope himself admitted that "the budget has increased in a marvelous way.")[44] In large part, this is due to his efforts to multiply the number of Coptic churches in the diaspora with a view to keeping émigrés connected to their roots. Whereas at the beginning of his reign the only contributions that reached the church were those of members of the upper middle class who had been successful in business overseas (the ancien régime upper class and its progeny in the diaspora are too secular to be interested in donating funds), today the churches in the diaspora act as funnels for the contributions of the numerous Copts of modest incomes living abroad. (Because of the weakness of the

Egyptian pound relative to the dollar, even modest contributions from the West translate into a lot of money for the church.) It is these monies and the profits from church investments that are not subject to any external monitor. As Ḥannā, an accountant who worked for such prestigious international firms as Price Waterhouse, says: "Millions of dollars in contributions come into the church. . . . They go into the patriarchal accounts with no receipts and no accountancy. Where does it go? Ask his Holiness."[45]

But so far the pope has refused to submit the budget to lay scrutiny, claiming that church government should continue to be based, as it has been from time immemorial, on "love and trust."[46]

The pope's words "love and trust" came back to haunt him, shortly after he uttered them, during a conflict in 1994 with the Communal Council over allegations of the corruption of the chief accountant at the patriarchate, his own nephew, Adel Raphael Gayid.[47]

While the pope himself has never been tainted by the slightest charge of corruption, his nephew was accused of illicit rapid personal enrichment in office. From a modest middle-class existence, based on a meager salary as an accountant in the district of Giza, he was rumored to have acquired considerable landed property, a gasoline station that caters to the papacy, and even a supermarket in the United States, after entering the pope's service.[48]

Within a year after his appointment as papal accountant, in 1972, the Communal Council was already calling for an investigation into allegations of his improprieties. But the pope turned down the request and went on subsequently to add to his responsibilities, naming him chief accountant for foreign aid and chief accountant for the Coptic Committee for Property in Mortmain. As allegations of misconduct continued to pour in over the years (when I was there, in 1994, the Front for Church Reform was accusing him of making illicit profit from the sale of church-owned lands), the once-tame Communal Council raised its voice from a mere whimper to a growl: from its initial demand for an investigation to one for his outright dismissal on the grounds that he was untrustworthy. Much to everyone's surprise, it proved that it had not become putty in the pope's hands: Despite his intensive lobbying on his nephew's behalf (he told them that "anyone who doubts in him, doubts in me"),[49] the council continued to hold its ground.

Thus the pope, who was once in the forefront of the church reform movement, which included a struggle against the corruption of the old guard, had begun to fight a rearguard battle to curtail change. He was sarcastically dismissive of objections of the reformers that "one man cannot do everything now, it is an outmoded system" and refused to listen to suggestions like Zakher's that the "church administration must be modernized." "Now all administration is in the hands of the clergy," Zakher said. "We need greater participation, particularly from the laypeople."[50]

For now the pope is able to hold off his opponents,aided by a reinforcement of his fiercely loyal spiritual sons who preside over his inner cabinet.

He continues to insist that the layman who serve the church defer to clerical judgment in all matters, big and small, and he will brook no suggestion that "love and trust" are no longer sufficient for the proper administration of church moneys. As one of the most perceptive of these layman, member of Parliament Mīlād Ḥannā, put it: "We are living in an age of transparency. Defects—not to say corruption—are a possibility in any institution. It is naive to say it's a Christian institution running on love and ethics. It has to have a self-correcting mechanism."[51]

It is uncertain just how large the opposition movement calling for a "white revolution"[52] is, because most of its members, in line with the Coptic age-old precept of caution, maintain a low profile. But judging from the growing number of articles in the press on the issue of church reform, their voices are on the rise. Even the church establishment cannot entirely shut them out.

The struggle for the democratization of the Egyptian Orthodox Church will be a long and bitter one; the reformers know this and seem resigned to sit it out: As the banned Father Abdel Sayed put it: "I don't expect Pope Shenuda to change his ways. . . . All we can do is to keep raising our voices and wait for the next pope."[53] But then the Sunday School generation itself, from which the pope hails, had to wait twenty years before it could begin to implement its reforms.

Just as in the introduction the point was made that this book is examining the *process* of modernization within the Orthodox Church, not its attainment, in the conclusion the point must be made that what is being claimed is the *process* of democratization has been set in motion, not that it has been attained. The cultural context of Egypt, in which the church is embedded, is authoritarian, and the yoke of that culture—to which must be added the high prelate's own monastic tradition of unquestioning obedience to one's superiors—still weighs heavily on the church, not only in its relationship to its congregation but also in its internal relationships.

That the lay church leadership is aware of the danger of this pressure to conform may be judged by the address of Dr. Magdi Isaac, one of Bishop Moses' chief church-servants, to a Sunday Youth meeting I attended, in the patriarchal headquarters: "Too many times we have been taught in our homes to obey without understanding, to carry out orders as though we were in the army. We (the church) don't want blind obedience, we want enlightened obedience."[54]

The democratization of the church depends, as many of the laymen involved in church service see it, not just on granting a stronger voice to the lay community along the lines of Protestant congregations but on changes in the rules governing elections and succession of both popes and bishops. The Front for Church Reform has been vociferously clamoring for the enlarging the electorate in papal elections as well as for the submission of the choice of bishops and priests to the electoral process.

Currently the choice of pope is based on a method according to which the Holy Synod puts forward the names of the candidates and then an electoral college of diocesan layman drawn from leading families is composed for voting purposes. The presumption is that the abbots and diocesan bishops, as well as the lay dignitaries who sit on church committees and the boards of church-run orphanages, educational establishments, old age homes, and other philanthropic endeavors are best acquainted with the qualities of the papal hopefuls. The fact that, after a short list is drawn up and voted on, the choice among the three candidates with the most votes is left to chance is not seen as a bad thing. The devout believe that the blindfolded little boy is only symbolically making the choice in picking out of a silver bowl one of the three papers inscribed in India ink with the names of the candidates—in actual fact God is making the choice—and the church is spared a destructive, all-out, last-minute electoral fight among the finalists, with all the mudslinging between ambitious rival bishops that would involve. (We have seen that even before they were up for election, when they were mere bishops, there was considerable acrimony between Bishops Shenuda and Samuel; because each bishop had his overzealous followers, it led to feuding and pulpiteering.)

Without the lottery, the electoral campaign would be even more charged, because the two finalists who do not make it to the papal throne are often relegated to obscurity thereafter. For example, in the election that brought Shenuda's predecessor, Pope Cyril VI, to the papal throne, Cyril had actually ranked third according to the electoral votes, behind two monks from the monastery of the Holy Family, Father Damien and Father Angelios. Though Father Damien was given a small consolation prize (he was made Bishop of Atbarra in the Sudan), Father Angelios was relegated to the back stalls of the patriarchal library for the rest of his life. Much the same thing happened in the case of the three hopefuls in 1971. Before the little boy's hand picked Bishop Shenuda's name out of the silver bowl, he had had considerably fewer votes than Bishop Samuel. And while Bishop Samuel had the Bishopric of Social Services to fall back on, the other candidate for the papal throne, who was a monk from the Monastery of the Holy Family, became an inconsequential general bishop; Bishop Timothy. He does not even figure as one of the men in the pope's inner cabinet.[55]

If the choice from among the finalists by lottery cannot be faulted, many feel that the pool from which the pope is recruited can be. The question of whether the pope should be chosen from the monks or the bishops has bedeviled the Coptic community for a long time. In theory, as Bishop Gregorios has pointed out in a learned historical discourse on the subject, a pope could even come from among the ranks of the laymen provided he was pious and celibate. And in fact, Ḥabīb Jirjis, the founder of the Sunday School Movement at the turn of the century, was at one time considered for the position. But after the corruption scandal associated with Pope Yusab, which ended with his banishment to the Monastery of the Holy Family by a decision of the Holy Synod, endorsed by the Communal Council in 1955, there was strong popular sentiment in favor of choosing the pope from among the monks. A missionary summed up popular sentiment against the selection of a bishop by saying, "They (the bishops) were already corrupt."[56] This sentiment was all the stronger in that all three patriarchs chosen before Pope Cyril VI had been diocesan bishops and all three reigns were—albeit in different ways—regarded as black marks in the Egyptian-Orthodox Church history.

After the death of Pope Yusab in 1956, the Holy Synod, reflecting popular opinion, opted for the choice of a monk as pope. But the Communal Council made it clear, loudly and publicly, that it disagreed with this and favored the choice of an experienced bishop. At any rate, the acrimony was so bitter and the rifts in the Coptic community ran so deep over this issue that the government stepped in and suspended the election.[57] When the election was allowed to resume its course in 1958, the government threw its lot in with the Holy Synod's preference and decreed that the candidate had to be a monk who had been in the monastery at least fifteen years and was over forty years of age. Each bishop was to choose twelve electors from among laymen close to the church, who either had university degrees (a restricted number, in those days) or paid over LE 100 (a respectable sum in those days) in taxes, and these electors had to have the approval of the Communal Council, which was to participate in the vote. In this way, a monk of impeccable reputation and unquestionable piety was chosen from among the list of monks who had presented themselves as candidates. He was to become Pope Cyril VI, a man who without any doubt contributed immensely to the moral elevation of the church. He had reached the spiritual mountaintop by living as a hermit in a cave and subjected himself to a harsh regimen of days of fasting and hours on end of prayer. Even after his ordination as pope, he continued to set a personal example of piety by waking up daily at 3 AM to celebrate Mass in public.[58]

But it was a long way from his spiritual heights to the priests of the Upper Egyptian villages. The realization of his vision had to await the more modern administration of Pope Shenuda and his revisions of diocesan boundaries which made possible the supervision of these priests at close range by young bishops steeped in moral valor. They saw to it that the priests lived off salaries, not *bakshish* (tips) for their services, so that they would serve the poor and the rich equally. Closer to the capital, Shenuda also appointed some of his most trusted bishops to head the church boards of administration so that they could supervise church collections. When Pope Shenuda appointed one of his most trusted spiritual sons, Bishop Bishio, a man known for his tough stance, as head of the committee set up to try priests for misdemeanors, loss of church funds greatly decreased. In one church alone, the church of St. Dimiana in Cairo (often referred to as the Papadopoulou Church), which received large donations because it was a very popular church in the Coptic community, the church revenue went up from LE 90 million to LE 220 million within a year after Bishop Bishoi issued a *ḥurman* against the priest, who was accused of pilfering from the collection box.[59] Whatever his shortcomings, Bishop Bishoi has done the church a great service in flushing out corruption.

The real question today in the mind of the opposition is whether the church, which has undergone a moral rehabilitation and is no longer as threatened with corruption as it once was, needs to weigh a man's record of public service alongside his spiritual achievements in choosing papal candidates. I asked Pope Shenuda if a diocesan bishop with administrative experience and exposure to state officials and overseas communities, donors, and foundations would not be better as a successor than a monk. He made it quite clear that he personally favored a bishop. But he rejected outright the idea of widening the suffrage, saying that the common people did not know enough about church affairs to participate in decision making.[60]

There is more to ensuring an effective papal or diocesan administration than the choice of the right man. There is also the question of transmission of power from one incumbent to the next, for which no satisfactory solution has yet been found. Both the pope and the bishops traditionally remain in office until they die. Even a senile pope like the former Pope Cyril V, or a bishop who has been incapacitated by a stroke like the current Bishop Domadios, cannot be removed from office. The idea of introducing a mandatory retirement age for high prelates, which has been put forward by the opposition groups, has not yet been seriously entertained by the Holy Synod. Though Pope Shenuda told me that a bishop whose capacity to serve was reduced by old age "should" retire to a monastery,[61] no one has so far chosen to do so. Bishops, like ordinary mortals, are reluctant to yield their power.

Before Pope Shenuda acceded to the papal throne in 1971, many bishoprics were ruled by saintly old men considered a *barakah* (blessing), who were so feeble they barely had the strength to stretch out their hands to the long cue of the faithful waiting for a chance to kiss them. In Minya, for example, Bishop Arsanios's predecessor, the aged, feeble-sighted Bishop Suweires, who lived to be 84, came completely under the sway of the janitor who attended to his corporeal needs. The latter eavesdropped on his telephone calls, spied on his financial records, and denied people whom the bishop wished to see access to him.[62]

As we have seen Pope Shenuda has come up with a solution: appointing a young monk as assistant bishop. But this kind of stopgap solution has not succeeded, because sooner or later the old bishops come to realize that they have been kicked upstairs to honorific positions, while the real power lies in the hands of their more dynamic assistant. If this was not at first evident to Bishop Mina, it was bound to strike the visitor of Girga who saw the hallway adjoining the two offices of Bishop Mina and his assistant Bishop Daniel. When I went to interview Bishop Daniel, the chairs of the hallway were all occupied with petitioners and complainants, who were waiting to be admitted by the janitor to his office; the true lord of the manor, Bishop Mina, received only one solitary visitor, an old lady who had come to ask him to pray for her ailing grandson.[63] So it comes as no surprise, that in both the cases of Ismailia and Girga the assistant bishops soon fell out of favor with the old bishops and were asked to leave the dioceses. In only one case, that of Shubra al-Kheima, was the aging Bishop Maximos, a kind, unambitious man, wrapped in simple piety, willing to settle for the handkissing and leave the management of this diocese to his young assistant, Bishop Murqus. The son in confession of the pope since the age of 16, Bishop Murqus had been told by the pope that he was being sent by him to a diocese in the vicinity of the patriarchate (Shubra al-Kheima is an industrial suburb of Cairo) so that he "would be able to consult him in all matters."[64]

Even when it is not a case of a youthful monk going to the assistance of an old bishop, this arrangement is problematic because the bishop comes to feel that the primary focus of loyalty of this man who has been sent to serve him is the pope, not himself. Hence, the diocesan bishop comes to regard the pope's gift as a Trojan horse that will divide up his principality into warring clans. This is what happened in the case of Bishop Athanasios of Banī Suwayf, who, when he lay gravely ill of a gall bladder ailment, asked the pope for an assistant and received Emile, a young medical doctor (Bishop Moses). The latter soon put into effect the best and most vigorous youth programs in existence in any dioceses. But in the tense years of the '70s, when the Sadat government seemed to be conniving with Islamic militants in the mounting persecution of the Christians, Bishop Athanasios and his assistant began to argue over the best policy for the church toward the government. Emile favored the pope's militant line, while the older Bishop Athansios favored the cautious diplomacy of his mentor and friend Bishop Samuel. The two men exchanged increasingly sharp words in the privacy of the bishop's residence.[65] When in 1980, a year that witnessed the bombing of several churches in Alexandria as well as the killing of a Christian priest and molesting of Christian students in Upper Egypt, Bishop Athanasios insisted on holding his customary annual reception for the governor Emile withdrew in protest to the monastery. The pope rewarded him later for his loyalty, by making him bishop of Youth.[66]

Some members of the opposition have therefore begun to raise the question of whether new rules such as those that govern retirement in civilian life ought to be worked out by the Holy Synod, to ensure that at a mandatory age, perhaps 70, a bishop retires from active service to a life of prayer, preaching, and meditation in the monastery, thus making way for a younger man in office. This, they feel, would spare the church the problems of maladministration that afflicted their past.[67]

On the eve of the new millennium, it seemed that the generation that launched a revolution against the old guard by insisting on a voice in church affairs had itself become a kind of old guard jealous of its prerogatives, resisting a democratization of the church. The question whether the church, which has shown a capacity to cultivate the strong roots that made possible its revitalization in the twentieth century, will be able to develop the flexible branches needed for sustained growth in the twenty-first century remains to be seen.

Churches by their very nature are old, inflexible institutions, inveterately resistant to change, as the West knows, with its bloody history of democratizing its own church and ridding it of corruption. Relative to the experience of the Catholic Church, the pace and price of change within the Egyptian Orthodox Church seems heartening. And it should also be pointed out that the struggle to democratize the administration of the church is part and parcel of the larger ongoing struggle to democratize the government of Egypt itself. The two are progressing at approximately the same pace.

17

Toward the Empowerment of Women?

In talking about opening the church to lay participation, one cannot fail to address the issue of female participation. For a place is being made for women in the service of the church, albeit grudgingly, but not as yet for women's voices in church affairs.

We have seen earlier that the Sunday School Movement reached its apogee in the '40s and early '50s, a period of the twentieth century marked by the breakdown of traditional controls and by a questioning of the hierarchic status and corporate privileges of the ruling class in Egypt. This phenomenon culminated in the 1952 revolution. The newly educated, pious youths who were caught up in the rebellious mood that swept over the country had, in joining the voluntary associations of the saintly, turned their backs on traditional relationships. There are countless stories about the angry confrontations between the fathers of novices, who wished to wrench their sons away from the monasteries before it was too late, and their abbots. Most of the parents frowned on their sons' single-minded pursuit of the Godly, which they had reason to fear would lead to a monastic vocation. What these fathers wanted for their sons was the same thing most parents want for their children: a successful career and a family. But in disobeying their fathers, in turning their backs on such primordial forms of traditional relationships as family—a rebellion symbolized by their adoption of new names in the monastery—the prospective saints had merely transferred their patriarchal system to the Sunday School Movement. It was in the image of the fatherhood of Christ and of his vicars on earth, as well as in the belief in a great chain of being that encompassed the angels and saints as mediators who interceded with God the Father, that the reformed church appealed to the loyalty of its members. And it is to a large extent a measure of the success of that ideology that the Copts today are loyal to their church and their pope, so that one can speak of a collective will and of a disciplined effort to implement a communal development program.

But once the prospective saints had succeeded in fastening on the necks of their followers the yoke of this new discipline, impersonal and ideological, not based on affective ties but on adherence to the Word, and no more open to spontaneity of expression and interpretation than to chaos—hence their abhorrence of Father Daniel—they still needed to fall back on the authority of a paternal prelate to enforce the Word (even if they did try to transform their congregations from passive, dependent, childlike subjects to willful, active, voluntary participants in their overall reform project).

At the top of the hierarchy sat the pope, the family patriarch to whom the children, both clergy and laymen, owed obedience. While he in return for the "trust" of his subjects was enjoined to govern with "love" (*mahabah*). The same relationship obtained between the bishop, who was "married" to his diocese and as such was the "father" of the Christians within its boundaries, and between the priest who was "married" to his church and governed his congregation (with the priest bound by the rules of obedience to the bishop and the bishop bound by those same rules to the pope). Needless to say, a relationship between children and their father is not grounded in the children's "right" to oppose their father. When a child is hurt by a father's arbitrariness, the only recourse is to cry. It is only very recently that the tearful entreaties of the children of the Orthodox Church (*awlad al-kanīsah* is the term used by its members in Arabic) have begun to change into angry voices of protest.

For the prospective saints who had vowed to remain celibate, genetic fatherhood was thus transmuted into a religious office and they taught their congregation that the male head of each family was the representative of God, whose duty it was to see to it that his family formed a little church within the larger church.

The problem with an order that relied on paternity as the most useful metaphor for authority, one in which, as bishop Moses liked to preach, a child must obey his father, a girl her older brother, and a wife her husband is that it did not encourage female participation. Within the context of an Egyptian culture in which children and women are not supposed to be heard, no one perceived this as a problem until the church's role began to change from a purely sacerdotal one to a developmental one, which generated a need for female church-servants—particularly in the villages and small towns of Upper Egypt, where female members of a household still live in a kind of purdah, which makes them out of bounds for male church-servants.

With the entrance of the Sunday School generation into the hierarchy, women's active participation in the service of the church was first allowed under the liberal aegis of Bishop Athanasios in Banī Suwayf, where as we have seen, the order of working nuns (*Banat Mariam* "the Daughters of Mary") was created in the late 1960s. For the first time, pious women were permitted to do something other than embroider the cowls of the monks and sacrosanctal robes of the bishops. During Pope Shenuda's reign, which began in 1971, women took a few more steps forward, albeit haltingly, toward a meaningful role in the church. Just how limited the pope intended that role to be may be gauged by the anecdote he likes to tell about his visit to the archbishop of Canterbury, shortly after the election of Margaret Thatcher. The Anglican Church had only recently begun to allow the consecration of women priest and in welcoming Pope Shenuda, the archbishop had quipped: "Today I am the one to greet you, but who knows, the next time you come you may find a woman in my place!" which had greatly amused Shenuda.[1]

The introduction of laywomen to a life of full-time church service as part of a non monastic order, the *mukarasat*, had to await the arrival of Bishop Bimen of Mallawi in 1976. The Orthodox Church as a whole only began to accept such women in the 1980s. Those bishops who did rely on them for services tended to be predominantly the bishops of Lower Egypt, such as those of Tanta, Damanhur, Menufia, and Port Said—regions where men mingle more easily with members of the opposite sex. All the bishops of Upper Egypt with whom I raised this issue expressed unease at the thought of having recourse to consecrated women, on the grounds that women are more emotional than rational, which rules them out for positions of churh leadership, and that they would make a poor workteam because their jealousy of each other would lead them to intrigue to curry favor with their bishop.

While some of these fears may not been entirely ungrounded inasmuch as girls who have been confined to their homes all their lives may be left with some of the same psychological scars as harem women had, bishops are also reluctant to admit women into their workteam because they themselves grew up in a segregated society and they are therefore ill at ease in dealing with members of the opposite sex. (Their experience as *khuddām* before they became bishops was limited to interaction with boys.)

The only exception was Bishop Athanasios, who tended to be unconventional in all ways and who seemed at ease in the presence of women. In contrast to Bishop Bishoi, who once made me follow him in a taxi on a four hour trek from Cairo to the village of St. Dimiana, because he said a bishop could not give a ride in his car to a woman, Bishop Athanasios felt sufficiently at ease in the company of women to make it a practice to sleep over once a week in the dormitory of Banat Mariam. I was startled one night when these women were hosting me during my fieldwork in Banī Suwayf to discover, as I was on my way toothbrush in hand, toward the bathroom area, that he was my next-door neighbor. He was seated dressed in a long white night-robe on the bed, with his door ajar, chatting gaily with a group of nuns in their nightdresses. When, the next morning I expressed surprise at this to the nuns in question, over the breakfast we shared in the refectory, their reaction was: "So what's the big deal?" (*ʿadi* was the Arabic word they used); the bishop, they said, was their "father."

There were a few Upper Egyptian bishops in my sample who felt comfortable with the idea of employing women, such as the bishops of Minya, Abu Tig, and Tahta. But Bishop Arsanios of Minya and Bishop Andrawis of Abu Tig were born and raised in Cairo and had traveled frequently to the West, and Bishop Isaiah of Tahta had also had some exposure to western culture during his term of service as a monk-priest in Australia.

The bishops' idea of where women should invest their energy may be judged from a pedagogical training session for church-servants who were to serve in the villages of the diocese Minya. The trainees were told that they should assign research on church history to the village boys, and needlework to the girls.[2] Even in a diocese such as that one, run by one of the most enlightened bishops in my sample, boys are given priority in the allocation of funds for services. For example, out of five orphanages, which have been established in Minya during the reign of Bishop Arsanios, only one admits girls and that one was built after two orphanages had been set up for boys.[3] The same preference for boys governed the aid to the handicapped in Minya. The first funds raised by Bishop Arsanios in 1989 from a German evangelical church in Bielefeld for handicapped youth was invested in vocational training for disabled boys. This is just one of many such examples.

Not only cultural bias in Egypt looks on the male as more important than the female and consequently on the male child as infinitely more desirable (hence the parents themselves seek out aid for their handicapped sons, whereas their handicapped daughters are left at home to writhe on the floor);[4] also, the Orthodox Church itself, so isolated from the debates and developments in western churches, has preserved many of the attitudes of ancient Christendom toward women. Just as in Orthodox Mass Communion is given to the men before the women and women's secondary rank is further made clear to them by the fact that the bishop gives the corpus Christi to the men while the priest attends to the women, in many of the churches of Upper Egypt the women are shunted to the back of the church, placed behind latticed wooden grills (*Mushrubiya*), through which they can barely see the priest performing the Mass or the wedding ceremony.[5] So it should come as no surprise that outside of spiritual life boys take precedence in receiving a share of the budget for services.

Those women who have been drawn to full-time church service have positions subordinate to their male counterparts. The church enshrines this place for women in its marriage ceremony, declaring the male to be "the head" of the woman, and enjoining her to obey and submit to him as did Sarah, the wife of Abraham, who called her husband Master.

Bishop Bula of Tanta once stated, in my presence, in a public conference at the papal headquarters on the role of women in the family, that God had cre-

ated Eve to serve Adam—to be his assistant and not his equal. He added that it was preposterous to conceive of women as equal to men, since there cannot be two heads of one household.[6] The idea of a partnership, of deciding things by mutual agreement, has not yet dawned on even the most enlightened of bishops; they uniformly maintain that just as Jesus is the head of the church, man must be the master at home. Being themselves men, the bishops tended, in most of the cases I observed, to side with the men in marital disputes, unless there was evidence of a severe physical injury (in one such case, a man had burned his wife),[7] or the man had committed adultery or was impotent. Bishop Moses, in an anecdote he recounted to the Sunday Youth meeting I attended in Cairo, cited, as an example of unseemly female conduct, a woman who ran howling to her neighbor because her husband had beaten her. The neighbor's child, who was in the midst of doing his homework, was "disturbed by" this, he said, and asked his mother why she didn't make this woman "go away."[8]

On the grounds that children need a serene atmosphere, woman are constantly admonished by the bishops to be meek and patient in adversity. To a woman who had been physically abused, Bishop Fam once said in my presence that marriage was a cross that she must bear.[9] Bishop Isaiah, in response to a plea from a Coptic woman who had come from Australia to obtain a church divorce from her husband, on the grounds that he was mentally disturbed and beat her (she had brought a psychiatric report with her) said that the church could not grant her a divorce because "What evidence have we that it is not the woman who drove her husband mad?"[10] (Unless a woman can prove that her husband was insane before he married her, she is forced to put up with him for life.) Even Bishop Tadros of Port Said, whose mental horizons have been considerably stretched by the seven years he spent as an immigrant to the United States, and who declares openly his admiration of certain American values such as punctuality and reliability, was horrified by the freedom he saw women enjoying there. He recounted to me how an Egyptian friend of his, whose wife had left him for a man she had fallen in love with, had complained to him that when he had called the Los Angeles police to ask them to bring her forcibly back, he was told, "Sir, you don't seem to realize that this is a free country."[11]

On the whole, the bishops tend to relate to their *mukarasat* the way a headmaster relates to girls in a boarding school. It is not just that they are always assigned the conventional female tasks—the supervision of nurseries, orphanages, old age homes, sewing workshops, and the like—but even within this restricted sphere of social work they have very little autonomy and very little space for growth and a feeling of self-worth. In contrast to consecrated males and male church-servants who are allowed to exercise some initiative in their work, the women must obtain the bishop's permission for every small thing they wish to undertake and they cannot leave town, even overnight, without his permission. Once, when I was returning from St. Dimiana to Cairo, I offered some of Bishop Bishoi's consecrated woman a ride. When I proposed a one-hour stopover in

Tanta to attend a church wedding conducted by Bishop Bula, they said they would be expelled from their order if Bishop Bishoi ever found out that they went without his permission.[12]

Tasoni ("Sister" in Coptic) Mary of Damanhour, an engineer who is a *mukarasa* there, once put it to me this way: "I know I'm every bit as smart as Father Theodoros [the monk-priest who is Bishop Bachomios's right hand] and I could easily be the bishop's assistant, but this will never come to pass because I'm not a man."[13] *Tasoni* Batul, a highly intelligent young graduate of the faculty of commerce, who hosted me in the home for consecrated women when I was doing fieldwork in Port Said, summed up the childlike relationship of the *mukarasa* to her bishop as follows: "What do you expect? We Egyptian women were brought up on the notion that to be submissive is to be a nice girl."[14]

The condescension toward women clerics is reflected by the public at large, which does not accord them the same regard as it does male clerics. For example, though in theory only the hands of bishops and priests are supposed to be kissed because these hands touch the body and blood of Christ during the Eucharist, in fact the public shows its respect for all monks—regardless of whether or not they celebrate Mass—by according them the same form of homage. Needless to say, it does not feel called upon to kiss the hands of cloistered nuns.

Conclusion

Toward a New Basis for National Equality?

The accomplishments of the Sunday School generation that took over the church proved the bleak prognosis of Wakin wrong. Observing the scene in the late '50s, under Pope Shenuda's predecessor Cyril IV, he wrote:

> Leaders recruited from pious monks are likely to resemble the present monk-Patriarch and the men he has chosen to assist him. An unshakable confidence that even passive faith guarantees ultimate victory may inspire monks, but it also paralyzes the community of Copts. . . . These monastic children of the desert are not made to sustain their fellow Copts in the modern social, economic, and political pressures they face. [T]heir inspiration is like the hashish used by Egyptian peasants; they pacify and weaken the will to act.[1]

Any assessment of Pope Shenuda's leadership has to take into account what he, together with his team of bishops, did for the Coptic character and capabilities, even if ultimately he failed to achieve equality for the Coptic people. I have tried to demonstrate the manner in which the church leadership restructured the social space into a political counterspace and a space for the socio-economic development of their community. To the extent that they succeeded this was due in part to the creation of more centralized and efficient clerical institutions but even more so to their ability to make use of the distinctive religious culture of the Coptic Orthodox Church for purposes of mass mobilization.

The subjective meanings of Egyptian-Orthodox symbols were greatly intensified, the Coptic language was revived not so much for use in everyday conversation as a way of perpetuating a glorious cultural heritage, and ancient Christian historical sites were transformed into sacred sites, with the visits to these sites not left, as in the past, up to individual family initiatives, but transformed into church-organized pilgrimages for pedagogical and socializing purposes. In short the Christian religion became not only a matter of personal belief, as it had been in the first half of the century, but a collective experience that created a community of believers out of the Copts.

It was during Shenuda's reign that the Copts moved from a mere ethnic category to a solidari community. (Some would argue that they are on their way to becoming a nation, inasmuch as nationality formation is one in which objective differences between groups take on increasingly subjective and symbolic significance and these become in turn the basis of group solidarity.) It was as a politicized ethnic community that the Copts, under Shenuda, began to make demands on the political system for recognition of their group rights. Their demands went beyond questions of individual civil rights, such as equal educational and economic opportunities, to more control over the system of education itself so that their history and culture be taught in the public schools and to the recognition, in the Egyptian constitution, of Orthodox Christianity as a national religion on a par with Islam.

The growth of such ethnic consciousness was itself a function of the creation of new social classes, the middle classes, that emerged out of the process of modernization in Egypt in the first half of the century, a process characterized by increasing urbanization, literacy, and government employment.

The disintegration of the "Arab Socialist" national framework in the aftermath of President Nasser's death in 1970, which coincided with Pope Shenuda's assumption of power, allowed the Copts more autonomy, which they used to fortify their own community. At the heart of this attempt was the church's socializing campaign, which manifested a desire to monopolize the creation of meaning for the faithful, to ensure the perpetuation of age-old religious values and to protect the Copts from the lure of competing national values and from secular "western" ones—including those of the modern Christian western denominations. This drive antedates, as I have tried to show in my discussion of the Sunday School Movement, the resurgence of political Islam, though the latter undeniably gave it further impetus. The danger of the annihilation of Coptic specificity, in an Islamic Egypt, appeared far greater at the end of the twentieth century than that of assimilation into a secular liberal Egypt had appeared at the beginning of the century.

But it was a deliberate, creative enterprise, not merely a defensive reaction to an Islamic threat—a withdrawal from the national scene into "the precarious safety of its ethnic boundaries," as the author R. B. L. Carter in her book *The Copts in Egyptian Politics* would have us believe. Nor was it a retaliatory, denomi-

national course of action to counter state-sponsored endeavors to Islamicize the Egyptian public space, as some of Pope Shenouda's Muslim detractors would have it. This interpretation of church action as conspiratorial, in the hands of a Machiavellian, power-hungry pope, is as simplistic as the opposite portrayal of a pathetic, submissive Coptic minority—even if the motive behind these interpretations differs, in as much as the first is inspired by resentment of the "arrogance" of Coptic claims and the latter by empathy for the Copts. In either case, a movement of reform and revival is reduced to the "reactive" impulse—whether retaliatory or defensive—of a threatened minority.

In my survey of the Coptic communal struggle over the course of the twentieth century, I have tried to show that the Egyptian modernizing venture was not a monopoly of the state. It should be seen, instead, as a confluence of many different trends—including the religious. Modernity is far more complex a phenomenon than many scholars have recognized. It is polymorphous.

I have also argued against those who would confine the communal movement to a simple return to origins. To the extent that that movement involved borrowing, selection, and adaptation from different sources, it aimed at far more than the perpetuation of an immutable church heritage. The reformers copied forms of organization from state and modern Protestant enterprises and they exerted themselves to work out new interpretations of religious fundamentals that would inspire modern endeavors.

What the Sunday School Movement wanted to achieve was not just the maintenance of church dogmas and the defense of church values, as Pope Cyril VI would have willed, but the creation of a new universe of meaning and of a compensatory space for the social ascension of the faithful. They also wanted to model an identity based on a revalorized Egyptian-Christian heritage, so as to fortify the Copts against any marginalization or exclusion they might experience within the nation state.

As they set out in the 1940s and early 1950s to conquer the religious spaces in which this new identify could be forged, they overran successively the seminaries, then the monasteries (which at first were wary of these educated monk-hopefuls and reluctant to admit them), and finally they took by assault that last bastion of conservatism, the papacy itself. Hassanein Heykal, the former editor of al-Ahrām newspaper, has described this takeover as an internal "coup d'Etat." I would go farther and call it a revolution, because it did not merely involve the replacement of the old guard by a new generation, but the creation of something totally new.

Equally important, I take exception in this book to that interpretation of Egyptian history, which, by idealizing the liberal phase of government (1919–1936), overestimated the integrative capacity of the Egyptian state at the beginning of the twentieth century. Many Egyptian and foreign scholars have looked at Egypt through such an idealizing prism. In the introduction, I pointed to Ṭāriq al-Bishri's work as among the very best on that period of Egyptian history. He and others, including eminent Coptic scholars like William Kīlādā, share this prism. The unfortunate result of the use of such a prism is to see Egypt as having progressed along a unilinear course, until it was derailed by the inexplicable dark forces of religious fanaticism. Carter's assessment of that same period, although more nuanced in its interpretation, does not eschew the pitfall of confusing the national with the political and, hence, of mistaking a temporary unification of Muslims and Christians behind anticolonial symbols, for an adherence to the same universe of meaning.

In focusing exclusively on the issue of the political participation of the Copts in a given historical period, one tends to look for villains to explain the failure of national integration—either individuals, as the Coptic social scientist, Samira Bahr, does, when she points an accusing finger at certain members of the post-1952 political elite who flirted with Islam, thereby presumably blocking the triumphalist course of Egyptian history toward enlightenment; or ethnic or religious groups, as in the more polemical book of the French journalist Peranceau, which takes to task the Muslims as a whole; or at conspiring outside powers, such as Britain, America, and Israel.

Such a line of thought explains the outrage expressed, in the al-Ahrām newspaper, by Muḥammed Heykal, its former editor, at the proposal that a conference on the problems of minorities in the Middle East, sponsored by Cairo's Ibn Khaldun Center, should include a panel on the Copts. Faced by a storm of protest in the press at the mere suggestion that Egypt's Christian minority, like other minorities all over the world, might be subject to the tyranny of the majority, the idea of the panel was scrapped and even the site of the conference was relocated to Cypress. Those familiar with the manner in which some Jews were compelled to practice the art of self-ingratiation (an art that at times bordered on self-hatred) to survive in a gentile state, will not be surprised to learn that a number of prominent Coptic intellectuals, including Dr. William Kīlādā, joined the chorus that decried the conference as a sinister, imperialist, covert operation. Even the church was, in the end, compelled to distance itself from the conference. For this, Pope Shenuda was praised as a "courageous" man in Rūz al-Yūsef (February 5, 1994).

The left, viewing the course of Egyptian history through a different prism, end up in the same pitfall as the liberals because, like the liberals, they never question the model of national integration that the Egyptian nationalists brought back from France at the turn of the century, namely a homogenizing one. They look upon religious movements in Egypt, both Muslim and Christian, as aberrations. Only if they are seen as the expression of the current socioeconomic ills of the middle classes can they be explained, in their view. One of the best examples of this kind of thinking is the book of Ghālī Shukrī, a brilliant Coptic intellectual,[2] *al-Thowrah al Muḍādah fi Misr* (Egypt's counter revolution).

By focusing on the Sunday School Movement, whose origins antedated the rise of political Islam in the Egypt of the 1940s, I have tried to show that neither the liberal interpretation, which falls short of a structural analysis of the flaws of the newly emerged nation-state, nor the Marxist interpretation of resurgent religiosity as a crisis of identity caused by social ills, provides a framework for comprehending the current Coptic drive to achieve integration on a new basis, the recognition of its specificity. This drive is indeed part of a worldwide end-of-century phenomenon: the politicization of ethnic identities.

Structurally, the kind of constitution that would have accommodated this need for the expression of Coptic specificity would have had to be drawn up more along American pluralist lines. However, one of the grounds for opposition to a system of proportional representation on the part of Abdel Ḥamid Badawi, the chief legal counselor on the committee that drafted Egypt's constitution after its independence from Britain in 1922, was that if such an allowance were made for the Copts, all of Egypt's other ethnic and religious minorities would have to be granted the same. And he did not believe that the committee had the competence to map out such complex arrangements. In this latter judgment he did not err. For the members of the French-speaking, upper-class elite—political, commercial, and cultural—who were the only people to count in an age when *democracy* was still a term whose meaning in Egypt excluded the have-nots, was made up of a mosaic of different ethnicities (a motley of peoples from the defunct Ottoman Empire Turks, Albanians, Circasians, and the like as well as Egyptians, Greeks, Italians, Armenians, and Ashkenazi and Sephardi Jews). In fact, the Wafd government of 1924, led by the nationalist leader Saad Zaglul, was the first cabinet of native Egyptians to come to power. Prior to this, all the cabinets had been dominated by the Ottoman aristocracy. My great-uncle Rushdi Pasha, who presided over the committee appointed by the king to draw up a constitution for Egypt after the 1922 declaration of independence, was the last prime minister of Balkan origin in a cabinet composed overwhelmingly of Ottoman aristocrats, during World War I. And the Egyptian syndicate of businessmen, which defended Egyptian commercial interests against the British Chamber of Commerce, was dominated by European permanent residents of Egypt and Jews. Cromer, the British agent, was not entirely wrong when he asked rhetorically who the real Egyptian was: the Greek, who had lived in Egypt for generations; the Turk; the Syro-Lebanese; the European whose adopted home it was? Granted that by emphasizing the cosmopolitan makeup of Egypt, Cromer was also serving British interests, which enabled him to argue that the British presence was the only guarantor of stability in a country with such ethnic, religious, and even linguistic cleavages.

Even if the constitutional committee had had the competence to draw up a constitution that would have accommodated this diversity, no amount of social engineering would have guaranteed the Copts a place of equality with their Muslim compatriots. For the members of the constitutional committee were not starting out with a tabula rasa. In 1922, Egypt was still engaged in an anticolonial struggle, encompassing efforts to end the legal and other privileges that the foreign ethnic and religious minorities had arrogated to themselves with the help of their consulates. The story of the abuse of those privileges has been amply documented by a number of foreign observers and scholars, most notably Harvard University's David Landes.[3] Up until the eve of the 1952 revolution, Egyptians had not even been able to to replace French with Arabic as the language of Egypt's commercial institutions (the language barrier was a major handicap for the native middle classes seeking employment).

It was inevitable, therefore, that once the leadership of the anticolonial struggle passed out of the hands of a restricted circle of upper-class politicians, predominantly of French cultural formation, to those of the Arabic-speaking middle classes—the first-generation graduates of the military academies and universities—there would follow a revivification of the religious component of the national identity. It was equally inevitable that the Copts, even though they had never been a party to the privileges of the European residents of Egypt, would be adversely affected once the 1952 revolution displaced the cosmopolitan upper classes from power and replaced them with members of the lower middle class. For the lower orders who had suffered the most from being lorded over by the Europeans, the Copts, by virtue of sharing the religion of the dominant race, were suspect, all of their sacrifices during the nationalist struggle and their vigorously professed Anglophobia notwithstanding.

It is this which, tragically, Badawi's generation was unable to grasp because it belonged, culturally, to a different nation. Badawi was sincere in his expression of fear that a system of proportional representation would give solidity and permanence to a religious distinction between Egyptians that would otherwise diminish in time. Neither he nor other upper-class members of his generation were perceptive enough to see that political unity was not necessarily synonymous with national unity, and to forecast that once Egypt was deprived of its external enemy (Great Britain), Coptic-Muslim cooperation would founder unless a new basis for political community was found.

Such a basis was not found. Quite the contrary, during the Sadat years, Islam became the predominant state ideology. This led to the restructuring of the Coptic Orthodox religious space as a political counterspace, a reversal of the trend during the first half of the century characterized by the passage of all Egyptians from traditional forms of organization to a modern national one. As the pressure on the Copts increased, communal bonds grew stronger and more relevant. And the creation of clerical institutions, which were at one and the same time centralizing and efficient, made it possible for the bishops not only to transform communal action into a vehicle for political expression but also, in the face of the relinquishment by the state of both its ideological and part of its economic role, to take over the functions of socialization and income redistribution.

These, under Nasser, had been the exclusive reserve of a "socialist" regime. The virtual collapse of the "Arab socialist" framework of the nation-state, after Egypt's crushing defeat in the Six-Day War of 1967 war at the hands of Israel, which discredited everything associated with his regime, not only permitted the Coptic community to free itself from state control, but also freed the Muslim Brotherhood, whose leaders had been kept in prison since their attempt on Nasser's life in 1954, as well as a whole gamut of political and professional associations. All of these associations began to mobilize their internal constituencies and to seek international support for their cause, to better exercise pressure on the state. Whereas Sadat, toward the end of his rule, lost patience with this pressure and tossed overboard his experiment with "democracy," Mubarak, perhaps chastened by the example of what happened to his predecessor, tried to reach a modus vivendi with their leaders, after releasing them from the prisons in which Sadat had confined them.

The political orbit at the beginning of the twenty-first century is therefore one in which the various particularistic and corporatist interests are pitted against the state. While the state has lost the all-powerful role of regulator it had under Nasser, it remains nonetheless a formidable protagonist with which—short of an all-out confrontation such as some of the Islamists seem to have opted for—one must seek compromises. Among all of the contending interest groups, the Copts are probably the weakest by virtue of their marginality in an overwhelmingly Muslim society (even if of late other secular liberal and left-wing groups, particularly the leftwing political party Tagamuʿ, which feel just as threatened by the possibility of an Islamic takeover have rallied to their support). Despite this, not only do the Copts lack the power of a Jewish lobby in the United States, but they do not even come close to the influence the Turkish Jewish community is able to exercise over the ruling establishment of a relatively secular polity.

Just as, with the rise of Muslim fundamentalist movements in the 1940s, the Copts began to realize that political action was ineffective, if not outright dangerous, and retreated into their community, so too the church's confrontational politics of the 1970s, based on publicly voiced recriminations, has given way to accommodation with the state. Pope Shenuda's stance of exemplary citizen, whose opinions are sought by the Egyptian press on every subject from how to solve the national debt crisis to how to cure Cairo's demographic problem, is not much different today from Makram Ebeid's—a man the pope by his own admission greatly admired and whose party (Kutla) he joined as a youth in the 1940s. Instead of mobilizing the Copts against discrimination, Shenuda now enjoins them to be good citizens and to participate in the national elections. He tells them not to fall prey to the pessimistic feelings that they don't make a difference. Coptic newspaper writers have been asked by him to refrain from criticism of the government, to help shore up the Coptic image of an exemplary minority that supports the regime. The same watchword has gone out to his constituencies overseas, with less success. Diaspora Copts, once securely anchored in the "Land of the Free," have been quick to exchange their fearful, submissive profile for a militant one. The pope has even been known to try to raise money in the diaspora (with equally poor success), to aid the state's effort to close the national debt. This continuing need of the Copts to demonstrate their exemplary loyalty to the state, which is in evidence also in the work of Coptic intellectuals like William Kīlādā, Mīlād Ḥannā, and Samira Bahr,[4] who focus on Coptic commitment to nationalist causes and their sacrifices, is familiar from the Jewish experience in Europe. It is, perhaps, the most damning proof of their continued subjugation.

Does that mean that the Copts have relapsed into the role of the pitiful victim? No. But faced with the hostility of the Islamic militants and the weakness and indifference of the state and of most of their Muslim compatriots (see the recent attack in Rūz al-Yūsef [February 11, 1998] on Bishop Wisa for having made "a mountain out of a molehill" over the killing of two Copts in the village of Kush), they have removed themselves once again from the political orbit. In answer to the Islamic references in the official discourse of the state and the growing threat of their annihilation at the hands of the Islamic militants, they have created their own orbit and their own metaphoric language of resistance, couched in the legends of the ancient Christian martyrs.

This is why, if we want to monitor the growing resistance to discrimination, we have to look beyond the space officially labeled "political." It is no longer in the state bureaucracy or in Parliament that the relevant Coptic political actors are to be found, but within the church, which has arrogated to itself the exclusive right to represent Coptic claims before the state. The relevant Coptic elite today is the clerical elite, which is not just a symbol of sanctity but a custodian of Coptic power. The Coptic cabinet ministers, technocrats who have been co-opted into the ruling establishment, are isolated and marginal to their communities. As token Copts, they do not have the leverage with the president of the republic that the clerical leaders have.

But neither the new tactical alliance of the church and the state against the Islamic militants nor their common rhetoric of national unity (*al-wehdah al-wataniyah*) can disguise the failure of the pope to achieve political equality for the Copts, let alone equality in other domains. They represent a strategy of survival, rather than genuine political integration. The pope is no fool; he understands better than anyone that the church is being manipulated by the government for its own ends. But he is forced into the embrace of the state, whose protection he needs for his people against the violent attacks of the Islamists.

The limited benefits of such an alliance are rooted in the very nature of the regime itself, one that is spent, exhausted, bankrupt—in short, a long way from the revolutionary ardor of its yesteryears. Without any new visions or dreams to offer its people, it derives its legitimacy from one thing only: being an alternative to an Islamic rule. While it may seek to curb Islamic militancy, and even go to extremes of brutality and human rights abuses to do so, it only wishes to contain the movement, to emasculate it, so as not to be endangered by it—but never to eliminate it. For the truth is that if the Islamic militants were not there, they would have to be invented to guarantee the regime both internal and external support.

Faced by a threat to their very physical survival, the Copts themselves have no choice. They cannot find a mode of political action that will prove viable in the long term. Instead, they come up with short-term tactics and adapt their strategies to changing circumstances. But the observers of the national scene should not fall into the trap of confusing temporary political alliances with national integration. And this is precisely the danger of the overly idealistic interpretations of a short period of liberalism in the 1920s and 1930s in Egypt.

It was fortunate that many of the Coptic leaders of that era, like Wisa Wasef, Wasif Ghālī, and Fakhri Abd al-Nur, who were strong believers in national integration, died in the 1930s. They did not live to see their hopes shattered. Makram Ebeid, who, perhaps, worked harder than any of them for the realization of that dream, must have been bitterly disillusioned by the end of his life. His enormous popularity within the Wafd party, among both Muslims and Christians—judging from the number of Muslims who followed him into the wilderness when he defected from the party—as well as his talents, which overshadowed those of the party leader Nahas, deluded him into thinking that, after years of playing second fiddle, he could make a bid of his own for party leadership. However, neither his aptitude, nor his influence over the Wafdist press and Wafdist youth groups, were enough to gain for him the office of prime minister, once he decided to form his own party (Kutla). For what he failed to realize was that while a Christian prime minister had been possible in the nineteenth century, when no one questioned the idea of submission to the autocratic will of the khedive, and even at the turn of the twentieth century, when the British ruler called the shots, it was no longer possible in the mid-twentieth century, once the will of the people was sovereign.

After the 1952 revolution, it was once more the gun, not the ballot, that determined political incumbency; but the ruling elite itself now hailed from the lower middle class and hence was bound to reflect popular will. There has been, since the 1952 revolution, a government by the people, if not always for the people. Mubarak's Coptic politicians, like Boutrous Boutrous Ghālī, who had stepped into the limelight once occupied by a Makram Ebeid, were more finely attuned to the call of the minaret than to their own people's cry of distress. As Boutrous Ghālī himself readily admitted to me in an interview for my *New York Times* article "Egypt's Angry Islamic Militants" in 1983 when he was "minister of State for Foreign Affairs": "It would be inconceivable for someone who could not inaugurate a meeting of Arab dignitaries in the name of God, the Merciful and the Compassionate to be named Foreign Minister." So he gracefully allowed himself to be skipped over three times in succession for the post of foreign minister, for which he was rewarded by President Mubarak by being kicked upstairs—outside the Egyptian political orbit.

In conclusion, by the end of the twentieth century, the Egyptian state has proved incapable of redefining its national ideal in such a way as to accommodate the particularities of its citizens. It would have had, during the course of that century, to move from the French homogenizing model on which it was based, to a pluralistic American model based on the recognition of diverse ethnic and religious communities and the legitimacy of mediation by their representative, on behalf of their particularistic interests. For historical reasons, which lie beyond the scope of this study, this proved impossible.

Instead, the Egyptian nation-state became increasingly one-dimentional, with a political discourse marked by a growing confusion between nationalism and Islam. The most obvious reflection of the ambiguity about what constitutes the nation-state and the criteria for citizenship within it can be seen in the Egyptian press which, alongside articles vindicating equality for the Copts, features others that question their loyalty to an Islamic country.

Just as America has moved away from the melting-pot ideal of the beginning of the twentieth century, which pressured members of minority immigrant groups to anglicize their names and accents to be assimilated, to an acceptance of multi-ethnicity as a basis for integration, so too the Copts are no longer willing to drop their Christian forenames and play down their religious affiliation to be accepted by the majority. On the contrary, Copts in recent times have returned to a choice of Christian names for their children and Coptic women and girls make it a point to wear their golden crosses outside their blouses and dresses.

Coptic political discourse has also changed in fin de siècle Egypt. It is no longer couched in terms of a plea for equality. Rather, it asserts *the right to be different* and to political expression as such. The Copts who, at the beginning of the twentieth century, when the Egyptian constitution was created, never disputed the claim of Islam to be the state religion, now demand the recognition of Christian Orthodoxy as a national religion on an equal footing with Islam. This is a far cry from the statements of the Coptic aristocracy of old, such as Makram Ebeid, that he was a Muslim by country and a Christian by religion, or those of Wisa Wasef, who was called a Judas by his correligionists for participating in Watani, a turn-of-the-century nationalist party with pan-Islamic leanings.

It is doubtful that the Copts have made much headway, in their century-long, tortuously slow trajectory toward citizenship with equal rights. This statement becomes even truer if one moves away from the national political scene to local politics, or to the level of social relations. Copts live to this day in kind of ghetto surrounded by a diffuse, but nonetheless palpable, atmosphere of Muslim prejudices.

Notes

INTRODUCTION

1. See Eric Hobsbawm's "Introduction: Inventing Traditions" in Hobsbawm and Terence Ranger, eds., *The Invention of Tradition* (Cambridge, 1983).

2. S. A. Arjomand, "Iran's Revolution in Comparative Perspective," *World Politics* (April 1986), p. 406.

3. See Emmanuel Sivan's introductory essay in Emmanuel Sivan and Menachem Friedeman, eds., *Religious Radicalism and Politics in the Middle East* pp. 1–9 (New York, 1990).

4. Lloyd I. Rudolph and Suzane Hoeber Rudolph, *The Modernity of Tradition: Political Development in India* (Chicago, 1967), pp. 3–14.

5. Edward Said, *Orientalism* (New York, 1985).

6. Tarek al-Bishrī, *al-Muslimūn wa-al-Aqbāṭ fiiṭar al-jamāʿah al-waṭanīyah* (Cairo, 1977).

7. B. L. Carter, *The Copts in Egyptian Politics 1918–1952* (Cairo, 1986).

8. For example, Nadia Ramsis Farah, *Religious Strife in Egypt: Crisis and Ideoıogical Conflict in the Seventies* (New York, 1986).

9. The exclusive focus on elites is not only characteristic of Carter's work but also of Samira Bahr, *The Copts in Egyptian Politics* (Cairo, 1979). In this respect, too Dina al-Khawaga's excellent work is the exception; see her "Le development communautaire Copte: Un mode de participation au politique?" *Monde Arabe: Magreb Mashrek* 135 (January–February 1992) and her "Renouveau Copte actuel."

PROLOGUE

1. Pierre Nora, "Entre memoire et histoire: La problématique des lieux de mémoire," in P. Nora eds. *Les lieux de mémoire: La République XVII–XXIII*, vol. 1 (Paris, 1984), pp. xvii–XLII.

2. Maurice Hallwach, *La mémoire collective* (Paris, 1950). See also his *Les cadres sociaux de la mémoire* (Paris, 1976).

3. See Benedict Anderson, *Imagined Communities: Reflections on the Origins and Spead of Nationalism* (London, 1992). See also Hobsbawm's "Introduction" in *The Invention of Tradition.*

4. This is a rough figure. Government censuses since the 1952 revolution have sometimes risen a little above this figure, such as in 1966 when the figure was 6.7, and sometimes fallen slightly below it—to 5.8 in 1968, for example. This sensitive and controversial issue has been very well addressed by the social demographer P. Fargues in *Chrétiens et Juifs dans l'Islam arabe et turc,* (Paris, 1992) See also a discussion of the problem of reliable statistics in a work of social demography by E. J. Chitham, *The Coptic Community in Egypt,* (Durham, England: 1986). See also J. D. Pennington, "The Copts in Modern Egypt," in *Middle Eastern Affairs,* 18 (1982), p. 159.

5. *The Census of Egypt 1917,* vol. 2 (Cairo, 1921). Subsequent British censuses continued to hover around this figure.

6. Lord Cromer (Evelyn Baring), *Modern Egypt,* vol. 2, (London, 1908), p. 206.

7. Lady Duff Gordon, *Letters from Egypt* (London, 1983), p. 66.

8. E. W. Lane, *Manners and Customs of the Modern Egyptians* (London, 1908), pp. 536–37.

9. Sir John Bowring, *Report on Egypt and Candia*: addressed to the Right Hon. Lord Viscount Palmerston, Her Majesty's principal Secretary of State for foreign affairs Series Parliamentary Papers, 1870, (v. xxi [277]), p. 8.

10. Chitham, *The Coptic Community in Egypt,* p. 83.

11. Ibid.

12. Samuel Rubenson, "Tradition and Renewal in Coptic Theology," in *Between Desert and City: The Orthodox Church Today,* Nelly van Doorn-Harder and Kari Vogt, eds. (Oslo, 1997), p. 44.

13. Bishop Arsanios told me this.

14. Safinas-Amal Naguib, "Martyr and Apostle: Victor Son of Romanos and Diocletian: A case of Intertertextuality in Coptic Religious Memory," *Temenos* 29 (1994), pp. 101–13 and the "The Martyr as Witness: Coptic and Copto-Arabic Hagiographies as Mediators of Religious Memories," *Numen* 41, (1995), pp. 223–54.

1. WHEN EGYPT WAS CHRISTIAN

1. The following historical sketch is derived from these main sources: L. Gonzalez, *The Story of Christianity: The Early Church to the Dawn of the Reformation,* vol.1 (San Francisco, 1984); Barbara Watterson, *Coptic Egypt* (Edinburgh, 1988); A. S.Atīyah, *History of Eastern Christianity* (New York, 1980); and E. L.Butcher, *The Story of the Church of Egypt,* vol. 1 (London, 1897); Henry Chadwick, *The Early History of the Church,* (London,1967), Pelegrino Rocaglia, *Histoire de L'Eglise Copte,* vols. 1 and 2, (Beirut, 1987); and R. P. Paul Cheneau, *Les Saints D'Egypte* (Jerusalem, 1923).

2. This is the viewpoint taken by the Coptic scholar A. S. ʿAtīyah in *History of Eastern Christianity.*

3. This is the interpretation of William Soliman Kīlādā, in his book *al-Kanīsah al-Miṣriyya tuwajāha al-isti'mar wa al-Ṣahyūniyya* (Cairo, nd)

2. THE DAWN OF A NEW ERA

1. For a good account of the role of the foreign workforce, see Joel Beinin and Zachary Lockman, *Workforce on the Nile* (Princeton, 1987). See also Jean Vallet, *Contribution a l'étude de la condition de la grande industrie du Caire* (Paris, 1911).
2. See Helen Ann B. Rivlin, *The Agricultural Policy of Mohammad Ali in Egypt* (Cambridge, Mass., 1961).
3. Ibid., pp. 126–27.
4. Ibid.
5. Samir Seikaly, "Prime Minister and Assassin: Butrus Ghali and Wardani," *Middle Eastern Studies* (1977), 13, pp. 112–123.
6. Carter, *The Copts in Egyptian Politics, 1918–1952*, p. 10.
7. Cited in ibid., pp. 14–15.
8. See Kyriakos Michail, *Copts and Muslims under British Rule* (London, 1911), p. 125. See also Jaques Taguer, *Coptes et Musulmans* (Cairo, 1954), p. 259.
9. Cromer, *Modern Egypt*, vol. 2, pp. 205–6.
10. Peter Mellini, *Sir Eldon Gorst, the Overshadowed Pro Consul* (Stanford, 1977), pp. 125–26, 128, 149, 152, 203–13.
11. Cited in Carter, *The Copts in Egyptian Politics*, p. 61.
12. S. H. Leeder, *Modern Sons of Pharaohs* (New York, 1973), p. 327.
13. Carter, *The Copts in Egyptian Politics*, p. 60.
14. Ibid., p. 106.
15. Leland Bowie, "The Copts, the Wafd, and Religious Issues in Egyptian Politics," *The Muslim World* 67 (1977), p. 108. See also Fakhri Abd al-Nur, "Mudhakirati," in *al-Muṣawwar*, March 12, 1969.
16. Carter, *The Copts in Egyptian Politics*, p. 63.
17. Ibid., p. 64.
18. Bowie, "The Copts, the Wafd," p. 111.
19. Ibid, p. 109.
20. Carter, *The Copts in Egyptian Politics*, p. 72.
21. Ibid., pp. 129–30.
22. Ibid., p. 109.
23. Bowie, "The Copts, the Wafd," p. 112.
24. Carter, *The Copts in Egyptian Politics*, p. 142.
25. For a good analysis of these intellectual currents, see Nadav Safran, *Egypt in Search of Political Community* (Cambridge, 1961), pp. 178–79.
26. Told to me by Victor Semeika, son of Murqus Semeika, in an interview at his home in December 1988.

3. THE VANISHED DREAM

1. Much has been written on this. See John Bowring, *Report on Egypt and Candia*; Rivlin, *Agriculatural Policy* pp. 201–5; and eyewitness accounts such as those

of James Augustus St. John, *Egypt under Muhammad Ali*, two volumes, London, 1834, and Gerard de Nerval, *Voyage en Orient*, (Paris, 1980).

2. Ibrāhīm ʿAmīr Kīlādā, *al-Arḍ wa-al-falāhīn al-masallah al-zirāʿiyah fiMiṣr* (Cairo, 1958).

3. André Raymond, "The Economic Crisis of Egypt in the Eighteenth Century," in A. L. Udovitch ed., *The Islamic Middle East 700–19000: Studies in Economic and Social History* (Princeton, 1981), pp. 687–788). See also his *Artisans et Commercants au Caire au XVII: ème Siècle* (Damascus, 1981), 149, 156–61, 178–9, 180–89, 190, 196f.

4. Raymond, "The Economic Crisis of Egypt."

5. Viscount Milner, *England in Egypt* (New York, 1970), p. 51.

6. E. R. Owen, "Lord Cromer and the Development of Egyptian Industry," in *Middle Eastern Studies*, 5.11, no. 4 (July 1966), pp. 282–301 and "The Attitude of British Officials to the Development of the Egyptian Economy," in M. A Cook, ed., *Studies in Economic History* (London, 1970), pp. 485–500.

7. Jean Ducruet, *Les Capiteaux Européens au Proche Orient* (Paris, 1943), p. 68.

8. A. E. Crouchly, *The Investment of Foreign Capital in Egyptian Companies and Public Debt* (Cairo, 1936), p. 32; see also his *Economic Development of Egypt* (London, 1938); Charles Issawi "Egypt since 1800, a Study in Lopsided Development," in *Journal of Economic History*, 21 (1961), pp. 1–25; Pierre Arminjean, *La situation économique et financière d'Egypte* (Paris, 1911); and Andre Eman, *L'industrie de coton en Egypte: Etude d'économie politique*, (Cairo, 1943).

9. See Jean Vallet, *Contribution a l'étude de la grande industrie du Caire* (Paris, 1911) and Athanase Politis, L'Hellénisme et l'Egypte moderne, (Paris, 1930).

10. Marious Deeb, "Bank Misr and the Emergence of a Local Bourgeoisie in Egypt," in *Middle Eastern Studies*, 12, no. 3 (October 1976), p. 74.

11. Robert Tignor, "The Revolution of 1919: New Directions in the Egyptian Economy," in *Middle East Studies*, 5.12, no. 3 (October 1976), pp. 59–60. See also his *Modernisation and British Colonial Rule in Egypt 1882–1914*, (Princeton, 1966).

12. Safran, *Egypt in Search of a Political Community*, 127–31.

13. On the growth of brigandage in the countryside, see Rheinhardt Schulze, *Die Rebellion der Ägyptische Fellahin, 1919* (Berlin, 1971).

14. Abd al-jalil al-ʿAmary, "La crise de chomage en Egypte," in *L'Egypte Contemporaine*, vol. 27, no. 164, p. 472.

15. Cited in Zaki Badawi, *La législation du travaille en Egypte* (Alexandria, 1951),pp. 8–9. See also Marcel Clerget, *Le Caire: Etude de geographie urbaine et histoire économique*, (Cairo, 1934), vol. 1, p. 159

16. FO 141/533/535/155 cited in MariusDeeb, *Party Politics in Egypt*, (London, 1979), p. 317.

17. See also Charles Isawi, *Egypt at Mid Century*, (London, 1954), pp. 66, 167, 261, and al-ʿImarī, "La Crise de Chomage," 472–75.

18. *Annuaire Statistique: 1932–33*, pp. 58–59, table 5.

19. E. R. Owen, *Cotton and the Egyptian Economy 1820–1914: A Study in Trade and Development* (Oxford, 1969), pp. 82–84.

20. Lord Cromer, (Evelyn Baring), *Political and Literary Essays*, Second Series, pp. 200–201.

21. These figures are from Malcolm Kerr, "Egypt," in James S. Coleman, ed., *Education and Political Development* (Princeton, 1967), p. 172.

22. Taha Husein, *The Future of Culture in Egypt* (Washington, 1954), p. 120.

23. *Annuaire Statistique*, 1932–1933, table 5, pp. 58–59.

24. Cited in Afaf Lutfi al-Sayyid Marsot, *Egypt's Liberal Experiment* (Berkeley, 1977), p. 87.

25. Safran, pp. 196–197.

26. ʿAbd al-ʿAẓīm Ramāḍan, *Taṭawwur al-ḥarakah al-Waṭanīyah fī Miṣr*, 1917–1936 (Cairo,1968), pp. 732–45.

27. Carter, *The Copts in Egyptian Politics*, p. 172.

28. Ibid., pp. 76–79.

29. Ibid., p. 77.

30. Ibid.

31. Ibid.

32. Beinin and Lockman, *Workforce on the Nile*, p. 182.

33. *Political and Economic Planning: World Population and Resources*, (London, 1954), pp. 45–46.

34. Mirit Ghali, *The Policy of Tomorrow* (Cairo, 1953), pp. 18–19.

35. Richard P. Mitchell, *The Society of Muslim Brothers*, (London, 1969), p. 53.

36. Beinin and Lockman, *Workforce on the Nile*, pp. 377–78.

37. See *al-Ikhwan al-Muslimun*, August 23, 1945 and December 6, 1948.

38. Ducruet, *Les capitaux européen*, p. 294.

39. Carter, *The Copts in Egyptian Politics*, p. 275.

40. Ibid., p. 181.

41. Ibid., p. 270.

42. Cited in Carter, *The Copts in Egyptian Politics*, p. 136.

43. Ibid., pp. 272–73.

4. REBELS AND SAINTS

1. Dina el-Khawāja, "Le développement communautaire Copte: Un mode de participation au politique?" in *Monde Arabe, Magreb Machrek*, no. 135 (January–March 1992), pp. 11–13.

2. See chapter 1 in Carter, *The Copts in Egyptian Politics*, on upper-class involvement in communal affairs.

3. Edward Wakin, *A Lonely Minority: The Modern Story of Egypt's Copts* (New York, 1963), p. 94.

4. For a colorful description of this, see Samir Seikaly, "Coptic Communal Reform: 1860–1914," in *Middle Eastern Studies* (October 1970), pp. 258–59. On the communal council, see William Soliman Kilādā, "Min Tarikh al-Maglis al-Milli," in *Majallat Madāris al-Ahad* (January–February 1983), pp. 11–18.

5. Carter, *The Copts in Egyptian Politics*, pp. 280–81.

6. Ibid.

7. Ibid.

8. el-Khawāja, "Le development Communitaire," pp. 11–13. The pedagogical mission of the diaconal corps had its beginnings in the mid-nineteenth century

when the enlightened pope Cyril IV, worried about the success of the Protestant missionary schools, set up schools patterned after theirs. These were meant to combine the teaching of Orthodox religious traditions and history with a modern education. He also created a seminary meant to raise the education level of the Orthodox deacons and priests.

9. Told to me by the pope, in an interview on his youth in March 1992. For a biographical account of Shenouda's early years, see John Watson, "Signposts to Biography—Pope Shenuda III," in van Doorn-Harder and Vogt, eds., *Between Desert and City*, pp. 243–53.

10. On this see Sivan and Friedeman, eds., *Religious Radicalism and Politics in the Middle East*, pp. 1–9.

11. Bishop Moses in a taped interview of a Sunday Youth Meeting I attended in Cairo, in February 1992.

12. Told to me by Bishop Arsanios's sister, Alexandra Nasr, in summer of 1993.

13. Stories told to me by a family of Bishop Paula's devotees (*muḥibīn*), in Tanta, with whom I visited when Father Tadros was in town for a series of talks that we attended together. I later heard these same stories from the photographer of the pope, Emad Nasr, who was lent to me by the pope for the purpose of taking pictures of the women dedicating their entire life to church service (*Banat Mariam*) in their home of consecration in Banī Suwayf.

14. Interview with the abbot of the Monastery of the Romans (Bishop Arsanios), in the monastery, in December 1991, before he "resigned" from that post at the pope's bidding.

15. I heard the question and reply in the course of one of Pope Shenuda's weekly general meetings, which I attended in winter 1992. When I attended the festivities at the Monastery of Bishoi in November of 1991, in honor of the twentieth anniversary of the pope's ordination, I tried to take a close-up picture of him flanked by his bishops eating cake. But Bishop Serapion, who sat next to him, looked up at me with an indignation that could not have been greater if I had surprised him in an indecent act. I realized then the acute embarrassment he felt at being exposed enjoying his food.

16. Told to me by Bishop Moses in an interview I conducted with him at the papal headquarters in February 1992, to ask him to justify his committee's recent excommunication of Father Daniel.

17. Interview with Bishop Arsanios, then the abbot of the Monastery of the Romans, December of 1991. He gave me this example of how a monk is taught humility when I expressed surprise at the sight of two monks who had entered the guestroom where we were seated and flung themselves at his feet. It was the first time I had ever witnessed such a thing, and I could not help feeling embarrassed.

18. The following information is derived from an excellent article by J. Van der Vliet, "Demons in Early Coptic Monasticism," in H. Hondelink, ed., *Coptic Art and Culture* (Cairo, 1990), pp. 135–55.

19. Ibid.

20. Wakin, *Lonely Minority*, pp. 128–29.

21. Carter, *The Copts in Egyptian Politics*, pp. 28–29.

22. Wakin, *Lonely Minority*, pp. 128–29.

23. Told to me by an old monk, from the Monastery of the Romans, who asked to remain anonymous.

24. Told to me by the monk in charge of taking foreign visitors on tours of the monastery, at the Monastery of the Syrians.

25. Saad Eddin Ibrahim, "Anatomy of Egypt's Militant Islamic Groups: Methodological Notes and Preliminary Findings" in *International Journal of Middle Eastern Studies* 12 (1980), p. 432.

26. On this phenomenon see Micheal Walzer, *The Revolution of the Saints* (Cambridge, Mass., 1965). The term *prospective saints*, which he coined, is used in this chapter to describe those Egyptians whose role models were the local saints of the Apostolic age, whom they actively strove to emulate.

5. ROOTS AND BRANCHES

1. On the role of the missionaries in Egypt, see William Soliman Kilādā, *Al Kinisa al-Misriya tewagih al-Iste' mar wa al-Suhyuniyah*. For the Sunday School Movement, see Samīr Murquṣ, "Tarikh Khidmet Madāris al-Aḥad" in *Majallat Madāris al-Aḥad* (November–December 1989).

2. Cromer, *Modern Egypt*, vol. 2, pp. 128–29.

3. Ibid.

4. Figures are cited in Kilādā, *Al Kinisa*, p. 12.

5. Taped interview of a Sunday youth meeting in Cairo with Bishop Moses, March 1992.

6. Cited in Wakin, *A Lonely Minority*, p. 142.

7. Ibid, pp. 138–39.

8. Interview I conducted with Father Maximos in April 1992, in the diocese of Shubra al-Kheima.

9. Wakin, *A Lonely Minority*, p. 145.

10. Murqus, "Tarikh khidmet."

11. Ibid.

12. Taped song, by the Coptic Institute.

13. Taped interview with Yassa Ḥannā, June 8, 1981 courtesy of Samir Murqus.

14. Ibid.

15. Taped interview with Yuhannā al-Rāhib August 21, 1982 courtesy of Samir Murqus.

16. Ibid.

17. The late Bishop Bimen in a videotaped interview conducted by the Bishopric of Youth in June 16, 1986, shortly before his death, courtesy of Samīr Murquṣ.

18. Yassa Ḥannā, June 8, 1981.

19. From my interview with William Soliman Kilādā, winter 1992.

20. Ibid.

21. Ibid.

22. Wakin, *A Lonely Minority*, pp. 144–45.

23. Ibid.

24. Ibid.

25. Yuhannā al-Rāhib, August 8, 1982.

26. Yassa Ḥannā, June 8, 1961.

27. Ibid.

28. Louis Awad, *al-Jāmiʿat wa-al-mujtamaʾ al-jadīd* (Cairo, n.d.), p. 48.

29. Cited in Raymond W. Baker, *Egypt's Uncertain Revolution under Nasser and Sadat* (Cambridge, Mass., 1987), p. 68.

30. These remarks of Nasser, February 12, 1969, were quoted in *al-Ahrām*, September 28, 1972.

6. THE WARRING FOUNDING FATHERS

1. The late Bishop Bimen, June 16, 1986.

2. Wakin, *A Lonely Minority*, p. 107.

3. Recounted to me by Bishop Gregorios, who was one of the young boys (then called Wahib Attalah) who sat at his feet, in a taped interview I conducted with him in February 1992.

4. Ibid.

5. Ibid.

6. Wakin, *A Lonely Minority*, p. 117.

7. Ibid., p. 118.

8. Samīr Murquṣ, "Tarikh khidmet Madares al-Ahad."

9. Told to me by Bishop Pachomios, in an interview in his diocese, Damanhour, spring 1993.

10. Told to me by the pope, in an interview about his youth, at the Monastery of Bishoi, December 1991.

11. Bishop Gregorios, in taped interview, February 1992. Bishop Gregorios was one of the founders of the Coptic Institute in 1954 along with professors Sami Gabra, Aziz Attiyah, and others. For more information about the institute see Christine Chaillot, "L'Institut des Etudes Coptes," in *Le Monde Copte*, .17, (1990), pp. 35–50.

12. Ibid, Bishop Gregorios.

13. Ibid.

14. Ibid.

15. Told to me by an old monk from the Monastery of St. Macarios, who asked to remain anonymous.

16. Ibid.

17. Ibid.

18. The monk in question has since become Bishop Johanna, the pope's secretary. He told me this when we were engaged in a conversation in the bishop's reception room, where I was waiting to be received by the pope. The other monk is today Bishop Bisante, who served as the pope's secretary prior to Bishop Johanna. He was unsparing in his criticism of Matthew the Poor, virtually depicting him to be a slave driver, in an interview I conducted with him in Cairo in December 1991.

19. Interview with Bishop Sherubim, in Kena, January 1994.

20. Told to me by Dr. Maurice Asʿad, a longtime friend and supporter of Bishop Samuel, in an interview at the Egyptian office of the Middle East Council of Churches in Heliopolis in 1994. He was the director of that center.

21. Ibid.

22. Ibid. See also Īzīs al-Maṣrī, *Qiṣṣat ḥayāt al-Anbā Ṣamūwil* (Cairo, 1988).

23. This is the way Pope Shenuda referred to it in his conversation with me in March 1992 at his monastic retreat, Deir el-Anba Bishoi.

24. Matt'a al-āb Maskīn, *Maqālāt bayna al-siyāsah wa-al dīn* (Wadi Natrun, 1966).

25. Shenuda III, *al-ḥurūb al-rūḥīyah* (Cairo, 1988).

26. al-āb Maskīn, *Maqālāt.*

27. Ibid.

28. Told to me by the aforementioned old monk from the Monastery of St. Macarios.

29. Told to me by the banker Fakhri Abd al-Nur, a friend of Bishop Samuel, who often contributed money to Bishop Samuel's projects and who accompanied him to the historic meeting with Pope John Paul II in the Vatican, in an interview in the winter of 1993.

30. My own observations and conclusions.

31. Matt'a al-āb Maskīn, *al Khidmah* (Cairo, 1980).

32. Shenuda III, *Ma'ālim 'alá al-ṭarīq al-rūhī* (Cairo, 1987) and *al-Sahar al-rūḥī* (Cairo, 1988).

33. Shenuda III, *Ḥurūb al-Shayṭān* (Cairo, 1986).

34. Shenuda III, *al-Khalāṣ fīmafhūm al-Urthūdhuksī* (Cairo, 1984).

35. Matt'a al-āb Maskīn, *Ma'a al-Masīḥ fī'alamihi ḥatt'a al-ṣalīb* (Cairo, 1986).

36. Matt'a al-āb Maskīn, *al Taqlīd al-kanasī wa-ahammīyatuhu fial ahmām al-Masīḥī* (Cairo, 1987).

37. al-Anbā Samuel, *Tanẓīm al-usrah min Wejhat nazar Masīḥīyah* (Cairo, 1975).

38. Bishop Moses, at one of his weekly youth meetings, which I attended in March of 1992.

39. In March 1992, in one of my visits to the pope at the Monastery of Bishoi to discuss an attack on me in the Egyptian press entitled "An Egyptian Woman in the Home of Israel's Leaders" (*Rūz al-Yūsef*, March 23, 1992), he told me this.

40. Bishop Bishoi told me this once, when all the bishops were assembled at the Bishoi Monastery to attend a conference the pope had convened on the subject of divorce.

41. Mohammed, Heykal, *Autumn of Fury* (New York, 1983), p. 134.

42. Fakhri Abd al-Nur, in a conversation at his home, the winter 1993.

43. Dr. Maurice As'ad, 1994.

44. Ibid.

7. DEALING WITH THE MUSLIM STATE

1. Wakin, *A Lonely Minority*, 148–53. On the cordial relations between Pope Cyril and Abd al-Nasser see Maḥmūd Fawzī, *al-Bābā Kīrillus wa-'Abd al-Nāṣir* (Cairo, 1993).

2. Heykal, *Autumn of Fury*, p.134.

3. Farah, *Religious Strife*, p. 4.

4. Ibid. See also Ibrahim, *'Isa, 'Amā'īm wa-khanājir* (Cairo, 1993).

5. Information from an interview I conducted with the pope in November 1992 in the Monastery of Bishoi.

6. Ibid.

7. Information from an interview I conducted with Bishop Arsanios, in the Monastery of the Romans in December 1991.

8. Jean-Pierre Peroncel-Hugoz, *The Raft of Muhammad* (New York, 1998), 111–13.

9. The pope gave me a copy of that tape.

10. Information from an interview with the pope at the Monastery of Bishoi, July 1992.

11. Muḥammad Anwar al-Sadat, *Speech Delivered on the Occasion of the Tenth Anniversary of the Corrective Revolution*, May 14, 1980, (State Information Service, Cairo 1980). See the pope's own statement on this subject in the Egyptian magazine *Rūz al-Yūsef* March 9, 1999. See also the discussion in the Egyptian newspaper *al-Ahram*, November 28, 1988. See further the article by Adel Hussein in the Egyptian newspaper *Al Sha'b* April 30, 1992. For good interviews with the pope on his strained relations with Sadat see Maḥmūd Fawzī, *al-Bābā Shanūdah wa-ḥiwār maḥzūr al-nashr* (Cairo, 1990) and *al-Bābā Shanūdah wa-tārīkh al-Kinīsah al-Qibṭīyah* (Cairo, 1992).

12. For an account of events of Zawya al-Hamra, see Hugoz, *The Raft of Muhammad*. Hugoz was a reporter for *Le Monde* stationed in Egypt before he wrote the book.

13. See Muḥammad Anwar al-Sadat, *Speech Delivered during the Joint Session of the People's Assembly and the Senate*, September 5, 1981 (State information service, Cairo, 1981).

14. This information was given to me by Fakhri Abd al-Nur in an interview at his home in the winter 1992. For a counterargument that Sadat himself may have been interested in ethnic conflict as a way to divert the attention of his critics from his raprochement with Israel, see *al-Ahālī* March 25, 1978.

15. Boutrous Ghālī is a friend of my family. I conducted this interview in his home in Cairo in 1983, when I was doing an article on the Islamic Militants for *The New York Times Magazine*. The same refusal to face up to unpleasant reality is manifest in his book *al-Sha'b al-waḥīd wa-al-waṭan al-waḥīd* (One people, one country) (Cairo, 1982).

16. Magdi Wahba was a friend of mine. He said this to me during a conversation in his home, over dinner, in the winter of 1992, on the plight of the Copts.

17. Abd al-Nur, interview, January 28, 1992.

18. Interview with Amīn Fahim in his office, winter 1992.

19. I was told this at a dinner I had with him and his family in my home in 1991.

20. The pope showed me a file with extracts of such writings, which he had just brought to the attention of the minister of Education, when I interviewed him at the papal headquarters in June 1994.

21. I was in Sohag interviewing Bishop Bachum at his residence in February 1993 and happened to overhear him talking on the telephone.

22. I was doing fieldwork in Tima when this happened in spring 1993, and the priest in question came to the bishop to ask for help.

23. Told to me by Bishop Tackla, during a lunch at his residence in the diocese of Dishna, in August 1993. The bishop's good relations with the governor and his

diplomatic skills were crucial in containing sectarian strife. In a later, bloodier, incident in the village of Kush in Upper Egypt, Bishop Wisa's more militant disposition led to his imprisonment and to vitriolic attacks by Muslims in the Egyptian press accusing him of exacerbating sectarian violence. See along these lines the article of ʿAbd Allāh Kamāl in *Rūz al-Yūsef*, November 2, 1998. For a more balanced account of the reasons for the failure to contain sectarian violence in Kush, see the articles by Adel al-Gohary in the journal *al-Mushāhid al-Siyāsī*, April 1, 2000.

24. Bishop Athanasios made this remark to me, over dinner at his residence in Banī Suwayf, October 1992.

25. In the course of 1991 and 1992, I witnessed this a number of times, when I happened to be seated in the office of Bishop Johanna, the pope's secretary. Pleas from Bishop Athanasios to be admitted to see the pope were denied.

26. I was present when Bishop Bisente scolded a priest and ordered him to remove Matthew the Poor's books from the church library.

27. Told to me by an old monk from the monastery of St. Macarios who wishes to remain anonymous. For the pope's own justification of his policies toward Matthew the Poor, see the interview with Maḥmūd Fawzī in *al-Bābā Shanūdah wa-al-muʿāradah fī al-kanīsah* (Cairo, 1992).

28. For a very accurate and detailed account of all the events leading up to the all-out confrontation between the pope and Sadat, see Farah, *Religious Strife in Egypt*, part 1.

29. For these charges see the National Security Report in *Mayo*, September 14, 1981; and also the discussion about the conspiracy to create divisions between Copts and Muslims in *al-Ahālī*, March 25, 1971, and March 18, 1987.

30. *al-Ahālī*, November 16, 1988 and November 23, 1988.

31. I attended this lecture at Minya's theological seminary in December 1992, while I was doing out fieldwork in that diocese.

32. I attended this general meeting during my fieldwork in Tanta in January 1992 and I heard the question-and-answer.

33. I attended this general meeting in Shubra al-Kheima during my fieldwork there in April 1992.

34. For attacks on tourists, see article in *Middle East Times*, March 23–29, 1993. See also *The Egyptian Gazette*, October 3, 1992, November 31, 1992; March 1, 1993; March 31,1993; May 26, 1993; and *al-Ahrām* Weekly, May27–June 3, 1992.

35. *The Egyptian Gazette*, April 13, 1993.

36. See, for example, *al-Ahrām*, July 20, 1993.

37. For one such incident, see *The Egyptian Gazette*, April 5, 1993.

38. *Civil Society*, 24 (December 1993).

39. *The Egyptian Gazette*, February 28, 1993.

40. Ibid., April 22, 1993, and July 20, 1993.

41. *al-Ahrām Weekly*, January 7–13, 1993.

42. Nagi Qumha, "Bulldozers Don't Hold the Answer," reprinted from *al-Gumhuria* in *The Egyptian Gazette*, December 14, 1992.

43. *The Egyptian Gazette*, November 2, 1992.

44. Ibid.

45. Ibid.

46. See M. K. Gandhi, *Self-Restraint versus Self-Indulgence* (Ahmedabad, 1956).

47. I have often heard them described in these terms in Muslim homes.

8. CENTRALIZING THE CHURCH ADMINISTRATION

1. Wakin, *A Lonely Minority*, 114.

2. Information given to me by Bishop Kyrilos of Naga Hammadi, whose diocese encompasses part of the land previously under the bishop of Girga's jurisdiction, when I went to interview him in Naga Hammadi in winter 1993.

3. H. Mussier, *Receuil des listes épiscopales de L'Eglise Copte*, Coptic Archeological Society (Cairo, 1989), pp. 67–68.

4. Taped interview with Bishop Fam, April 1993, when I was doing fieldwork in his diocese.

5. Told to me by Bishop Athanasios in a taped interview during my fieldwork in Bānī Suwayf in October 1992. He said that the bishops of Upper Egypt had raised the strongest objections in the Holy Synod because they had the most to fear from the competition of the Protestant churches. He added that he himself disagreed with the pope on this and applied a much more liberal policy in his diocese. For Pope Shenuda's views on the subject of marriage and divorce, see *al-Muṣawwar*, March 2, 1992

6. *al-Kirāzah*, June 16, 1989 and November 25, 1989 and April 21, 1989.

7. Ibid.

8. Told to me by the pope during a conference he had organized in the Monastery of Bishoi for bishops and priests on how to deal with disputes between spouses.

9. I visited these homes during my fieldwork in Abu Tig, in June 1993.

10. I visited these homes during my fieldwork in Tima, in April 1993.

11. Told to me by the pope on the earlier-cited occasion.

12. Told to me by Bishop Bimen of Nagada during a lunch we shared in his residence at the bishopric in Nagada when I was based in Luxor for my fieldwork in March 1994.

13. The late Bishop Bimen, videotaped interview cited earlier.

14. Conversations with the church servants of the various dioceses where I did fieldwork.

15. Such is the case not only in Cairo, but also in Minya, where I met the salaried church servants in the Community Development Center.

16. This happened during my trip to the Monastery of Bishoi with a group of university students who lodged at the Giza church-hostel, to meet Bishop Isaiah.

17. Arsani Ghabour, a deacon in Minya, said this to me during a conversation at his apartment, winter 1994.

18. These words were spoken by the pope in my presence on November 14, 1991.

19. The pope said this to me during a stroll on the grounds of the monastery the next day.

20. *al-Kirāzah* is a very useful source for finding out who is in and out of favor at any given time.

21. See *Egypt Today* (April 1985).

22. Told to me by Mīlād Ḥannā, the head of the most important Coptic philanthropic organization, al-Tewfikiyah.

9. ḤARAKA WA BARAKAH

1. al-Anbā Athanasios, *al-iman wa al-Tanmiya* (Banī Suwayf, n.d.).

2. Because the demographic question is a very sensitive one, since the greater the number of Copts, the more vociferously they will demand equal rights, it is impossible to rely on the statistics collected by government agencies, in whose interest it is to under-represent the Copts. The only other choice is to rely on the figures at the disposal of the bishops of each diocese, which are based on computations by each church of the Christian families in its neighborhood—both those who attend Mass and those who do not. But the accuracy of these figures is questionable, since they depend on the competence of the church servants who collect them and the zeal with which the priest in each parish pushes them to do so and monitors them.

3. This conclusion is based on observations made during my fieldwork in Banī Suwayf in October 1992 and a series of taped interviews with Bishop Athanasios at his residence in Banī Suwayf.

4. Observed during my fieldwork in October 1992 in Banī Suwayf.

5. Taped interview with Bishop Pachomios at his bishopric in Damanhour, August 1992.

6. I attended the summer camp for village children during my fieldwork in Damanhur in August 1992.

7. This is my judgment based on my fieldwork in Damanhur during that period.

8. Taped interview with Bishop Arsanios, December 1992.

9. Interview with the monk Abdel-Mesih, carried out in the Monastery of the Romans in November 1991.

10. Ibid.

11. Taped interview with the program director, Raef Hinawi, in Minya in December of 1992.

12. Based on my own observations.

13. Ibid.

14. Witnessed during my fieldwork in Minya in December 1992.

15. For information about the multipurpose school see *St. George Multipurpose School*, a project submitted for funding by the Community Development Center of Minya, 1992.

16. See the *Development Training Farm*, a project submitted for funding by the Department of Community Development in the Coptic Orthodox Diocese of Minya, 1994.

17. See *Hand in Hand*, a project submitted for funding by the Community Development Center of Minya, 1991.

18. Told to me by Bishop Arsanios.

19. Ibid.

20. See *al-Ahrām Weekly*, February 20–26, 1997, *The New York Times*, March 15, 1997, and *The New York Times*, March 15, 1993.

21. *Hand in Hand.*

22. Ibid.

23. Ibid.

24. Told to me by Bishop Arsanios in July 1994.

25. Ibid.

26. Ibid.

27. Told to me by Bishop Bimen of the diocese of Nagada, at a lunch at his residence, when I was doing fieldwork in his diocese, in April 1994.

28. I witnessed this scene in April 1992 during this meeting, which Bishop Murqus had allowed me to attend.

29. Taped interview with Bishop Tackla, Dishna, July 1993.

30. Told to me in January 1995 by engineer Fahmi Basili, who was vice minister of housing. He was present when these contributions were made.

31. Told to me by Bishop Tackla during a lunch at his residence in Dishna, July 1993.

32. Taped interview with bishop Murqus, at his residence in Shubra al-Kheima, fall 1993.

33. Interview with Bishop Murqus, April 1992.

34. Told to me by Raef Hinawi.

35. This is my judgment as a Harvard-trained political economist, based on a thorough study of all of his projects.

36. Told to me by Bishop Arsanios.

37. I have chosen not to reveal the name of this bishop to avoid embarrassing him.

38. Told to me by Bishop Arsanios.

39. This is the estimate given to me by the engineer in charge of its construction, Fahmi Basili, when we visited the site in June 1994 in Abu Talat where the construction had begun.

40. Told to me by Bishop Arsanios and Bishop Tackla.

41. Interview with Bishop Serapion, carried out in the headquarters of the bishopric of Social and Ecumenical Affairs in Cairo, February 1992.

42. Bishop Tackla showed me the project proposals.

43. I witnessed this during my fieldwork in Tima, April 1993.

44. Told to me by Bishop Fam in the monastery of Bishoi, in the presence of Bishop Serapion, March 1992.

45. I witnessed the delivery of the chocolates in Sohag during my fieldwork in Tima in April 1993.

46. Told to me by Tasoni Imtisal, who was in charge of the girls' workshop.

47. I visited these hovels repeatedly, during my fieldwork in Tima, with the representative of the Orthodox Brothers of Jesus Association (Ikhwāt al-Rabb), called Om Nasr, in March 1993.

48. Taped interview with Bishop Besada in Akhmim, January 1993.

49. Ibid

50. Ibid.

51. Ibid.

52. Ibid.

53. Witnessed by me during my fieldwork in Minya.

54. Ibid.

55. Ibid.

56. Cited in Walzer, *The Revolution of the Saints*, pp. 313–14.

57. Published in the magazine of the Orthodox Church Youth movement of Minya, *al-Raja'*, July 1977.

58. Taped interview with Bishop Bachum in Sohag, February 1993.

10. THE RECRUITMENT OF BISHOPS

1. Interview I conducted with Coptic member of Pariament Mīlād Ḥannā, November 1991.

2. Taped interview with Bishop Lukas in Abnub, December 1993.

3. Taped interview with Bishop Tackla in Dishna, August 1993.

4. Information given to me by these bishops.

5. Information about Bishop Dimitrios given to me by Bishop Bishoi, and that about Bishop Amonios provided to me by Bishop Fam.

6. Videotaped interview by Samir Murqus, with Bishop Bimen shortly before his death in 1986. Courtesy of Mr. Murqus. See also Anba Bimen, *al-Khidmah fi al-qaryah* (Cairo, n.d.).

7. Told to me by one of his consecrated women (*mukarasa*), who after his death left the service of his successor Bishop Dimitrios, in protest against his dismantling of some developmental programs the late Bishop Bimen had launched. She moved to Cairo, where she entered the service of the more progressive Bishop Moses. She asked me not to name her.

8. Ibid.

9. Told to me by one of his devotees (*muhibin*), a Coptic notable in Luxor who owns Hotel Emile.

10. Told to me by Bishop Fam, during my fieldwork in Tima in April 1993.

11. Ibid.

12. Ibid. I spent time in the major towns of Luxor and Aswan studying and comparing their developmental and cultural activities in summer 1994; I also carried out a prolonged interview with Bishop Hidra, the bishop of Aswan, in May 1994, at his residence. It proved impossible, however, to interview Bishop Amonios. He twice set up appointments for an interview while I was in Luxor and twice did not appear, as I was told by several of his priests was his habit.

13. Most of the church-servants (*khuddām*) I interviewed were of this opinion.

14. See Lee Keath, "Honor Thy Father," in *Egypt Today* (April 1989), p. 89.

15. Interview with Bishop Bachum, when I was doing fieldwork in Sohag, his diocese, February 1993.

16. This is my evaluation based on my own observations.

17. Information based on my interviews with these bishops.

18. Based on my observations during my fieldwork in Abu Tig, June 1993, and my conversations with its bishop, Bishop Andrawes.

19. Ibid.

20. Story told to me by a family of Bishop Bula's devotees, whom I visited when I was doing fieldwork in Tanta in January 1992. He was their patron saint.

21. Based on my observations during my fieldwork in Tahta, in May 1993 and my conversations with Bishop Isaiah.

22. Told to me by Father Abraham in Tima in March 1993.

23. Told to me by Bishop Isaiah during an interview I conducted with him in May 1993, when I was doing fieldwork in his diocese.

24. Interview conducted with Bishop Bula in his residence, January 1992.

25. I witnesses this when I lived in the home for consecrated women, in Tanta, in the days that preceded the 1992 Orthodox Christmas (January 7).

26. I observed this during my fieldwork in Qusia in October 1993.

27. Ibid.

28. Taped interview with a group of church servants, during fieldwork in Qusia in November 1993.

29. Told to me by Dr. Maurice, the director of the development projects carried out by the Bishopric of Social Services throughout the country, in a taped interview in December 1991, in Cairo.

30. Bishop Thomas, taped interview, October 1993.

31. Taped interview with Bishop Bula, during fieldwork in Tanta in January 1992.

32. Dr. Maurice, taped interview, December 1991.

33. Told to me by Father Joseph of Tima.

34. Dr. Maurice, taped interview, December 1991.

35. Videotaped interview in 1986 with the late Bishop Bimen, courtesy of Samir Murqus.

36. I was present when this conversation took place, which occurred during my fieldwork in Abu Tig in June 1993.

37. Interview with Bishop Lukas, December 1993.

38. Told to me by Fathers Malak of Sohag and Dimian of Kena in the course of a conversation, about the condition of women in Upper Egypt, in the monastery of Bishoi during a two-day colloquium the pope had organized for the priests of Upper and Lower Egypt on the policy of the Orthodox Church toward divorce.

39. Told to me by church-servant Mīlād Murqus during my fieldwork in Tima in April 1993.

40. Told to me by Bishop Thomas in Qusia in November 1993.

41. Ibid.

11. CULTURE AND HEGEMONY

1. This reason was given to me by Mājid ʿAṭīyah, the Coptic associate editor of the weekly magazine *al-Muṣawwar*.

2. Wakin, *A Lonely Minority*, p. 65.

3. Cited in ibid., pp. 66–67.

4. Told to my father by Amin Fikry.

5. Wakin, *A Lonely Minority*, p. 45.

6. I watched many of these programs on television as part of my research for this book during the period 1992–1994.

7. Told to me by Magdi Wahba.

8. *al-Ahrām Weekly*, May 3, 1993.

9. See, for example, *al Wafd* June 25, 1992, and *al-Ahrām* February 19, 1992, *al-Ahrām Weekly*, June 18–24, 1992; *al-Sha'b*, October 6, 1992.

10. *The Egyptian Gazette*, May 7, 1993, and February 11, 1993.

11. *Middle East Times*, August 17–23, 1993.
12. *The Egyptian Gazette*, March 21, 1993.
13. *The Egyptian Gazette*, November 12, 1992.
14. *al-Ahrām Weekly* May 3, 1993.
15. *al-Ahali*, November 23, 1988.
16. *The Egyptian Gazette*, November 17, 1992.
17. *Middle East Times*, August 3–9, 1993.
18. *al-Ahrām*, June 12, 1992.
19. *al-Ahrām* Weekly, June 12, 1992.
20. *al-Ahrām* Weekly, May 3, 1993.
21. *Middle East Times*, October 8–14, 1992.
22. Information from an interview with Farag Foda in March 1992.
23. *Middle East Times*, July 13–19, 1993.
24. Ibid.
25. Ibid.
26. *The Egyptian Gazette*, January 15, 1993.
27. *The Egyptian Gazette*, November 8, 1992.
28. *The Egyptian Gazette*, January 15, 1993.
29. *Middle East Times*, August 3–9, 1993.
30. Ibid.
31. Bishop Gregorios sent the government a long letter of protest against the slurs on the Christian faith by Sheikh Sha'rawi, of which he gave me a copy.
32. *The Egyptian Gazette*, May 2, 1993.
33. Cited in *Middle East Times*, March 21–28, 1993.
34. Ibid.
35. *al-Sha'b*, April 20, 1993.
36. *The Egyptian Gazette*, May 21, 1993.
37. Ibid.
38. For best coverage of this incident, see *Middle East Times*, March 21–28, 1993.
39. *The Egyptian Gazette*, November 17, 1992.
40. Ibid.
41. Farah, *Religious Strife in Egypt*, p. 128.

12. "THE GLORIOUS AND THE SACRED"

1. Information given to me by Dr. Emile, who was a friend of Dr. Shafik (doctors are called by their first names in Egypt).

2. This is the way Pope Shenuda expressed himself in an interview I conducted with him in October 1992, when I asked him about his motive in creating the Bishopric of Youth.

3. See the *Egyptian Gazette*, May 7, 1997. I witnessed a similar phenomenon after the excommunication of Father Daniel, when a good number of his youthful followers left the Orthodox Church in protest and attended prayer meetings in private homes, where he officiated. Bishop Arsanios of Minya told me that often some parents would come to him in tears, begging him to try to persuade their

children to return to the mother church. And he did try with varying degrees of success.

4. Information from taped interview with Bishop Moses, February 1992.

5. Ibid.

6. Information from taped interview with Bishop Murqus, April 1992.

7. Bishop Moses, interview, February 1992.

8. Ibid.

9. Taped conference for the youth leaders (*Umana' el Khidmah*) of secondary school (high school) and university students held in Cairo in March 1992.

10. Ibid.

11. Ibid.

12. Ibid.

13. See *Majallat Madāris-al-Aḥad*, January 1967.

14. See *Risālāt al-Shabāb al-Kanasī*, January 1993.

15. Told to me by church servant Samir Murqus, one of the editors of *Risālāt al-Shabāb al-Kanasī*, to whom Bishop Bishoi expressed his displeasure.

16. Bishop Moses in a Sunday youth meeting I attended in February of 1992.

17. Youth leaders' conference March 1992. See also his *al-Shabāb wa-ḥayāt al-ṭahārah* (Cairo, n.d.).

18. See *Middle East Times*, November 20–26, 1994.

19. Cited in ibid.

20. Cited in ibid.

21. Address to university students, at the Patraiarchate in Cairo in March 1992. A plethora of publications is put out by the Bishopric of Youth about the proper moral conduct between the sexes. See Rāghib ʿAbd al-Nūr, *Naḥwa al-ṭāhāra* (Cairo, 1970); al-Qumus Yūsuf Asʿad, *Kayfa yataʿāmil al-khaṭībān* (Cairo, 1998); *al-Tarbiyah al-jinsīyah lil-fatrah al-murāhaqah* (no author); Majlis Kanā'is al-Sharq al-Awsaṭ, (Cairo, 1986); al-Anbā Mūsā, *Al-Shabāb wa-ḥayāt al-ṭahārah*, (Cairo, 1989) and by the same author *al-Ma'na al-Masīḥī lil-zawāj* Cairo 1991), *al Taʿāmul bayna al-jinsayn* (Cairo, 1990), and *al-Ma'na al-Masīḥī lil-jins* (Cairo, 1991). Ṭalʿat Zakarīyā Mīnā, *al-Muḥafazah ʿala al-usrah al-Masīḥīyah*, (Cairo, 1988).

22. See *al-Malā'ikah* no. 2 (n.d.) and *al-Malā'ikah* no. 5 (n.d.).

23. See *Dunyā al Ṭifl*, July 1991 and October 1992. The Bishopric of Youth puts out a whole series of publications in this vein. Examples are Klayr Fahīm, *al-Umūmah wa al-ṭufūlah* (Cairo, 1988) and, by the same author *Dar al-ḥadānah wa-al-usrah* and *al-Mashākil al-nafsīyah li-ṭifl al-ḥadānah* (Cairo, 1988). See also Ṭal'at Dhikrī *al-Tilīfizīyūn fiḥayāt al-aṭfal*, (Cairo, 1988), and *al-ṣiḥḥah al-nafsīyah al-fata al-murāhiq* (Cairo, 1989).

24. I observed this during my fieldwork in Girga, where Nagib was an instructor in an institute set up by Bishop Daniel to train church-servants.

25. Bishop Moses in a lecture, "The Complete Personality" (February 1992).

26. This scene took place during those same lectures, February–March 1992.

27. Narrated by Bishop Moses at the youth leaders conference in March 1992.

28. This question was asked in a Sunday youth meeting in February 1992.

29. Youth leaders conference, March 1992.

30. Bishop Moses, "The Perfect Personality."

31. Ibid.

32. Interview with Bishop Bachum in Sohag in February 1993.

33. Interview with Bishop Thomas in Qusia in October 1993.

34. I witnessed this during my fieldwork in Tanta.

35. I witnessed this during my fieldwork in Damanhour.

36. I witnessed this during my fieldwork in Shubra al-Kheima.

37. I witnessed this when Bishop Bishoi put me up in St. Dimiana's church-run guest house, when I went to the latter's diocese to observe his pastoral activities.

38. "The Complete Personality," February 1992. Here again, the Bishopric of Youth publishes a whole series of books on the local saints and martyrs used as a pedagogical material in the Sunday schools, Examples are Sāmiḥ Kamāl, *al-Shahīd Abū Fām*, (Cairo, 1989); *al-Shahīdān Dīsqūrūs wa-Isqlābīyūs* (The Monastery of St. Anthony, 1986 Abādīr Siryānī *al-Shahīdān Abādīr wa-ukhtuhu Ayrīnī* (Monastery of the Syrians, 1990).

39. He said this during one of his lectures in the series *The Characteristics of Orthodoxy* (March 1992).

40. Ibid.

41. Bishop Moses' address to university students on the occasion of their graduation, which I attended in March 1992. Compare the way he addresses the problem of the youths' anxiety about their future in a pamphlet entitled *Anxiety* in a series published by the Bishopric of Youth called *Pamphlets for Your Life.*

42. Magdi Isaac, in a series of lectures entitled *Christianity and Psychology*, March 1992.

43. Ibid.

44. The frequent use of this term by Orthodox prelates presents an interesting parallel with Ben Gurion's telling the Jewish nation that they should be a light to the *goyim*. In a private birthday party the pope held for me in his Anba Ruweis residence in May 1994, he offered me a Christmas candle engraved with a snowman and said he wanted me to be a "light" (in the Christian sense of this word) unto the world.

45. Graduation address to university students, March 1992.

46. *Middle East Times*, January 2–7, 1994.

47. Ibid.

48. Ibid.

13. COPTIC CULTURAL NATIONALISM

1. See Anba Shenuda, *Hayat al-Iman* (Cario, 1986).

2. Raymond Stock, "Preserving Pharaohs' Psalms," in *Egypt Today* (April 1997).

3. Ibid.

4. Ibid.

5. This information is based on my interviews with church-servants in charge of the duplication and sales of tapes at the Bishopric of Youth and in the different churches throughout the dioceses.

6. For example, when I visited the Abu Talat summer resort with Bishop Tackla in July 1993, the youngsters gathered around him on his arrival and sang such a song. The same thing happened when I visited Nazlit Ebeid in December 1992 with Bishop Arsanios.

7. I observed this during my stay with three families close to the church that were putting me up overnight in Aswan, Tima, and Kafr al-Sheihk.

8. Ibid

9. Wakin, *A Lonely Minority*, p. 154.

10. This was said to me by both Fakhri Abd al-Nur and Magdi Wahba in the aforementioned interviews.

11. Interview with Bishop Gregorios, (Cairo, February 1992).

12. *Egyptian Gazette*. January 14, 1997.

13. Ibid.

14. THE CHURCH AS BATTLEGROUND

1. Told to me by a priest in Assiut in November 1993.

2. Told to me by Bishop Arsanios in March 1995.

3. Told to me by the journalist Majid Aṭīyah in December 1991.

4. I observed this when I was doing fieldwork in Minya in November–December 1992 and in Tima in March–April 1993. I then asked the bishops of these two dioceses about the state of these churches.

5. Information given to me by Bishop Arsanios in March 1975.

6. I witnessed this in several of the dioceses I visited.

7. Bishop Kyrilos of Naga Hammadi told me this in an interview in February 1994.

8. Mark Francis Gruber, "Coping with God: Coptic Monasticism in Egyptian Culture," in Doorn-Harder and Vogt, *Between Desert and City*, p. 65.

9. This account of the increase in the number of Masses held was given to me by Bishop Arsanios.

10. See Anba Shenuda, Ḥayat al-Iman.

11. This conversation took place when the building engineer took me to visit the complex he was building for the Bishop of Minya and then led me on a tour of some of the other resort establishments of the diocese, which were either operative or still being built.

12. He said this in a talk he gave for blue-collar workers in the Church of the Virgin in Shoubra, which I attended in March 1992.

13. Pictures given to me by the family of Abu Hisham, which hosted me in Tima.

14. Told to me by Bishop Tackla, in a taped interview in July 1993.

15. Told to me by Bishop Tadros in a taped interview in Port Said in June of 1992.

16. Narrated by Bishop Moses at one of the weekly youth meetings at the papal headquarters, which I attended in February 1992.

17. Told to me by Bishop Arsanios.

18. This woman arrived at the papal headquarters with her daughter one evening when I was waiting to see the pope.

19. I met this woman at the pope's monastic retreat, where she had gone to show him her son, then two years old, and we had some pictures taken together with the pope.

20. See article by J. Van der Vliet, "Demons in Early Coptic Monasticism: Images and Reality," in H. Hondelick ed., Coptic Art and Culture (Cairo, 1990), pp. 135–55.

21. Episode related by Bishop Moses at one of the Sunday Youth Meetings in the papal headquarters, which I attended in February 1992.

22. Gruber, "Coping with God," p. 53.

23. See *Muʾjizāt al-Bābā Kīrilus* (Cairo, 1981)

24. The family of Abu Hisham with whom I stayed in Tima in March–April 1993 often brought such gifts of food to the neighboring monastery.

25. Told to me by the Coptic dignitary who owned Hotel Emile in Luxor. He himself was called Emile.

26. I witnessed this when I accompanied Bishop Tackla and his mother in July 1993 to the Monastery of the Romans on his birthday.

27. Bishop Arsanios once boiled some guava leaves for me, when I visited him in Minya on a cold winter day. The concoction tasted a little like licorice.

28. Gruber, "Coping with God," p. 53.

15. THE CHURCH AS AMPHITHEATER

1. My estimate after paying two church-servants to count the audience, independently of each other, row by row, on three consecutive Wednesdays.

2. Pope Shenuda, in a conversation with me at his monastic retreat, in February 1993. He told me that he had had to give asylum in his monastery to a Muslim convert named Nahed. Later he spirited her out of the country because she was in danger of being killed.

3. Heykal, *Autumn of Fury*.

4. Bishop Arsanios told this to me one evening, when I was visiting him at the Anba Ruweis guest house for bishops from out of town, and a young woman was just leaving, in tears, as I was entering. When I asked why she was crying, he said that he had rebuked her because she wanted to convert to marry a Muslim.

5. For example, when I was in Kena in January 1994, the local church choir was on every video screen, because Kena had just won the competition.

6. Based on my interview of the church-servant in charge of the duplication and sale of tapes at the Bishopric of Youth, in the patriarchal headquarters.

7. I have witnessed this at a variety of family get-togethers to which I was invited: birthdays, graduation parties, parties for visiting immigrant sons, and so on.

8. All that follows is a description of the Wednesday General Meetings, which I've attended innumerable times.

16. TOWARD A MORE DEMOCRATIC CHURCH?

1. Told to me by Bishop Tackla, in a taped interview in August 1993.

2. Told to me by Bishop Bula in a taped interview in his residence in Tanta in January 1992.

3. I witnessed this during my fieldwork in Banī Suwayf in October 1992.

4. Ibid.

5. Ibid.

6. Ibid.

7. Bishop Athanasios showed me his room once, during a dinner in October 1992 at his residence and told this to me.

8. I witnessed this many times, when I myself was at the papal headquarters.

9. Ibid.

10. Told to me by the pope, when I was visiting him at his monastic retreat in the Natrun valley in March 1995.

11. This happened even to me, an outsider, at the hands of Dr. Nabila, who as the only woman who had the pope's ear, because she wrote for the papal organ *al-Kirāza*, was jealous of my access to him.

12. Told to me by Bishop Athanasios, who was one of the few bishops sympathetic to Father Daniel.

13. This is how I heard the pope refer to his preaching style during a videotape display of one of Father Daniel's sermons, which he aired in defense of his excommunication edict, for his Tuesday theological seminary.

14. Told to me by Bishop Arsanios.

15. Told to me by Bishop Bula one day in January 1992, when he arrived from Tanta at the papal headquaters for a meeting of the committee on divorce (referred to as the Family Status Committee) and I noticed him asking the *Mukarasa* attached to his service to bring him some aspirin.

16. I've been told this many times, both by his internal critics and by Copts in the United States.

17. Wakin, *A Lonely Minority*, p. 130.

18. This discussion took place in my presence at the end of the Tuesday theological seminary, given by the pope.

19. I chanced to be at the papal headquarters when the pope stalked out of his first-floor reception room, visibly upset. I asked him why he seemed so irritated and he told me what had happened.

20. See the interview about sports with the pope in *al-Ahrām Weekly*, March 30–April 5, 1995.

21. For the best account of the growing voices of opposition to the pope see Lee Keath, "Honor Your Father," in the April 1995 issue of *Egypt Today*. For this, in particular, see p. 91.

22. Ibid.

23. Ibid.

24. Ibid, p. 90.

25. Ibid, p. 113.

26. The dignitary in question was Abu Hisham.

27. Told to me by Father Angelios at his sister's house in spring 1993.

28. Ibid.

29. Told to me by the pope, at the papal headquarters in spring 1993.

30. Scene I witnessed at the patriarchal headquarters in winter 1992.

31. Told to me by Bishop Arsanios over dinner at his residence in Minya in January 1999.

32. Told to me by the pope, at his monastic retreat in December 1993, when I pleaded on behalf of Bishop Arsanios.

33. See Father Daniel, *Leisa siwah* (Cairo, n.d.), *Ma agmaluh* (Cairo, 1976), *al-Fach inkasar* (Cairo, 1977), and *La Ataza'za'* (Cairo, n.d.).

34. Father Zakaria's story was told to me by one of his devotees in Alexandria, whom I met at the Sporting Church. By the time I arrived to do my research, Father

Zakaria had been spirited out of the country; he was dispatched by the pope to be a priest in Australia, because the secret police was pursuing him, having been apprised of his success in converting Muslims.

35. Told to me by William Nasr, Bishop Arsanios's brother.

36. Taped interview with Yassa Ḥannā, June 8, 1981.

37. *Egypt Today*, April 1995, p. 113.

38. See interview in the *Middle East Times*, June 27–July 3, 1977. See also article by Majid Aṭīyah in *al-Muṣawwar* July 7, 1994 and Maḥmūd Fawzī, *al-Bābā Shanūdah wa-al- muʿāradah*, (Cario, 1992).

39. *Egypt Today*, April 1995, p. 89. See Raʾfat Butrous's article in the magazine *Ākhir Saʿah* July 27,1994.

40. *Egypt Today*, April 1995, p. 89.

41. Ibid.

42. See *The Egyptian Gazette*, May 7, 1997 and *Egypt Today*, p. 89.

43. Information from my interview with Bishop Serapion, the Bishop of Social and Ecumenical affairs, in November 1994.

44. Interview in *Egypt Today*, April 1995, p. 113.

45. Interview in ibid., p. 90.

46. *Egypt Today*, p. 89.

47. I was carrying out my research at the time the scandal broke and I had conversed with Adel Raphael a number of times, when we met in the pope's reception room, during the feasts, when he received the cabinet ministers and other state officials as well as members of the Muslim religious establishment. But I never broached this subject with him. See the article by Alfi Anwar Atalah in *Rūz al-Yūsef*, August 1, 1994.

48. These were allegations by some of the people who were lobbying the papal headquarters to get him ousted, while I was carrying out my research.

49. *Egypt Today*, p. 9.

50. Ibid., pp. 113 and 88.

51. Ibid., p. 113.

52. *Egyptian Gazette*, May 7, 1997.

53. *Egypt Today*, p. 113.

54. Dr. Magdi Isaac during a lecture he gave following Bishop Moses Sunday youth meeting. This lecture was part of a series I attended in the winter of 1992.

55. Based on my own observations.

56. Wakin, *A Lonely Minority*.

57. Ibid.

58. Ibid.

59. Told to me by Bishop Bishoi.

60. Told to me by the pope in a conversation at his monastic retreat in May 1994.

61. Ibid.

62. Told to me by Bishop Arsanios, who was Bishop Suwereis's most trusted church-servant.

63. Based on my own observations when I did fieldwork in Girga in September 1992. I later discussed it in an interview with Bishop Daniel.

64. Told to me by Bishop Murqus, during an interview in his diocese in April 1992.

65. Told to me by Bishop Athanasios.

66. Ibid.

67. Told to me by members of the Front for Church Reform.

17. TOWARD THE EMPOWERMENT OF WOMEN?

1. Told to me by the pope when I visited him at the Monastery of Bishoi in March 1992.

2. I witnessed this during my fieldwork in Minya in November–December 1992.

3. This information about the orphanages and rehabilitation centers was given to me by Bishop Arsanios.

4. I witnessed this when I was doing fieldwork in Minya November–December 1992.

5. I saw this in several of the dioceses of Upper Egypt where I did fieldwork: Akhmim, Tima, Abu Tig, Tahta, Abnub, and Minya, among others.

6. Bishop Bula said this in a conference on marriage and the Orthodox family held at the papal headquarters in March 1992.

7. This discussion between a priest and Bishop Bishoi about a woman who had been burned by her husband took place in my presence in the Monastery of Bishoi, during a conference on how priests should deal with troubled marital relationships sponsored by Pope Shenuda in winter 1992. The priest was urging Bishop Bishoi to put her up in one of the shelters for abused women under his auspices.

8. Incident recounted by Bishop Moses in one of the youth meetings I attended at the papal headquarters in February 1992.

9. I overheard him telling her this after a general meeting I attended in Tima, when I was doing fieldwork in spring 1993.

10. He said this to me when he came in August 1994 to give a talk in the church of the old papal headquarters of Clot Bey. I had brought up the problem of the woman from Australia at the end of the talk when he accepted questions from the audience, as part of an argument that the Orthodox Church should liberalize its divorce laws.

11. Bishop Tadros told me this in the course of an interview in Port Said in June 1992.

12. This happened when I was doing fieldwork in St. Dimiana in July 1992.

13. Told to me by *Tasoni* Mary when I was doing fieldwork in Damahour in August 1992.

14. Told to me by *Tasoni* Batul, who was hosting me in the home for consecrated women in Port Fouad, where Bishop Tadros put me up in June 1992.

CONCLUSION

1. Wakin, p. 122.

2. Ghālī Shukrī, al-Thowrah al-muḍādah fīMiṣr (Cairo, 1987).

3. David Landes, *International Finance and Economic Imperalism in Egypt* (Cambridge, Mass., 1979).

4. See in this vein William Soliman Kīlādā, in his book *al-kanīsah al-miṣrīyya tuwājih al-isti ʿmār wa al-Suhyuniyah* (Cairo, n.d.); Mīlād Ḥannā, *Na ʿam Aqbāṭ wa-lakin Miṣrīyīn* (Cairo, 1980); and Samira Bahr, *The Copts in Egyptian Politics* (Cairo, 1979).

Select Bibliography

Interviews recorded by me in Egypt (except with the pope, who would not allow recording). Interviews with church servants are too numerous to list.

Pope Shenuda III	November 1991, December 1991 October 1992, February 1993 June 1994, March 1995
Bishop Johanna (pope's secretary)	December 1991
Bishop Bisente (formerly, pope's secretary)	December 1991

LOWER EGYPT

Bishop Bula (diocese of Tanta)	January 1992
Bishop Moses (Bishopric of Youth, Cairo)	February/March 1992
Bishop Serapion (Bishopric of Social Services, Cairo)	February/March 1992
Bishop Murqus (assistant bishop, diocese of Shubra al-Kheima)	April 1992
Bishop Butrus (assistant bishop, diocese of Ismailia)	May 1992
Bishop Tadros (diocese of Port Said)	June 1992
Archbishop Bishoi (diocese of Kafr al-Sheick)	July 1992
Archbishop Bachomios (diocese of Damanhour)	August 1992

UPPER EGYPT

Bishop Athanasios (diocese of Banī Suwayf)	October 1992
Bishop Arsanios (diocese of Minya)	November/December 1992
Bishop Besada (diocese of Akhmim)	January 1993
Bishop Bachum (diocese of Sohag)	February 1993
Bishop Fam (diocese of Tima)	March/April 1993

Bishop Isaiah (diocese of Tahta)	May 1993
Bishop Andrawes (diocese of Abu Tig)	June 1993
Bishop Tackla (diocese of Dishna)	July/August 1993
Bishop Daniel (assistant bishop, diocese of Girga)	September 1993
Bishop Thomas (diocese of Qusia)	October/November 1993
Bishop Lukas (diocese of Abnub)	December 1993
Bishop Sherubim (Diocese of Kena)	January 1994
Bishop Kyrilos (Diocese of Naga Hammadi)	February 1994
Bishop Bimen (Diocese of Nagada)	March/April 1994
Bishop Hidra (Diocese of Aswan)	May 1994

INTERVIEWS RECORDED BY ME WITH PROMINENT CHRISTIAN LAYMEN (EXCEPT AS NOTED)

Interview with civil rights activist Farag Foda (a Muslim), December 28, 1991.

Interview with member of Parliament and veteran of the Sunday School Movement Mīlād Ḥannā, December 13, 1991.

Interview with Fahmi Basili, vice minister of Housing, winter 1994.

Interview with Majid ʿAṭtiyah, vice editor of *al-Muṣawwar* magazine, December 14, 1991.

Interview with William Soliman Kīlādā, a promiment intellectual who is a veteran of the Sunday school Movement, March 20, 1992.

Interview with Dr. Maurice Asʿad, Director of Middle East Council of Churches (Cairo branch), April 12, 1992.

Interview (unrecorded) with the banker Fakhri Abd al-Nur, son of prominent Wafdist parliamentarian by the same name, January 28, 1992.

Interview with Boutros Boutros Ghālī, grandson of Prime Minister Boutros Ghālī, then acting foreign minister, January 18, 1983

Interview with Amīn Fahim, founder of a chain of Christian schools in Upper Egypt.

Interview (unrecorded) with Magdi Wahba, grandson of Prime Minister Yūsuf Wahba, former vice-minister of culture, Februay 24, 1992.

Interview (unrecorded) with Victor Semeca, son of the founder of the Coptic Museum in Cairo, December 30, 1991.

Interview (unrecorded) with the medical doctor Akil Yūsuf, grandson of former minister of Defense Sami Salib.

UNPUBLISHED MATERIAL

Videotape of interview with the late Bishop Bimen June 16, 1986, shortly before his death (courtesy of Samir Murqus).

Tape of interview with veteran Sunday School leader Yassa Ḥannā, June 8, 1981 (courtesy of Samir Murqus).

Tape of interview with veteran Sunday School leader the late Yuhannā al-Rāḥib, August 21, 1982 (courtesy of Samir Murqus).

RECORDED LECTURES OF THE CLERGY AND CHURCH-SERVANTS

Bishop Moses' lecture series at the papal headquarters, winter 1992, to the "Youth Meeting," "The Complete Personality" and "The Characteristics of Orthodoxy."
Bishop Moses' lecture to the blue-collar workers in the Church of the Virgin in Shoubra, Cairo "No One Is Too Small to Give a Helping Hand."
Dr. Magdi Isaac's lectures on Christian psychology in the papal headquarters, winter 1992, "Christianity and Self-Knowledge."
Bishop Arsanios's lecture to the Theological Seminary of Minya, November 11, 1992, "White Points in Muslim History."
Pope Shenuda's lecture to the Tuesday Theological Seminary, March 17, 1992, "The Grounds for Father Daniel's Excommunication."

PRIVATE PAPERS

Defense of Father Daniel, presented by Bishop Arsanios to the Pope, December 1991 (in Arabic)

PUBLISHED MATERIAL

Church Publications: Newsletters and Magazines in Arabic
Dunyā al-Ṭifl
al-Kirāzah
Majallat Madāris al-Aḥad
al-Malā'ikah
al-Rajā'
Risālat al-Shabāb al-Kanasī

NEWSPAPERS, MAGAZINES, AND PERIODICALS IN ARABIC

Ākhir Sā'ah
al-Ahālī
al-Ahrām
el-Akhbār
al-Da'wa
Fikr ma'a al-Rusul
al-Ikhwān al-Muslimūn
el-kash kūl
Majallat Uktūbir
Māyu
Miṣr
al-Muṣawwar
al-Mushāhid al-Siyāsī
Rūz al-Yūsuf
Sabāḥ al-Khayr

al-Sha'b
al-Siyasa
al-Wafd
al-Watan
Watanī

ARAB NEWSPAPERS AND JOURNALS IN ENGLISH AND FRENCH

al-Ahrām Weekly
Civil Society
Dossier du CDEJ (Centre D'Etude Economique et Juridique)
The Egyptian Gazette
Egypt Today
Magreb-Mushrak
The Middle East Times
Proche Orient Chrétien

DOCUMENTS

Muḥammad Anwar Sadat, *Speech Delivered on the Occasion of the Tenth Anniversary of the Corrective Revolution*, May 14, 1980, State Information Service. Cairo, 1980.

Muḥammad Anwar Sadat, *Speech Delivered during the Joint Session of the People's Assembly and the Senate*, September 5, 1981, State Information Service. Cairo, 1981.

St. George Multi-Purpose School Project, submitted for funding by the Community Development Center of Minya. 1992.

Development Training Farm Project, submitted for funding by the Department of Community Development in the Coptic Orthodox Diocese of Minya. 1994.

Hand in Hand, Project submitted for funding by the Community Development Center of Minya. 1991.

John Bowring. *Report on Egypt and Candia: addressed to the Right Hon. Lord Viscount Palmerston, Her Majesty's principal Secretary of State for Foreign Affairs*. London, 1840, Series Parliamentary Papers, 1870, fo.xxi[277].

H. Mussier. *Receuil des listes episcopales de L'Eglise Copte*. Societé d'Archeologie Copte, Cairo, 1989.

Annuaire Statistique. Maslahat al-Ihsā wa-al-Ta'dād, Cairo, 1932–1933.

The Census of Egypt taken in 1917. Two volumes. Maṣlaḥat 'Umum al-Iḥsā, Cairo, government press, 1920–21.

World Population and Resources: A Report/by PEP. London: Political and Economic Planning, 1955.

CHURCH PUBLICATIONS: BOOKS IN ARABIC

Abnā' al-Kanīsah al-Qibṭīyah. *Bustān al-ruhbān*. Muṭranīyat Banī Suwayf, 1977.

al-'Abd, 'Āṭif 'Adlī. *al-I'lām wa-al-usrah*. Cairo, 1989.

'Abd al-Nūr, Rāghib. *Naḥwa al-ṭāhārah*. Cairo, 1970.

Asʿad, Mūrīs. al-Usrah *wa-al-ṭifl al-Masīḥī*. Cairo, Majlis Kanāʾis al-Sharq al-Awsaṭ, 1981.
Asʿad, Yūsuf, al-Qumuṣ. *Kayfa yakhtāru al-insān sharīk ḥayātuh*. Cairo, 1988.
———. *Kayfa yataʿāmilu al-khaṭībān*. Cairo: Kanīsat al-ʿAdhrāʾ al-ʿUmrānīyah, 1988.
[Athanasios] Athanāsiyūs, al-Anbā. *al-iman wa al-Tanmiya*. Banī Suwayf, n.d.
———. *Fī ḥubb Miṣr*. Muṭranīyat Banī Suwayf, 1991.
Barsūm, al-Anbā. *Shahīd al-ḥubb al-amīr Tāwḍurūs*. Dayr al-Shahīd Ṣanbū, 1991.
[Bimen, Bishop] Bīmin, al-Anbā. *al-Ḥayāh al-ijtimāʿīyah al-Urthūdhūksīyah*. Muṭrānīyat Mallāwī, 1971.
———. *al-Kāhin al-Qibṭī*. Kanīsat al-Adhrāʾ bi-al-ʿUmrānīyah, 1986.
———. *al-Khidmah fī al-qaryah*. Cairo: Muṭrānīyat Mallāwī, 1981.
———. *al-Masīḥīyah wa-bināʾ al-shakhṣīyah*. Muṭrānīyat Mallāwī, n.d.
———. *al-Qiyāmah wa-mushkilāt al-shabāb*. Muṭrānīyat Mallāwī, 1977.
———. *al-Tarbiyah al-Masīḥīyah khilāla marāhil al-namūw*. Cairo: Muṭrānīyat Mallāwī, 1987.
[Cyril, Pope] Abnāʾ al-Bābā Kīrilus al-Sādis. Hayāt al-Bābā Kīrilus. Cairo, 1975.
———. *Muʿjizāt al-Bābā Kīrilus*. Cairo, 1981.
———. *Muʿjizāt al-Bābā Kīrilus*. Cairo, 1988.
[Daniel, Father]. *Al-Fach Inkasar*. Cairo, 1977.
———. *La Atazaʿzaʿ*. Cairo, n.d.
———. *Leisa Siwah*. Cairo, n.d.
———. *Ma Agmaluh*. Cairo, 1976.
Dayr al-Anbā Anṭūnīyūs. *al-Shahīdān Dīsqūrūs wa-Isqlābīyūs*. Cairo, 1986.
Dhikrī, Ṭalʿat. *Mushkilāt al-abnāʾ al-nafsīyah wa-al-tarbawīyah*. Cairo, 1989.
———. *al-Ṣadāqah min wajhat Masīḥīyah*. Cairo, 1988.
———. *al-Ṣiḥḥah al-nafsīyah li-ṭifl ibtidāʾī*. Cairo, 1989.
———. *al-Tanshiʾah al-usarīyah wa-āthāruhā fī ḥayāt al-aṭfāl*. Cairo, 1989.
———. *al-Tilīfizīyūn fī ḥayāt al-aṭfāl*. Cairo, 1988.
Fahīm, Klayr. *Dār al-ḥaḍānah wa-al-usrah*. Cairo, 1988.
———. *al-Mashākil al-nafsīyah li-ṭifl al-ḥaḍānah*. Cairo, 1988.
———. *al-Numūw al-nafsī lil-raḍīʾ*. Cairo, 1989.
———. *al-Ṣiḥḥah al-nafsīyah lil-fatʾa al-murāhiq*. Cairo, 1989.
———. *al-Umūmah wa-al-ṭufūlah*. Cairo, 1988.
[Gregorios, Bishop] Ghrīghūriyūs, al-Anbā. *al-Ishtirākīyah fī al-Masīḥīyah*. Cairo, n.d.
———. *al-Intikhāb al-baṭrīyark*. Cairo, 1971.
———. *al-Kanīsah wa-qaḍāyā al-waṭan wa-al-dawlah*. Cairo: Usqufīyat al-Dirāsāt al-Uly'a, 1979.
——— *al-Masīḥīyah wa-al-tadkhīn*. Cairo: Usqufīyat al-Dirāsāt al-Uly'a, 1988.
———. *al-Raʾy al-Masīḥī fī aṭfāl al-anābīb*. Cairo: Usqufīyat al-Dirāsāt al-Uly'a, 1988.
———. *al-Shabāb wa-rūḥ al-ʿaṣr*. Cairo: Usqufīyat al-Dirāsāt al-Uly'a, 1972.
Ḥabīb, Kamāl. *al-Ḥayāh al-ijtimāʿīyah min minẓar al-Urthūdhūks*. Cairo, 1971.
Ḥabīb, Raʾūf. *al-Rahbanah al-dīrīyah fī Mịr*. Cairo, 1976.
Ḥannā, Nabīl Ṣubḥī. *al-Shakḫsīyah*. Cairo, 1988.
Kamāl, Sāmiḥ. *al-Shahīd Abū Fām*. Cairo, 1989.
Kanīsat al-Qiddīs Taklā Hīmānūt. *Ṭaqs usbūʿ al-ālām*. Cairo, 1991.
Khalīl, Murqus ʿ*Azīz. Falinaṭmaʾin*. Cairo : Kanīsat al-Adhrāʾ bi-al-muʿallaqah, 1991.

———. *Li-na'mal ma'ahu*. Cairo: Kanīsat al-Adhrā' bi-al-mu'allaqah, 1991.

Majlis Kanā'is al-Sharq al-Awsaṭ. *al-Tarbiyah al-jinsīyah lil-fatrah al-murāhaqah*. Cairo, 1986.

Manṣūr, Yūsuf. Tārīkh al-kanīsah lil al-Shammāsīn. Cairo, n.d.

Maskīn, Matt'a, al-Āb. *Ḥayāt al-salāh al-Urthūdhaksīyah*. Dayr al-Qiddīs Anbā Maqār, 1986.

———. *al-Khidmah*. Dayr al-Qiddīs Anbā Maqār, 1980.

——— *Lamaḥah sarī'ah 'an Dayr al-Qiddīs Anbā Maqār wa-al-rahbanah fī Mṣir*. Dayr al-Qiddīs Anbā Maqār, 1966.

———. *Ma'a al-Masīḥ fī alāmihi ḥatt'a al-salīb*. Cairo, 1986.

———. *Maqālāt bayna al-siyāsah wa-al-dīn*. Dayr al-Qiddīs Anbā Maqār, 1977–1980.

———. *al-Mar'ah ḥuqūquhā wa-wājibātuha*. Dayr al-Qiddīs Anbā Maqār, 1982.

———. *al-Ni'mah*. Dayr al-Qiddīis Anbā Maqār, 1991.

Matāwūs, al-Anbā. *al-Shahīdah al-'aẓīmah al-Umm Dūlājī wa-awlāduhā*. Muṭranīyat Banī Suwayf, 1991.

Mīnā, Ṭal'at Zakarīyā. *al-Muḥāfaẓah 'ala al-usrah al-Masīḥīyah*. Cairo, 1988.

Murjān, Binyāmīn. *al-Jihād wa-al-ni'mah*. Cairo: Baṭrīyarkīyat al-Aqbāṭ al-Urthūdhūks, 1991.

Murqus, Samīr. *Aḥādīth al-Bābā il'a al-sahāfa al-Mṣrīyah*. Cairo : Baṭrīyarkīyat al-Aqbāṭ al-Urthūdhuks, 1991.

Mūs'a, al-Anbā. *al-Azmāt al-nafsīyah*. Cairo : Usqūfīyat al-Shabāb, 1991.

———. *Kayfa ittakhadha qarāran*. Cairo: Baṭrīyarkīyat al-Aqbāṭ al-Urthūdhuks, 1989.

———. *Kayfa nuwājih al-'ạr*. Cairo: Baṭrīyarkīyat al-Aqbāṭ al-Urthūdhuks, 1989.

———. *Kayfa nakhdimu al-shabāb*. Cairo: Baṭrīyarkīyat al-Aqbāṭ al-Urthūdhuks, 1989.

———. *Khādim jamā'ī*. Cairo: Baṭrīyarkīyat al-Aqbāṭ al-Urthūdhuks, 1992.

———. *Khādim al-shabāb*. Cairo: Baṭrīyarkīyat al-Aqbāṭ al-Urthūdhuks, 1992.

———. *Khādim yahtamu bi-al-nafs al-waḥīd*. Cairo: Baṭrīyarkīyat al-Aqbāṭ al-Urthūdhuks, 1992.

———. *al-Ma'nā al-Masīḥī lil-jins*. Cairo: Baṭrīyarkīyat al-Aqbāṭ al-Urthūdhuks, 1991.

———. *al-Ma'nā al-Masīḥī lil-zawāj*. Cairo: Baṭrīyarkīyat al-Aqbāṭ al-Urthūdhuks, 1991.

———. *Naḥwa usrah sa'īdah*. Al-Tarbiyah al-Kanīsīyah bi-Jīzah, 1991.

———. *al-Shabāb wa-ḥayāt al-ṭahārah*. Cairo: Baṭrīyarkīyat al-Aqbāṭ al-Urthūdhuks, 1989.

——— *Shakḥīyatuka*. Cairo: Baṭrīyarkīyat al-Aqbāṭ al-Urthūdhuks, 1988.

———. *al-Ta'āmul bayna al-jinsayn*. Cairo: Baṭrīyarkīyat al-Aqbāṭ al-Urthūdhuks, 1990.

———. *Ta'līm lītūrjī*. Cairo: Baṭrīyarkīyat al-Aqbāṭ al-Urthūdhuks, 1991.

———. *Ta'līm mutakāmul*. Cairo: Baṭrīyarkīyat al-Aqbāṭ al-Urthūdhuks, 1991.

———. *Yumkinuka an tahzima al-qalaq*. Cairo: Baṭrīyarkīyat al-Aqbāṭ al-Urthūdhuks, 1988.

Muṭrānīyat Banī Suwayf. *Niẓām idārat al-ībrāshīyah*. 1984.

Nasīm, Sulaymān. *al-Shabāb wa-al-qaḍāyā al-ijtimā'īyah*. Cairo, 1988.

Raflah, Jirjis. *Ma'a Abī al-kāhin*. Cairo, 1988.

Rāghib, Nabīl. *A'midat al-usrah al-sab'ah*. Cairo, 1989.

———. *al-Khawf min al-majhūl*. Cairo, 1989.

al-Raja', Ibrāhīm Fransīs. *Nubdhah ʿan ḥayāt al-Anbā Arsānīyūs.* Muṭrānīyat al-Mīnā, 1977.

[Samuel, Bishop] Ṣamū'īl, al-Anbā. *Maʿa al-shabāb.* Kanīsat Mār Jirjis Muṭranīyat Jīzah, 1988.

———. *Tanẓīm al-usrah min wajhat naẓar Masīḥīyah.* Cairo, 1975.

[Shenuda, Pope] Shanūdah al-Thālith, al-Bābā.*Ḥayāt al-Iman.* Cairo,

———. *al-Ḥurūb al-rūḥīyah.* Cairo, 1988.

———. *Ḥurūb al-Shayṭān.* Cairo, 1986.

———. *al-Khalq fī mafhūm al-Urthūdhuksī.* Cairo, 1984.

———. *Maʿālim ʿala al-ṭarīq al-rūḥī.* Cairo, 1987.

———. *al-Sanawāt maʿa as'ilat al-nās.* Cairo, 1983.

———. *al-Sanawāt maʿa as'ilat al-nās.* Cairo, 1989.

———. *al-Sanawāt maʿa as'ilat al-nās.* Cairo, 1993.

———. *al-Sahar al-rūḥī.* Cairo, 1988.

———. *Tajallī al-Sayyidah al-Adhrā' fī Shubrā wa-al-muʿjizāt al-khāriqah.* Cairo: Kanīisat al-Qiddīisah Dumyānah bi-Shubrā, 1986.

———. *Ẓāhirat tajalli Umm al-nūr wa-muʿjizātuhā fī Shubrā athnā' wa-baʿd al-ẓuhūr.* Cairo: Kanīisat al-Qiddīsah Dumyānah bi-Shubrā, 1986.

al-Siniksār: akhbār *al-anbiyā' wa-al-rusul wa-al-shuhadā' wa-al-qiddīsīn.* Cairo, 1978.

Siryānī, Abādīr. *al-Shahīdān Abādīr wa-ukhtuhu Ayrīnī.* Dayr al-Siryān, 1990.

[Anon.] *al-Tarbiyah al-jinsīyah li-fatrah al-murāhaqah.* N.p., n.d.

Yūnis, *al-Anbā. Bustān al-ruhbān.* al-Anbā Ruways al-ʿAbbāsīyah. 1985.

ARTICLES FROM ARABIC LANGUAGE PERIODICALS

ʿAbd al-Samīʿ, Amr. "Tashjī' al-Aqbāṭ li-khidmat bilādihim fī kull al-majāllāt wa-ishtirāk fī al-aʿmāl al-siyāsī." *al-iqtisādi,* July 18, 1988.

ʿAṭā Allāh, Alfī Anwar. "al-Taḥqīq maʿa ibn shaqīq al-Bābā." *Rūz al-Yūsuf,* August 1, 1994.

ʿAṭīyah, Mājid. "Azmat al-bābā wa-al-ruhbān wa-al-qasāwisah wa-al-ʿulamānīyīn", *al-Muawwar,* July 15, 1994.

———. "Salbīyat al-Aqbāṭ naʿam wa-lakin li-mādhā." al-Ahālī, March 25, 1978.

al-Badrī, Hannān. "Baʿḍ al-Aqbāt qad yusāfirūn il'a Isrā'īl bi-munāsabat iḥtifālāt ʿām 2000." *Rūz al-Yūsuf,* September 3, 1999.

Būlā, al-Anbā. "al-Sayyid al-Masīḥ al-Khādim." *al-Kirāzah,* April 23, 1993.

Buṭrus, Rifʿat. "Muḥāwalah yā'isah li-hadm al-Kanīsah wa-narfūd al-wiāyah ʿala al-Kanīsah." *ākhir sāʿah,* July 27, 1994.

Ḥannā, Mīlād. "Li-mādhā hamashtum al-shabāb wa-al-Aqbāṭ." *Rūz al-Yūsuf,* June 13, 1994.

Ḥusayn, ʿĀdil. "Man yaḥmī al-Aqbāṭ? Hal taḥmīhim ummatuhum am al-Amrīkān?" *al-Shaʿb,* June 3, 1992.

al-Jawharī, ʿĀdil. "Ghiyāb al-qiyādāt al-maḥallīyah al-fāʿilah warā'a tikrār al-aḥdāth al-damawīyah." *al-Mushāhid al-Siyāsī,* April 1, 2000.

Kamāl, ʿAbd Allāh. "Tamthiliyāt iḍtihād al-Aqbāṭ fī al-Kushṇ." *Rūz al-Yūsuf,* November 2, 1998.

Kīlādā, [William Soliman] Wilyam Sulaymān. "Min Tarikh al-majlis al-Milli." Majallat Madāris al-Ahad (January-February 1983).

Luṭfī, Wā'il. "Zawāj al-ruhbān." *Rūz al-Yūsuf*, June 20, 1998.

Murquṣ, Anṭūniyūs. "Qaḍīyat al-Kanīsah fī Ifriqiya." *al-Kirāzah*, March 12, 1993.

———. "Qaḍīyat al-Kanīsah fī Ifriqiya: Ṣalīb Qibṭī fawqa burj." *al-Kirāzah*, June 4, 1993.

———. "Siyāmat al-abā' al-asāqifah al-judud". *al-Kirāzah*, September 16, 1992.

Murquṣ, Samīr. "al-Aqbāṭ wa-al-intikhābāt." *al-Ahālī*, 28/3/1984.

———. "Dawā'ir qaḍā'īyah lil-Muslimīn wa-ayḍān lil-Masī ḥīyīn." *al-Ahālī*, June 6, 1984.

———. "Tarikh Khidmat Madāris al-Ahad." *Majallat Madāris al-Aḥad* (November–December 1989).

Mūsā, al-Anbā. "al-Masīhīyah wa-al-thimah." *al-Kirāzah*, October 18, 1994.

———. "al-Qirā'ah wa-al-sama' wa-al-ḥawās (al-Bābā Shanūdah)." *al-Kirāzah*, November 29, 1991.

———. "al-Ta'līm al-Urthūdhuksī." *al-Kirāzah*, March 27, 1992 and June 5, 1992.

Rif'at, Salwa. "'Ilm al-Qibṭīyāt wa-al-ḥaḍārah min al-qarn al-awwal wa-ḥatt'a al-qarn al-tāsi'ashar." *al-Waṭanī*, April 13, 1988.

Salāmah, Usāmah. "al-Aqbāṭ fī Miṣr wa-maṭālibuhum: ti'dāduhum, mashākiluhum, ṭalabātuhum." *Rūz al-Yūsuf*, May 2, 1994.

———. "Ma'rakah jadīdah bayna al-jam'īyāt al-Qibṭīyah wa-al-Kanīsah." *Rūz al-Yṣuf*, March 3, 1995.

Sarābīyūm, al-Anbā. "Riḥlat al-Bābā ilā-Urūba wa-Amrīkā." *al-Kirāzah*, February 21, 1992.

Shanūdah al-Thālith, al-Bābā. "Laysa ṣahīh anna hunāka qunbulah mawqūtah fī Asyūṭ." *al-Aḥrār*, November 28, 1988.

———. "Siyāmat al-asāqifah al-judud 'ala 'Ayd al-'Unṣsurah". *al-Kirāzah*, November 4, 1977.

Tawfīq, Ra'ūf. "Aqbāṭ al-mahjar, ṭalāq al-Masīḥīyīn, nasha'at al-kanīisah fī al-mujtama' al-Miṣrī." *Ṣabāḥ al-khayr*, August 25, 1994.

ASSORTED UNATTRIBUTED ARABIC ARTICLES

Aghābī.

"al-Ḥubb fī ḥayāt al-rajul wa-al-mar'ah wa-al-usrah al-shāmilah," 1990.

"al-Kanīsah wa-khidmat al-fuqarā'," September 1989

"al-Kanīsah wa-mushkilāt al-biṭālah," September 1990.

"al-Maḥabba bayna al-zawjayn wa-al-tafāhum al-zawjī," 1991.

"al-Mustaqbal: barāmij al-ṭufūlah," July 1991.

"Riḥlat al-Bābā il'a al-kanā'is al-Urthūdhuksīyah bi-al-mahjar," January 1990.

"al-Tanmiyah wa furaṣ al-'amal," February 1991.

"Zuhūr al-'adhrā' fī al-Zaytūn," April 12, 1982.

al-Kirāzah

"Kanā' isunā fī ūrubā," November 1, 1991.

"Niyāfat al-Anbā Maksīmūs rakada fī al-rabb," May 22, 1992.

"Riḥlat il'a thalāth qārāt," September 24, 1993.

"Risāmat al-asāqifah al-khamsā'," July 3, 1992.

"Siyāmat 60 usquf," November 15, 1991.
Risālat al-Shabāb al-Kanasī.
"Ḥāwil an tuḥiba nafsaka," September 1988.
"al-Ḥayāh al-jāmiʿīyah," October 1988.
"al-ʿIlāj li al-qalaq," August 1987.
"al-Īmān wa-al-shuʿūr bi-al-farāgh," November 1991
"al-Jins," 1987.
"al-Kambyūtir lughat al-ʿaṣr," December 1988.
"Khaṣā'iṣ al-zawāj al-Masīḥī," August 1988.
"al-Shabāb wa-ʿaṣr," 1992.

BOOKS (NON-CHURCH PUBLICATIONS) IN ARABIC

Awad, Louis. *al-Jāmiʿat wa-al-mujtama ʿal-jadīd*. Cairo, n.d.
al-Bishrī, Ṭāriq. *al-Muslimūn wa-al-qawmīyah al-ʿArabīyah*. Cairo, 1987.
———. *al-Muslimūn wa-al-Aqbāṭ fī iṭār al-jamāʿah al-waṭanīyah*. Cairo, 1977.
[Boutros Ghālī, Boutros] Buṭrus Ghālī, Buṭrus. al-Shaʿb al-waḥīd wa-al-waṭan al-waḥīd. Cairo, 1982.
Fūdah, Faraj. *al-Ḥaqāʾiq al-ghāʾibah*. Cairo, 1987.
———. *al-Suqūt*. Cairo, 1985.
*Fawzī, Maḥmūd. al-*Bābā Kīrillus wa-ʿAbd al-Nāsir. Cairo, 1993.
———. al-Bābā Shanūdah wa-ḥiwār maḥzūr al-nashr. Cairo, 1990.
———. *al-Bābā Shanūdah wa-al-muʿāraḍah fī al-kanīsah*. Cairo, 1992.
———. *al-Bābā Shanūdah wa-muḥākamāt al-qasāwisah*. Cairo. 1994.
———. al-Bābā Shanūdah wa-tārīkh al-Kanīsah al-Qibṭīyah. Cairo, 1991.
Ḥabīb, Rafīq. *al-Iḥyāʾal-dīnī fī Mịr*. Cairo, 1991.
———. *al-Masīḥīyah al-siyāsīyah fī Misr*. Cairo, 1990.
Ḥannā, Mīlād. *Dhikrayāt Sibtimbirīyah*. Cairo, 1987.
———. *Naʿam Aqbāṭ wa-lakin Misrīyīn*. Cairo, 1980.
'Īs'a, Ibrāhīm. *ʿAmāʾim wa-khanājir*. Cairo, 1993.
Kīlādā, Ibrāhīm *ʿAmīr. al-Arḍ wa-al-falāhīn al-masallah al-zirāʾiyah fī Mịr*. Cairo, 1956.
Kilādā, [William Soliman] Wilyam Sulaymān. al-KanIsah al-Misriya tuwājaha al-istiʿmār wa al-Suhyuniyah. Cairo, n.d.
al-Mịsrī, Īzīs. Qisat ḥayāt al-Anbā Ṣamū'il. Cairo, 1988.
Ramāḍan, 'Abd al-ʿA zīim. *Taṭawwur al-ḥarakah al-waṭanīyah fī Mịsr, 1917–1936*. Cairo, 1968.
Shukrī, Ghālī. *al-Aqbāṭ fī waṭan mutaghayyir*. Cairo, 1991.
———. *al-Thawrah al-muḍādah fī Mịr*. Cairo, 1987
Yūsuf, Abū Sayf. *al-Aqbāṭ wa-al-qawmīyah al-ʿArabīyah*. Cairo, 1987.

BOOKS AND ARTICLES IN ENGLISH, FRENCH, AND GERMAN

Anderson, Benedict. *Imagined Communities: Reflections on the Origins and Spread of Nationalism*. London, 1992.
Arjomand, S. A. "Iran's Revolution in Comparative Perspective." *World Politics* (April 1986), pp. 383–414.

Arminjean, Pierre. *La situation economique et financière d'Egypte*. Paris, 1911.
ʿAṭīyah, A. S. *History of Eastern Christianity*. New York, 1980
Badawi, Zaki. *La législation du travaille en Egypte*. Alexandria,1951.
Bahr, Samira. *The Copts in Egyptian Politics*. Cairo, 1979.
Baker, Raymond W. *Egypt's Uncertain Revolution under Nasser and Sadat*. Cambridge, Mass., 1987.
Beinin, Joel, and Zachary Lockman. *Workforce on the Nile*. Princeton, 1987.
Bowie, Leland, "The Copts, the Wafd and Religious Issues in Egyptian Politics." *The Muslim World* (1977), 67.
Butcher, E. L. *The Story of the Church of Egypt*. Two volumes. London, 1897.
Carter, R. B. L. *The Copts in Egyptian Politics 1918–1952*. Cairo, 1986.
Chadwick, Henry. *The Early History of the Church*. London, 1967.
Chaillot, Christine, 'L'Institut des Etudes Coptes.' Pp. 35–50. *Le Monde Copte*, 17(1990).
Cheneau, R. P. Paul. *Les saints d'Egypte*. Two volumes. Jerusalem, 1923.
Chitham, E. J. *The Coptic Community in Egypt*. Durham, England, 1986.
Clerget, Marcel. *Le Caire: Etude de geographie urbaine et histoire économique*. Cairo, 1934. Volume 1.
Crouchly, A.E. *The Investment of Foreign Capital in Egyptian Companies and Public Debt*. Cairo, 1936.
———. *The Economic Development of Egypt*. London, 1938
Cromer, Lord (Evelyn Baring). *Modern Egypt*. Two volumes. London, 1908.
Deeb, Marious. "Bank Misr and the Emergence of a Local Bourgeoisie in Egypt." *Middle Eastern Studies*, 12, no. 3 (October 1976), pp. 69–86.
Ducruet, Jean. *Les Capiteaux européens au Proche Orient*. Paris, 1943.
Eman, André. *L'industrie de coton en Egypte: Etude d'économie politique*. Cairo, 1943.
Emary, Ahmad. "La Crise dé Chomage, ses causes et ses remédes en Egypte." *L'Egypte Contemporaine* 27, no. 164 1936, pp. 465–483.
Farah, Nadia Ramsis. *Religious Strife in Egypt: Crisis and Ideo1ogical Conflict in the Seventies*. New York, 1986.
Fargues, P. *Chrétiens et Juifs dans l'Islam Arabe et Turc*. Paris, 1992.
Gandhi, M. K. *Self-Restraint versus Self-Indulgence*. Ahmedabad, 1956.
Ghali, Mirit. *The Policy of Tomorrow*. Cairo, 1953.
Gonzalez, L. *The Story of Christianity: The Early Church to the Dawn of the Reformation*. Two volumes. San Francisco, 1984.
Gordon, Lady Duff. *Letters from Egypt*. London, 1983.
Gruber, Mark Francis. "Coping with God: Coptic Monasticism in Egyptian Culture." In Van Doorn-Harder and Vogt, *Between Desert and City*, pp. 52–65.
———. "The Monastry as the Nexus of Coptic Cosmology." In Van Doorn Harder and Vogt, pp. 66–83.
Hallwach, Maurice, *La mémoire collective*. Paris, 1950.
———. *Les cadres sociaux de la mémoire*. Paris, 1976.
Heykal, Mohamed Hassanein. *Autumn of Fury* New York, 1983.
Hobsbawm, E., and T. Ranger, eds. *The Invention of Tradition*. Cambridge, UK, 1983.
Hugoz, Jean-Pierre Peroncel, *The Raft of Muhammad*. New York, 1998.
Husein, Taha. *The Future of Culture in Egypt*. Washington D.C., 1954.

Ibrahim, Saad Eddin. "Anatomy of Egypt's Militant Islamic Groups: Methodological Notes and Preliminary Findings." *International Journal of Middle Eastern Studies* 12, no. 4 (1980), pp. 423–453.

ʿIsā, Ibrahim. Maʿāim wa Khanaik. Cairo, 1985.

Issawi, Charles. "Egypt since 1800, a Study in Lopsided Development." *Journal of Economic History*, 21 (1961), pp. 1–25.

Kerr, Malcolm. "Egypt." In James S. Coleman, ed., *Education and Political Development.* Princeton, 1967. pp. 169–194.

el-Khawaga, Dina. "Le renouveau Copte Actuel; Raison d'émergence et mode de fonctionnement." *Dossier du CDEJ* 1991.

———. "Le développement communautaire Copte: Un mode de participation au politique?" *Monde Arabe: Magreb Mashrek* 135 (January-March 1992), p. 135.

Landes, David. *International Finance and Economic Imperialism in Egypt.* Cambridge, Mass., 1979.

Lane, E. *Manners and Customs of the Modern Egyptians.* London, 1908.

Leeder, S. H. *Modern Sons of Pharaohs.* New York, 1973.

Marsot, Afaf Lutfi el-Sayyid. *Egypt's Liberal Experiment.* Berkeley, 1977.

Mellini, Peter. *Sir Eldon Gorst, the Overshadowed Pro Consul.* Stanford, 1977.

Michail, Kyriakos. *Copts and Muslims under British Rule.* London, 1911.

Milner, Viscount. *England in Egypt.* New York, 1970.

Mitchell, Richard P. *The Society of Muslim Brothers.* London 1969.

Naguib, Safinaz-Amal. "Martyr and Apostle: Victor Son of Romanos and Diocletian: A case of Intertextuality in Coptic Religious Memory." *Temenos* 29 (1994), pp. 101–13.

———. "The Martyr as Witness: Coptic and Copto-Arabic Hagiographies as Mediators of Religious Memories." *Numen* 41(1994), pp. 225–49.

Nerval, Gerard de. *Voyage en Orient.* Paris, 1980.

Nora, Pierre. "Entre mémoire et histoire: La problématique des lieux de Mémoire." In Pierre Nora et al., eds., *Les lieux de memoire: La république XVII–XXIII.* Vol. 1. Paris, 1984, pp. xvii–xlii..

Owen, E. R. "Lord Cromer and the Development of Egyptian Industry" *Middle Eastern Studies* 5.11, no. 4 (July 1966), 282–301.

———. *Cotton and the Egyptian Economy 1820–1914: A Study in Trade and Development.* Oxford, 1969.

———. "The Attitude of British Officials to the Development of the Egyptian Economy." In M. A Cook, ed., *Studies in Economic History* London, 1970, pp. 485–500.

Pennington, J. D. "The Copts in Modern Egypt." *Middle Eastern Affairs* 18 (1982), pp. 158–79.

Politis, Athanase. *L'Hellénisme et l'Egypte moderne.* Paris, 1930.

Raymond, André. *Artisans et commerçants au Caire au XVIIiéme siécle.* Two volumes. Damascus, 1981.

———. "The Economic Crisis of Egypt in the Eighteenth Century" In A. L. Udovitch, ed., *The Islamic Middle East 700–1900: Studies in Economic and Social History,* Princeton, 1981, pp. 687–788.

Rivlin, Helen Ann B. *The Agricultural Policy of Mohammad Ali in Egypt.* Cambridge, Mass., 1961.

Rocaglia, Pelegrino. *Histoire de l'Eglise Copte*. Two volumes. Beirut, 1987.

Rudolph, Lloyd I., and Suzane Hoeber Rudolph. *The Modernity of Tradition: Political Development in India*. Chicago, 1967.

Safran, Nadav. *Egypt in Search of Political Community*. Cambridge, Mass., 1961.

Said, Edward. *Orientalism*. New York, 1985.

Schulze, Rheinhardt. *Die Rebellion der Agyptische Fellahin, 1919*. Berlin, 1971.

Seikaly, Samir. "Prime Minister and Assassin: Butrus Ghali and Wardani." *Middle Eastern Studies* 13 (1977), pp. 112–23.

———. "Coptic Communal Reform: 1860–1914." *Middle Eastern Studies* (October 1970), pp. 247–75.

Sivan, Emmanuel, and Menachem Friedeman, eds. *Religious Radicalism and Politics in the Middle East*. New York, 1990.

St. John, James Augustus. *Egypt under Muhammad Ali*. Two volumes. London, 1834.

Taguer, Jaques. *Coptes et Musulmans*. Cairo, 1954.

Tignor, Robert. *Modernisation and British Colonial Rule in Egypt 1882–1914*. Princeton, 1966.

———. "The Revolution of 1919: New Directions in the Egyptian Economy." *Middle East Studies* 5.12, no. 3 (October 1976), pp. 41–68.

Vallet, Jean. *Contribution a l'étude de la condition de la grande industrie du Caire*. Paris, 1911.

Van Doorn-Harder, Nelly, and Kari Vogt, eds. *Between Desert and City: The Coptic Church Today*. Oslo, 1997.

Vliet, J. Van der. "Demons in Early Coptic Monasticism." In H. Hondelink, ed., *Coptic Art and Culture* (Cairo 1990), pp. 135–55.

Wakin, Edward. *A Lonely Minority: The Modern Story of Egypt's Copts*, New York, 1963.

Walzer, Michael. *The Revolution of the Saints*, Cambridge, Mass., 1965.

Watherson, Barbara. *Coptic Egypt*. Edinburgh, 1988.

Watson, John. "Signposts to Biography—Pope Shenuda III." In van Doorn-Harder and Vogt, *Between Desert and City*, pp. 243–53.

Index